Finding
Chief Kamiakin

To David,

With warmest personal
regards and sincere appreciation
for your valued fellowship.

Blessings,

Richard Scheuerman

17. XI. 08

Finding
Chief Kamiakin
The Life and Legacy of a Northwest Patriot

Richard D. Scheuerman
and Michael O. Finley

Washington State University Press
Pullman, Washington

Washington State University Press
PO Box 645910
Pullman, Washington 99164-5910
Phone: 800-354-7360
Fax: 509-335-8568
E-mail: wsupress@wsu.edu
Web site: wsupress.wsu.edu

Library of Congress Cataloging-in-Publication Data

Scheuerman, Richard D.
    Finding Chief Kamiakin : the life and legacy of a northwest patriot / text by Richard D. Scheuerman and
  Michael O. Finley ; introduction by Albert Redstar Andrews ; foreword by Robert H. Ruby ; photographs by
  John Clement.
       p. cm.
    Includes bibliographical references and index.
    ISBN 978-0-87422-297-5 (alk. paper)
  1. Kamiakin, Yakama chief, ca. 1800-ca. 1877. 2. Yakama Indians--Kings and rulers--Biography. 3. Yakama
Indians--Wars, 1855-1859. 4. Yakama Indians--History. 5. Washington (State)--History. I. Finley, Michael O.,
1978- II. Title.

E99.Y2K367 2008
979.7004'9741270092--dc22
[B]
                                                                                    2008029025

Fine Quality Books from the Pacific Northwest

Front cover photograph: The Mid Columbia, *John Clement.*

Contents

Introduction vii

Foreword.. ix

Preface.. xiii

A Note xvii

Prologue.. 1

Chapter 1: Rocks that Glisten 5

Chapter 2: A Highly Desirable Field 23

Chapter 3: Peace and Friendship 35

Chapter 4: Common Cause 43

Chapter 5: Forests Must Fall 55

Chapter 6: Lake of Fire 69

Chapter 7: Home in the Hills 91

Chapter 8: Deceived and Deserted 103

Chapter 9: Salmon Out of Water 115

Chapter 10: Travois on the Trail 125

Chapter 11: Artists and Authors 137

Chapter 12: Rivers Rise 145

Chapter 13: The Essence of Life 153

Epilogue.. 173

Family Lineages.. 177

Chapter Notes... 184

Bibliography 191

Index.. 197

The Authors and Photographer 205

To the Kamiakin family elders.

WSU Press acknowledges the contribution of
The McGregor Company in helping make publication
of *Finding Chief Kamiakin* possible.

Royalties from this book will support
the Chief Kamiakin Memorial Fund.

Introduction

Albert Redstar Andrews

I grew up on the Colville Indian Reservation hearing about our Kamiakin relatives living on the Yakama, Umatilla, and Nez Perce reservations and elsewhere. When we traveled to these places and met with Longhouse people, I listened to their "teachings" and stories, which immersed me deeper into our heritage. I also learned about those of my family who fought all the way through to the Bears Paw in Montana during the 1877 Nez Perce War. Some of our people escaped to Canada, and then came back down and lived on the Umatilla Reservation. I remember going to some of their homes as a boy with my grandparents. After a brief time for weeping, I listened to them tell of our family members who died all along that trail, and in Kansas, in Oklahoma, and at Ft. Spokane. These are sacred places.

I also heard elders speak of what life was like before all this happened to us. My hope is that our children better connect to their past, so it can inform their future. Maybe this knowledge can strengthen them as well. There are not many elders left amongst us who "carry" the stories of our past. Perhaps we must rely on books for these things.

Often I ask myself, "What is the way out of the struggles we have?" Our lore and ways of hunting and root-digging were our life for millennia. Then we were thrown into the modern age with all its challenges and potential social ills. How do we contend? There was such evil done removing us from our ancestral homes. We never considered ourselves "owners" of the land. We sought to care for what the Creator entrusted us.

While traveling in my ancestral homelands in 2004, I met Richard Scheuerman as he was passing through Lapwai on a camping trip across the Lolo Trail. I had read the book he wrote with Clifford Trafzer about the Palus people, *Renegade Tribe*, and learned about his work on area reservations with Colville tribal historian Michael Finley, telling the story of the Kamiakin family.

My mother's father, Charley Kamiakin Williams, was a grandson of Chief Kamiakin. He was born near present-day Starbuck, in a fishing camp on the Tucannon River near its confluence with the Snake. He later moved to the Colville Reservation. I remember Chief Kamiakin's son, Cleveland Kamiakin, and his wife, Alalumt'i, living up by the old Longhouse in Nespelem, and also my father's father and mother, Willie Red Star Andrews and Hattie Paween, who resided by the concrete bridge. Grandma was a sister to Alalumt'i and Annie Owhi. These women were from the Wawawai and Almota areas of the Snake River—the people of Chief Hetelexkin (Hahtalekin). He helped lead the Palus band in the 1877 war and was the first one killed at the Big Hole in Montana.

I grew up speaking my people's language as a child. The elders would say, "This young man can speak good Indian!" (I learned of this observation years later.) Those visits are treasures to me now. My family, my people, and my home became a coherent, meaningful story through those experiences with the Old Ones and my travels to their former home places. I had seen these locations on maps when I was younger, but never visited many until I worked for the National Park Service some years ago. During that time, my home remained on the Colville Reservation, but I often resided for long periods in the Wallowa Valley. My role involved editing and writing terms in our language for brochures and graphics. My duty station was in Joseph, Oregon, and I loved being in that beautiful place.

There is a well-worn traditional path northeast of the Wallowa Valley, leading over a bunchgrass-covered saddle to the Snake River crossing at Dug Bar. Going up there once on a trip, I stood in this deep rut of a trail looking back over the Imnaha River locality. I realized this might have been the last view my ancestors had of their homeland, when taking their final leave from the Wallowa country in 1877.

An elder, Joe Redthunder, once observed: "Be very careful when you walk that land because we have people buried all over down there." Too many of these sites have been looted by "treasure seekers," who disturb what is sacred. Today, I want to bring my children to those places; just to go and be there. It would be something good to move back there, unencumbered. This is our ancestral homeland.

But I was homesick for my family and friends in Nespelem and Coulee Dam, many of whom are descendants of the original Palouse people and the Joseph band of Nez Perce. Eventually I decided to move back to the Colville Reservation.

But in connection with my work in the Wallowa country, I explored the areas inhabited by my ancestors and examined many of their trails and campsites.

I have visited the Kamiakin family's Palouse River place and also Rock Lake, and imagined what my people (on my maternal grandfather's side) were like when they lived there and along the Snake River. Those visits have impressed upon me an understanding of why our people always looked to their old homes. I came to realize why my grandparents wept when they talked about where they once lived in the Palouse country, the Wallowa Valley, and along the Snake River— they could never return.

But our elders also taught us important lessons about respecting others in spite of the many tragedies and indignities they experienced. At the old Longhouse, a dispute had arisen between the traditional Longhouse people and those of a local church, who wanted to enter and pray before a wake service. The traditionalists wanted no part of "those people" praying inside the Longhouse.

After much discussion my grandfather, Charley, rose. He spoke of a great rope descending from above. He related that as this great rope got nearer to Mother Earth, it came apart into various strands. He said that to each strand is a religion—the Catholic, the Protestant, the Pentecostal, and the Longhouse. And all are connected to this great rope as it ascends above them to the one Creator. The traditionalists allowed the church people to enter with their prayers before continuing with the services led by my grandfather. From him and other family elders I have learned religious tolerance.

My work with the National Park Service, and hearing stories such as in this book, have provided something like a homecoming, and further renewed my interest in our heritage. We never saw our Nez Perce, Palus, and Yakama elders as famous people, and they did not seem to affect any special privilege. To be sure, circumstances of the 19th century cast Chief Kamiakin as a figure of great significance in the history of our people and land. But as this story shows, his remarkable life was connected to a wide realm of family members and friends. There were many other men and women of kindness, courage, and wisdom, and their experiences are also related here. These qualities made them honorable people, and books like *Finding Chief Kamiakin* flesh out their history—what I call the "documented record."

Some readers in both the Indian and White communities may object to how a name or term is spelled, or question a specific date given for an event. History seems to have many "knowing" eyes. All of these written words, however, will not change our true history. But for me, the matter of greater significance is that this work validates the story of our people, and helps us contend with the influences still threatening to scatter us further.

I knew Cleveland Kamiakin, Charley Williams, and Willie Red Star Andrews as living persons—not as mere figures in a book. But younger people today who did not know them in life can still make their acquaintance through stories like these, and better understand the responsibility to uphold our honored traditions. *Renegade Tribe* helped in important ways to do this and these persons now emerge again in *Finding Chief Kamiakin*. Their descendants will, in turn, provide the next chapter of our people's enduring story.

Nespelem, Washington
July 10, 2007

Foreword

Robert H. Ruby

*T*his book is the first inclusive biography of Chief Kamiakin, a major Indian leader of the 19th century Inland Northwest. This remarkable story portrays his life from birth to death. It is an astounding presentation, since the search for elusive facts has come from countless oral histories and interviews, and required sorting through innumerable sources in libraries, archives, and depositories, revealing primary information never before appearing in published form. A.J. Splawn's pivotal biography, *Ka-Mi-Akin: The Last Hero of the Yakimas* (1917), was mainly limited in its time-scope to what Splawn wrote in the preface: "It is to present the Indian side of the war of 1855–58." There are brief segments of Kamiakin's story in many other books, but these also are largely restricted to the wars in that era.

Richard Scheuerman and Michael Finley have reconstructed the full dramatic saga of Kamiakin's long life, as well as an extensive genealogy of the chief's extended family. At first glance, such an effort would seem impossible today, after the passage of so many years. It was accomplished, however, by a very persistent and patient recording and review of Native people's oral histories.

This was fused with original source materials and accounts written down by Whites who played roles in 19th century Plateau history. Scheuerman and Finley also consulted the work of later historians and researchers, such as Cull White and Okanogan County Judge William C. Brown, who interviewed first and second generations of Native people who lived from the time of their late-19th century restriction to reservations, up to their passing by the mid-20th century. Indians now also interpret that information themselves with their own perspectives.

Scheuerman is among the cadre of non-Indians who have collected Native history through oral interviews over many years, and who has worked with tribal historians such as Michael Finley to bridge gaps in the continuity of the available historical accounts. Scheuerman, a professor at Seattle Pacific University, has spent over three decades documenting the Kamiakin story. Finley, a member of the Confederated Tribes of the Colville Indian Reservation, is a professional historian and cultural advisor, and serves on the Colville Business Council.

They are among the emerging authors and historians of both cultures who are gathering, interpreting, and writing Indian and frontier history. The future assures more Indian history will be written from the Native perspective, adding to or altering aspects of the history previously seen or written only through the eyes of Whites, some of which was biased, or unintentionally faulty due to a shortage of primary sources.

Scheuerman and Finley have impressively told the story of Chief Kamiakin's role in the fur trade and missionary eras, the coming of American governance, the Pacific Northwest Indian treaties and wars, and the spread of White ranching and settlement in the post-Civil War era. They correct common misrepresentations of his controversial life, depicting the leadership and humanity of an individual whose life spanned a time of unprecedented cultural change. The book explains how Kamiakin sought to retain the homes and culture of his family and people against overwhelming odds and circumstances. *Finding Chief Kamiakin* also explains how his sons, daughters, and grandchildren endeavored to maintain their cultural identity in the 20th century, in the face of early oppressive education policies, federal termination efforts, and other persistent challenges.

In my own regional travels and studies over the years, I had many opportunities to visit with members of the extended Kamiakin family. I have had a lifelong interest in Native Americans. As a small boy, I remember local Indians coming to my father for assistance at our farm near Mabton, close to the east side of the Yakama Indian Reservation. Klickitats also often came down from the Horse Heaven Hills, riding their mounts from Bickleton and Cleveland. My father furnished provisions as they visited when passing through. In wintertime, their horses would drift down from the hills, looking for fodder under the snow and in my father's alfalfa fields.

In summer, Yakamas came looking for farmers wanting to rent Indian allotments, seeing if they could get advance payment. This usually was unsuccessful, as payments were required to be handled by the Indian agent; any money given directly to an Indian owner was not credited as prepayment. On Flag Day in June, Whites visited Cleveland, joining in the assemblage of Indians dressed in colorful beaded clothing, and watching the horse races, gambling, drumming, and chanting at the holiday gathering. Visitors tasted Native foods—combined with lots of carbohydrates such as macaroni, potatoes, bread, sweet desserts—and venison, as well as the best salmon I ever tasted. On the Fourth of July, our family joined the combined community celebration in Toppenish, where with boyhood wonder I watched the elaborately costumed Indians in the parades.

Later, I began recording conversations with my Indian friends and neighbors. This endeavor became a fascination for me in 1953, when the Public Health Service assigned me to the Pine Ridge Indian Reservation, where I had charge of the hospital for eighteen months. I wrote a small book based on my research there, *The Oglala Sioux: Warriors in Transition* (1955), which Alvin Josephy Jr. used as one of his references for *The Patriot Chiefs* (1961). This later encouraged me to write more, using the raw information I gathered here in the Pacific Northwest.

Almost immediately on returning to Washington State in 1955, I settled in Moses Lake, which then was a small agricultural town just beginning to expand with irrigation from the Grand Coulee Dam Project. Some early comers thought Moses Lake was named after the biblical Moses. Knowing better, I immediately started to research the life of Chief Moses, for whom the lake and town actually were named, in order to set the story straight. I began making numerous acquaintances and friends on the Colville Indian Reservation, including many of those noted in this book. I talked to Billy Curlew many times. It was a thrill to know he was Chief Moses' horse handler. I attended Billy Curlew's funeral, joining others in sprinkling soil on his grave.

I drove Cleveland Kamiakin, Chief Kamiakin's youngest son, around the Columbia Basin as he pointed out traditional trails, campsites, and other places. Quite elderly, Cleveland spoke slowly, in a quiet voice. Peter Dan Moses, another elder, also traveled with us. I particularly remember a sweathouse location he pointed out south of Soap Lake.

On a hot June 2, 1957, I also joined Cleveland and Peter Dan for the dedication of a monument to Chief Moses' sister, Sinsinq't. The burial site is situated at the edge of a high bank of the Columbia River at the mouth of Moses Coulee, not far from Wenatchee. Men at the dedication mostly wore heavy felt, broad brimmed, brown hats, the usual attire at the time. Cleveland's hat, however, was black with a high, cone-shaped crown and decorated with a bright green scarf stretched around it.

Emily Peone, another Kamiakin descendant whom I visited several times in Auburn, Washington, was very expressive, remembering places, names, and dates. She was a walking reference for history, a "professional" Indian storyteller. Another person with that talent was Isabella Arcasa. She was devoted to her faith, and told me that one time she flew to Alaska to see Pope John when his plane landed there. She raised many orphaned children on the Colville Reservation, as well as youngsters whose parents were unable to care for them. She was a great preserver of foods, mostly Native staples, and canned each summer and fall, including salmon.

Prodded by a story Isabella told, I made a most rewarding trip to New Zealand. When only four years old, Isabella was staying one day at Billy Curlew's home, near the cemetery south of Nespelem. She discovered that Chief Moses' grave had been opened and disturbed. Beads and other items were scattered on the ground. Upon hearing Isabella's story, I recalled that clothing belonging to Moses was owned by the Otago Museum at Dunedin, New Zealand. It was said to have been purchased in Yakima long before Moses' death in 1899. But I wondered about this; could the garments have been the same that Moses was buried in, and later stolen, but sold with a false story that it was older clothing?

I immediately made reservations to fly "down under." There, I met with Otago anthropologist Wendy J. Harsant, and then went to the museum to meet anthropologist G.S. Park, who showed me the designs on the coat, which easily were identifiable as belonging to Moses. It was of a small size, however, something that Moses would have worn in mid-life, nor were there any soiled spots or burial mold. Whatever its provenance, I hope that someday the regalia might be returned to its original Northwest home.

One of my favorite persons to visit was Madeline Covington, the widow of Robert Covington. Her husband had provided information to anthropologist Verne Ray for the book, *The Sanpoil and Nespelem* (1932). Members of the extended Covington family, such as Madeline, knew many details about the Moses and Kamiakin families. After a horse accident, Madeline had lost her right arm, and her left elbow was so stiff that her fingers could not reach her mouth. She used a thin stick at least a foot long with a notched end, fitting a cigarette into it to smoke. This device even outdid President Franklin Roosevelt's famous cigarette holder. She resided in Nespelem, and always had a smile and pleasant, low-key giggle.

Henry Covington, Robert's brother, lived up the Sanpoil River at the mouth of Cache Creek. He also had a fine memory, sharing information with me. I remember a pair of snowshoes that he made out of stout willow stems and laced with rawhide strips. He was a delightful person, who had been a great friend of amateur historian Cull White. Henry had papers showing that he had been employed by the military at one time, stationed at Ft. George Wright outside of Spokane.

Others that I became acquainted with on the reservation included Chief Jim James, whose aristocratic demeanor exuded authority, yet he was soft-spoken. I remember driving into James' yard one winter day to visit and seeing his buggy dusted with snow under a tree. Helen Toulou resided in the southeast part of the reservation where the town of Kewa once was located. She was the descendant of a Lake mother and the son of a high profile British official connected with the fur trade. Helen was a sturdy woman, as was Clara Moore who lived at Belvedere. At the time, Clara was a champion huckleberry picker and most talented weaver of baskets. She told me about a trip to Spokane in November 1926, taking part in a grand reception for Queen Marie of Romania. Clara showed me the leather dress that she had made for the occasion. It now is preserved at the Museum of Arts and Culture in Spokane. The authors of *Finding Chief Kamiakin* made notable use of accounts left by these people and other families.

Life is constantly evolving. A half-century ago, it was difficult for a White person to enter a reservation and receive any attention, and almost impossible to get answers to questions. Rightfully so, because Indian people thought most Whites only came there to take advantage of them. After being introduced around by Cull White, however, I got along fine on my own.

Cull had been a sheep man, moving seasonally around the region and becoming a friend to many Indians, knowing their ages and backgrounds. Cull had two homes—in Ephrata and at Coulee Dam on the Colville Reservation. I often stayed at his house in Coulee Dam. The menu usually was a tasty, ribsticking, camp stew. Cull also stayed overnight at my home in Moses Lake, often unexpectedly arriving in the evening while on a trip. Cull recorded his talks with Indians and today those valuable notes are retained at Washington State University and have been used by the authors of this book.

As early as the 1880s, the U.S. government began forbidding Indian children to speak their Native tongue when they were placed in boarding schools far from their homes. This dismantling of Native American culture also was an assault on the retention of tribal history. The boarding school rules in those days were harsh. Eventually, Indian storytellers who transferred histories verbally from generation to generation almost became a thing of the past. Their place now has been largely taken over by educated Native people. Many tribes are now resurrecting their history by consulting elders for any remembrances that they retain. The new tribal historians are also gleaning libraries, archives, and other repositories, appreciative of the historical sources and materials that were gathered earlier.

Scheuerman and Finley's research inspires me, because of their persistence and the great amount of information they were able to find. I had pangs of nostalgia, wishing I could start another go-round in recording and writing Indian history. However, "you can't go home again."

But things have changed. Indian people are writing their own history. The people I knew and worked with, the first- and second-generation descendants of those Indians of the last half of the 19th century, have passed away. The demeanor of the people today has changed as well. They are managing for themselves, on their own determination. When visiting the agencies years ago, I would need help finding an Indian employed there. Today this is reversed. Now I have to hunt through the offices a bit to find a White employee, as it should be.

I made trip after trip in all seasons to gather information at Spokane, Lapwai, Yakima, Wenatchee, and Nespelem. Driving in midwinter from Moses Lake up to Grand Coulee was rather treacherous on highways glazed with slippery ice. I crossed the Columbia River at Coulee Dam to drive onto the reservation. The high, steep banks of the river would be shrouded with snow, flashing sparks from the sun. Turning north toward Nespelem, the snowy countryside became even more eye-blinding white. There was quietness, as if everything were at rest. Nothing moved but for a wandering horse, while other horses hunkered in groups or stood under trees. Only an infrequent slow-moving automobile passed by. When coming into town, I could see small houses with wood smoke vapors slowly swirling from chimneys.

Gravel and dirt off-roads were traveled with caution. One always carried overnight supplies in case of problems. Inside the homes, however, there was warmth and comfort. In the yards stood abandoned cars and discarded items, covered with snow. Paths led to woodpiles and outhouses. One blind lady had a rope attached to her house; she could hold onto it in finding her way when outside.

When springtime warmth swept away the snow, however, there was lots of movement outdoors, and in midsummer the daytime temperatures were high. Green grass on the hillsides turned yellow, before fading to autumn rust brown. I brought along my children when they were old enough to swim, hike, and camp. They played and socialized with Indian children. It was safe then to drive on the off-roads visiting families. Birds sang and other wild creatures scampered about. Wagons and cars were on the roads, and there was a cacophony of rodeos, celebrations, sport events, and other gatherings.

When visiting the reservation, I talked to storytellers who had a special ability to keep and pass on vocal history. This has faded, after new technology took over—long-time memory is no longer necessary. Tribes I worked with, such as the Colvilles, Umatillas, Spokanes, and Yakamas, today are determined to resurrect their history. They also have programs attempting to recovery lost or diminishing Native languages. Some dialects have been revived enough to use; others are only remnants of what once was spoken.

There is another reason I cannot return to doing research as it once was for me. It would be lonesome. I have lost my writing partner, John Brown. I first met John about 1960, when he was head of the Wenatchee Valley College history department. John called me one day after returning from a trip to the Washington State Library in Olympia, where he had been researching Chief Moses. A librarian told him that I was doing similar research and had used the same materials. John then contacted me by mail. I answered with a perfunctory reply, however, thinking he was a student at the college.

He persisted and wrote again, telling me of his position and interests. We agreed to meet and he came to Moses Lake.

We decided then and there to work together on a Chief Moses biography. Our common interest led to a lengthy collaboration—the partnership was flawless. I was the luckiest person to have worked with John. We worked at the same speed—without computers, of course—sharing the same passion for some forty years.

By the time of our first meeting, I had spent half a decade or more interviewing knowledgeable people on the Colville Indian Reservation. Since I already had done most of the interviews for the Colvilles, John and I spent more time together on the Spokane Reservation, then the Umatilla Reservation, and so on. But we kept up visitations to the Colvilles, whose people are related to families on the other Plateau reservations. The last time that John Brown and I visited the Colville Reservation together was in 1989, for a grand celebration of Isabella Arcasa's 100th birthday.

In *Finding Chief Kamiakin*, I revisit Indian people whose lives have deeply enriched my own—the first- and second-generation descendants of those who struggled through the Indian wars and the early decades of reservation life. We read biographies of Joseph, Moses, Leschi, and other great leaders in the Pacific Northwest, but until now there has been no definitive, close-up account of Kamiakin. Though Kamiakin's people were pushed to their knees by overwhelming waves of Euro-Americans in the 19th and early 20th centuries, they were not beaten. Today, they retain a distinctive, thriving culture. Time has brought together two authors, one of each culture, to do justice to Chief Kamiakin.

Moses Lake, Washington
July 15, 2006

Preface

*K*amiakan Butte. Owhi Lake. Leschi Point. Qualchan Road. Located on maps depicting a vast and varied landscape from the Bitterroot Range to Puget Sound, place names such as these commemorate Indian leaders and evoke the Pacific Northwest's enduring Native American heritage. It is less widely known that these individuals, whose names are also attached to many additional places across the region, were members of the same extended family. In some instances, names such as Spokane and Walla Walla are recognitions noting traditional tribal homelands.

Such designations were applied by surveyors, cartographers, civil engineers, and local residents, who sought to pay tribute to leading figures among the region's First Peoples. A century ago, for example, pioneer banker James Perkins of Colfax, Washington, recommended that a wedged-shaped prominence near Pullman be named "Kamiak Butte." He respected the historical past and suggested that any area possessing a "Steptoe Butte," honoring the commander of an ill-fated 1858 expedition, should also pay tribute to Chief Kamiakin, the Yakama-Palouse leader popularly credited with the Army's defeat.

In the Cascades east of White Pass, an imposing basalt dome, "Kamiakan Butte," separates Rimrock Lake from Clear Lake. Over the years, Kamiakin's name also has been attached to schools, parks, and streets from Pullman to Seattle, and now identifies premium regional wines and prize-winning racehorses.

Names such as Kamiakin and Owhi sound vaguely heroic to today's Northwest residents. Written histories describe them in the context of the dynamic times in which they lived, and tell about their struggle to maintain cultural autonomy in the face of an overwhelming flood of Euro-American settlement. This epic sweep of human history would violently claim the lives of a number of prominent Indian leaders, including Owhi, Leschi, and Qualchan, whose deaths occurred through the treachery of their adversaries. They did not die on the battlefield, although Kamiakin and Qualchan were severely wounded in battles in 1858. Rather, Indian leaders were captured and sometimes executed in a conscious effort to break Native resistance to American rule.

"The soldiers tried to catch and kill all our good fighters," recalled Mary Owhi Moses, daughter of Yakama Chief Owhi and Qualchan's sister, at a distance of sixty years when inter-

viewed by Judge W.C. Brown at Nespelem in 1918. In many instances they succeeded, and the victims' widows and young children were left to fend for themselves.

The remarkable story of the life of Chief Kamiakin before and after the Northwest Indian wars, and of other participants and their descendants, is less known. In Eastern Washington, it might seem that when open conflict came to an end in the fall of 1858, virtually all Indians accepted relocation as their fate, and the displaced soon afterward moved to area reservations. But for many Indian families this was not the case. In addition to exercising treaty rights arising from the 1855 Walla Walla Council guaranteeing seasonal hunting, fishing, and gathering on ceded lands, many Indian families, such as the Kamiakins, tenaciously clung to outposts in their old homeland for many years. Chief Kamiakin's story also represents constancy in the face of so much misfortune, and a moral challenge to the great national theme of continental conquest.

At the dawn of the 20th century, significant numbers of Indian families still lived at the ancient village of *Palus* at the mouth of the Palouse River, at *Samuya* not far from present-day Ice Harbor Dam on the lower Snake River, at the White Bluffs village of *Tacht*, and further upstream at *P'na* near Priest Rapids along the Columbia River, as well as other locations in the region. While most of these places are now flooded by hydroelectric-dam reservoirs, some Indian families still own properties in these localities under the terms of the Indian Homestead Act.

After the 1855–58 battles and a year of exile in the Bitterroots of Montana and Idaho, Kamiakin returned with his family in 1859 to the Columbia Plateau, where he lived for the remainder of his life, independent of tribal, reservation, or government authority. This is a biography of that man. It also is the story of his sons and daughters during their challenging transition to life on reservations, principally the Colville reserve, but also among the Yakama and Coeur d'Alene confederated tribes. Kamiakin's descendants became prominent in Indian cultural and political affairs in the 20th century, and often sought, under difficult circumstances, to assert treaty rights negotiated by Kamiakin and other Plateau leaders in 1855.

Chief Kamiakin's effort to steer an independent and honorable course for his people was undertaken against the backdrop of cataclysmic change, which threatened the cultural existence of the region's First Peoples. His actions drew the wrath of Oregon and Washington territorial officials, a number of whom could not abide the presence of an articulate and defiant spokesman for Indian sovereignty.

While acknowledged by Governor Isaac I. Stevens at the 1855 Walla Walla Council as the "Head Chief" of the Yakamas and Palouses, a designation Kamiakin would not have sought, he also had close family relationships with the Nez Perces and Spokanes, while his marriages likewise brought important alliances with the Klickitats and Moses-Columbias. Ironically, Kamiakin's resolute course of action in defense of his people, homeland, and traditions led to disaffected relationships with some members of these tribes, who were seeking other accommodations with the newcomers. Because of these circumstances, Kamiakin came to have few confidants among his own people, fewer with the British, and none among the Americans during the late 1850s.

Outside of his personal family relationships, only a handful of individuals emerge from historical accounts as people knowing Kamiakin well during the pivotal years of conflict—the Oblate missionary Father Charles Pandosy, Hudson's Bay Company trader Angus McDonald at Ft. Colvile, and Chief Piupiu Maksmaks of the Walla Wallas. But the circumstances of American conquest caused the British subjects to eventually withdraw from the area, and the war claimed Piupiu Maksmaks under despicable circumstances at the hands of Oregon Volunteers. For these reasons, and because he fought a generation before reporters from national newspapers or such Eastern publications as *Harper's Weekly* covered the exploits of Chief Joseph and Sitting Bull, Kamiakin has remained an enigmatic figure.

Descriptions of his character by Indian and White, by friend and foe, however, are almost universally admirable. To Isaac Stevens, Kamiakin's "countenance" had "an extraordinary play," reminding the governor of "the panther and the grizzly bear." The intrepid traveler Theodore Winthrop, who journeyed through the Yakima Valley prior to the war period, noted that Kamiakin was "every inch a king," yet imbued with a profound humility that enhanced his regal bearing.

Winthrop's words hint at the family's remarkable Star Brothers origin in the night sky, which fostered a special sense of dignity and responsibility among fabled Chief Weowicht's descendants, such as Owhi, Kamiakin, and Mary Moses. Trader McDonald described Kamiakin as "well-formed and powerful," and possessing a "sagacious intellect" of "clear foresight." Kamiakin's assumed premonitions suggests a fig-

ure of tragic heroism, but McDonald's portrait of Kamiakin also showed him to be "a hospitable man and fond of fun and anecdote," and who enjoyed a glass of wine.

Yakima Valley pioneer A.J. Splawn—whose youthful and accidental encounter with Kamiakin led to succor when Splawn and a companion were lost on an 1865 trek through the Palouse region—characterized the chief as a man of "genius and devotion," and "the strongest personality of his time west of the Rocky Mountains." But even contemporaries such as Splawn and McDonald lamented the lack of documentation about Kamiakin's profound life.

Kamiakin was a great and good man—a devoted father and patriarch, who resourcefully provided for his substantial clan in times of need. The Yakama-Palouse leader invited the first missionaries to his homeland and protected them in the face of opposition from fellow tribesmen and territorial officials. He easily moved between worlds ancient and modern, guiding his adolescent sons and daughters on traditional spirit quests, but seeking Catholic baptism for his newborn children. He speared salmon at Kettle Falls with tools of archaic design, while also selectively breeding horses and introducing cattle and crop irrigation to his people.

The example of his life and other traditional influences would guide his descendants, included among them sons Tomeo and Cleveland, granddaughters Sophie (Wakwak) and Nellie (Friedlander), and great-grandchildren Frank George, Emily Peone, and Lucy Covington. All later provided insightful oral history and played leading roles in the 20th century struggles against termination and other federal policies designed to "pulverize" tribalism (as Theodore Roosevelt aptly termed it).

Kamiakin's youngest son, Cleveland, possessed a rare ability to skillfully serve his people's interests in the political convulsions of a new century. First, he kept alive the wisdom and traditions handed down from his parents and other elders, who had endured warfare, exile, and the uncertainties of life in a changing era. Much like his father, Cleveland possessed an ability to adjust to new times. He did not settle for short-term views and agreements of convenience with government and agency officials, when mid-20th century congressional legislation and federal power development along the Columbia River threatened the treaty rights negotiated in 1855. In the face of recurrent defeat in political affairs, ranging from salmon protection and tribal governance to off-reservation land claims and Bureau of Indian Affairs corruption, he remained a person of hope and supreme patience, who imparted the prospect of a fresh beginning each day.

Cleveland's agile mind was informed—but not constrained—by other opinions, past utterances, and previous defeats. Cleveland had strong associations with the Colville and Yakama reservations' last traditional chiefs, including Willie Red Star Andrews, Alex Saluskin, Peter Dan Moses, Alec Shawaway, Charley Williams, and Jim James. He drew from misfortune itself a will and a way for future success in a modern era of hard-fought battles in state and federal courts. The organizing of the Affiliated Tribes of Northwest Indians in 1947 contributed to the defeat in the 1960s of the federal government's reservation termination policy, testimony to the Indian Claims Commission in the 1950s led to decisions in favor of Indian petitioners in 1963, and the tribes' 1952 suit for Coulee Dam revenue-sharing finally prevailed four decades later.

As Cleveland grappled with challenges to his people's life along the region's great rivers and the threats to traditional values, Cleveland and also Tomeo adroitly guided Indian children in understanding their special heritage. The Kamiakin brothers patiently shared the wisdom and knowledge that they themselves had gleaned from their elders in earlier decades. They also gave of their time and provided invaluable assistance to a new generation of historians and anthropologists, such as Cull White, Verne Ray, and Robert Ruby, who were seeking understanding for themselves as well as for the general public.

While many essential and important details about Chief Kamiakin were recorded in A.J. Splawn's *Ka-Mi-Akin: The Last Hero of the Yakimas* (1917) and William C. Brown's *The Indian Side of the Story* (1961), other significant information has emerged in recent years. In the 1980s, historian Clifford Trafzer of Washington State University organized a research project among elders at the Nez Perce, Colville, and Yakama reservations, which introduced scholars and both the Indian and White communities to the profound significance of Indian oral histories. This work led to several important publications by Trafzer and his students regarding Chief Kamiakin and 19th century Indian policy.

Father Edward Kowrach's investigation into the life of Oblate Father Pandosy resulted in *Mie. Charles Pandosy, O.M.I., a Missionary of the Northwest: Missionary to the Yakima Indians in the 1850s* (1992). This led to Kowrach's discovery in Seattle's Catholic Chancery Archdiocese Archives of Kamiakin's letter, *Les Yakamas aux Soldats*, dictated to the Oblate black robe in the tense aftermath of Major Granville O. Haller's autumn 1855 campaign. The document is remarkable for Kamiakin's extensive recitation and commentary on events leading to the outbreak of war and his perspective on means to resolve the conflict. At the Oblate Archives Deschaletets in Ottawa, Kowrach uncovered other relevant letters from fathers Pandosy and Chirouse during their years at St. Joseph's (Ahtanum) Mission, which had been founded at Kamiakin's behest.

The writing of *Finding Chief Kamiakin* greatly benefited from the contributions of family elders residing on the Colville, Yakama, Coeur d'Alene, and Nez Perce reservations. They generously and patiently gave of their time to share stories about Kamiakin and members of his immediate family. We especially thank the late Arthur Tomeo Kamiakin, Emily Friedlander Peone, and Andrew George. These individuals deeply enriched our lives and provided important commentary on matters related to the family's experiences in the Palouse country after the war, the relocation to reservations, and their involvement in tribal cultural and political affairs.

Other tribal elders whose guidance and kind fellowship is gratefully acknowledged include Barbara Aripa, Sharon Redthunder, Agnes Davis, Albert Redstar, Tanya Tomeo, Carrie Jim Schuster, Gordon Fisher, Wilson Wewah Jr., Agatha Bart, Frank Andrews Sr., and Ronald "Duckie" Friedlander.

Most special thanks to Cliff, Frank, and Merle Sijohn and to Thomas Connolly S.J., Mahlon Kriebel, and Glen Leitz for sharing insights and organizing an unforgettable fieldtrip on the sesquicentennial of the Steptoe Battle.

Also of special relevance to this study is a 1984 WSU Libraries accession consisting of interviews conducted by central Washington historian Cull White with Kamiakin and Moses descendants in the 1940s and 1950s. We likewise give tribute to Robert H. Ruby and the late John A. Brown for their unfailing generosity and fellowship throughout our endeavor, as well as for providing historical resources they gathered while completing their unprecedented number of contributions to the University of Oklahoma's acclaimed Civilization of American Indians Series.

Other scholars whose works have significantly contributed to this study include Bruce Rigsby, Eugene Hunn, Ronald Grimm, David Stratton, Roderick Sprague, Dan McDermott, and Greg Cleveland. We also give recognition to Ron Pond, Barbara Aston, Debbie Brudie, and Mary Collins of WSU's Plateau Center for American Indian Studies for their dedicated efforts in preserving Indian culture and history.

We also thank Alex McGregor, Greg Partch, Gary Libey, Jerry Moss, Gary Schneidmiller, Robert Eddy, Andrew Joseph Jr., Jackie Cook, Geraldine Gabriel, Cato Tomeo, Gene Nicholson, Kenneth Tollefson, Bernie Griffith, Walter Gary, Eric Sorenson, Steve Emerson, Jerry Galm, James Payne, and the Homer Splawn family.

Valued archival and institutional services were provided by Camille Pleasants, Connie Johnston, Milton Davis Jr., John Sirois, Don Shannon, and Guy Moura of the History and Archaeology Office, Colville Confederated Tribes, Nespelem; Pamela Fabela, Yakama Nation Museum, Toppenish; Mike Mahaney, Ft. Simcoe State Park, White Swan; Michael Rule, Turnbull National Wildlife Refuge, Cheney; Mike Siebol and Summer Hahn, Yakima Valley Museum; Diane Mallickan and Jim Speer, Nez Perce National Historical Park, Lapwai, Idaho; Patty McNamee, National Archives and Records Administration, Seattle; and Laila Miletic-Vejzovic, the late Larry Stark, Cheryl Gunselman, Trevor Bond, and Patsy Tate of Manuscript, Archives, and Special Collections, Holland-Terrell Library, WSU.

We also wish to thank Rose Krause and Jane Davey of the Northwest Museum of Arts and Culture, Spokane; Charles Mutschler, Kennedy Library Archives, Eastern Washington University, Cheney; Rayette Sterling, Northwest Room, Spokane Public Library; Robert Leopold and Vyrtis Thomas, National Anthropological Archives, Smithsonian Museum, Washington, D.C.; and John Amita, Museum of Anthropology, Pennsylvania State University, Philadelphia.

Other important information for *Finding Chief Kamiakin* was gleaned from regional newspapers. For their patient consideration of our requests, we express appreciation to Wilfred Woods of the *Wenatchee Daily World*; Gordon Forgey and Jerry Jones, *Colfax Gazette*; and Carla Richerson and Nicole Bouche, Special Collections Division, Suzzallo Library, University of Washington, Seattle. The abiding encouragement and suggestions provided by Palouse country native Donald Meinig, author of Yale University's magisterial Shaping of America Geographical Series, is likewise gratefully acknowledged.

The Gustavus Sohon portraits from the 1855 Walla Walla Treaty Council were provided courtesy of the Washington State Historical Society, Tacoma; we thank WSHS director David Nicandri and staff members Gary Schalliol, Joy Werlink, and Elaine Miller for their encouragement and valued assistance. The epic series of Palouse War murals featuring vivid scenes of the Steptoe Battle and Wright Campaign are the masterful work of Spangle artist Nona Hengen, who spent years studying original accounts and the actual landscapes depicted in each painting. We also are very thankful for the patient copyediting by Vicki Cibicki and Kerry Darnall.

This project was motivated in part by educational opportunities recently formulated through Washington Senate House Bill 1495 for "the teaching of tribal history, culture, and government in the common schools." We especially acknowledge the cooperation of Northwest tribal officials in our efforts, and the institutional support and encouragement provided by Editor-in-Chief Glen Lindeman of the Washington State University Press, and Art Ellis, Chris Sink, Frank Kline, and Rick Eigenbrood of Seattle Pacific University.

We are deeply grateful for family and friends whose encouragement has supported us throughout our endeavor, including Lois and Jackie, and Richard Johnson, Bill Schmick, Keith Merritt, John Waldren, and Jennifer Ferguson.

Richard D. Scheuerman
Seattle, Washington

Michael O. Finley
Inchelium, Washington

A Note

Historical Illustrations, Epigraphs, and Spellings

The remarkable images drawn by German immigrant Gustavus Sohon (1825–1903) and other artists of Isaac Steven's Northern Pacific Railroad Survey in the 1850s provided the first comprehensive visual documentation of the land and peoples of the Columbia Plateau. Sohon skillfully drew images of the region from 1852 to 1863, and sketched Chief Kamiakin and tribal leaders participating in the Walla Walla Treaty Council of 1855. In many cases, these portraits are the only known visual depictions of these individuals.

Replete with such documentation as names, dates, and color codes, Sohon's work is considered among the finest technical and artistic renderings of the Northwest and its indigenous peoples. It is as significant as the work of the expedition's official artist, American landscape painter John Mix Stanley (1814–72). Sohon's linguistic studies and artistic works are preserved today at the Washington State Historical Society in Tacoma, Washington State University in Pullman, and the National Anthropological Archives in Washington, D.C.

The monumental Senate reports for the transcontinental surveys, published between 1855 and 1861, bear the ponderous title *Reports of Explorations and Surveys to Ascertain the Most Practicable and Economic Route for a Railroad from the Mississippi River to the Pacific Ocean*. The multi-volume set contains a number of Sohon and Stanley lithographs, including such views as the Grand Coulee, the Columbia River, and the Palouse Hills. Detailed drawings of western flora and fauna were contributed by J.H. Richard (zoological) and John Young (botanical). Three-plate lithography often was used, with images separately colored in black and sienna with either olive green or sky blue. Other Sohon lithographs were included in John Mullan's *Report on the Construction of a Military Road from Fort Walla-Walla to Fort Benton* (1863).

In *Finding Chief Kamiakin*, italicized epigraphs at the beginning of each chapter feature portions of a Salmon origin myth that has been related for generations among the Kamiakins and other Plateau Indian families. This version was told in 1980 by Andrew George, late at night around a small kitchen table at his home on the Yakama Indian Reservation near Toppenish.

Kamiakin's name is variously spelled in the historical records (e.g., Kamiahkin, Kamiakun), but is pronounced by family elders as *K'əmáyaqən*, which is most closely rendered in standard English as "Kamiakun." However, the written form "Kamiakin" is used in this story, since it appears most commonly that way in period documents and tribal records. Similarly, this also pertains to Owhi (*Áwxay*), Teias (*Tiyáyaš*), Showaway (*Sháwaway*), Skloom (*Shklúum*), Kanasket (*Kánašq't*), Qualchan (*Kwálchŭn*), and Quiltenenock (*Qwiltnínak*).

The place name "Yakima" is used here as a geographic reference to the Pacific Northwest valley and city, while the spelling "Yakama" refers to the Indian tribe of that name and their traditional homeland. Some 19th century references that remain in conventional use, such as the "1855 Yakima Treaty," retain the original spelling in the text.

Ft. Colvile refers to the upper Columbia fur trading post established at Kettle Falls in 1825 and named for a Hudson's Bay Company official, Andrew Colvile. On the other hand, the spelling "Colville" refers to the upper Columbia Indian tribe, the reservation, and the U.S. military fort.

Words and expressions exist in any language for which there is no true equivalent in others. Indian names in translation and seemingly close synonyms can have different connotations, misrepresenting a word or even an entire concept. For these reasons, use of indigenous terms sometimes seemed reasonable, with an explanation of its meaning in the text where appropriate.

The Columbia Plateau was divided linguistically with Sahaptin-speaking tribes, including the Yakamas, Palouses, and Nez Perces, to the south, and Interior Salish peoples to the north, such as the Moses-Columbias and Spokanes. Although these two language families were mutually unintelligible, many Indians in the region, including some members of the Kamiakin clan, were bilingual due to intertribal family connections and seasonal travel patterns. Places throughout the region, therefore, often had more than one traditional name. Unless otherwise noted, geographical names are used in the language of the tribal area where located and appear in italics. In addition, the Chinook trading jargon was spoken in many places—a simplified polyglot of several hundred Chinook, French, and English words used by both Indians and White frontiersmen.

Most of the letters for spelling Sahaptin and Interior Salish personal and place names appear in Standard English, but several symbols and diacritical marks shown in the following chart indicate some sounds in these languages unfamiliar in English. Among Native speakers there may be several ways to spell the same word, since some have only recently been rendered in written forms, and individuals and families maintain distinct phonetic structures. We acknowledge the contributions of Virginia Beavert, Tillie George, Agnes Davis, Albert Redstar Andrews, Margaret Gore, Dale Kincaid, Bruce Rigsby, and Noel Rude for systemizing the alphabet and lexicons for these languages and dialects.

á	short "a," as in "**a**rise"
áa	long "a," as in "p**ay**"
íi	long "i," as in "b**ee**"
k'	closing throat glottal stop, pronounce "k"
q'	closing throat glottal stop, pronounce "q"
c	"ts" sound, as in "hi**ts**"
č	"ch" sound, as in "**ch**urch"
ə	unaccented "uh" sound, as **a**bout
t'	closing throat glottal stop, pronounced "t"
u	short "u," as in "l**oo**k"
š	"sh" sound, as in "**sh**ape"
úu	long "u," as in "tr**ue**"
x'	guttural "kh," as in German "a**ch**"
ł	"lh" sound, as in "phi**lh**armonic"
´	phonemic accent
ʔ	glottal stop, as in the middle of "uh-oh"

Prologue

*In the time of the Animal People
there was a big village
down along* Pik'úunen [Snake River].
Salmon Man lived there.

*Many maidens wanted him
because he was strong and brave.
But Salmon only had eyes for
the beautiful sister,
the sister of the Wolf Brothers.*

Sk'olumkee, "Snake River Kamiakin," 1937.
WSU Libraries (L.V. McWhorter Collection)

*W*hen he arose at dawn, Sk'olumkee told Pemalks this would finally be the day. After washing themselves in the waters of nearby *Elatsaywitsun* (Sprague Lake), the old couple returned to their canvas-covered wagon and finished dressing. Pemalks put on a loose fitting, tan gingham shift with orange flower print and fastened her leather *dalpas* money pouch around her ample waist. She combed her long black hair, while her husband put on a dark evergreen shirt with ruffled sleeves. Even around their Johnson Lake place on the Colville Reservation, Sk'olumkee often wore such fancy shirts. He was a proud, aloof man, and how peculiar it was that this was the one luxury he allowed himself.

Accommodations in the wagon were not much different from their one-room shack back home. The unpainted frame house where they had lived for years featured a single square four-paned window. Inside, it was devoid of even a single piece of furniture—no table, no chairs, not so much as a footstool. They needed only a steamer trunk for Sk'olumkee's shirts, an apple box of pine slats to hold an extra blanket, a bottle of his liniment, and a small corner closet to hang her things. The same wool blankets they now were using on this trip covered a straw mattress on the floor back home. What more was really needed? Sk'olumkee could hang his wide-brimmed felt hat from a nail on the wall, next to the roots Pemalks dried every spring.

The trip from Nespelem to Rock Lake, 175 miles to the southeast, was only a few hours' quiet drive by automobile through gently rolling hills south of the Columbia River. But the old couple had been traveling by horse and wagon on their peculiar pilgrimage for at least a week now. The last stretch from Edwall to Sprague had incited more roadway chaos than usual. Seeing a decrepit vehicle crawling along the pavement in June 1941 was enough to slow most drivers down. Sk'olumkee's wife was not eager to head back to the highway past Sprague's two downtown blocks of stately brick buildings.

For a few moments, Pemalks thought about how proud she was of Sk'olumkee. He was still handsome in his seventy-fourth year, and she was a little older. She had not seen him wear this particular shirt during the trip, but she liked the smart look—narrow lines connected tiny red spangles that ran the length of the sleeves.

As Pemalks finished combing her hair, Sk'olumkee fastened the brass buttons on his red-brown leather vest that fit tightly against the slight hump of his back. His shoulder-length braids of gray-streaked black hair dangled onto the two orange and purple stars Pemalks had deftly beaded on the vest. She risked commenting on her husband's fine looks that morning when gazing upon his lean face. "So *Khwe̓sat* (Old Man)," she said raising both eyebrows, "Your grandfather's waters have restored your youth."

Sk'olumkee slightly smiled and shook his head. "*Sma̓wíc!* (Old Woman!), I still feel like a grandfather," he said with a slight slur in his speech.

He left the tent and gathered their cooking gear from the fire pit, while Pemalks neatly folded the blankets. They then worked together to take down the canvas, and in a familiar routine loaded their belongings into the box wagon.

The previous evening, Sk'olumkee had built a fire from wood and dry tules scavenged along the water's edge, and they consumed the last morsels of tasty camas cakes she had hoarded in recent days. They still had enough dried salmon stored in large cedar root baskets in the wagon, but the camas flour was almost gone. She had not expected the trip to take so long and now their supplies were running low. Pemalks knew that her husband kept a small bag of bitterroots in a pine box with some dried berries, as well as a steel-strike and matches that he packed with his things. She also remembered his curt response when asking him about using the roots for their next meal.

"You may have all that is left when we are finished!" he scolded. "You brought the money. You can buy White man's flour at the Ewan store tomorrow."

Pemalks was hoping they would move along and wanted to avoid driving back through the middle of town. She watched as Sk'olumkee threw some hay from a broken bale stashed in the back of the wagon to a pair of sway-backed mares, whose patient labor had somehow brought them this far. The horses looked tired even in the morning, and Pemalks wondered how they would fare the rest of the trip. As the mares munched on the tender stalks in the brisk morning air, Sk'olumkee threw the black leather harness across their backs and soon had connected them to the trace chains.

Moving on, the old couple could see the town folk beginning to stir and worried that their presence might become something of a spectacle. A band of low gray clouds brushed against the horizon to the north, but the early morning sunlight brilliantly shone off the white steeple of Mary, Queen of Heaven Catholic Church, towering even higher than the town's grain elevators. Shortly after starting to move through town, Sk'olumkee turned the team left to avoid Main Street and passed by the imposing brick edifice.

"The windows are beautiful," Pemalks whispered, just as a young boy rushing from an alley stopped in front of them. A look of wonder filled his eyes and he hesitated to cross until Sk'olumkee jerked the reins with a "*Hup-hey!*" and waved the startled lad by with a smile. In a few moments, they reached a gravel road leading east toward open prairie and the horses settled into a familiar plodding tempo.

Nearly an hour later, they came to a railroad crossing five miles beyond town. Sk'olumkee drew the reins to one side and led the team along a dirt trail following the tracks for a mile to the northeast. At the end of the trail he pulled back on the iron lever brake and handed the reins to Pemalks. "We need to make the lake by nightfall so I will not be long," he said. "Stay here with the horses."

He then reached behind to the pine box stored near his feet and took out two small bags. He slowly crawled down the side of the wagon and walked ahead toward a small aspen grove. In a couple of minutes he disappeared beyond the trees. Pemalks picked out a large canvas bag she kept behind the seat and pulled out a tangled pile of steel knitting needles and thick gray thread, used to repair a large wool stocking. In twenty minutes, Sk'olumkee returned to the wagon and pulled himself up into the seat. He returned the bags to the box and grabbed the reins without saying a word.

Soon they were on their way headed southeast, and in another hour approached a rise in the road. A meadowlark perched on a barbed wire fence sang its familiar springtime welcome. The jolting cadence of the iron-rimmed wheels slowed and the horses began to breathe more heavily, but Sk'olumkee snapped the reins as he exclaimed, "*Akailu!*" Pemalks felt a stiff breeze hit her face and was surprised that the ancient creatures seemed to take on new life.

In a moment, the grade leveled and a broad expanse of green and yellow pastureland, bisected by deep basaltic coulees, appeared before them. Far to the east, the pyramidal shape of Steptoe Butte stood prominently above the surrounding hills. Sk'olumkee knew he was finally home. "*Yáamuštas*, my power mountain! The Wolf Brothers will not get us now," he said with obvious delight, pointing so she would know.

"Yes, I see it" she said, "and I shall have a special meal for us tonight." She clutched her money pouch. "I have saved more than you think, and you said we will find a store by the lake."

Sk'olumkee raised his eyebrows and nodded with a smile just as a pickup truck passed them and honked, flushing a white-tail jackrabbit from the brush along a fence line.

"How long has it been since you were here?" Pemalks asked.

"Only last night," Sk'olumkee replied matter-of-factly. "I came in a dream and met an old boyhood friend I had long forgotten."

Then he explained to Pemalks what he had seen. Sk'olumkee had been wandering along a trail where a cluster of willows grew near his family's Rock Lake camp of long ago. He turned a corner and saw a bald-headed man clad in ragged buckskin staggering along, a short distance ahead. Sk'olumkee hollered something and the man turned and hobbled back a few steps. Then Sk'olumkee noticed he had no feet. The man grinned a great toothless smile of recogni-tion and began shouting and waving his arms. Sk'olumkee saw one hand also was missing, but ran to embrace his old friend. Then the dream had ended.

"So who was this pitiful creature?" Pemalks asked.

"Atween," sighed Sk'olumkee, as if she should have known. "He lived with us here in the old days; helped our mothers tend the children."

Without thinking, Pemalks said, "Well, at least he had a head." But she no sooner had spoken the words than pursed her lips with regret, and they rode the rest of the way in silence.[1]

Si'lailo (Celilo Falls) on the Columbia River, seven miles upstream from The Dalles rapids.
Museum of Arts & Culture, Spokane

Chapter 1
Rocks that Glisten

Salmon Man thought it over
when the Wolf Brothers were away.
They were away gathering
firewood for sweatbaths.
Salmon made up his mind
to go to their sister's lodge.

He wore a fancy headdress,
feathers green and red.
He stood outside, and she knew.
She could tell by the sound of his walk
and his pleasing scent.

Much of the talk during that Moon of Falling Needles in villages clustered along the Yakima River concerned an amazing encounter with a stranger who had come from lands beyond the buffalo country. Their Palouse and other tribal relatives farther to the southeast reported he rejoined a party of others, who plied the treacherous currents of *Nch'i-Wana*—"Big Water," the mighty Columbia—in dugout canoes headed toward the ocean.

The man with peculiar clothes and alien tongue had ventured up the Columbia within sight of the Yakima River (*Tape-tett*). The water was "remarkably clear and crouded with salmon," and in customary fashion he had feasted inside a tule-mat lodge on "boiled fish which was delicious," courteously offered to newcomers. William Clark and two men had left the main exploring party at the mouth of the Snake River on October 17, 1805, and were among the first Euro-Americans to witness one of the Pacific Northwest's mysteries—the return of immense numbers of fall salmon to the precise place of their origin. Evading a host of ocean predators, jumping towering cataracts, and escaping Indian spears, nets, and baskets, these majestic creatures now ended one of nature's epic quests by scattering their eggs and milt to birth a new generation.

For the Native peoples of the Columbia Plateau, the return of *sinux* (silver) and *kálux* (sockeye) salmon during the moons of Salmon Coming (August) and Salmon Spawning (October) was an experience to marvel, and was honored with sacred feasting; to the English-speaking pathfinder the phenomenon was to be observed and recorded as he had done for solar and lunar positions earlier that morning. For similar reasons, he had bagged an enormous sage grouse—"Size of a Small turkey" with a wingspan of 3½ feet—to describe yet another species new to Eastern scientists. Clark thanked his hosts for their hospitality, and noted they were fashionably clad with beads and shells, lived "in a State of comparative happiness," and "respect the aged with veneration."

Now in the spring of 1806, the reappearance of the inquisitive hat-wearing strangers was greatly anticipated by those who eagerly sought to learn more about the visitors' ways and intentions. But when word reached the Yakama in late April 1806 that the travelers had returned up the Columbia and were moving overland through the lands of their Walla Walla neighbors, the news was hardly a distraction for another bunch of explorers.[1] The child of a Palouse father and a Yakama mother ran with his playmates along a stream bank near their camp. The youngsters shouted while watching their willow branch miniature canoes float downstream on currents glinting with the golden lambency of sunny afternoons.

The valley landscape Kamiakin shared as a boy with his elders, brothers, and a wide circle of young friends was a vibrant wonderland of stirring adventure. Older family members commented on his vitality and intelligence as the boy pursued his playful, inquisitive ways in games of *kalilásh*, racing with willow wheels and poles. The bluebunch wheatgrass bottomlands along the *Aha-tah-num* (Ahtanum), the placid "Stream by Long Mountain," hosted a diverse flora, with clumps of ponderosa pine, towering cottonwood, and majestic white oak, brightened by the seasonal blossoms of golden currant bushes, as well as tangled honeysuckle vines with rows of fiery tubular flowers. Meadows burst redolent with wildflowers, beginning in the Moon of Buttercup Blooming (March) and continuing into summer with bluebells, sunflowers, purple iris, and yellow asters. Sugar bowl clematis grew among riverbank conifers on southern exposures.

Sometimes Kamiakin helped his mother gather fuzzy purple heads of lupine growing in stony places to decorate and purify nearby graves of their ancestors. The appearance of colorful blossoms occasioned lessons from elders, including the sorrowful tale of delicate Yellow Bell. The flower did not heed the warnings of Lily, Violet, and others, who pleaded with her to prepare for the hazards of springtime. When Chinook Wind suddenly appeared, these others were prepared in all their colorful finery, but Yellow Bell was left wearing a hastily fashioned costume of faded and drooping yellow.

Kamiakin's people also shared the land with the four-legged and winged tribes and other creatures. The riparian habitat offered sanctuary to migratory fowl such as geese, canvasbacks, and redhead ducks, as well as jackrabbits, marmots, and sometimes the troublesome *wáxpuš*—rattlesnake. Mourning doves, crows, and mergansers were common along the flatland brambles, where badgers sometimes lumbered along trails to their hillside burrows among copses of serviceberry and scraggly hackberry. Incomprehensible numbers of wraithlike mayflies, midges, and damselflies appeared in the spring and summer to feed larger winged neotropical creatures nesting in the Yakima Valley during seasonal journeys. Bluebirds, goldfinches, and the shimmering Rufous hummingbird, known to the Yakama as *q̓mamsa-lí*, fascinated the children.

Low trees along streambeds hosted the spherical twig-and-mudded mansions of magpies. Draped in distinctive feathered robes of iridescent black and white, magpies were ever anxious to ridicule the children who raced around these abodes. Kamiakin and his young hunting companions sometimes wished to shoot these annoying disputers, who swooped close to them whenever the boys approached springtime nests. Just as Kamiakin wanted to master his shooting skills, the young birds were tending to flying lessons and their parents would brook no interference. One of the boys once took aim at a hapless juvenile and struck him with an arrow, only to be sternly disciplined by his grandmother for violating a sacred fellowship. Like many birds known to Kamiakin, a distinctive magpie cackle was voiced in their name—*ach'ay*. But his friend's grandmother informed them that the bird's peculiar call came from the time of the Animal People, when ancestral Magpie lost an important race to Coyote.

Spilyáy and *Xaslú*

Kamiakin sought to learn from *Spilyáy*—Coyote—just as his elders did. When traveling with his grandfather in the shadow of sacred *Páhto*—"Standing High" (Mt. Adams)—they sometimes encountered a coyote in the distance. The boy observed his grandfather and the coyote staring intently at each other when the animal inevitably turned to watch. "We will have good luck hunting today," or "Someone needs

Jim family fishing camp at Fishhook Bend, looking north across the Snake River to the site of T'siyiyak's famed horse race. Ice Harbor Dam inundated Fishhook Rapids in 1961.
Washington State Historical Society (Roger Chute S1991.51.2.533)

us back home," his grandfather would report, and so it would come to pass. The boy wanted to know how to acquire these understandings, and slowly did so by learning from his elders' stories, carefully observing the animal and plant nations, and listening to *wesl'yawau*, the cries of the wind that bore news from distant places. But Kamiakin also wanted to know these far places directly.

Growing into adolescence, he continued to impress those around him. No youth his own age could best him at wrestling, nor many who were older. Yet Kamiakin's ready wit and cheerful presence balanced his competitive spirit and won him a wide circle of friends. Young Kamiakin took special pride in his father's fabled horseracing exploits among his native Palouse people. He heard the story of how the intrepid T'siyiyak had faced capture or death in battle with enemies, or from men jealous of his skills.

T'siyiyak's cunning in a celebrated Snake River horse race of champion riders was legendary. The young man from the village of *Hasúutin*, an eel fishery at present-day Asotin, had entered a heavily wagered contest held near *Samuya*, upstream from today's Pasco where two great rocks formed the ends of the course. T'siyiyak rode a spirited mount entered by a different owner, but claimed it as his own as part of the substantial gambling stakes that piled up where the horsemen lined up to start the race. T'siyiyak pulled ahead of the field, but fearing the owner would not part with the horse, he turned away at the far turn and left his other winnings unclaimed.[2]

This unexpected episode led to his legendary foray westward, where he first found sanctuary with a Wanapum headman, Swaptsa, at Priest Rapids. The young adventurer

next continued on to the land of the Yakamas where he fell in love with Com-mus-ni, the daughter of legendary Chief Wiyáwiikt (Weowicht) and his wife (who possibly was of Wenatchi background). The brash young Palouse eventually earned the respect of the Yakama leader, who allowed the two to marry. According to some family accounts, the couple soon journeyed east to dwell among T'siyiyak's Palouse people.[3]

Kamiakin, born about 1800, was the couple's first child, followed by sons Showaway (*Sháwaway*) and Skloom (*Shklúum*). About ten years later, Kamiakin and his brothers apparently relocated with their mother Com-mus-ni back to Yakama country.[4] From his mother's people, Kamiakin

Chief Wiyáwiikt (Weowicht) Family*

SONS—

Teias (Kittitas Valley)
 children: Sunk-hay-ee (*m.* Kamiakin *c.* 1825), Tom-teah-kuin, Josephine (Ye-mow-at), We-sham

Owhi (Kittitas Valley)
 children: Wow-ya-q'yah, Sq'ue-malks (Mary), Lo-k'out, Qualchan, Lesh-hi-hite, Q'uo-mo-lah, Si-een-wat (Mollie), Sanclow (Mary Owhi Moses), Yan-um-tk'o (Cecelia)

Tuh-noo-num (Kittitas Valley)

Te-wi-net (Kittitas Valley)

Sluskin ("Nachez and mountains at its source")

Sko-mow-wah ("Cowiche and Tieton")

Wi-na-ko ("Wenas, Umptanum, and Pahato")

Showaway ("Ahtanum down the Tapteal as far as Pisco")

DAUGHTERS—

Com-mus-ni (*m.* T'siyiyak)
 children: Kamiakin (born *c.* 1800), Showaway, Skloom, Kayoutonay

Su'q'um

* The Chief Wiyáwiikt family lineage with homeland designations is based on information recorded by Yakima Valley rancher and historian A.J. Splawn (1917) in interviews with Tomeo Kamiakin and other elders in the early 20th century. Splawn gave 1808 as the approximate date of Chief Wiyáwiikt's death. The children of Teias, Owhi, and Com-mus-ni are added to this list because of special pertinence to the *Finding Chief Kamiakin* story.

learned why the Wiyáwiikt clan was treated with a deference that bespoke their unique Star Brother ancestry.

Clear night skies held an incredibly sequined universe full of wonder along the *Lschchit* (White Path), explained to the boy in terms of mystical beings. Near the Milky Way shone the three bright stars of Orion's Belt, which were the "Cold" Wind Brothers; their canoe descended toward faint Salmon Star, located near blue-white Alnitak. The bright stars of Orion's Bow were the "Chinook" Wind Brothers, who attempted to thwart the movement of the Cold Winds.

The five stars of the Big Dipper's Handle were the five Wolves (*Xaliishyama*); they were led by Coyote along a trail of arrows that Chickadee shot to pierce the sky in order to hunt the Two Grizzlies, the Dipper's two side stars. On the other side of the pole star from the Wolves were the five white and pink stars of Elk Hide. These and the other principal stars of Cassiopeia appeared where light shone through holes, made when a legendary Yakama hunter used wooden stakes to dry the skin before casting it into the sky for all to admire.

Wherever Kamiakin's family roamed throughout the region, he could often see *Xaslú*, the bright evening star. He heard elders tell of a young Yakama woman named Tah-pal-lauw; she was mystically transposed to the celestial world—where *Xaslú* lived with his older brother star—when she and a younger sister, Yas-lam-mas, were on a root digging outing with her grandparents. The boy learned how Tah-pal-lauw later escaped back to earth on a rope fashioned of hazel withe.

Stone remnants of the rope could still be seen piled on Rattlesnake Mountain, located west of the Cascades near the confluence of the north and middle forks of the Snoqualmie River. The woman later gave birth to Kamiakin's ancestor in the vicinity of Chief Mountain, *Miyáwax* (Cowiche Mountain), in the Yakima Valley, where an outcropping of resinous black rock glistened as evidence of his remarkable birth. The baby's father was one of the Star Brothers. The evil Frog Women came from the coast to kidnap the child, but the boy was rescued by Blue Jay and restored to his mother.[5]

The name of the important fishing camp of *Miyáwax* near present Rimrock may have been derived from this story. It was the easternmost Yakama village on the

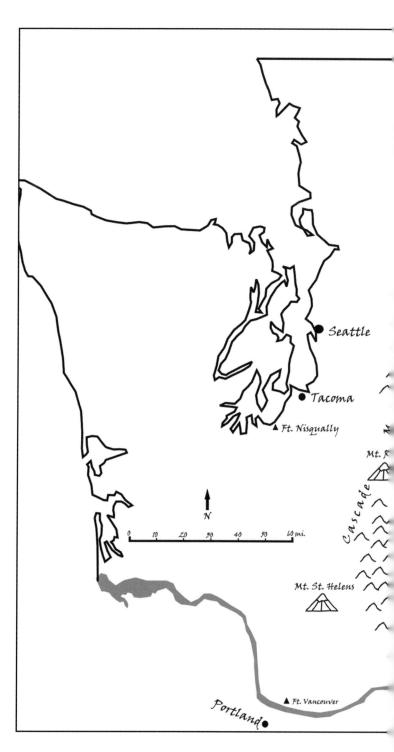

Tieton River, along an ancient Cascade trail forking above *Miyáwax* to Cowlitz, White, and Tieton passes. Wiyáwiikt's people sometimes frequented the rugged environs of White Pass and the Goat Rocks in the fall, where huckleberries grew in abundance and young men from the camps hunted

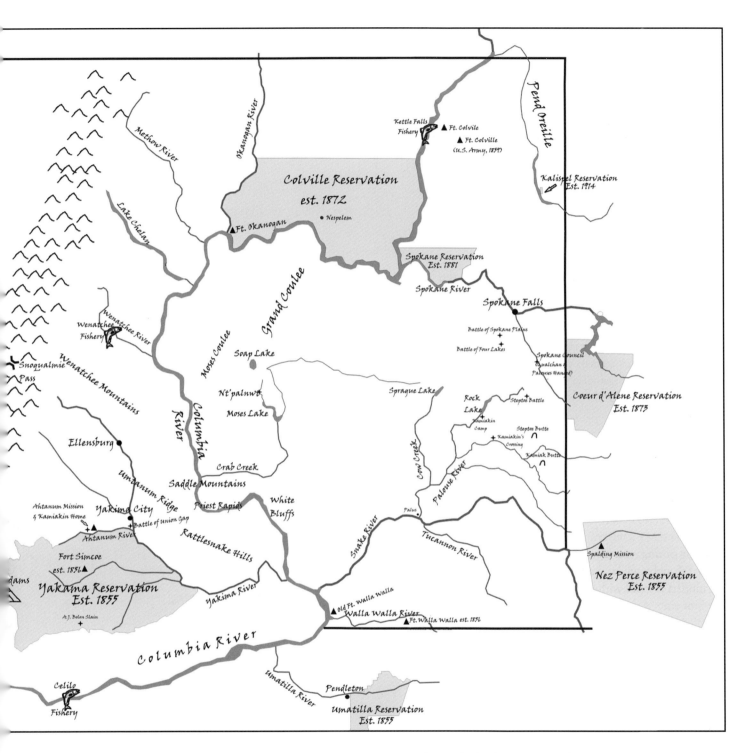

Methow River

Okanogan River

Kettle Falls Fishery

▲ Ft. Colvile

▲ Ft. Colville (U.S. Army, 1859)

Pend Oreille

Kalispel Reservation Est. 1914

Lake Chelan

Colville Reservation est. 1872

▲ Ft. Okanogan

• Nespelem

Spokane Reservation Est. 1881

Spokane River

Spokane Falls

Wenatchee River

Wenatchee Fishery

Grand Coulee

Moses Coulee

Soap Lake

Battle of Spokane Plains +

Battle of Four Lakes +

Spokane Council (Qualchan & Palouses Hanged)

Coeur d'Alene Reservation Est. 1873

Snoqualmie Pass

Wenatchee Mountains

Columbia River

Nt'palnwš

Moses Lake

Spraque Lake

Rock Lake

Kamiakin Camp

Steptoe Battle

Steptoe Butte

Kamiakin's Crossing

Kamiak Butte

Ellensburg •

Crab Creek

Cow Creek

Palouse River

Umtanum Ridge

Saddle Mountains

Priest Rapids

White Bluffs

Ahtanum Mission & Kamiakin Home

Yakima City •

+ Battle of Union Gap

Ahtanum River

Rattlesnake Hills

Palus

Snake River

Tucannon River

Spalding Mission ▲

Nez Perce Reservation Est. 1855

Fort Simcoe est. 1856 ▲

dams

Yakama Reservation Est. 1855

A.J. Bolen Slain +

Yakima River

Old Ft. Walla Walla ▲

Walla Walla River

▲ Ft. Walla Walla est. 1856

Columbia River

Celilo Fishery

Umatilla River

Pendleton •

Umatilla Reservation Est. 1855

mountain goat and other large game; the snowy wool of the elusive *wáaw* was highly prized for weaving into blankets of heavy twine.

The Star Brothers tale may also relate to Chief Wiyáwiikt's preference to reside seasonally at *Wapatukš* on the northern periphery of Chief Mountain. The village served as an important council ground in historic times. Some of the region's most striking panoramas of colorful *puh-tuh-num*, or pictographs, were prominent on a monumental gallery of lichen-encrusted, basaltic rock above Cowiche Creek along the

Ahtanum-Wenas trail. Multicolored human figures of ancient origin and crowned with concentric rayed arcs in red, black, and white adorned the columnar panels beneath stylized four-point stars that may have reminded young Kamiakin of his family's stellar ancestry.

Wiyáwiikt had sought to marry his sons to the daughters of headmen from similar villages as these. These alliances among the region's *miyawaxpamáma*, or "chiefly people," involved the elaborate exchange of many horses and valuable trade items, and gave special prominence to the Wiyáwiikt clan among the Yakamas.[6]

As Kamiakin grew older, he helped relatives tend the Wiyáwiikt clan's rapidly expanding herds foraging on prairie tablelands in the Yakima and Kittitas valleys. The blue-flowered camas (*Camas quamash*) and the wild onion (*Allium acuminatum*), members of the lily family, blossomed in prodigious resurrection in early spring on open ground and meadows, and their highly nutritious roots were collected. Camas was either cooked while fresh, or dried for use throughout the year.

Other roots vital to the Yakama diet were bitterroot (*Lewisia rediviva*) and the lomatiums, a genus of "Indian celery" including yellow-flowered *kouse* (*L. cous*) and *sk'okl* (*L. canbyi*); these latter two important plants were among some forty native to the Yakima Valley and the Columbia Plateau. These roots and other food resources grew seasonally, causing Plateau families to follow an annual semi-nomadic cycle of gathering, fishing, and hunting.

For Kamiakin's family, this "seasonal round" typically involved wintering in tule mat lodges at family camps in the Kittitas and Ahtanum valleys, spring root gathering on the surrounding prairies, salmon fishing along the Columbia River and among the Spokanes in the summer, and fall hunting and berrying in the higher elevations of the Cascades. Less predictable were the gathering trips among the middle Columbia tribes, who *Náami Piap*, "Elder Brother," had blessed with many favored gathering areas.

The people were profoundly grateful. They had been taught since time immemorial by "great prophets" about "laws that had been established" to know of the Creator's existence: "First, the water; second, the salmon; third, the big game; fourth, the roots; and fifth, the berries." Each gift contributed to the sustenance of Kamiakin's people and their consumption "when first taken" required a communal act of thanksgiving.

The Yakamas further reckoned time based on a yearly lunar cycle, with names of thirteen moons reflecting the Native peoples' intimacy with the natural world. Like other Plateau women, Com-mus-ni may have recorded special events in her family's life by fashioning a "counting" ball of hemp string, or *itatamat*, on which knots, beads, shells, and other talismans were carefully spaced—a valuable remembering device to recall marriages, births, and other significant events.[7]

Horse Herds and Fisheries

The Yakama and Kittitas prairie lands were ideal for horse herding, as the earth was cloaked in dense pine grass, elk sedge, and ubiquitous Poaceae, including members of the wheatgrass and ryegrass genera, on which creatures of horn and hoof had thrived for ages. These formed a diminutive universe of *waskú* forage grasses with slender stalks, emerging petioles, and curling leaves inhabited by herbivorous armies of crickets, beetles, and grasshoppers. Equipped with tiny serrated sickle jaws, these creatures were integral to the region's ecological renewal. Their ingestion of vegetative growth and its deposition into forms essential to plant nutrition eventually fed the horses of the Yakama and neighboring tribes.

The Kamiakin family's legends and wealth were closely associated with horses. In addition to the principal colors of black, bay, brown, sorrel, buckskin, gray, and white, they also distinguished animals in their herds by a host of other descriptive names—the popular spotted-rump appaloosa (*máamin*), chestnut sorrel (*siwíw-siwíw*), orange buckskin (*páatk'wiki*), strawberry roan (*qaas-qáas*), huckleberry roan (*wíwlu*), pinto, and palomino. Even slightly different shadings warranted distinctive names, including faded white, pure white, blue-gray, faded blue-gray, and dun.[8]

Family tradition held that the region's first appaloosa, a spotted colt, was brought from the Plains in the mid 1700s by the Palouse chief Khalotash, a close relative of the Kamiakins. Since his people previously had no horses, Khalotash had crafted a clever plan to obtain the beautiful and powerful creatures. He procured the services of an expert bone-and-stick game gambler. The two journeyed across the Rockies to the Missouri River, where they met a group of Plains Indians with horses and who were eager to gamble for Northwest furs and other trade items brought by Khalotash. The Palouses purposely lost the first round and then significantly raised stakes the second time. Among the participants was a White trader from the Plains whose bet rose to six horses and then to

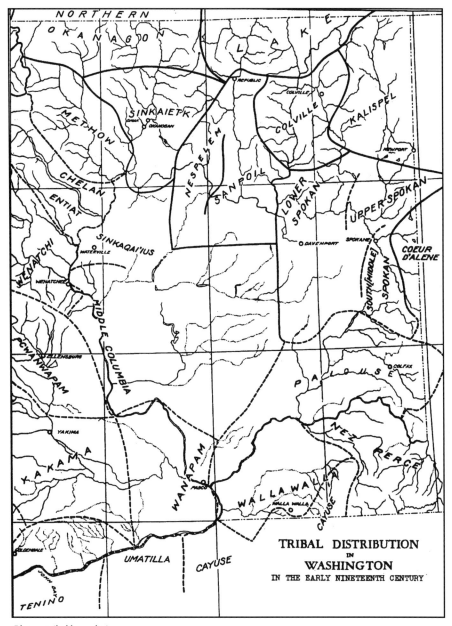

Plateau tribal boundaries.
Modified from Leslie Spier (1936)

other Indians may have obtained them from Shoshone, Utes, or other Great Basin peoples far to the southeast where the Latter Day Saints settled by the late 1840s.)[9]

As had been the case on the Great Plains, the introduction of the horse transformed Indian life throughout the Inland Northwest, as travel was facilitated both within the region and across the mountains. Members of the Wiyáwiikt clan would sometimes "go to buffalo" for extended visits, sometimes staying more than a year in the lands of the Blackfoot and other sometimes hostile Plains tribes.[10] Through such contacts, the Yakamas, Nez Perces, and other groups adopted certain aspects of Plains Indian culture, including the use of tipis, feathered headdresses, and concepts of a more formal tribal organization. The horse also enabled Plateau tribes to trade more bulky, but valued, items on the coast, such as buffalo robes and root-cakes, as well as smaller items like stone pipes, tobacco, and Indian hemp, in return for white dentalium, iridescent abalone jewelry, and other items from Puget Sound peoples.

Horses became a measure of wealth and the Wiyáwiikt clan maintained some of the largest herds in the Yakima Valley, with men and women alike caring for the animals. Horses were selectively bred for strength, speed, and intelligence. Although breeding horses for color alone was unlikely, some Indians prized the beautifully spotted appaloosa, named in pioneer days for T'siyiyak and Khalotash's Palouse homeland, and recognized their value as a medium of trade. In September 1831, a prominent Palouse chief, likely a descendant of Khalotash and bearing a legendary name—Simon McGillivray's "Talatouche"—appeared at the gates of Ft. Nez Perces to make restitution for an appaloosa and company horse taken the previous year by a member of his band. As a goodwill gesture, the traders provided a reward of musket balls and powder, a yard of tobacco, a large knife, and a measure of red cloth shrouds.[11]

eight, including the appaloosa female. The visiting gambler's strategy prevailed and Khalotash returned with his prize to the Palouse country.

The animal became the matriarch of the tribe's herd, and Khalotash became a prominent horse breeder. The Palouse called the creature *tamsilpiin*, for its spotted appearance. (To neighboring tribes, the appaloosa eventually became known as *máamin*, likely derived from the word "Mormon," since

Traveling by horseback led to larger intertribal gatherings near the great Columbia River fisheries around The Dalles and at Kettle Falls, a location on the upper Columbia favored by the Kamiakin family. Situated far upriver, the Kamiakins gathered beneath the foaming, tumbling waters at Kettle Falls, taking spring Chinook salmon often weighing over one hundred pounds from the channeled fury. Here the family met their Salish relatives in grand gatherings to share news, race horses, and gamble against a backdrop of rainbowed spume and pine forests.

Kettle Falls

An Englishman, once present when Kamiakin visited in June, described Kettle Falls as "most beautiful, the whole river falling over a ledge of quartz into a cauldron in which the water bubbles & boils in a most remarkable manner…. [A]ll day long you see one continual stream of fish in the air, many of them clear the whole in a single leap…. They hand a basket made of willow or crab apple, over the rock at the side of the falls, the salmon in jumping strike their noses against the top part & fall into the basket below; they catch from 700 to 1,000 salmon a day in this manner which are equally divided amongst them in the evening by one of the chiefs."

Yakama families also frequented the Wenatchi fishery, the most popular site in the mid Columbia region where as many as 3,000 Indians gathered in historic times above the forks of the Wenatchee and Icicle rivers. Indian camps regularly dotted the river banks along Tumwater Canyon, where miles of precipitous ledges provided ideal positions for spearing and netting fish during the spring and fall runs.

Five members of the genus *Oncorhynchus* ("Hooked Snout") migrated profusely throughout the Columbia and its tributaries, including the Yakima River, Toppenish Creek, and Ahtanum Creek. Salmon were known collectively to the Sahaptin-speaking Yakama as *núsux*, but Yakama nomenclature also had names for four species (Chinook, silver, chum, and sockeye), as well as for seasonal variations of the annually migrating Chinook, or blueback jack. Valley residents also named a sixth, the humpback or pink, though few of these ascended beyond the lower Columbia. Other fish commonly taken included steelhead, rainbow, and brook trout.[12]

Salmon was a principal staple of all the Plateau peoples and supplied at least a third of their nutritional needs. But, in addition to the essential root harvests, the gathering of other foods also was important. Numerous varieties of wild berries abounded along the Yakima River in autumn, while others were prevalent at higher elevations in the eastern Cascades.

Among the earliest to ripen was the serviceberry, which bursts forth white blossoms in spring. Two blackberry species also were prized by the Yakama—the trailing blackberry and mountain blackberry, both commonly gathered in late summer and fall—as were huckleberries, raspberries, and elderberries. Many Indians traveled to the present-day Easton vicinity to pick plump, abundant loganberries. Other mountain treats that Kamiakin knew from his youth were whipped, sweet tasting foamberries, and tamarack and pine black moss pounded and dried into *k'unch*, forming hardtack like pieces resembling a nutty licorice. Provisions often were stored in baskets fashioned from coils of narrow cedar-bark strips, willow fiber, and split tules, and in pouch-shaped bags of Indian hemp. Much of this basketwork bore exquisitely imbricated, geometric designs in contrasting earth tones.

Armed with double-curved or flat-type bows usually made of juniper, and with arrows fashioned from serviceberry or greasewood and carried in deerskin quivers, skilled Yakama hunters took deer and bear on fall hunts, and sometimes high country game such as mountain goat and elk. Smaller animals hunted throughout the year included beaver, marmot, and rabbit, as well as geese, ducks, grouse, and sage hens.[13]

T'siyak's Palouse Homeland

Though Kamiakin was raised among his mother's people in the Kittitas and Yakima valleys, he also visited the Palouse country during his adolescence, becoming acquainted with his father's relatives and their ancestral campsites. In such journeys, Kamiakin may have found an outlet for his adventurous spirit and quenched his boyhood curiosity regarding his nomadic father's past.

One camp was known to the family as "T'siyiyak's Place," located near Dixons Pond in the coulees several miles east of *Elatsaywitsun* (Sprague Lake), a refreshing expanse of blue and green for travelers crossing the stony plains and coulees. From Sprague Lake, ancient thoroughfares forked northward to Kettle Falls or east to *Tekam* (Spokane Falls). Another favored place, eventually called "Kamiak's Flat," was on the southeastern shore of *Tax'liit* (today's Rock Lake).

These bodies of water and many other pothole lakes in the western Palouse country were seasonal habitat for now rare white pelican, trumpeter swan, whooping crane, and other migratory fowl. Narrow ledges tucked into the immense northern cliffs above mysterious *Tax'líit* provided one of the region's few nesting places for vultures; the bald and black *q'spali* could be seen for great distances circling on vagrant air currents, where they were sometimes joined by the high gliding *khwama'* ("High Above"), or golden eagle. Wild currants, serviceberries, and gooseberries abounded in the deep canyon north of the lake, where travelers passed beneath circular basalt promontories, a natural stone bridge, and other peculiar formations fashioned in the time of the Animal People.

T'siyiyak and his family also camped on the northernmost stretch of the broadly meandering *Mo-ho-li-šah* (Palouse River) between present-day St. John and Endicott. Later known to pioneers as "Kamiak's Crossing," the vicinity abounded in native trout, whitetail deer, great blue herons, and other wildlife.[14] From their Palouse River camp, the family could range in any direction during springtime to dig the nine "winged seed" species of the nutritious lomatium family, which were native to the Palouse and favored shallow lithosoils among rocky outcroppings along the stream and its tributaries. In addition, over twenty major camas and bitterroot grounds were located in vernal meadows throughout the Palouse country.

Edible roots also grew at *Mox-mox* near a revered place for spirit quests—mystical *Yáamuštas* ("Elk's Abode"). Frontier explorers later called the peculiar formation "Pyramid Peak" and eventually it became "Steptoe Butte," a strange island-like prominence standing above an oceanic-appearing maelstrom of earthen waves crested with wind-pulsed native grasses. It served much as a mariner's landmark for travel-

ers crossing the region. With its 3,600 foot summit often shrouded in purling clouds, Steptoe Butte consists of sandpaper-orange quartzite, a billion years old. It is geologically related to Kamiak Butte, located twelve miles to the south, which pioneers later named in honor of Chief Kamiakin.

Steptoe and Kamiak buttes are surrounded by titanic fingerprints of earthen whorls and swirls with mystical origins for Indian people. Stories passed down in the Kamiakin family told how Coyote created this incredible labyrinth of swales, ridges, and slopes—unique to Palouse topography—in a vain effort to prevent other Animal People from winning a great race in ancient times. The course ran from the mouth of the Palouse River to Spokane Falls. The land was flat until Coyote went out the night before the race to scoop it into a series of barriers that he could easily leap over. But the six clever Turtle Brothers learned of his scheme; they placed themselves along the route before the race began and were able to claim victory. The story instructed young listeners about the consequences of false pretenses, and explained the appearance of the remarkable landscape known to the Palouse people as *Mukwnísha*.[15]

Localities to the northeast of the Palouse River camp also were utilized by T'siyiyak's people to dig camas; here the Coeur d'Alenes, Spokanes, and Palouses gathered in the springtime at such places as *Ni'lukhwaqw* ("Cut in the Woods") near present-day De Smet, Idaho, and at *T'celiyutum* ("Woodpecker Place"), located at the confluence of Latah and Rock creeks.

T'siyiyak's other family camping place in the Palouse country was at the Snake River village of *Pinawáwih*, an important fishing site at the mouth of Penawawa Creek, an area that also abounded in serviceberries, blackberries, and prairie elderberry. Many varieties of fish were taken from *Pik'úunen*, the "Great Water," including trout, steelhead, whitefish, and eels. Penawawa also was known for its white sturgeon, which when mature could reach twelve feet in length and weigh a half-ton—making them virtually impossible to catch. Three genera of the Salmonidae family were native to the Snake River including the genus *Oncorhynchus* with the five species of Pacific salmon.

The Palouse people's principal fishing site on the Snake River, however, was their ancient and largest village of *Palus*, located at the mouth of the Palouse River. Here, young Kamiakin would have resided among dozens of tule mat lodges on his periodic visits to his father's people.[16] The Palouse people called themselves *Naha'úumpúu*, or "People of the River." Located just out beyond the river's sandy shoreline stood the

Sprague Lake

〰〰〰

A passing frontiersman noted that Sprague Lake was ringed by basaltic cliffs and tall reeds, "which the breeze was moving with a melancholy rustling noise." In inspiring appreciation, he viewed "the most beautiful sunset I ever saw on shore, the sun going down over a plain behind a bank of clouds, bringing out the edges as if they had been carved with a knife & tipping them with points of gold."

Palus village's namesake, *Ehpelutpa*—the massive petrified heart of the legendary Beaver, *Wishpushya*.

In the time of the Animal People, the five Wolf Brothers armed with spears attacked Beaver, who was peacefully residing near his lodge at Hole-in-the-Ground above Rock Lake. A terrific fight ensued during which Beaver clawed and chewed out Rock Lake, one of the deepest lakes in the region with depths of 325 feet. Beaver ripped his way down the channel toward the Snake River. Where he beat down his tail, small falls were formed in the Palouse River. He was struck again at *Apútaput* ("Falling Water"), where in his pain Beaver cut the castellated formations and sheer cliffs that formed Palouse Falls. The massive creature finally fell from his wounds at the confluence with the Snake and his heart turned to stone. Beaver's remains were transformed into the ancestors of all the area's tribes; the Palouses were said to have sprung from his heart.[17]

In his travels as a boy, Kamiakin came to know his Palouse relatives and others among the Wallas Wallas, Nez Perces, and Spokanes. He was about five years old when word reached his village of the peculiar appearance of the strange people, who entered their lands from the east in the fall of 1805. Their Nez Perce kindred had fed the starving Corps of Discovery, and chiefs had guided them down the Snake and Columbia rivers in the direction of the ocean. Because of the newcomers' attire, and that of French Canadian traders who soon followed, Kamiakin's people came to call them *Shuyapo*—from *chapeau*, French for hat. The actions of many Whites who came later also led to the designation *Wasichu*, "Greedy Ones."

Sacred Landscapes

In his adolescence, Kamiakin acquired his *tah*, or tutelary spirit, from the power of Buffalo, seen in a dream during a vision quest on the majestic but treacherously icy heights of *Takhuma*—"Snow Peak," Mount Rainier. Divulging specific details of such a personal matter risked losing one's power, but on one occasion years later, when pressed about this experience, Kamiakin did say the ordeal was the "severest feat of his life." In later years, he lifted up the song imparted in his dream to summon strength needed for the battles and struggles of a life that would witness unprecedented and cataclysmic cultural change.

One of Kamiakin's sons later described the elaborate, solemn preparations necessary for successfully participating in a spirit quest. Usually, the ancient ritual was undertaken by males and females in early adolescence, and often during the autumn when families moved to the high country to gather berries and hunt large game. The seeker needed to draw up uncommon strength of character and endurance. For this reason, prolonged preparations preceded a vision quest, consisting of austere physical conditioning each day, followed by a purifying sweat bath. This regimen included counseling by a deeply spiritual tribal elder, who would admonish a youth with instructions about the humility and judgment necessary to receive a spirit guardian.

After this training was completed, the youth was sent to a remote high place to fast. Amidst mountain winds, clouds billowing in mythical mosaics, the fluttering of wings, and the sounds of animals, the seeker kept lonely vigil under a vast lodge of sun and star light, while fighting against the numbing effects of fatigue and hunger.[18]

Native peoples understood that all of nature, both terrestrial and beyond, was mysteriously imbued by *Náami Piap* with spiritual force—animals and plants, rocks and weather, moon and stars. Their worldview of reverential animism meant that Plateau people felt a high moral obligation to these life powers in recognition of their creation and sacrifice for human benefit. Cutting fir boughs for bedding and drinking fresh mountain water were preceded by respectful words of thanks to a tree and stream for their benevolence, just as the elders gave thanks in proper season during First Root, First Salmon, and First Berry ceremonies. But not everyone seeking to abide by the stringent expectations of a vision quest could abide by these demands; success was by no means certain. In the case of young Kamiakin's five-day ordeal and for many others of his time, however, the search was rewarded with a profoundly life-changing vision of imparted power.

Poetic expressions of awesome encounters, seen and heard in dream-like flashes when in high places among wild creatures and the elements, are suggested in the names of Kamiakin's contemporaries—Eagle of the Dawn, Red Star, Whistling Swan, Yellow Grizzly Bear. The sounds of many such names are onomonapoetic suggestions of their meaning, as with Pahka Qohqoh, or Five Crows, and Chief Joseph's Nez Perce name, Hin-mah-too Yah-lat-kekt, or Thunder Rolling in the Mountains.

The designation of some names may have been associated with atavistic or traditional ancestral powers, while others were bestowed uniquely through the sacred quest. The origins of Kamiakin's adult name are obscure, but the word is linguistically related to *k'əmáyaqən*, the Columbia Salish term for "skull." Over time, its pronunciation was reshaped in con-

Mt. Rainier

John Clement

In August 1870, the Taidnapam-Yakama warrior Sluskin (*Salúskin*), a headman from today's Packwood area who possibly was one of Kamiakin's relatives, guided Hazard Stevens and P.B. Van Trump to the base of Mt. Rainier's glaciers. From there, the two Whites set out to complete the first recorded ascent to the summit. They reached slopes with "lofty walls and precipices whence avalanches of snow and vast masses of rock were continually falling," and where "a furious tempest continually swept the crown of the mountain."

When guiding the explorers to the slopes of Mt. Rainier, Sluskin had told them of "a great chief and warrior, and a mighty hunter"—perhaps this was Wiyáwiikt or Kamiakin—who "had ascended part way up the mountain," farther than anyone had been known to venture.[19]

More than a decade earlier—during the Plateau wars—Sluskin's hand was permanently mangled by a gunshot in fighting with teritorial militiamen. Hazard Stevens' father, Governor Isaac Stevens, had organized the volunteers from Olympia. Nevertheless, Sluskin's interaction with the two courageous mountain climbers was unequivocally positive.

formity with Yakama Sahaptin phonetics, but the name likely further distinguished him among his young Yakama peers.[20] The spirit quest manifested a profound appreciation for the sanctity of all life. Following this experience, young Kamiakin would have participated in the tribe's Winter Spirit Dance (*Wanpt*), called by a shaman for the sacred singing and dancing of *tah* songs by all the *tánish*.

These vigils may strike modern minds as spectral experiences caused by stress-induced trances blurring the borders of imagination and reality. But relationships between the Plateau people and nature fashioned a world view that communed with the land, and steeled them to the virtues of fortitude and restraint. In some ways this also was known to the cultural forbearers of the Euro-American newcomers. Numerous classical accounts relate stories, such as that of the Athenian Phidippides, whose encounter with Pan on Mt. Parthenium led to a shrine built at the Acropolis. The American Northwest of two millennia later also was akin to the mystical realms of Pasternak's taiga—"settled so sparsely that nature was not eclipsed by man"; a place where the elemental forces of water, wind, and earth still struck mortals fiercely and tangibly.

Continental and Maritime Fur Trade

As the sons of Chief Wiyáwiikt established their own families in camps along the principal streams of the Kittitas and Yakima valleys in the 1820s and 1830s, important decisions affecting their future already had been the focus of deliberations in smoke-filled offices of Eastern entrepreneurs. Early in the century, the interior Northwest had attracted the attention of various fur trade merchants, traders, and trappers.

Wealthy New York financier John Jacob Astor incorporated the American Fur Company in 1808 in order to gain a foothold for his personal ambitions and the national interest in the continental fur trade, which at the time was largely controlled by foreign firms. The oldest and most securely established was the Hudson's Bay Company (HBC), a London owned concern with interests throughout Canada's eastern woodlands and into the Great Plains. A rival enterprise to the HBC, the North West Company (or "Nor'Westers"), had been organized by Montreal merchants of Scottish ancestry in 1783. Both firms employed numerous French Canadian boatmen, traders, and laborers, and had sights on reaching the Rockies and the Pacific Coast, and eventually transporting furs directly by sea to the lucrative Chinese market.

Astor formed a subsidiary of his firm in 1809, the Pacific Fur Company, and outfitted expeditions for the Northwest, which in addition to Americans, included numerous British and French Canadian employees. The first contingent to arrive, following a voyage around the Horn to Hawaii and then to the mouth of the Columbia, was led by Duncan McDougall, and included such later frontier notables as David Stuart, Robert Stuart, and Alexander Ross. They immediately founded Ft. Astoria on the Columbia's south bank in the spring of 1811.

The following summer, a detachment of about a dozen Astorians, including among their number several Indians and Hawaiians, journeyed up the Columbia to establish trading relations with the Plateau tribes. In August, they passed the mouth of the Yakima River, but continued up the Columbia to establish Ft. Okanogan near the mouth of the Okanogan River in September. The crude post was built with driftwood, while the Stars and Stripes were permanently raised for the first time within the boundaries of present-day Washington. Alexander Ross assumed responsibilities as the small post's chief trader. During the first year, trade with the Yakama, Wenatchi, Okanogan, and other tribes yielded 1,550 beaver hides "besides other peltries, worth in the Canton market 2,250 pounds sterling."[21]

Shortly, due to wartime and economic threats from the British when the War of 1812 erupted, the Astorians were forced to relinquish control of their Northwest operations in 1813 to the Nor'Westers, who by this time had pushed their operations across the Rockies into the Columbia region. However, many of the Astorians, such as Ross, were allowed to enter the employ of the new owners.

Trade continued with the Yakama and other interior tribes, but in 1813 an event occurred in the Plateau region that disaffected their amiable relations with the traders. In the spring, word reached the Yakamas of a fatal incident involving Kamiakin's Palouse relatives to the east, perpetrated by the trader John Clarke. En route with a party to Astoria from the Spokane country, Clarke had camped at *Palus* on the Snake River. Finding a goblet missing from his belongings in the morning, the ill-tempered trader demanded its return. The offender meekly obliged, but was promptly hung by Clarke from a gallows crudely fashioned out of the man's own lodge poles, a harsh action later widely rebuked by Clarke's compatriots in the fur trade. Though he actually was a Canadian, Clarke was employed by the Astorians; thus the Indians

viewed the Americans as the perpetrators of this outrage. News of this episode quickly spread and fired resentment among many Indians, who began viewing the Whites more as intruders than as friends.

The following spring, a large group of Nor'Westers in fourteen boats departed the lower Columbia on an overland express to the firm's Canadian headquarters at Ft. William on Lake Superior. Alexander Ross accompanied them as far as Ft. Okanogan, where he joined others in continuing the trade with neighboring tribes. Having no packhorses available for transporting furs and goods, he decided to obtain them from Indians in the Yakima Valley who were "rich in horses." Moreover, Ross knew that at this time of year the Yakama held a "great national rendezvous" of Indians throughout the region, "when thousands meet and on such occasions horses can be got in almost any numbers."

He was accompanied by two French Canadian companions and their Indian wives and a young clerk, Thomas McKay. After four days of travel, they were met by two couriers sent by Chief Sopa of the Wenatchi, a friend of Ross's, who warned, "White men, turn back, turn back, you are all dead men!" Tribes to the south had expressed hostile intentions against the Whites since the Palouse killing, and Sopa wanted the traders to avoid tragedy. But Ross was undeterred.

Two days later they descended into the Kittitas Valley and came upon an immense camp several miles long at *Ch'iláxan*, northwest of present-day Ellensburg, where plumes of smoke trailed from lodge fires, while a dreamy susurrus rustled the leaves of aspen and cottonwood. Ross estimated that the gathering "could not have contained less than 3,000 men, exclusive of women and children, and treble that number of horses. It was a grand and imposing sight in the wilderness," which featured horse and foot races, gambling, hunting, root gathering, councils, singing, dancing, drumming," and a thousand other things."

But Ross received a cool reception from his hosts and was lectured by sullen chiefs, possibly by Wiyáwiikt himself or a relative. Unaware of Ross's new Canadian company affiliation, an Indian leader accused him of being among those "who kill our relations, the people who have caused us to mourn." The trader became the object of other accusations and provocative actions, and found his restive hosts reluctant to release the horses after exchanging ownership for steel knives, glass beads, fishhooks, or other goods.

Ross remarked that his patience "was put to the test a thousand times," though he finally wrangled twenty-five horses through skillful diplomacy. Still wary of his hosts' intentions, Ross then sped northward to join his companions, who had gone ahead toward Sopa's country. Ross later described the ordeal as "the most trying and hazardous of trips I ever experienced in the country."[22]

Every Inch a King

As Kamiakin matured into adulthood, his captivating presence and wisdom distinguished him, even as a young man. Fur trader Angus McDonald described the Yakama-Palouse leader as standing "five feet eleven in his moccasins" and weighing "about two hundred pounds, muscular and sinewy," with black hair bearing streaks of auburn "twisted down over his shoulders." McDonald had come to know Kamiakin well when the wiry Scot served as chief trader at Ft. Colvile, founded near Kettle Falls in 1825. Four years earlier, the Nor'Westers had merged into the Hudson's Bay Company to extend British monopolistic control and Catholic influence across the region.

Like his father, Kamiakin had become a skilled competitor in horseracing and feats of agility, and acquired considerable wealth measured in horseflesh. His physical strength was expressed in Odyssean terms by one contemporary, who observed: "In his prime, none of his people could bend his bow." As early as 1840, the greater portion of the Yakamas recognized him as their headman, and "the young men flocked to Kamiakin, with his power extending from Nahcheez to Tap-tat [Prosser]."

The young leader had taken his first wife, Sunk-hay-ee, at the age of about twenty-five. The daughter of Chief Teias (*Tiyáyaš*), she was Kamiakin's cousin and also a grandchild of venerable Chief Wiyáwiikt. Marriage between relatives was not uncommon among Plateau peoples in order to consolidate political and economic power.[23]

A few years later, Kamiakin also married Kem-ee-yowah, the oldest daughter of the Klickitat Chief Tenax, and, in accordance with the custom of Plateau sororal polygyny, also inherited as wives her three younger sisters—Wal-luts-pum, Hos-ke-la-pum, and Colestah. The youngest, Colestah, became a revered *twati* and confidant to her husband; her spirit power would be used to restore health to children and others when disease threatened. She was said to be able to

Fur trader Angus McDonald, Ft. Colvile.
WSU Libraries (cage 196, 9-45)

change huckleberries into red glass beads and bitterroot into lustrous shells.

Kamiakin's marriages brought more children into the Wiyáwiikt clan. In about 1840, a son was born to the chief by Kem-ee-yowah —one of an eventual dozen children. The son became known as We-yet-que-wit (Talking Hunter) and also as "Young Kamiakin." A special protective power was imparted to We-yet-que-wit in adolescence during his spirit quest. He ventured into the mountains and found an abandoned hunter's camp where deer bones were scattered about. A great tempest later arose and he sought refuge in the crude shelter.

During the rain and hail, he heard a voice cry out: "You do as I tell you, and I will give you my power. You see that I am all old and weather-checked, but this hail does not enter me or hurt me. I resist the beating hailstones which beat upon me without harm. Do as I tell you, and with my power, although the bullet of the enemy strike you like a hailstone, you will not be harmed."[24]

Possibly because of a special friendship between Kamiakin and his uncle, Chief Showaway, the Yakama leader established his home on Ahtanum Creek where Showaway had long resided.[25] The stream abounded in trout and seasonal runs of coho. Kamiakin located his home along a bend a couple miles east of present-day Tampico, where his camp was sheltered by stands of cottonwood, Oregon white oak, and isolated pines. The place was known as *Yi-kŭp-yí-kŭp-pam*, or Salmonberry Place, for this delicate fruit that grew near stands of hardy elderberry and chokecherry. In historic times an enormous grave mound, likely of a notable family member, was located on the west side of the camp.[26]

Kamiakin first appears in the written historical record in an 1841 travel account kept by an American military explorer, Lt. Robert E. Johnson. His party had been dispatched from Puget Sound to Ft. Colvile by Charles Wilkes, commander of the four-year-long United States Exploring Expedition, which had been commissioned by naval officials in 1838 to conduct a cartographic world tour. Johnson's party departed the Hudson's Bay Company's Ft. Nisqually on May 17, and, traveling via Naches Pass, reached the Kittitas Valley by June 1.

A day later, they visited a camp of twenty Indians near present-day Ellensburg. "The chief, Kamaiyah, was the son-in-law of old Tidias [Teias], and one of the most handsome and perfectly-formed Indians" they met. The explorers, however, found Kamiakin "gruff and surly" in his manners. They were impressed with the band's fine horses, but the Indians "could not be induced to part with any of them."[27]

Explorers and traders who penned descriptions of Kamiakin often commented on his dignified manner, cordiality, and attire. He was seen in fine buckskin clothing with a fisher-pelt cap; other times he was dressed in a Hudson's Bay broadcloth coat with red trimming and brass buttons; and sometimes he wore a single eagle feather in his hair. Territorial pioneer Francis Chenowith and three friends encountered Kamiakin in late June 1851, while on an excursion from The Dalles to the Simcoe Valley. Chenowith noted the Indians' bountiful crops of ripening wheat and flax, and judged the area's climate "perhaps as near perfect as any in the world." He marveled at the "large bands of fat horses and cattle that rove unmolested upon the rich pastures."

The party chose a different route to return to the Columbia River, venturing west to the "splendid country" around Camas Lake (modern-day Conboy Lake) in the shadow of Mt. Adams' "dazzling whiteness." Here Chenowith found Kamiakin, the "principal chief" among the "lords of creation," overseeing horse races and the gathering of roots on a vast camas prairie known as *Taht*. Kamiakin treated his guests with "politeness and hospitality" and tea with sugar, while pointing out "the pile of blankets and other articles he had won at the races."

Theodore Winthrop, a well-educated adventurer with literary talent, described Kamiakin in regal terms after meeting him in the Yakima Valley in 1853. The traveler was introduced to Kamiakin by the missionary Father Pandosy, after the Yakama chief rode up on a "white pacer" wearing "a long tunic of fine green cloth" with patches "of all shapes." "He had…an imposing presence and bearing, and above all a good face, a well-lighted Pharos at the top of colossal frame." He was, Winthrop declared, "every inch a king."[28]

Increasingly, Kamiakin became more prominent among the Yakamas and other Sahaptin and Salish tribes, whose headmen often sought his counsel. Through personal ability as well as family connections, Kamiakin had emerged as one of the most influential leaders in the entire region. But growing authority also invited jealousies. The principal rivals were his uncles—Teias, who also was his father-in-law, and Owhi

(*Áwxay*), a highly respected leader of the Yakamas living upstream in the Kittitas Valley.

Over the years, Kamiakin and his brothers traveled widely, acquiring cattle and horses from the Willamette Valley and perhaps journeying as far as California. Long-horned "Spanish" cattle and milk cows that Kamiakin brought back are believed to have been the first in the valley. Rev. Alvan Waller, Jason Lee's co-worker at the Wascopam Mission, rode north from The Dalles to the Yakima Valley in the spring of 1845, where he noted small herds of livestock belonging to Kamiakin, Showaway, Skloom, and others. The Wiyáwiikt men also introduced potatoes, peas, and other crops to the area. During Waller's visit, "Kamiacan" showed the Methodist circuit-rider a few sacks of crib corn remaining from the previous year's harvest.[29]

Some privileges accorded to men of Kamiakin's time and standing are repugnant to modern sensibilities. He might acquire a slave from other tribes on faraway excursions, and he wielded power over life and death in instances where a shaman summoned to heal family members could not bring about a recovery; execution of the shaman could occur. Accounts of Kamiakin's life by priests who knew him well make no reference to such practices, but other reliable contemporaries do. Perhaps on one of his journeys southward, Kamiakin obtained a slave named Atween, whom the chief later punished for recurrent thieving by forcing him to sleep outside in bitter weather. The unfortunate man lost both feet and a hand to frostbite and afterward was known as Askolumkee, or "Cut-Off." In spite of his condition, Askolumkee, also called Atween, became an able horseman and valued family member.[30]

Visits by Owhi to Ft. Nisqually on southern Puget Sound were noted in that post's journal as early as June 1833. It is likely that Owhi's nephew, Kamiakin, would have accompanied the chief on such journeys to their Coastal Salish relatives, and to acquaint himself more fully with the peculiar and perhaps useful ways of the *Shuyapu*.

Relationships between the Indians and the traders varied with the newcomers' origins. Generally, the closest ties developed with the French Canadians, whereas the "King George" men (the British) and "Bostons" (Americans) might often stand more at arm's length, though the American mountain men got along famously well with the Nez Perces and other Plateau peoples who journeyed to the Rockies and Northern Plains. Of growing concern after 1840, however, were the increasing numbers of American settlers who year after year were willing to risk the months-long trek over the

Oregon Trail. As they passed through the region toward the Willamette Valley, many of them noted and would remember the fertile hills and valleys of the Columbia Plateau.[31]

Perhaps indicative of an abiding identity with his father's Palouse people, Kamiakin also is known to have often traveled substantial distances to the northeast and east. For example, he was a frequent guest of trader Angus McDonald at Ft. Colvile, where the chief impressed the affable Scotchman as "a well-formed and powerful Indian" possessing a "sagacious intellect."[32] Kamiakin prized the spring Chinook taken at nearby Kettle Falls as the choicest salmon on the entire river.

In the Ahtanum country, Kamiakin raised potatoes, squash, pumpkins, and corn in substantial garden plots, irrigated by spring water from below the principal fork in the stream. Given the rocky terrain and primitive tools available to the workers, the digging of a half-mile long canal was a monumental undertaking—it snaked from the spring to the gardens along a contour just north of the chief's camp. The canal later was dubbed "Kamiakin's Ditch" by pioneers. Like some other Plateau Indian leaders, Kamiakin believed his people could benefit from the practical knowledge and spiritual power of the Whites; yet Kamiakin also felt a sacred commitment to safeguard his people and the natural world fashioned by *Náami Piap*.

Kamiakin cautiously welcomed White newcomers in the region, while seeking to learn about those aspects of their culture that he considered advantageous. He befriended Nathan Olney, who in 1843 had "overlanded" to the Willamette Valley at age nineteen, only to return to The Dalles in 1847 and open a small store to provision a burgeoning number of Oregon Trail immigrants. This enterprise helped give birth to a strategic settlement located at this important Indian fishery. Olney soon married Twawy (Annette Hallicola), daughter of the local Wasco chief, Chalalee, and the relationship gained him the trust of area Indian leaders. In June 1851, the enterprising frontiersman procured a trading license from the Oregon Superintendent of Indian Affairs, Anson Dart. Chief Kamiakin traveled frequently to The Dalles to fish, trade, and to visit in-laws, and he came to regard the young Iowa native "as a son."

In the spring of 1850, Olney's closest White neighbors had settled downstream, about halfway to Ft. Vancouver. Here, Francis Chenowith founded fledgling Cascades City on the north side of the Columbia near modern-day Stevenson.

In May, the U.S. Army established a small military outpost at The Dalles, named Camp Drum. A mounted rifle unit maintained peace along the heavily traveled route along the Columbia.

Ft. Colvile

In 1825, Ft. Colvile replaced Spokane House as the center of trading activity on the Columbia Plateau. Following a strategic tour of the region in 1824–25, London-based Sir George Simpson of the Hudson's Bay Company had recommended this site on a broad flat of fertile loam near scenic and strategic Kettle Falls, the largest Indian fishery on the upper Columbia. It was a better locale for agriculture and more strategically situated for the Indian trade than Spokane House.

By 1840, Ft. Colvile employed 20 men on a 400-acre farm and at the company store and gristmill. The first grain harvested in the Inland Northwest, fifteen bushels of barley, was grown here in 1826, planted with seed from the company's eponymous regional headquarters at Ft. Vancouver. Wheat, oats, potatoes, and other vegetables also flourished on Big Prairie across from the fort, where horses, cattle, and hogs sent by John McLoughlin and from abandoned Spokane House also were herded.

The HBC also operated Ft. Nez Perces (later Ft. Walla Walla), founded in 1818 by the Nor'Wester Donald McKenzie at the mouth of the Walla Walla River on the Columbia's east bank. Here in the 1830s, Chief Trader Pierre Pambrun supervised a substantial horse raising operation and the cultivation of small vegetable plots.[33]

A year earlier, Astoria native William C. McKay also had established a trading post near the mouth of the Umatilla River. McKay's venture would continue to flourish, until his prominence in subsequent treaty negotiations aroused the suspicions of Kamiakin and other regional tribal leaders.

Kamiakin warily observed these Columbia River outposts on the periphery of Yakama territory. At Cascades City, the Columbia's hazardous rapids blocked steamboat traffic from proceeding further upstream, but the enterprising Chenowith shortly completed a 2½ mile wooden portage tramway, with cars pulled by oxen, to facilitate transportation. Cascades City soon boasted a store, blacksmith shop, and some half-dozen families, whose men found employment at this strategic point. Kamiakin frequently traversed through these localities on trading and fishing excursions to *Si'lailo* (Celilo Falls), The Dalles, the Great Cascades, and to Ft. Vancouver, while maintaining cordial relations with the local residents, such as Chenowith, who was elected to the Washington Territorial Legislature in 1853 and served at the first Speaker of the House.

St. Joseph's Mission

Kamiakin also knew of Marcus and Narcissa Whitman, who in 1836 had established a Presbyterian mission at Waiilatpu in the Walla Walla Valley. Their colleague, William Gray, was invited to start similar work among the Yakama. When the Protestants declined, Kamiakin and Skloom eventually turned to the Catholics, as would Owhi and Chief Piupiu Maksmaks. After a disaffected group of Cayuses massacred the Whitmans and others at Waiilatpu in November 1847, Kamiakin spurned their overtures to join in a war against the Whites.[34]

In the summer of 1848, two Oblate missionaries, Eugene Casimir Chirouse and Charles Marie Pandosy, answered Kamiakin's call and established St. Joseph's Mission on Simcoe Creek. Kamiakin pledged to "be responsible for everything." In a short time, these men developed strong bonds of mutual respect and cooperation. A structure with a simple wood steeple crowned with a cross soon arose along the glassy stream winding through the Simcoe bottomlands.

Father Pandosy, a 23-year-old native of Margerides in southern France, was a vigorous individual, gifted with a keen intellect and amazing physical strength. His full black beard did not conceal a ready wit and likeable personality showing through his large, deep-set eyes. The priest was a gifted musician and classical scholar, and had also studied botany, medicine, and linguistics while a student at Arles' College Bourbon and as a novitiate at Notre Dame de l'Osier at Grenoble. He aspired to the motto of the recently founded Oblate order, "to preach the Gospel to the poor," and received the order's distinctive black and gold crucifix upon his vows in 1843.

Four years later, he ventured to North America in response to pleas from Bishop A.M.A. Blanchet for missionaries to serve in the vast Walla Walla Diocese covering the inland Pacific Northwest. Life for the missionaries was far from idyllic on the Columbia Plateau frontier. Their letters mention long bouts of illness, bitter winter cold, and quarrels over the distribution of provisions among the Yakama mission outposts. But they also laughed and sang, discussed divine grace and the Last Judgment, raised melons and potatoes, and made bread and cheese.[35]

The priests especially delighted in the children. Father Pandosy opened a mission school, where Yakama youths could be heard reciting the catechism and the Lord's Prayer in Sahaptin (Pandosy's *Náami Psht*, or "Our Father"), singing Gregorian chants, and intoning a "Yakama Peace Song." Pandosy frolicked with the children, and described Kamiakin's little girl, Catherine—probably his daughter Yam'naneek by Sunk-hay-ee—as "a playful, joyful, happy child, who likes to play tricks beyond all imagination and all sensible limits; Catherine, the true daughter of Kamiakin by her temper, pride, anger, and sulking, is a consolation to me."

The priest found especially heartwarming his young assistant's celebration of Mass with other children, and her baptism of a dying child. "I love them with a consuming heart," he wrote of the Yakamas, seeing the Indians on equal terms. "I am not better looking, nor am I more spiritual, than they are."[36]

By 1852, St. Joseph's Mission was relocated to Ahtanum Creek about two miles east of Kamiakin's streamside camp. Also known as the Ahtanum Mission, it consisted of a log church with clay-plastered walls on the interior, plus an adjacent residence. The priests also built a horse corral and raised large gardens, probably planted with seeds from Kamiakin's fields. Kamiakin described the habits of the great elk herds roaming on the adjacent mountain slopes, and hunted them to provision the blackrobes. "We can get everything from him," Pandosy wrote appreciatively. The same brass spyglass used to locate animals also revealed lunar craters and Jupiter's moons, to aid in demonstrations of celestial motions from the inquisitive blackrobe's hand and finger orrery showing the position of planets. Pandosy also shared information about world affairs with the inquisitive chief.

With Kamiakin's assistance, the priests constructed Indian vocabularies and a dictionary, and set Native words to music and prayer. Pandosy's mastery of kinship terms and his organizing of Yakama grammar according to Greek and Latin rules fostered discussions about classical history and cardinal virtues. Pandosy and Kamiakin learned much from each other, developing a close personal friendship in evening conversations in the mellow radiance from Adam candles.

Pandosy stayed with Kamiakin's band during the harsh winter of 1851–52. At that time, Pandosy's penning of a succinct exposition on basic tenets of faith in a letter to Father Pascal Ricard likely reflects the nature of Pandosy's conversations with Kamiakin and other Yakamas. "Grace is the main point, fundamental, unique, because if it were lacking, everything would be missing. Even if grace was the only thing we had, we would have everything, and everything without it would be nothing. Man is human, earthly, and grace is invisible, that is why in man's eye it has not value. Take a man purely spiritual or who knows how to subdue his body to his spirit and this invisible grace will sustain him."

Pandosy's epistle was a plea to continue work among the Yakamas after learning of his superiors' skeptical review of St. Joseph's viability. His arguments prevailed and Ricard consented to extend the Ahtanum ministry.

Pandosy's passionate persistence bore fruit. Kamiakin, a proud man often feared by others throughout the region, found the missionary's message compelling. He and his family had their own profound personal reasons to identify with the biblical account of origins not of this world. "[They] know and acknowledge the existence of God," Pandosy wrote of his hosts, "This is a real fact…. They recognize the necessity of religion, but do we try to make it pleasing to them, and make it easier for them to practice it?"

Pandosy evidently made it so. Soon, Kamiakin's presence was noted at morning and evening prayers, which "he never misses" and "always attends the instructions." Kamiakin insisted that his band's milk cows be tended on Saturday evening in order "to keep the Sabbath clean," and forbade others to pick berries and gather wood or water on Sunday. He also had his children baptized, but, when the missionaries demanded monogamy for adults, Kamiakin refused to give up his wives. He could point to the example of the ancient patriarchs in the Bible for justification of this Plateau tradition. (When later faced with the same choice, Kamiakin's friend Quetalican, or Chief Moses, would respond: "How can I choose just one from among them? I love them all.") Still, Kamiakin often hunted for the blackrobes, shared other provisions with them, and remained a lifelong advocate of the Oblates.[37]

Lt. Johnson and Theodore Winthrop were just two of a rather limited number of newcomers whom Kamiakin and the Yakamas warily observed passing through their lands in the 1840s and early 1850s. During the rest of the decade of the 1850s, however, an unprecedented number of Whites were attracted to the Pacific Northwest in quest of land, gold, and empire. Hundreds of dissatisfied California miners, who had arrived late and were busted after the Sierra strikes of 1849 and the early 1850s, moved northward across Indian lands in search of precious metal, joined by Willamette and Puget Sound settlers also excited by gold rumors. As early as the summer of 1850, Henry Spalding, the former missionary to the Nez Perce, wrote from the Willamette: "Great nos. went from this country last June to explore the Spokane and Nez Perce countries for gold."

These prospectors were unlike other groups of Whites who had lived among the interior tribes for decades, and they would continue to enter the region in following years. Often enough they were a coarse lot, seeking gold along the many streams where Indian villages were located. A number of them brought whiskey to appease Indians, with some soon devoting their full energy to the profitable business of selling liquor to the tribes.

Land was the other attraction for newcomers. On September 29, 1850, Congress passed the Oregon Donation Land Act in order "to provide for the survey, and to make donations to settlers of the said public lands" of the territory. This law granted to every eligible citizen who settled before December 1850 a half-section (320 acres); if a married couple, the wife was entitled to an additional 320 acres. For those occupying lands before 1853 (later amended to December 1, 1855), they obtained quarter-sections—again a settler's wife was entitled to an added 160 acres. News of these liberal provisions led to a pioneer onslaught over the Oregon Trail, and the territorial population rose from approximately 8,000 in 1850 to nearly 30,000 in 1855.

Most of the first immigrants settled in Oregon's fertile Willamette Valley. By 1853, however, enough Americans had settled north of the Columbia River in the Puget Sound country to warrant the carving-out of Washington Territory from Oregon. In that year, a large wagon train deviated from the Oregon Trail route, heading directly toward Puget Sound over Naches Pass, thereby proceeding through Yakama country. Some Indians considered this trespass an affront to their rights. Increasing encounters between Indians and Whites led to a rise in violent incidents. Six Americans were reported killed by Indians in the region in both 1851 and 1852, while forty-seven were killed in 1853. Friends and relatives of the victims informed territorial authorities of the violence and pressed for intervention.

About 1853, Chief Kamiakin contacted military authorities at newly established Ft. Dalles, situated on a grassy knoll overlooking the Columbia. The chief asked for the removal of a settler who had established a claim on land about twenty miles north of the river. Over the objections of some officers as well as civilian residents in the tiny community, the camp commander decided against provoking an incident and complied with Kamiakin's request.

Many Plateau Indian leaders, however, perceived an air of foreboding in the increased pulse of White settlement on the Columbia, along with rumors of new arrangements for American settlers in the lands north of the river. In fact,

Father Pandosy feared for his safety on a trip from the Ahtanum to the Coeur d'Alene mission in April 1853, saying "the clouds are gathering on all lands. The winds begin to lower, the tempest is pent up. Ready to burst."

He informed Father Mesplié, in a letter passed on to military officials at Ft. Dalles, "The cause of the war is that the Americans are going to seize their lands."[38]

Rattlesnake Canyon, a tributary of Toppenish Creek.
John Clement

Mt. Adams—Páhto, "Standing High" over the Yakama homeland.
John Clement

Ahtanum Mission bronze.
John Clement

Ahtanum Mission (rebuilt 1868–70).
John Clement

"Grand Coulee"—artist John Mix Stanley accompanied Lt. Richard Arnold's detachment of railway surveyors, autumn 1853.
Stevens, Report of Explorations, Vol. 12

Dry Falls escarpment.
John Clement

Cowiche Mountain.
John Clement

Manashtash Creek, Kittitas Valley.

John Clement

Pvt. Gustavus Sohon depiction of the Walla Walla Council, 1855.
Washington State Historical Society

Ft. Simcoe parade ground and officers' quarters.
John Clement

Battle of Tohotonimme, by Gustavus Sohon.
Washington State Historical Society

Bead design by Cleveland Kamiakin's wife, Alalumt'i (1885–1977), daughter of Tom Paween.

"T'siyiyak's Place" in the Dixons Pond vicinity near Fishtrap Lake, burial place of Chief Kamiakin's Palouse father.
Richard D. Scheuerman

Chapter 2

A Highly Desirable Field

Salmon Man waited outside.
He stood at the Wolf Sister's door for a while.
Then he decided to leave.
But the Wolf Sister knew he was there.
She pulled back the door.
"Do you want to visit me?" she asked.

Salmon told her, "I want you
to come with me. If you want to come,
then get ready to leave."
The Wolf Brothers were jealous of Salmon Man.
He knew they would try to get him.

Isaac I. Stevens, Governor of Washington
Territory, 1853–57.
WSU Libraries (78-215)

*I*n an effort to proceed with orderly settlement on what
federal officials considered the public domain in Washington Territory, the government sought to extinguish Indian
title to these lands. This responsibility fell to the territory's
first governor, Isaac Ingalls Stevens. As an Army major, Stevens had become knowledgeable about the Pacific Northwest
after his 1849 appointment to the U.S. Coast Survey as chief
assistant to the director, Professor Alexander Dalles Bache.

The survey was an ambitious federal project, based out of
Washington, D.C., to obtain detailed geographical information about the West for economic exploitation and for routing a transcontinental railroad. Over the course of three and a
half years, Stevens had cultivated friendships with influential
leaders in the nation's capitol, and came to view the Pacific
Northwest as a region with great agricultural and commercial
potential, which also would serve as a strategic link in new
U.S. international trade with the Orient, inaugurated by
Commodore Perry's visit to Japan in the early 1850s.

With the organization of Washington Territory in 1853,
Stevens recognized an unparalleled opportunity to become
involved in these dynamic events, and he secured appointment as the first territorial governor, consequently resigning
from the Engineers and the U.S. Army. Though slight of stature, Stevens was highly
energetic and a prodigious learner; he had
ranked first in his West
Point class upon graduation in 1839. But while he
demonstrated an amazing
aptitude for mathematics
and engineering, Stevens
also could be short-tempered, impatient, and
demanding—qualities not well suited for diplomacy with the
proud leaders of the Columbia Plateau tribes.

On his overland journey to Olympia in 1853, while leading railroad survey parties across the prairies and ranges,
Stevens would learn that the interior tribes opposed White
settlement on their lands. Like most of his countrymen in
the day of Manifest Destiny, however, the governor equated
progress with settlement. At the first session of the Territorial
Legislative Assembly in 1854, he would declare: "In this great
era of the world's history, an era which hereafter will be the
theme of epics and the torch of eloquence, we can play no
secondary part if we could. We must of necessity play a great

part if we act at all." A man of fecund versatility, Stevens had far-reaching plans for his own role in the grand drama.

When Stevens became the governor of Washington, he also was named the territory's superintendent of Indian affairs, as well as supervisor of the Northern Pacific Railroad Survey to lay out the most northerly of several potential routes across the West then under consideration by Congress. While successfully undertaking any one of these official roles would be a daunting task to many, Stevens reveled in the challenge and sought these responsibilities because they mutually served his goals. Completion of a northern transcontinental railway would guarantee for Washington Territory "the best geographical position to control the trade of Asia and the Pacific." In an unprecedented achievement, Stevens' 1853–54 railroad survey project used the skills of 240 men to map and record more data on the northern route than was thought possible in such a short time.

Stevens also believed that extinguishing Indian title to lands east of the Cascades was essential to clear the way for his grand vision of railroads and settlement. Since the federal courts recognized the legitimacy of Indian land claims, Stevens had the legal means to negotiate land cessions in council with the tribes. Reflecting national policy, his plan was to establish two vast Indian reservations distant from the proposed main railway line through the Columbia Basin. Stevens also believed that the development of transportation networks and creating reservations would benefit Indians by forcing them to adopt a sedentary, agricultural lifestyle and thus avoid what appeared to many Americans as their inevitable decline. He argued that the government should act as a benevolent guardian, which in his view would uplift Native peoples from savagery to civilization. He would soon learn, however, that many Indians preferred confrontation to accommodation.

Council with Nez Perces in the Bitterroots, by artist John Mix Stanley of the Stevens railroad survey expedition.
Isaac I. Stevens, Report of Explorations

The Northern Railway Surveys

In early summer 1853, the newly appointed governor-super-intendent-surveyor made his way west from St. Paul, Minnesota, leading the main northern transcontinental survey party exploring potential railroad routes across the northern Plains and Rockies. Meanwhile on the West Coast, a second survey group was dispatched eastward from Ft. Vancouver under the command of Stevens' friend and fellow West Pointer, Captain George McClellan, who had arrived in late June following a sea journey via the Isthmus of Panama. McClellan was a man of caution, which some of his military associates would unfairly equate with a lack of initiative. His style contrasted sharply with Stevens' headstrong approach in fieldwork and diplomacy. The petulant governor's iron will and strict scheduling would not yield to indecision or the contingencies of topography or Indians. Disagreements between the two men on policy issues and the pace of the surveys would soon emerge.

On July 18, 1853, McClellan and a column of 61 men and 161 horses and pack mules left Ft. Vancouver to cross the Cascades to the Great Columbia Plain, in accordance with Stevens' instructions to survey the middle Columbia region and passes in the Cascade Range. The expedition's scientific complement included a talented a 38-year-old ethnographer and geologist, George Gibbs, a Harvard-trained lawyer with a lifelong interest in Indian cultures. Accompanying him was Dr. James Cooper, the party's surgeon and naturalist, who was undertaking a substantial study of the long-term effect of diseases on the tribes.

Townsend's Striped Squirrel (Yakama/Sahaptin: *tsii-lá*).
Isaac I. Stevens, Report of Explorations

McClellan was concerned about the overly large contingent of men accompanying him, and wrote Stevens regarding uncertainties about the "disposition of the Indians among" whom they would travel. After a month on the trail, McClellan sent most of the military escort back to Ft. Vancouver when pressing ahead through thick evergreen forests southeast of Mt. St. Helens, before reaching the scenic bunchgrass and sage-covered ridges of the Yakima Valley.

The group descended down the Simcoe Valley, and reached Ahtanum Creek on August 17, where they camped near the mission. Fathers Pandosy and D'Herbomez greeted the party, and introduced McClellan and Gibbs to "Kammaiahkan, the principal chief of the country." McClellan

found his Indian host to be "generous and honest." The two men had a long conversation regarding the purposes of the American expedition. McClellan truthfully explained that the Whites sought suitable routes over the Cascades for a road to Puget Sound. He did not explain the railway, but assured the Yakama leader that Americans would not settle in the interior because, as Gibbs observed, "it is difficult to imagine" that the area would ever serve any "useful purpose." The Americans failed to grasp the significance of Kamiakin's gardens and grain fields, the tribe's cattle and vast horse herds, or the priests' bountiful orchard.

The military and civilian leaders in the party were much impressed with Kamiakin. Gibbs noted that the chief "expressed very friendly feelings, and I have no reason to doubt his sincerity for, in a number of instances, he displayed an honesty not often found." McClellan was equally impressed, reporting to Stevens: "He is very friendly and well disposed and may, I think, be relied on far more than the generality of the Indians."[1]

Kamiakin perceived there was more to McClellan's professed intentions than might be accomplished with brass sextants and transits. Though he would provide Indian guides for survey forays to the Cascade passes, he grew increasingly disturbed as he considered the implications for his people. Kamiakin decided to ride north to confer with Owhi at his camp on lower Naneum Creek in the Kittitas Valley. (Meanwhile, Teias was traveling west of the Cascades.) In this council, Owhi informed Kamiakin that he would accompany the soldiers north to the Wenatchee Valley in an attempt to better ascertain their plans—the Star Chiefs had relatives there among both the Wenatchis and Columbias, and they frequently visited at the great *Winátsa* fishery during spring and summer salmon runs.

Moreover, Owhi had recently married off his daughters, Q'omolah and Sanclow, to Quetalican (Moses), scion of the prominent Columbia Half-Sun family. Quetalican's older brother, the warrior Quiltenenock (*Qwiltnínak*), lately had been staying with Owhi's fiery son and Kamiakin's *stoq'uay*, brother-friend, Qualchan (*Kwálchǔn*). When meeting them, the Whites would describe them as "tall, handsome men" clad in "profusely ornamented dress."[2]

They were fearless patriot warriors, disturbed over recent reports that the Americans planned to take over the country and by the sudden appearance of McClellan's men. Owhi, "a man of very considerable understanding and policy" and aware of settler takeovers in Oregon's Willamette and Rogue River valleys, assured the younger chiefs that he would accompany the soldiers and investigate the matter more fully.

Explorers and Guides

In spite of any misgivings, Kamiakin had treated his American guests with hospitality and respect that summer of 1853. Father D'Herbomez wrote soon after their departure: "they took a portrait of Kamiakin to send it to the President of the United States. We have made Kamiakin known as the most powerful chief in the country, being at the same time feared and loved by his subjects. These gentlemen happened to notice it and intended to make him recognized as the big chief of the whole country. Teias, Owhi, Skloom, and others would be but chiefs of small power and influence."

This likely would have frustrated Kamiakin, who was well aware of jealousies within the Wiyáwiikt clan over his prominence at the expense of Owhi and his brothers. But Kamiakin had impressed the soldiers and missionaries like none other. The chief also had sought to provide sufficient provisions for McClellan's men during their time on the Ahtanum. The blackrobes had no meat to feed the hungry surveyors, so D'Herbomez and Kamiakin went bird hunting. Notwithstanding the priest's sure aim that could claim three hens with one shot, they returned shorthanded. But Kamiakin "found a quicker way to provide...food. He had a bull of one year slaughtered" and the surveyors feasted.[3]

On August 20, Captain McClellan and his party departed St. Joseph's Mission for the long ride northward, traveling along the Yakima River to the Kittitas Valley, where Owhi ceremoniously met them several days later. While other members of Owhi's family wore "profusely ornamented" buckskin, Owhi uncharacteristically donned an American suit coat and hat. Gibbs was impressed by his "very considerable understanding and policy" and his tall stature sons. During the next couple of weeks, McClellan explored possible routes across the Cascades, assisted by Indian guides accompanying him to the headwaters of the Yakima River.

When McCllelan returned to Owhi's camp in early September, the surveyors recorded a change in the weather as colder winds blew from the west. McClellan seemed to sympathize with Kamiakin and Owhi's plight, since he and Gibbs were well aware of tragic patterns elsewhere when Native

peoples resisted White settlement. McClellan and Gibbs could only hope that the pioneers who followed them would deem these lands unsuited for farming. Perhaps things could turn out differently here.

"It is a fortunate circumstance that there has yet been little or no negotiation with the Indians of the Territory," wrote Gibbs soon after his Columbia tour, "and that their official relations with the government have been few.... The evils arising from the want of a consistent policy, from constant changing of agents, and from the rejection of treaties entered into with them, have not arisen here. The field is new, and it is highly desirable, both for the sake of the Whites and Indians, that it should be entered upon with judgment."

The White and Indian perspectives could not have been more different than the contrasting landscapes of lush Cascade forest and grass-covered Kittitas prairie. The officers and civilian scientists, engaged in plans to transform the landscape to their bidding, met tribal elders hesitant to change ancient ways and who spoke of encounters with Animal People. Each embraced a different way of knowing. Americans, such as Stevens and McClellan, sought rational explanations for natural phenomena, and adhered to grand schemes to alter the world their God had given over to them. On the other hand, leaders of the First Peoples, such as Kamiakin and Owhi, who already were facing social and cultural change with the introduction of horses, guns, and epidemics, now heard stories of roads to be built across landscapes they deemed sacred. During that week in September 1853, however, each side sought peaceful means to accommodate the interests of the other, while sharing camp space, meals, and stories.

Owhi soon would decide that the Whites could have their road across his people's lands, as long as they did not stray far from its course. This seemed a reasonable compromise in order to avoid the tragedies that had befallen tribes in California, western Oregon, and in the East. For their part, McClellan and Gibbs voiced support for vast permanent reserves in the region, where Indians could freely reside and roam, fishing in the valleys, gathering roots and berries, and hunting on the plains and in the mountains. After all, few settlers would ever venture onto the "vast sage desert" of the Columbia Plateau.

Grave doubts lingered, however, in Kamiakin's mind. Even if the Whites could be trusted to keep to their roads, perhaps an unlikely prospect, their very presence in passing through the region represented a threat to the well-being of his people. From his cousin, Chief Leschi of the Nisquallies, whose wife, Sloletsa, and mother were of Yakama heritage, Kamiakin knew how whiskey men plied their trade among the tribes of the coast and lower Columbia, with devastating results. Even worse were the prospects of new waves of infectious diseases. Indeed, Dr. Cooper and an associate with Stevens' party, Dr. George Suckley, would learn a great deal about the spread of illnesses in the Puget Sound area resulting from White contact over the years. Introduced Old World diseases were a grave problem not restricted to the coastal regions, though the effects there were more acute.

Plateau Indians likewise had suffered from the scourge of disease. According to Cooper and Suckley, sickness had spread up the Columbia in the late 1840s, infecting and killing many Indians. "The Indian tribes on the Columbia river, below Fort Colville," wrote Suckley in 1853, "are rapidly becoming depopulated by the smallpox, intemperance, and syphilis." All three of these diseases—and others—had been introduced by Whites, and the sicknesses were killing Indians by the hundreds.[4]

Smallpox, Measles, and Fever

According to an Indian report, disease killed all the residents of one village along the Snake River. Illnesses indiscriminately took other men, women, and children throughout the region, including among the Yakamas. Measles had been the major killer among the Cayuse and other inland tribes during an 1847 epidemic.

Six years later, smallpox swept up the Columbia River, prevailing "in every direction, carrying off the natives by hundreds." Some of the Indians living along the Columbia River "buried more than one-half of their numbers." Dr. Cooper noted, "of the diseases prevalent among the Indians, the smallpox was the most common and fatal in its effects." He maintained: "Whole tribes have been exterminated by it on the Columbia River." He personally witnessed the affects; "we met with it among all those inhabiting" the region.[5]

Cooper also observed, "those creatures who have been longest in isolation suffer most." These populations had little natural immunity, and they died as a result. No one will ever know the total number of people who succumbed, but clearly the Yakamas and Palouses were tragically affected by the 1853 smallpox epidemic. Survivors and the yet to be afflicted watched in terror as their family and friends suffered the horrors. Smallpox spread easily, quickly transforming a healthy person's flesh into a disfigured mass of oozing pustules. Indians felt a great sense of helplessness, while suspecting the diseases had been introduced by Whites. On a grand scale, epidemics demoralized and decreased Native populations, adversely affecting their overall social organization and strength.

While McClellan journeyed across the Cascades toward the mid Columbia area, other American soldiers under the command of Lt. Rufus Saxton had marched up the lower Columbia toward Ft. Walla Walla. Better equipped and mounted than McClellan's group, Saxton's party consisted of fifty-one men and a large pack train loaded with provisions to resupply Governor Stevens' overland expedition in the Rockies.

When Saxton reached the Umatilla River on July 25, he met an Indian delegation wanting "to ascertain our object in passing through their country." Rumors had spread that the soldiers "were coming to make war upon them, and take away their horses." The lieutenant told them he "had been sent by the great Chief of us all, at Washington, on a mission of peace to all the Indian tribes on both sides of the mountain." The Indians listened and smoked a pipe with the officer, while one "said that he was glad our 'hearts were good.'" Saxton did not discuss the government's plans for building a railroad across the region.

PICA HUDSONICA, Bonap.
Magpie

"Carrion affords its principal food. The dead cattle, so numerous along the great Oregon emigrant trail some years ago, afforded them an abundant supply of food during half the year.... When in the Rocky Mountains I frequently noticed these birds assembling on the trees around us.... Instinct, or, perhaps, experience, had taught them that on our departure they would have 'full swing' at the...culinary refuse of the deserted camp."—Dr. George Suckley, in Stevens, *Report of Explorations*

Following several days rest at Ft. Walla Walla, Saxton proceeded eastward in the Snake River area, led by Antoine Plante, a mixed-blood scout and future Spokane River ferryman. Guides also were provided by Chief Piupiu Maksmaks of the Walla Wallas, who had expressed his goodwill to Saxton at the fort. Near the mouth of the Tucannon River, the soldiers were met by "a delegation of fifty Pelouse and Nez Perce warriors, who came in full costume, and with great formality, to hold a grand 'war talk.'" The council took place the next day, with Saxton explaining that his purpose was to meet the new governor, "chief of all the country between the mountains and the Pacific ocean."

After exchanging formalities, a "fine young Indian" told everyone that his father had "extended the hand of friendship to the first White man that was seen in that country, and they must follow his example." Pleased at the hospitable reception, Saxton handed out tobacco and beads before ordering his men to display the firepower of their new Sharps and Colt firearms. The Palouses helped the soldiers and their horses safely across the Snake River. The column continued without incident on a well-worn trail to the Spokane country, where they met Spokan Garry before moving across the mountains to rendezvous with Stevens' surveyors at Ft. Benton on the Missouri.[6]

Lessons from the Sound

In late September, Stevens departed from the main survey party and proceeded west to assume his new duties as governor at Olympia. He arrived among the Coeur d'Alenes on Columbus Day, 1853, and held a council with some Indians at Father Ravalli's Sacred Heart Mission. Stevens told them he had "come four times as far as you go to hunt buffalo, and I have come with directions from the Great Father to see you, to talk to you, and to do all I can for your welfare." He promised that "every family will have a house and a patch of ground, and every one will be well clothed."

He gave a similar speech to the Spokanes after arriving at the HBC's Ft. Colvile, adding, "the government would do for them what it had done for the other Indians." This pledge did not ease the minds of the Indians, as a number of them knew from accounts told by traders, missionaries, Indians from the east, and mixed bloods such as Plante that the Americans had forced thousands of Indians to give up their homes and move far from their traditional homelands.

Stevens then proceeded into the Palouse country accompanied by Spokan Garry, who explained the land's legendary origins and described mystical places, such as *Encush-*

eluxum—"Never Freezing Water," Rock Lake. The Palouses assisted Stevens across the Snake River, and, when the governor camped on the south bank near the mouth of the Tucannon, the Palouse Chief Witimyhoyshe expressed his amity in unique fashion. He "exhibited a medal of Thomas Jefferson, dated 1801, given to his grandfather, as he alleges, by Lewis and Clark." The medallion bore the inscription "Peace and Friendship," and the Palouses wished to affirm these values. Stevens continued with Garry to Ft. Walla Walla and then hastened down the Columbia.

At The Dalles, Stevens was informed by Major Gabriel Rains that trouble was brewing east of the Cascades as more and more Whites traveled through the region. The Indians had long feared that once the Americans secured all the land they wanted west of the Cascades, they would turn their attention to the Columbia Plateau. McClellan and Saxton's activities did not put their minds to rest. When among the White settlers, the governor noted that he "met several gentlemen—men who had crossed the plains, and who had made farms in several States and in Oregon or Washington—who had carefully examined the Yakima country for new locations." These men impressed Stevens "with the importance of it as an agricultural and grazing country."

The governor was well aware that the government was obligated to secure title to Indian land by negotiating treaties. Moreover, his dream of a northern transcontinental railroad could only be realized when such agreements were arranged. With news of settlers eyeing plans to occupy the region, his mission took on more urgency as the governor completed his journey to Olympia on November 25, 1853, where he began organizing the new territorial government.

In 1854, Stevens and Joel Palmer, Oregon's superintendent of Indian affairs, arranged to have Nathan Olney from the flourishing settlement at The Dalles appointed as Indian agent for the interior. Because of Olney's good relations with the Indians, he provided valuable information to both Oregon and Washington's governors about the growing belligerence of some tribal leaders east of the Cascades. In late August 1854, two wagon trains were attacked by Snake Indians on the Oregon Trail in southern Idaho and eighteen Whites were killed. Olney helped lead a party in retaliation that killed several Indians believed to be complicit in the raids.

Kamiakin, in addition to hearing such disturbing reports, also soon learned about Stevens' treaty negotiations with the coastal tribes, forcing them to accept hardly favorable terms imposed by the government. In late 1854 and early 1855, Stevens conducted a rapid tour of Puget Sound, making formal agreements with the Indians, including Leschi's people. Kamiakin surely heard of these developments from his Nisqually relations.

The Medicine Creek, Point Elliott, and Point No Point treaties deeply affected Puget Sound Indians, and also had ramifications for later tribal negotiations east of the Cascades. Stevens, having virtually no experience in treaty making, had simply studied treaties recently concluded with the Oto, Omaha, and Missouri tribes. The governor and his staff drafted documents for the Puget Sound Indians based on these models. By and large, the coastal treaties were nearly identical—each called for the end of tribal warfare, the cession of Indian lands, and the establishment of reservations. The government, however, recognized the Indians' right to fish, hunt, and gather "at common and accustomed places" on the lands they had ceded. The documents promised to establish an agency on each reservation, and provide instruction for Indians to learn farming and trades. In addition, medical care was guaranteed.

Although Stevens and his agents said the treaties would benefit Indians, many Native peoples were unconvinced. Some openly defied the governor. Such was the case of Kamiakin's Nisqually relatives, Leschi and Quiemuth—it was rumored their names were forged on the Medicine Creek Treaty.

Chiefly Counsel

The rapid dispossession of Puget Sound tribal domains confirmed Kamiakin's suspicions that the polite rhetoric of White officials concealed other motives. For Stevens, the "great end to be looked to is the gradual civilization of the Indians, and their ultimate incorporation with the people of the Territory." The reservation system represented a temporary means to the grand design. Kamiakin understood

that the Whites wanted control over most of his people's lands, and they would be unyielding in achieving it. But was calamity inevitable? Once again Kamiakin sought the advice of his trusted friend, the blackrobe Father Pandosy.

The priest's response was disturbing, but not unexpected: "It is as I feared," Pandosy told Kamiakin, "the Whites will take your country as they have taken other countries from the Indians…. Where there are only a few here now, others will come with each year until your country will be overrun with them…. [Y]our lands will be seized and your people driven from their homes. It has been so with other tribes; it will be so with you.

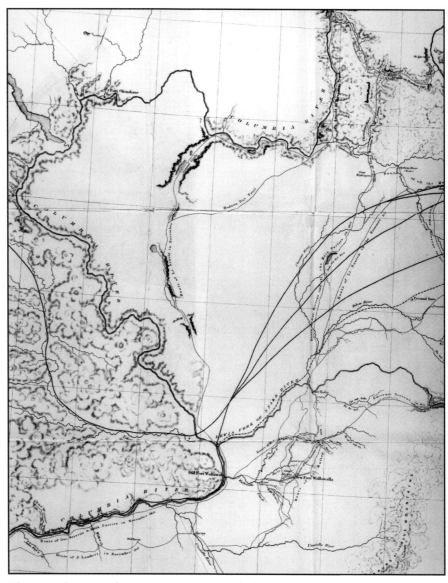

The 1853–54 mapping of approximate transcontinental railway routes in the Columbia Basin.
Isaac I. Stevens, Report of Explorations

Chronology

c. 1800	Kamiakin born to T'siyiyak and Com-mus-ni and raised in the Yakima Valley.
1805	Lewis and Clark Expedition descends Snake and Columbia rivers.
c. 1825	Kamiakin marries Sunk-hay-ee, daughter of Yakama Chief Teias.
c. 1830	Kamiakin marries daughters of Klickitat Chief Tenax.
1830s–40s	Yam'naneek, We-yet-que-wit, and Yumasepah born to the Kamiakins.
1841	Explorer Lt. Robert Johnson meets Kamiakin.
1843–44	First significant waves of American immigrants over Oregon Trail, followed by scarlet fever and measles outbreaks across the southern Plateau.
1848	Kamiakin invites missionaries Chirouse and Pandosy to establish St. Joseph's Mission on Simcoe Creek.
1850s	T'siyiyak, Tespaloos, and Lukash born to the Kamiakins.
1850	Congress passes Donation Land Law for Oregon Territory. Camp Drum (Ft. Dalles) established by U.S. Army.
1852	St. Joseph's Mission relocated to Ahtanum Creek, close to Kamiakin's camp.
1853	Washington Territory organized, with Isaac Stevens appointed governor. Writer/adventurer Theodore Winthrop visits Kamiakin. Northern Pacific railway surveys begin under Stevens, George McClellan, Rufus Saxton, et al. Capt. McClellan confers with Kamiakin, who furnishes guides.
1854	Grande Ronde Indian council.
1855	Walla Walla Treaty Council, May–June. Miners and Agent A.J. Bolon slain on Yakama lands, August and September. Haller's defeat, October. Battle of Two Buttes (Union Gap), November. Oregon Volunteer raids in Yakima and Walla Walla valleys, November–December.
1856	Battle of Seattle, January; and The Cascades, March. Wright expedition to Yakama country. Kamiakin withdraws to the east, May-June. Grande Ronde Battle, July. General John Wool closes interior to White settlement. Kamiakin visits Spokane, Nez Perce, Walla Walla, and other Indian leaders.
1857	Stevens elected Washington Territorial Delegate to Congress. General Wool replaced by General Newman S. Clarke. Kamiakin remains north of Snake River.
1858	Lt. Col. Edward Steptoe defeated at Battle of Pine Creek (Tohotonimme), May. Col. George Wright campaign, August–October. Kamiakin retreats to northern Rockies.
1858–61	Northern Overland (Mullan) Road survey and construction.
1859	Father Pierre DeSmet peace mission. Kamiakin visits Ft. Walla Walla, May.

c. 1860s	Tomeo, Kiatana, Petescot, Tomomolow, and Sk'olumkee born to the Kamiakins.
c. 1860–65	Kamiakin resides on the Palouse River at Kamiak's Crossing.
c. 1865	Colestah dies at Palouse River camp. Kamiakin family relocates to Rock Lake.
1870	Piupiu K'ownot (Cleveland Kamiakin) born to the Kamiakins.
1872	Colville Indian Reservation established.
1877	Chief Kamiakin dies at Rock Lake, April. Nez Perce War, June-October.
1878	Sternberg fossil expedition to Pine Creek; Kamiakin grave desecrated.
c. 1882	Lukash Kamiakin marries Sinsinq't, daughter of Chief Moses.
1884	Major J.W. MacMurray and others prepare Indian homestead entries for members of non-reservation bands, including Kamiakins.
1885	Moses-Columbia band moves to Colville Indian Reservation. Chief Joseph and Chief Húsis Kute return with Nez Perce and Palouse exiles from Indian Territory to the Northwest, May–June. Tespaloos, Tomeo, Sk'olumkee, and Piupiu K'ownot and other families relocate to Colville Reservation.
1887	General Allotment (Dawes) Act.
1906	Burke Act.
1917	A.J. Splawn publishes *Ka-Mi-Akin: The Last Hero of the Yakimas*.
1933–42	Construction of Grand Coulee Dam.
1934	Indian Reorganization (Wheeler-Howard) Act (IRA).
1937–41	WSC Nespelem Art Colony.
1938	Mitchell Act. Colvilles adopt IRA and establish elected Tribal Business Council.
1944	National Congress of American Indians (NCAI) formed in Denver. Yakamas adopt IRA and establish elected Tribal Council.
1946	Indian Claims Commission Act.
1947	Affiliated Tribes of Northwest Indians organizational meeting in Nespelem.
1950	Cleveland Kamiakin, et al., present "Truman Scroll."
1951–53	Frank George serves as NCAI executive director.
1955	Stevens treaties centennial commemorations held on Northwest reservations. NCAI convention in Spokane.
1957	The Dalles Dam completed.
1959	Cleveland Kamiakin dies at Nespelem, September.
1961	W.C. Brown's *The Indian Side of the Story* published.
1965	Indian Claims Commission final judgment on consolidated Yakama and Colville tribal Palouse claims cases.
1969	Chief Charley Williams dies at Nespelem, June.
1975	Indian Self-Determination and Education Act.
1989	Andrew George named Washington Centennial Commission's first "Living Treasure."

You may fight and delay for a time this invasion, but you cannot avert it. I have lived many summers with you and baptized a great many of your people into the faith. I have learned to love you. I cannot advise you or help you. I wish I could."[7]

Because of the political impropriety of such warnings, Pandosy would later be reprimanded by Father Ricard, the Oblate superior. But Kamiakin valued his friend's brutal honesty.

The situation was bleak, and Kamiakin surely left the mission with a heavy heart. He had little interest in further dealings with the Whites, but knew his people's very existence was at stake. Relations in his own family were strained, as most of the older chiefs argued for accommodation with the Americans. Now, dire warning stirred within him.

About this time, he also sought the counsel of another trusted King George's man, Chief Trader Angus McDonald at Ft. Colvile where the Hudson's Bay enterprise was still allowed to operate by mutual consent of the British and Americans. The canny Scotsman had years of regional experience in dealing with Americans and a "curious mixture" of company employees—English, Orkney men, French mixed-bloods, Iroquois, and other Indians from the East. He had married Catherine Baptiste, sister of a Nez Perce chief, Eagle of the Dawn. Kamiakin often had visited the post in earlier years and enjoyed sharing dinner and wine with the Scottish laird's family, whose hospitality was as legendary as the nighttime dancing to his piping of Scot reels and Irish jigs. The company store and warehouses held a "vast collection" of saddles and bridles, guns and pistols, shirts and leggings, and other items. If Kamiakin already possessed enough of these things, perhaps the pictures from the *Illustrated London News* papered on the walls aroused his curiosity.

Kamiakin would trade most anything for a solution to his people's dilemma, but the trader spoke from the same script as Pandosy. Again he heard, "it was hopeless for the Indians to fight the whites; that to kill a white man was like killing an ant, there would be hundreds more pour up out of the nest; that the whites would eventually overrun the country."[8]

T'siyiyak's son stood between two worlds. His father had passed down to him the ancient *walsákt* lore of the Animal People. Now it was Kamiakin who told these same stories of Coyote and Blue Jay to T'siyiyak's namesake, Kamiakin's oldest son by one of his Klickitat wives, Wal-luts-pum.

The elderly T'siyiyak himself, blind and infirm in old age, may have passed away by this time at the campsite named for him east of Sprague Lake. As Salmon Man had confronted the Wolf Brothers, so now Chief Kamiakin must rise, also, to meet forces inexorably forming against him. For the well-being of the children and the future of his people, he must summon his *wyak* powers and not despair. Kamiakin resolved to not passively submit to the overrunning of his people and desecrations of the land as described in the warnings from the blackrobes and traders.

Surely, tribal leaders elsewhere in the region were weighing options in this season of whirlwind change and he would now confer with them. Kamiakin knew from his youthful days when traveling in the Palouse country that his relatives and friends among the Palouses, Nez Perces, and Walla Wallas had considerable experience in dealing with Americans. They included his Nez Perce cousin, Tuekekas, known to the Whites as Joseph. Spokan Garry had been educated at White schools and spoke the newcomers' language. Other elders he had grown to respect from his youth also could be consulted. He knew the revered Nez Perce war chief and buffalo-hunting leader, Apash Wyakaikt (Looking Glass, the Elder), who resided at *Hasúutin* where Kamiakin's father had close ties; Kamiakin also knew the Asotin band's ally, Chief Piupiu Maksmaks (Yellow Bird), who lived near the mouth of the Walla Walla River.[9]

The Walla Walla leader had more experience with the Americans than most of the others. His son had been educated at Reverend Jason Lee's mission school in the Willamette Valley, but was later slain by Whites in California. Piupiu Maksmaks had long observed the ways of overlanders on the Oregon Trail, who often passed through his domains. Leaders such as Piupiu Maksmaks and Apash Wyakaikt were experienced, fearless, and wise. Kamiakin would seek their counsel and solicit support for his idea of forming a Plateau confederacy to prevent the Americans from seizing lands. The future as described by Father Pandosy need not be hopeless— "There are only a few here now," he had told Kamiakin. Perhaps by combined action, the tribes could prevent the priest's ominous prediction.

The prospect for forming such an alliance was not favorable. The tribes were separated by vast distances, some disputes, and the Sahaptin-Interior Salish language barrier and other cultural differences and viewpoints. Even within each tribe, individual bands essentially functioned autonomously, as village headmen made decisions affecting the welfare of the families under their guidance. Yet there seemed to be no other choice than to attempt the improbable. As Kamiakin reflected on his particular circumstances, relationships, and abilities, he realized few others were in a position to attempt what he might.

Schemes and Dreams

Years later, Andrew Jackson Splawn—one of the Yakima Valley's earliest White settlers who was on good terms with his Indian neighbors—said the Yakamas learned in 1854 that the governor planned to return to the east side of the mountains to hold a council, and talk over the purchase of Indian lands. Apparently, a chief replied that the Indians were not interested in selling their lands, and simply "wished to be left alone." But a government official supposedly said: "If the Indians would not sell, the Whites would take the lands anyway and the Indians would get no return; also, that if they refused to make a treaty with him, soldiers would be sent into their country to wipe them off the earth."

Stevens may well have held such beliefs, but it is unlikely he said such things to the Yakamas, at least not to their faces. For much of 1854, in fact, he was in Washington, D.C., working out details with government officials for the forthcoming treaty negotiations and for other territorial business. Nevertheless, it is possible that someone in a survey party might have made such remarks, and, even if the statements were mere rumors, they were highly unsettling to the Indians.[10]

Kamiakin's idea of forming an Indian alliance among the Plateau tribes was not new. A year earlier, in 1853, Father Pandosy had expressed alarm to Father Mesplié about a "gigantic scheme" threatening the safety of Whites in the region, including the missionaries. He described an enormous recent gathering where a "chief of the Upper Nez Perce" endeavored to "unite the hearts of all the Indians together, to make declarations of war against the Americans." Father Pandosy doubted that "all the tribes could be united as one body" because of old antagonisms and since "they do not themselves love war."[11] The Plateau tribes and bands often had come together for root harvesting, hunting, and gathering, and for forming war parties, but never had they created a large political confederation of Salish- and Sahaptin-speaking peoples.

In 1854, according to Splawn, Kamiakin met with several prominent regional leaders at Wallula and urged them to join him a month later in a large inter-tribal council. Evidence that such a meeting occurred is sketchy, but the council reportedly met for several days along the Grande Ronde River in northeast Oregon, far removed from White interference. A point of discussion supposedly related to the question of whether or not to meet with Stevens. Most of the chiefs were in favor of boycotting such a meeting, except for Lawyer of the Nez Perces, Stickus of the Cayuses, and Garry of the Spokanes. These leaders, who had long accommodated the Whites, took "the view that if all were in a position to hear directly what the emissary of the Whites had to say, war might, perhaps, be avoided."[12]

The council participants finally consented to meet with Stevens, but refused to cede any land. They would "mark the boundaries of the different tribes so that each chief could rise in council, claim his boundaries and ask that the land be made a reservation for his people." In this manner, the Indians felt "there would be no lands for sale, the council would fail, and the contentions of Lawyer and Stic-cas, at the same time, be met."

Splawn's account of a great 1854 council is the only one to survive. He received this information directly from the Yakamas who in later years orally shared it with him. The Indians likely had such discussions, since inter-tribal gatherings and the sharing of important news were common when the bands congregated at customary fishing, gathering, and hunting places.

Certainly there was good reason to council, as this was an extraordinary period of suspicion, fear, and threatening change. Kamiakin surely understood that support from such prominent leaders as Stáquthly (Stockwhitley) of the Teninos and Piupiu Maksmaks was indispensable. What vivifying oratory Kamiakin intoned cannot be known, but the effect of his arguments, with the additional pronouncements of others, effected a widespread commitment to stand up to the newcomers. For the moment, jealousies over tribal influence and squabbles between bands were irrelevant indulgences.

Word soon reached the tribes that Stevens planned to hold a council east of the Cascades in 1855. Correspondence among the Oblate missionaries indicates that Kamiakin's efforts to form tribal alliances were bearing fruit, and that attitudes were becoming combative. In March 1855, Father Paul Durieu at St. Joseph's wrote, "Kamiakin is getting ready to declare on the Americans, they want his lands and they will only get them, he says, when they have killed me on them. So, several appeals are made on all sides. Since Easter, we see every day, going through Ahtanum, some bands of Palouses, Nez Perces, who are going to the camp to plot and get ready to fight."[13]

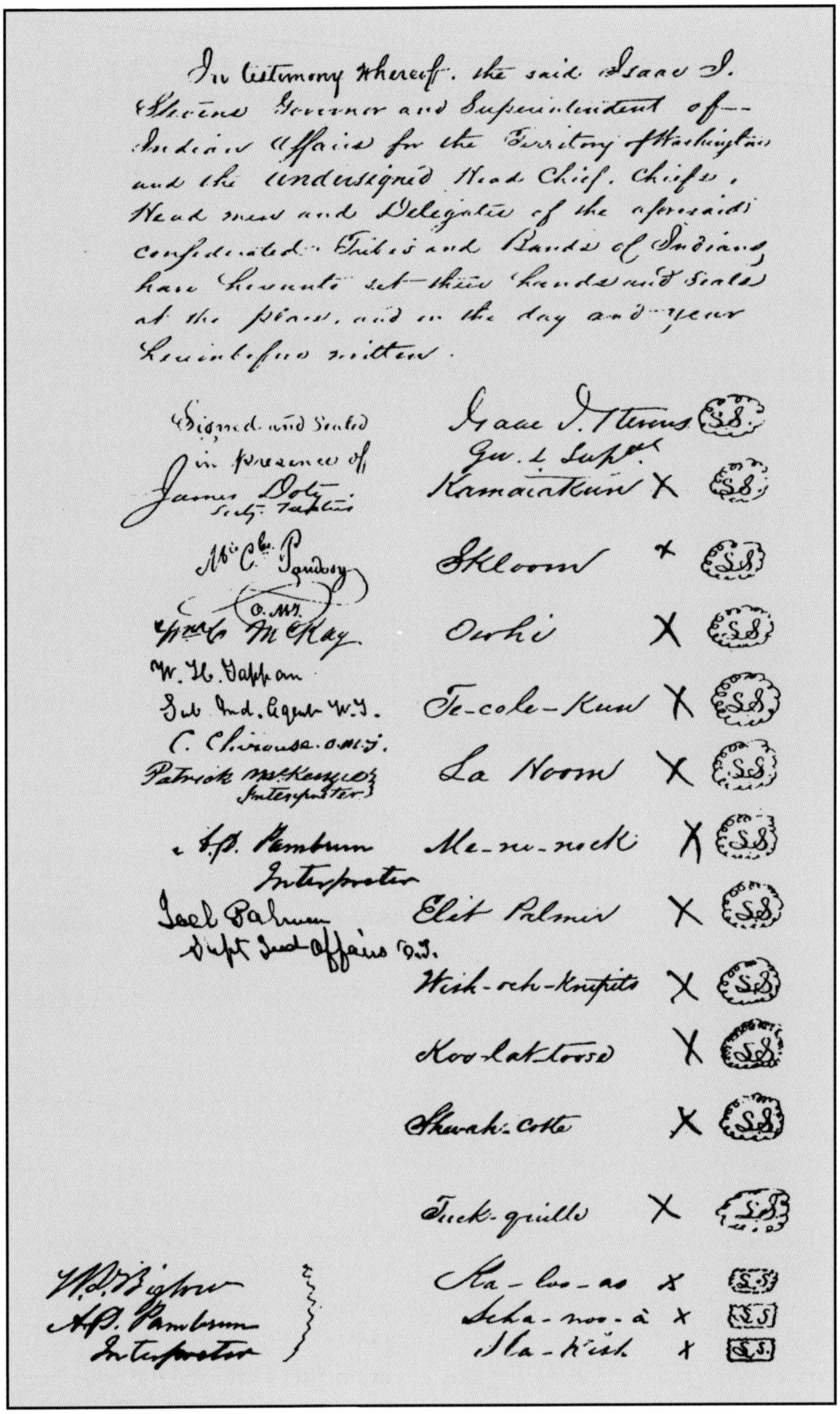
In testimony whereof, the said Isaac I. Stevens Governor and Superintendent of Indian Affairs for the Territory of Washington and the undersigned Head Chief, Chiefs, Head men and Delegates of the aforesaid confederated Tribes and Bands of Indians, have hereunto set their hands and seals at the place, and on the day and year hereinbefore written.

Signed and Sealed in presence of
James Doty, Secty. Treaties
Mie. Cles. Pandosy, O.M.T.
Wm. C. McKay
W. H. Tappan, Sub Ind. Agent W.T.
C. Chirouse, O.M.T.
Patrick McKenzie, Interpreter
A. D. Pamburn, Interpreter
Joel Palmer, Supt. Ind. Affairs O.T.
W. D. Biglow
A. D. Pamburn, Interpreter

Isaac I. Stevens (L.S.) Gov. & Supt.
Kamaiakun X (L.S.)
Skloom X (L.S.)
Owhi X (L.S.)
Te-cole-kun X (L.S.)
La Hoom X (L.S.)
Me-ni-nock X (L.S.)
Elit Palmer X (L.S.)
Wish-och-kmpits X (L.S.)
Koo-lat-toose X (L.S.)
Shee-ah-cotte X (L.S.)
Tuck-quille X (L.S.)
Ka-loo-as X (L.S.)
Scha-noo-a X (L.S.)
Sla-kish X (L.S.)

Yakima Treaty signatures.
National Archives

Chapter 3
Peace and Friendship

The Wolf Sister gathered her things
while Salmon Man watched outside.
Soon she was ready to go
and called for his help
to carry the bundles.
But one of the Wolf Brothers returned,
came along the river with firewood.
He saw her clothing wrapped in hides.
"Are you planning to go with him?"

The Wolf Sister saw he was angry,
so she walked over to Salmon Man.
"You belong with us," her brother said.
Salmon Man says, "She is
coming downriver with me."
And they loaded the bundles in a canoe.
"They will not get far!"
the Wolf Brother told the others.
He ran off to tell his brothers.

On March 7, 1855, a small group of men, including James Doty, Andrew Jackson Bolon, and Dr. Richard H. Lansdale, left The Dalles for the interior. These envoys were under instructions from Stevens "to organize a party with a view to vigorous action in the Indian country east of the Cascades, explaining to the Indians the objects of the Government in proposing to treat with them, and collecting them at some point favorable for holding Treaties."

During the last week of March, the *Shuyapo* met with Piupiu Maksmaks of the Walla Wallas, who learned that "Stevens was coming to hold a treaty with his tribe." They reportedly received consent from the headman to participate in such a gathering. Word spread quickly among the interior tribes, for they had been expecting the conference with Stevens. The Palouses, who had relatives living with the tribes south of the Snake, particularly among the Walla Wallas who recognized Piupiu Maksmaks as their leader, also learned of Doty's message.

When the Whites had completed their parley with Piupiu Maksmaks, they turned northwest toward Yakama country. On the last day of March, Doty dispatched an Indian to Skloom's camp, asking Kamiakin's younger brother to meet with him on Ahtanum Creek.

Doty arrived at St. Joseph's Mission on Palm Sunday, April 1, 1855. Kamiakin and his father-in-law, Teias, were at the mission, where Father Charles Marie Pandosy was celebrating Mass. Following a short discussion with the priest, Doty talked with the two chiefs for some time, explaining the purpose of his assignment and asking them to meet with him again after Owhi and the other headmen arrived. Doty was favorably impressed with Teias, an old man by this time, who "was cordial in expressions of friendship and readily acceded" to deal with the Whites. Kamiakin, however, "was either silent or sulky and declined meeting the Whites or discussing the subject of a Treaty."[1]

An Envoy's Entreaties

Doty recognized the divisions among the Yakamas and was determined to secure "the friendly presence of all the other chiefs and if Kam-i-a-kun, then stood aloof, it would be alone." Doty was correct about the intra-tribal divisions— "there was a very considerable amount of family rivalry existing between Kamiahkin and his wife's people." Kamiakin was only half Yakama through his mother. There were those Yakamas who reminded the chief that he was not a full blood and thus had less claim to leadership than Owhi or Teias. There also were "smoldering family discords" because Kamiakin was a wealthy and powerful figure whose prestige rivaled the other Yakama leaders. The details of this were unknown to Doty, but he easily perceived that the Yakamas were divided along family lines. Like so many official agents before, he determined to make the best of this situation to foster his government's objectives.[2]

The second day, Doty and Bolon, a brash, red-bearded Pennsylvanian, met with Kamiakin's brothers, Skloom and Showaway, at Ahtanum. Teias also was present, and the three headmen reportedly "were very friendly." But Kamiakin remained uninterested in socializing with Doty, stayed about a quarter of a mile away from the mission, and paid "no attention to an invitation" to visit Doty's camp.

The chief remained at his own camp and awaited the arrival of Owhi, before they all finally met in council. Owhi and other important chiefs now met with Doty, including Kamiakin, who came bearing arms and in a stern mood. "He entered the lodge," observed Father Durieu, and "spoke only twice. When the time came to choose a place for the meeting, he absolutely wanted it to be held at Walla Walla while the Agent wanted to have it at Simkoe, and when the Agent offered gifts, Kamiakin said he did not want any."

Everyone listened as Doty told the Indians that Stevens wished to meet with them "to purchase all their country." Then the government would give back a portion of the land as reservations, which would "belong to them forever." The Indians "would be required to live" on the reservations where "they could build their houses, cultivate farms, and pasture their cattle and horses." In addition, the Indian bureau would "manage" the reservations "for the exclusive benefit of the Indians." The Indians were promised a "schoolhouse, blacksmith and carpenter shop, farm house and mills."[3]

All this was to be "given" to the Indians "without charge." Doty felt that he and the government were doing the Indians a favor, by helping them along "the White man's road."

Indeed, Doty believed that the "beneficial results" would soon be seen among the Indian "children, who would learn" manual trades, such as smithing, building, and farming. In addition to learning to read and write, this would enable them to take positions "among the whites, and earn for themselves and families a comfortable subsistence." Doty assumed the Indians would soon abandon their traditional way of life for the benefits of Euro-American culture.

According to Doty, Kamiakin suggested that the treaty council be held in the Walla Walla Valley along with the Nez Perce, Cayuse, Walla Walla, Palouse, and other tribes. Kamiakin previously had declared: "He had never had much to do with the Whites," and "he knew but little of them; he had heard that the soldiers were coming to take their lands and had believed it, but was glad to hear that we [the Americans] wished to treat fairly for them, and that it was all a lie about the soldiers."

Perhaps Doty convinced Kamiakin that it was in his own best interest to meet with the governor. More likely, Kamiakin largely agreed to attend because he did not trust the other chiefs to prevail against Stevens. He feared the consequences if Stevens should make an unacceptable agreement with the other leaders.

Before leaving the Yakamas, Doty distributed clothing, tobacco, cloth, and other gifts, a common practice for government agents. Kamiakin believed that Indians from other parts of the country had lost lands by accepting gifts. For this reason, he refused to accept any, with the sentiment "he had never accepted from the Americans the value of a grain of wheat without paying for it." He maintained "that the Whites gave goods in this manner, and then claimed that the Indian lands were purchased by them."

Doty denied that this was true, telling Kamiakin that the presents "were given to indicate our friendship." The other leaders followed Kamiakin's example and refused gifts, until the next day when Teias received some because "he did not wish to offend them [the president and the governor] and make them think his heart bad." Owhi also accepted gifts. They stated when taking the presents that they were slaves of no man, a likely reference to Kamiakin's own words. Skloom and Showaway likewise received gifts in spite of Kamiakin's objections.[4]

Kamiakin had decided to meet with Stevens, but the chief was unwilling to sell lands or permit Whites to displace his people. Doty left the Yakama country believing that Kamiakin was the "head chief" of the Yakamas, which was a serious misconception, for Kamiakin was "chief" of only one band of Yakamas. No one claimed to be "head chief" of the whole tribe. Certainly, Kamiakin never would have said he could speak "on behalf of and" be "acting for" the fourteen different tribes and bands that Stevens later claimed were under the chief's leadership, including the Palouses with whom he did maintain close ties. The Palouses looked to Kamiakin as a leader, but they also were ably represented by local chiefs such as Khalotash, Tilcoax, and Húsis Paween.

The designating of "head chiefs" was an important element of Stevens' Indian policy. In his 1854 report to Commissioner Manypenny, Stevens wrote: "In making the reservations it seems desirable to adopt the policy of uniting small bands under a single head.... When they are collected in large bands it is always in the power of the government to secure the influence of the chiefs, and through them manage the people."

Kamiakin's aversion regarding treaty-making concerned Doty and Stevens, while the chief's own anxiety grew as the appointed time approached. Father Pandosy informed Stevens that the Yakamas "were generally well disposed towards the Whites, with the exception of Kam-i-ah-kan." The priest also told Stevens that Kamiakin had said: "If the governor speaks hard, I will speak hard, too." Some Indians likewise allegedly warned the governor that the chief "will come with his young men with powder and ball." The governor knew that Kamiakin opposed the treaty council and land cessions, and that some individuals worried that the chief planned hostilities, but no evidence exists to prove that there actually was any such plan.[5]

The Walla Walla Treaty Council

Prior to when the council opened, Governor Stevens stated: "I confidently expect to accomplish the whole business." But treaty making was not a mere formality. Ever since the Supreme Court's seminal 1823 ruling in *Johnson v. McIntosh*, Indian tribes were recognized as "rightful occupants of the soil, with a legal as well as just claim to retain possession of it," representing shared title with the United States. However, Stevens did not intend to deal with the chiefs as equal partners. While the tribes were considered sovereign nations, in the eyes of most civilian and military officials their rights were superseded by the preeminence of the federal government.

In late May 1855, as the opening of deliberations approached in the Walla Walla Valley, the governor reassessed his position, concerned that Piupiu Maksmaks, Kamiakin, and Young Chief of the Cayuses were opposed to any treaties and land sales. The vast number of Indians camped at this traditional Cayuse gathering place along Mill Creek impressed the governor; several thousand near Stevens' small military detachment formed a pulsing panoramic throng of tribal finery amongst the springtime landscape.

Kamiakin expressed suspicion toward the Americans in subtle ways. He was cordial when talking and smoking with the governor, and "shook hands in the most friendly manner." But the chief purposely refused tobacco offered to him, fearing that Stevens would later say Kamiakin had accepted the gift in payment for lands.

The day before the council opened, Piupiu Maksmaks and Kamiakin asked tribal leaders to assemble. They hoped to revisit the issue of presenting a united front, but most Nez Perces were unwilling to join the assembly. Cayuse leaders approached Utsinmalikin, a noted Nez Perce chief, to ask the Nez Perces to attend the meeting. "What are their hearts to us? Our hearts are Nez Perce hearts," Utsinmalikin retorted, "and we know them. We came here to hold a great council with the Great Chief of the Americans, and we know, the straight forward path to pursue and are alone responsible for our actions." He concluded by noting that the Nez Perces "will not have the Cayuse troubles on our hands."[6]

Under cloudy skies on May 29, 1855, the Walla Walla Council commenced with a brief meeting attended by leaders from the Yakama, Nez Perce, Palouse, Walla Walla, Cayuse, and related bands. Observers from the Deschutes and other lower Columbia peoples, as well as Spokanes and Kettles from the north, also were present. They assembled near Stevens' tent under a post and brush arbor erected for the occasion. At 10 a.m., however, rain caused an adjournment.

The following day, Stevens and Oregon Indian Affairs Superintendent Joel Palmer sat on a wooden bench, while hundreds of warriors were seated on the ground "in concentric semi-circles," with the chiefs up front and women and children behind. Stevens had asked the Oregon superintendent to attend the council because many eastern Oregon Indian bands were involved in the treaty making. Fathers Chirouse and Pandosy also had arrived. After smoking a ceremonial pipe, the governor participated in the welcoming speeches, with translation supplied by Andrew Pambrun for the Cayuses, William Craig in Nez Perce, and John Whitford for the Yakamas and Palouses.

Superintendent Palmer acknowledged Chief Lawyer of the Nez Perces, Piupiu Maksmaks, and Kamiakin by name in his opening remarks. Stevens found Kamiakin's demeanor difficult to penetrate as the chief sat in silent deliberation. "He is a peculiar man, reminding me of the panther and the

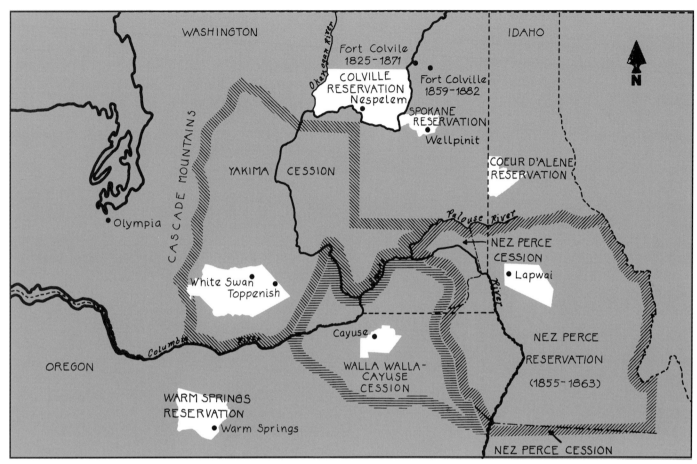

Yakama, Walla Walla-Cayuse, and Nez Perce cessions and reservation boundaries, 1855 Walla Walla Treaty Council. The Warm Springs Reservation also dates from 1855, while the Colville, Spokane, Coeur d'Alene, and reduced Nez Perce reservations were established later.
From Trafzer & Scheuerman, Renegade Tribe *(WSU Press, 1986)*

grizzly bear. His countenance has an extraordinary play, one moment in frowns, the next in smiles, flashing with light and black as Erebus the same instant."

An observer noted that Kamiakin was "the great impediment in the way of any cession of Indian lands," and while "other chiefs, one by one, came into the measure,…nothing could move Kamiaken. With more far-reaching vision than the rest, he probably saw that this surrender of their lands… would be the final step in destroying the nation."

On this second day of negotiations, Lawyer rose and reaffirmed his people's friendship with the Whites and trust in their leaders. The chiefs knew of Kamiakin's less effusive views: "I have been afraid of the white man[,] their doings are different than ours. Perhaps you have spoken straight, that your children will do what is right, let them do as they have promised."[7]

For more than a week Stevens would drone on with theatrical aplomb about the federal government's Indian policy and how it would be to the tribes' advantage to be provided with farms, mills, and schools. On June 2, they gathered again in council with Stevens and Palmer to hear the specific proposals about reservation boundaries and fishing rights. The chiefs had been annoyed with the governor's condescending tone and generalities that tended to cloud rather than clarify issues. A generation of economic interaction with traders and missionaries also had changed their status from bygone days; leaders such as Kamiakin, Owhi, Teias, and Piupiu Maksmaks now were honored men of wealth and they would not passively allow newcomers to dispossess them.

The governor's braggadocio and promised benefits had little effect on Kamiakin's steely nonchalance and few words were attributed to the chief in Stevens' "Official Proceedings." However, Owhi's warrior son, Lokout (*Luqaiôt*), remembered aspects of the council exchanges that did not appear in the governor's account. According to the young Yakama,

Kamiakin rose to tell the governor, "Captain Stevens, this is what I understand you to mean: if we agree to your words, you are going to bring white people. That is why I will not agree with the words of these chiefs. That is what I want to find out, if you are going to do that."[8]

The son of Chief Meninock, who also was present, remembered that Kamiakin responded with words of concern about his people's future. "I am afraid that the white men are not speaking straight," he told the governor, "that their children will not do what is right by our children; that they will not do what you have promised for them."

Young Meninock also recalled Stevens' answer: "You and your children will not be troubled in the use of your streams. The Indians will be allowed to take fish from them at the usual fishing places, and this promise will be kept by the Americans as long as the sun shines, as long as the mountains stand, and as long as the rivers run." Indeed, the final text of the treaties, modeled on agreements with eastern Plains tribes but with profound later implications in the Pacific Northwest, specified the "right of taking fish at all usual and accustomed places, in common with the citizens of the Territory."

Piupiu Maksmaks then addressed Stevens in blunter terms: "I do not see anything with which you are going to pay me for this land. Why should I take up a little farm? I will never do it, and let this land go, unless you pay for it. That is all I have to say. I will never let my country go!"

By June 5, a keen observer noted, "the hostile feeling at the counsel increases, how long will it be before we have an actual outbreak?" Having grown with the times, these proud chiefs were no longer "naïve primitives, but…owned horses, cattle, and cultivated lands." Rather, the council proceedings involved negotiations between representatives of two peoples whose shared perspectives about the future use of the land were somewhat closer than often assumed.[9]

Nevertheless, old factions within the tribes were evident and Stevens worked them to his advantage. The governor's Nez Perce and Yakama reservation proposals were well

Gustavus Sohon's depiction of Owhi, June 3, 1855.
Washington State Historical Society (Sohon 1918.114.9.66)

received by Chief Lawyer of the Nez Perces, although subsequent challenges by a late-arriving Looking Glass almost ended the proceedings. Kamiakin was suspicious of loyalties expressed by some Nez Perce leaders because of the tribe's long history of liaisons with Americans, from when the Corps of Discovery first descended the Clearwater River. Some Yakama leaders demonstrated a willingness to reside on a reservation including their village homelands, but seemed to be holding out for better terms. Kamiakin and the Wenatchi-Entiat leaders Tecolekun (*Taqúliqan*) and Lahoomt (*Laxumt*) also sought a separate reserve at the confluence of the Wenatchee and Icicle rivers, "where the Indians take many fish," the largest fishery on the middle Columbia and a popular summer destination of the Wiyáwiikt family.

Meanwhile, Walla Walla, Umatilla, and Cayuse leaders expressed dismay at the prospects of their people being removed to either the Nez Perce or Yakama reserves, and rumors circulated that the Cayuses were plotting to rise up and massacre the commissioners. These tribes later acquiesced when Stevens proposed that a third reservation, the Umatilla, be established for their use.[10]

Arguments and Threats

After days of tedious deliberations and promises of more land, houses, and money, including Stevens' offer of a $500 annual salary to Kamiakin for twenty years "to perform many services of a public character," the more northerly chiefs tended to oppose treaties ceding their lands at this time. To these leaders, matters of such great significance in such perplexing circumstances required more time for consideration. Word arrived, however, of new gold strikes in the Colville country, which meant more miners would be flocking from the lower Columbia and Puget Sound across Yakama, Wenatchi, and Columbia-Sinkiuse lands. It was now more important than ever for Stevens to break the deadlock.

On June 8, the arrival of Chief Looking Glass of the Nez Perces caused Stevens further grief since "a new explosive element dropped into the little political caldron." Owhi had risen to address the council: "Shall I say that I will give you my land? I cannot say, I am afraid of the almighty.... My people are far away, they do not know your words." Similar troubling expressions were voiced by other chiefs who met Stevens' metallic gaze, but the governor chided them for indecision and pressed for rapid resolution.[11]

As Stevens concluded the afternoon session, he announced with hands astir and eyes ablaze, "the papers will be drawn up tonight." Negotiation had become dictation, and that night there was "violent confusion" in the Indian camps. Owhi, Teias, and, according to A.J. Splawn, even Piupiu Maksmaks leaned toward making an agreement, while Kamiakin at the time refused to concede so much as a stand of pine or sage.

According to Lokout, Kamiakin's resolve was reinforced by the words of the Cayuse leader Tahwat-tus-son, who addressed a council of the chiefs: "I have heard that some of you are agreeing to [Stevens'] words.... If you do this there will be thousands and thousands of white people here." He then grasped a handful of sand, and continued: "You will never count this, but the white people will be like this. You know that I can read and know what the white people know. If you agree to the Captain's words, the white people will come like great waves of water, and sweep us out of our country."

Most of the other leaders, however, remained unconvinced, and sought an accord with Stevens. Lokout remembered that the younger warriors at the council became increasingly "eager to fight," but "the chiefs held them back."[12]

Realizing the futility of further debate, Kamiakin decided to leave the council before the next morning's formal assembly, but, as a courtesy, he visited Stevens before departing. The events associated with this audience were of monumental importance, for Stevens considered Kamiakin the head chief of many tribes. The day before, Stevens' assistant, James

Skloom, June 11, 1855.
Washington State Historical Society (Sohon 1918.114.9.67)

Doty, believed that Kamiakin was "in favor of some Treaty, but does not agree directly to the one proposed."

When Kamiakin visited Stevens, he said he "was tired of talking—tired of waiting, etc." and was prepared to ride home. Stevens demanded to know why Kamiakin, "the acknowledged Head Chief of the Yakimas did not speak his mind in Council as became a Great Chief, why he did not take a decided course for or against the Treaty." Stevens told Kamiakin that it was time for the chief to make "a Treaty of Peace and Friendship with the Whites, to endure forever." Stevens asked Kamiakin if he would leave the council "without doing anything."

Kamiakin gave the governor's words "considerable deliberation" before replying: "All say that I am the Head Chief of the Yakimas. They look to me to speak. Owhi and Skloom are Chiefs but they will not talk. They say let Kam-i-ah-kun speak. Well let it be so." According to Doty, Stevens' arguments carried the day, convincing Kamiakin to sign the treaty.

Interpreter Pambrun provided another account of the discussion between Stevens and Kamiakin. Like his father Pierre, Andrew Pambrun had served as a Hudson's Bay Company trader at Ft. Nez Perces. He was Métis, had taken an Indian wife, and was well acquainted with area tribal leaders. Years later he claimed that that the governor had to resort to "a great deal of urging" and said: "If you do not accept the terms offered and sign this paper (holding up the paper) you will walk in blood knee deep."

Perhaps the invective of possible confrontation with the Whites, combined with advocacy for accommodation among other tribal elders, eventually prevailed upon Kamiakin to sign the Yakima Treaty. With great reluctance he finally "touched the pen" to affix a simple "X" by his name. The crossing of the black lines marked the point of a cultural collision, and represents the only physical remnant of anything recorded directly by Kamiakin's hand. Although the chief's name appears at the top of a list of fourteen Indian signatories, Pambrun claimed that "Kamiakin was the last, and as he turned to take his seat, the Priest [Pandosy or Chirouse] hunched me and whispered, look at Kamiakin, we will all get killed, he was in such a rage that he bit his lips that they bled profusely."

The priests in attendance thought that the governor's approach was a mistake, for Stevens had incited the Indians. "The Priest remarked that this is an error, he should not make such a threat." Doty made no record of this incident, stating only that there was "considerable deliberation" as the commissioners sought to reorder ages of Indian sovereignty.[13]

Under the terms of the Yakima Treaty of 1855, the fourteen tribes confederated into the "Yakima nation" ceded to the United States approximately 17,000 square miles from the crest of the Cascades to the Palouse River in exchange for their exclusive use of about 2,000 square miles of reservation lands, $200,000, two schools and other amenities, and fishing and gathering rights at "all usual and accustomed places." (Ahtanum Creek was designated the northern boundary of the Yakama Reservation although Kamiakin's camp at *Yi-kŭp-yí-kŭp-pam* on the left bank of the stream lay just outside its border.) Article X of the agreement also designated "a tract of land not exceeding…one township of six miles square, situated at the forks of the Pisquouse or Wenatshapam River, and known as the 'Wenatshapam fishery.'"

Similar agreements—the Nez Perce and Walla Walla-Cayuse treaties—were drawn up by the Americans to be signed by "head chiefs," including Lawyer, Piupiu Maksmaks, and other leaders. In this way, the domain of Kamiakin's Palouse relatives was trisected into vast irregular shapes, since the boundaries of all three cessions converged at the mouth of the Palouse River. The identities of the Palouse signatories reveal how these designations would later help foster the tribe's disintegration, and why Kamiakin's sons would one day campaign in vain for a reserve in their homeland. Chief Tilcoax signed the Walla Walla-Cayuse Treaty, while Khalotash made his mark with Kamiakin on the Yakima Treaty,

Chief Kamiakin.
Washington State Historical Society (Sohon 1918.114.9.65)

and Hahtalekin from *Wawáwih* appears on the Nez Perce Treaty. The northwestern part of the Nez Perce Reservation extended about twenty-five miles west from the Snake-Clearwater confluence to the village of *Wawáwih*, an area along the Snake River that actually was homeland of the Upper Palouses.

According to provisions in the three Walla Walla Council treaties, the agreements would not come into effect until the documents were ratified by Congress. Due to delays as hostilities soon developed on the Plateau, the Yakima Treaty would not be ratified into law by President Buchanan until 1859. Within weeks of the treaty signings at Walla Walla, however, a wave of sometimes ill-tempered White fortune seekers rode across the agreed-upon reservation lands. Word recently reached Ft. Vancouver from Angus McDonald that an HBC man discovered gold when washing a pannikin of gravel near the post. The news quickly spread to the Americans. The Indians, unaware of the delays of federal treaty ratification procedures, considered them trespassers, or even worse, because of some of their actions.

In the years to come, much of the Yakama's appropriated financial settlement was lost through bureaucratic mismanagement, while operations of the schools were delayed. The Wenatshapam Fishery Reservation was never properly surveyed (and remains in federal litigation today), and fishing at other "accustomed places" would lead to contentious and continuing disputes with local White homesteaders. (In the years not long after congressional ratification in 1859, agency officials would plead with Kamiakin to take a leading role on the new reservation and accept the salary offered to him as head chief of the Yakama Nation, but he steadfastly refused.)

Striking in Simplicity

The only certain pictorial image known to exist of Kamiakin was rendered at the council by Stevens' remarkable interpreter-artist, Gustavus Sohon, who had been serving as an Army private at Ft. Steilacoom. Sohon's artistic legacy is highly acclaimed, since his Indian subjects are shown with particular attention to ornamental clothing and ceremonial paraphernalia. Sohon's artwork at this historic gathering of Plateau leaders in the 19th century immortalized Owhi, Piupiu Maksmaks, Looking Glass, Stáquthly, and other leaders of the Yakama, Walla Walla, Nez Perce, and various tribes.

The peculiar combination of period adornment and styles illustrates the influence of French Canadian, British, and American culture on the Plateau peoples, as chiefs are depicted wearing choker necklaces of French brass, Hudson's Bay visor caps, and colored glass beads. Lawyer is festooned in a Whiteman's top hat wrapped with colored ribbons that support three ostrich plumes, a popular if incongruous trade item. Spokan Garry, his head crowned with a knitted toque, proudly signed his name to the portrait done by Sohon in a flowing script, attesting to his mission schooling.

Kamiakin's portrait, however, is striking in its simplicity. His long unbraided hair falls freely upon a shirt without the fringed and beaded epaulets seen on others. Sohon's drawing expresses uncommon authority and intelligence bereft of accouterments shown elsewhere as badges of affluence. Kamiakin's eyes look far beyond the viewer. The calm gaze is of an over-comer, one possessing a resilient determination to defend his people from a maelstrom of cataclysmic change.

On the treaty document, Stevens' young secretary, James Doty, identified the fourteen Indian groups comprised together under the leadership of Kamiakin, calling the Yakamas a confederated tribe. This was done for the convenience of government officials, not the Indians, and Kamiakin specifically disputed this point. Oregon Superintendent Joel Palmer observed: "It is pretty evident that the signing of the treaty was adverse to the will of the [Indian] nation." Even

Gustavus Sohon (1825–1903).
Sohon Family and the Smithsonian Institution

Stevens ally and secretary, George Gibbs, later concluded that the governor's "grand blunder" was bringing together so many different tribes "into one council, and cramming a treaty down their throat in a hurry."[14]

According to Stevens, the Indians had united under one leader "for the purposes of this treaty," and were "to be considered as one nation, under the name of 'Yakima,' with Kamaiakun as its Head Chief, on behalf of and acting for said bands and tribes, and duly authorized thereto by them." This statement, directly from the Yakima Treaty of 1855, is misleading. Plateau chiefs acted as representatives of their own bands, and Kamiakin signed the treaty with great reluctance. Kamiakin himself declared that he did "not speak this for myself[, but] it is my people's wish[—]Owhi and Teias and the chiefs. I, Kamiakin do not wish for goods myself. The forest knows me, he knows my heart, he knows I do not desire a great many goods…. I have nothing to talk long about. I am tired, I am anxious to get back to my garden."[15]

During his speech, Kamiakin reportedly said he hoped the Americans would "settle on the wagon route…so that the Indians may go and see them." His comment may have been offered sarcastically to those Indians willingly signing the treaty, which would allow Whites to pass through the region. Kamiakin again refused to accept any gifts during the council, and to his dying day he took no presents from the Americans, fearing that if he did so, they would say he sold his lands.[16]

"The forest…knows my heart" was not a fanciful platitude. Kamiakin communed in the woods with life forces empowering the towering firs, granite precipices, and the four-leggeds. *Náami Piap's* handiwork abounded in mountain solace through the power of the wind and the voices of sacred creatures, such as the oriole, the orange and black-winged harbinger of spring. Kamiakin might have wondered what *wawshukla* could possibly see from the skies in one year's time.

Chapter 4

Common Cause

The Wolf Brothers made plans,
they wanted to kill Salmon Man
for taking their sister.
They ran to Old Lady Spider,
all of them, and said to her,
"You can do anything;
your poison can kill Salmon."

But the old lady said,
"How can I do this to my friend?"
So they went to Grandfather Coyote.
They said, "You must help us,
Salmon Man took our sister."
"You are all my relatives," he said.
"How can I hurt anyone in my family?"

Following the Walla Walla Treaty Council, Governor Stevens left the valley on June 16, 1855, and with habituated energy made his way northeast toward the Snake River and the Bitterroots to meet with the Flatheads and Blackfoot. He reached the confluence of Alpowa Creek with the Snake, where the Nez Perce headman Red Wolf ferried his party across the great river. As Stevens proceeded north through the Palouse region, he found it to be "a delightful rolling country, well grassed and arable," and was convinced that the hills would make "a remarkably fine grazing and wheat country."

While Stevens journeyed across the Bitterroot Mountains, the various tribes on the Columbia Plateau returned home to ponder their treaties. An added irritant was that some bands not on good terms with each other would be consolidated together on the different reservations, a complaint that Kamiakin later presented in an epistle recorded by Pandosy. Many among the Indians as well as a number of Whites soon concluded that Stevens had negotiated the treaties with too much haste.

Within days of the council's ending, however, the Puget Sound press was heralding a new era of regional development. In late June, Olympia's widely circulated *Pioneer and Democrat* proclaimed that because of the treaties, "the land ceded is now open for settlement.... The whole scope of the country...presents great attractions for settlers." This account and others in the regional press reported words from a Stevens' emissary that the tribes had agreed to open their lands immediately, a claim later disputed by the Indians and contradictory to provisions in the treaties themselves (settlement on ceded lands could not legally proceed until after congressional ratification).[1]

Gold Strikes and Strife

Kamiakin reacted by hoping for peace while organizing his allies for the likelihood of war. A month after the treaty council, area headmen assembled at his Ahtanum camp, and then emissaries were dispatched. The Yakama chief would send messengers to various tribes in the Puget Sound country, the Columbia Plateau, and the Bitterroot Valley. Like Pontiac and Tecumseh before him, Kamiakin hoped to organize a tribal confederacy to act as a bulwark against the Whites.

In July and August 1855, the tribes became further alarmed for yet another reason. Gold had been discovered north of the Spokane River near Ft. Colvile. After the treaties were signed, some Whites rushed to the new diggings. Many Northwest Indians were aware of what had happened to California and southwest Oregon tribes during earlier gold rushes and feared a similar fate. Miners often were a hardy, ruthless lot, who let nothing—heat, hardship, mountains, rivers, or Indians—stand between them and their El Dorado. Many brought with them typical frontier prejudices and a disregard of Indian rights and property. Their recurrent malfeasance stirred the Natives' contempt of foreigners. Most would have little interest in the Indian dictionaries and drawings of Pandosy and Sohon. "For one that comes with a pencil," Henry David Thoreau was then lamenting in New England, "a thousand come with an axe or rifle."

The Northwest gold seekers were one more wave in the advancement of White settlement, to be followed shortly by ranchers and farmers. Most conceived of themselves as agents of regeneration, making the wilderness useful for private ambition and beneficent civilization. However, as the Concord sage postulated—in language that men such as Pandosy and Kamiakin would have comprehended—true human greatness also depended on a balance of primordial vitality with cultural appreciation. What an Oblate and an artist may have contributed through books and sketches, Kamiakin knew from experiencing natural landscapes. He would have agreed with Thoreau's celebrated observation—that places "where the pine flourishes and the jay still screams" were necessary for the human spirit.[2]

During the summer of 1855, missionaries at St. Joseph's Mission on Ahtanum Creek reported several "bands of Palouse and Nez Perces passing the Mission going to… [Kamiakin's] camp to plot, to get ready." Such references likely related to the chiefly conclave convened by Kamiakin in the Yakima Valley about a month after the Walla Walla Council. Participants included Owhi and Teias as well as Quiltenenock and Quetalican of the Columbias, and the Wanapum leader Suxaapí (Sohappy).

Kamiakin asked: "What of us then?" Shall we become "a degraded people. Let us stop their coming, even if we must fight. You are all brave men and most of you great chiefs. Let me know your hearts."

Owhi and Teias were opposed to fighting unless soldiers were sent against them. Sohappy was even more adamant: "We cannot win…they are thicker than the leaves on the trees… When one of them dies, ten come in his place."

But Quiltenenock expressed the sentiments of younger warriors. The white men "will take our lands and no place will be left to pitch our lodges," he told the assembly. "The white man's plow will disturb the bones of our people. If our fathers could speak to us, they would say, 'Fight.'" Speaking next, Moses said his brother "has spoken my heart."

Qualchan, the son of Owhi, followed by expressing his confidence in Kamiakin to choose the correct course of action.[3] Kamiakin silently pondered the various perspectives for some time before responding, and again sought a path toward reconciliation. "Let us send men to the mountain passes to warn the white men to go back," but "if they persist" and the soldiers come, "we will fight."

In accordance with this hope to forestall conflict, Yakama messengers were sent along the routes to the Naches and Snoqualmie passes and elsewhere to carry the warning. Several sources confirm the spreading of this message, and suggest it may have been carried in person by Kamiakin to his Klickitat relatives to the south. At the time, a band was digging roots at Camas Prairie, south of Mt. Adams; elders later recalled, "to that place came Kamiáikǐn…. Five nights he remained in council with the old men, and said his people should not fight."[4]

But prospects of making a fortune in new strikes beyond the Cascades outweighed any consideration to the contrary, and parties of miners continued to cross Yakama lands. Kamiakin traveled eastward to confer with the Walla Wallas and Nez Perces, while Skloom counseled with Wasco, Wishram, and Warm Springs leaders, and Qualchan carried the message to Leschi, Stahi, and others on Puget Sound. Chief Looking Glass of the Nez Perces offered a horse in battle array, with the request that Kamiakin give it to his leading warrior. Kamiakin presented the animal to Qualchan after the chief returned to Yakama country from a circuit that also included visits with Palouse, Spokane, and Coeur d'Alene leaders. Red Wolf of the Spokanes reported that emissaries of Kamiakin came "to get all the people to go to war." Tilcoax later pledged horses to them as inducements to support the cause.[5]

Catholic priests, close observers of tribal sentiments, feared that the gold strikes and the opening of the interior Northwest to White settlers would cause war. In a prophetic statement, Father Ricard of Olympia wrote, "the mines of Colville will become a new cause of trouble." Certainly, he exclaimed, "there will be a lot more bloodshed." Unfortunately, he proved correct.

Press reports during the summer of 1855 seemed to confirm that the Colville gold strikes were genuine and attracting a rakish lot, while other newspaper articles about the Stevens treaties seemed to allay the threat of Indian trouble. Olympia and Portland newspapers also recommended various routes to the strikes, including a trail from Ft. Steilacoom over Naches Pass to the Columbia River. This route led close to the country that the Indians considered their exclusive domain, as stipulated in the Yakima Treaty.

During August 1855, as six miners traveled into the Yakima Valley en route to Colville, several warriors led by Qualchan attacked the party at the confluence of Wenas Creek and the Yakima River, and killed them. One month later, three Indians including Mámunashat (Charley Nason), the young son of Kanasket and Chief Teias's nephew, killed Henry Matisse and O.M. Eaton north of Umtanum Ridge in Yakama country. Father Chirouse said this occurred because Matisse had assaulted Owhi's niece, the daughter of Chief Teias. Although allegations would later appear in Olympia's *Pioneer and Democrat* that Kamiakin was involved in the killings, a Colville miner penned an August 6, 1855, letter to a Portland newspaper describing his meeting that same week on the Spokane River with Kamiakin, who stressed hope "for peace with the whites."[6]

Charles Mason, acting governor of Washington Territory while Stevens held council among the Flatheads and Blackfoot, called upon Major Gabriel Rains at Ft. Vancouver to investigate a report "that 3 American citizens have been murdered by Yakima Indians on the eastern side of the Cascades, while going to the Colvile mines." Closer to the scene at Ft. Dalles, the recently appointed Yakama Indian agent, A.J. Bolon, left to investigate on September 20. A former territorial legislator who joined in Indian athletic contests, Bolon was openly critical of Catholic priests, most of whom were French Canadians or from Europe. Like many Whites in the Northwest, he believed they were actively encouraging the tribes to resist Americans. One of the resident priests at St. Joseph's, Father Louis D'Herbomez, however, countered by characterizing Bolon as a man of "little prudence and wisdom," whom many Yakamas disliked because of the sometimes overbearing way he treated Indians.

As Bolon rode to Toppenish Creek, where he visited Kamiakin's brother Showaway, he was told that the Indians were in an ugly mood and his life might be in danger. Heeding the warning, he headed back south toward The Dalles on September 22. Along the way, however, Bolon fell in with a small band of Yakamas led by Mushíil (Mosheel), Showaway's son, also heading in that direction to acquire fish on the Columbia. According to Owhi's son, Lokout, Mushíil knew and hated Bolon because he held the agent responsible for the hanging of some of his Cayuse relatives in the wake of the Whitman killings. According to another Wiyáwiikt family account, Mushíil sought retaliation for miners who recently had killed his wife, daughter, and an infant confined to a cradleboard. Soon after the group made camp at Wahk-shum spring north of present-day Goldendale, Mushíil and some of his companions wrestled Bolon to the ground and cut his throat.[7]

Old Levitical Law

When Bolon failed to return to The Dalles, his colleague, Special Agent Nathan Olney, sent a delegation of Deschutes Indians to spy on the Yakamas. Kamiakin's young acquaintance, Olney, soon learned the alarming news about Bolon's murder from an Indian woman who arrived from the north side of the Columbia. Days later, a Deschutes chief returned to The Dalles bearing a letter from Father Brouillet in the Yakima Valley. The Deschutes man had been disarmed by Kamiakin and taken to the Ahtanum Mission in order to carry the Indians' defiant message back to the Whites. Oregon Superintendent Palmer was informed of Bolon's demise, and that the tribes were uniting to make war upon the Whites, as well as those Indians not joining the effort to drive out the Americans. At the same time, Kamiakin dispatched an envoy to Olney warning his young friend to avoid participation in the anticipated hostilities, advice Olney would not heed.[8]

Like the killing of Marcus and Narcissa Whitman in 1847, Bolon's death was a watershed moment in Pacific Northwest history. The incident was the most immediate cause of the "War against the Northern Indians," fought between 1855 and 1858. It prompted Acting Governor Mason's initial call for two companies of mounted volunteer soldiers. Many Whites believed the Indians were planning a war of extermination and that Kamiakin was the primary instigator. For many years following Bolon's death, Whites perpetuated the erroneous claim that Kamiakin had directed Qualchan to murder the agent, but this was based on information supplied to Palmer and Army officials by a rival chief among the Wascos.

The charge, however, contributed to Qualchan later losing his life, and altered Kamiakin's reputation among Whites after it was widely reported in the regional press. An October 1855 issue of the *Pioneer and Democrat* in Olympia printed the text of an October 3 letter from Palmer stating: "There can be no longer any doubt as to the hostile intention of the Yackamas and Clikitats, nor can there be of Agent Bolon's death, and that he was killed by direction of Camackan." In the following week, Editor J.W. Wiley arrogated the views of many settlers in more vitriolic terms when calling for "no leniency or quarters to be shown to the adult male members of the tribe. We trust they will be *rubbed out—blotted from existence* as a tribe…no good [can] result by the adoption of *half-way* measures—the old Levitical law should have full and free force."

This inflammatory rhetoric reflected the vicious nativist sentiment sometimes expressed in antebellum America. Wiley's alarm was fueled by erroneous reports of further casualties east of the Cascades. The murders of frontiersmen William McKay, Victor Trevit, "and several others" were said to have occurred "at the Umatilla" in "the general war for exterminating the whites," but the incident never happened.[9]

Around this time, news also reached Puget Sound and the Willamette Valley about the capture at Ft. Vancouver of a prominent Klickitat leader, Time-i-tas, on the charge of "acting in concert with Camackin and Skloom" in efforts to unite Indians of the lower Columbia against the Whites. The Klickitat leader had long been a trading partner and close friend of Kamiakin, as well as of Hudson's Bay personnel, but the charge of his complicity in warring against the Americans could not be reliably substantiated. Yet the Whites' penchant for guilt by association served as a sufficient indictment to imprison Time-i-tas in the stockade under deprived conditions. Time-i-tas was confined with a ball and chain; an Indian observer reported "it went hard with him."

A younger leader in Time-i-tas's band, White Swan, came to plead with military officials for the prisoner's release and his persistent efforts eventually succeeded. White Swan was told, indeed, that "some Klickitats have joined the Yakimas in the war,'" and concluded that Time-i-tas's only crime was "being friendly with Kamiakun." The Klickitat leader died at The Cascades about a year after his release. During the months of Time-i-tas's confinement, Chief Kamiakin gave sanctuary to his wife and sister at his camp in Yakama country.[10]

The Haller Fight

Fearing that Indians planned "to join in a general uprising against the Americans," Acting Governor Mason and the ter-

ritorial legislature demanded that the U.S. Army launch an expedition to "punish these Indians, and to check their murderous intentions." They hoped a determined response would "prove sufficiently strong to inflict a severe punishment upon the Indians, and thus check the war at the outstart."

Major Gabriel Rains answered the public outcry by ordering Major Granville O. Haller at The Dalles, where Camp Drum had been renamed Ft. Dalles in 1854, to take two companies of soldiers north to investigate. Haller would be supported by Lt. W.A. Slaughter and a force of fifty men from Ft. Steilacoom. Slaughter's column would march from Puget Sound toward Naches Pass with the intent of joining Haller in the Yakima Valley. Thus, in response to rapidly developing events east of the Cascades, the military invasion of Yakama country commenced on October 1, 1855.

On the evening of October 3, an Indian rider reached Kamiakin's camp on Toppenish Creek with the disturbing news. Kamiakin immediately dispatched couriers to the Kittitas country to gather Owhi, Qualchan and his fighters, and the Columbia-Sinkiuse warriors with Quiltenenock and Quetalican (Moses), who were in the vicinity. Kamiakin also sent two messengers south to summon Klickitat warriors "with five horses and five ropes, which they distributed among the head-men. The promise that each man who would come to their help should receive five horses and five rawhide ropes." Some sixty men responded to join Kamiakin on the Toppenish. A number were exiles from Oregon, who had been driven out of the Clackamas Valley. Owhi's men paraded on horseback in battledress and sang their equestrian songs.[11]

One of Haller's objectives was to "prevent a combination of the various tribes," since territorial officials feared that the Yakamas would soon "be joined by a large portion of the Walla Wallas, Palouses, and Conguses [Cayuses], all of whom are turbulent." Whites believed that the Palouses were in league with the Yakamas, as many likely were. As the Indian allies mobilized, Haller's soldiers traveled north from The Dalles, led by Cutmouth John, a Cayuse scout who earned his sobriquet when shot in the mouth while aiding soldiers during the Cayuse War. On Sunday afternoon, October 6, 1855, Haller's force steadily moved northward, meeting Indians before Qualchan was able to arrive at Pisco Meadows near the trail's Toppenish Creek crossing, several miles west of Satus Peak.

Here, a force of about 300 Indian fighters under Kamiakin, Skloom, and the Half-Sun Columbia-Sinkiuse leaders held their ground into the next morning despite "fierce fighting." By midday, Haller threatened to break out of a position taken on higher ground near an ancient Indian burial ground, the present Colwash Cemetery. At this point, Kamiakin harangued the scattered warriors in a voice "heard above the noise of battle, urging his braves to stand."[12]

A short time later, some 200 reinforcements arrived under Qualchan and turned the day against Haller's soldiers. (According to Haller's exaggerated account, he met "nearly 2,000 Indians in the field.") A Yakama eyewitness reported that Kamiakin's horse became winded during the fight and the chief risked being overtaken by soldiers. Qualchan recognized the danger and rode to join his cousin. Drawing on his power from the *Stáaha*, or Stick People, he saved Kamiakin's life by killing one of the riders bearing down on the chief.

Haller's situation was becoming desperate. While supervising fire from the unit's mountain howitzer to scatter the warriors, he risked sending a courier back to Ft. Dalles to summon Lt. Edward Day with reinforcements. Haller then decided to salvage his out-numbered command by escaping under cover of darkness. The soldiers hastily retreated that night back toward The Dalles after burying the howitzer and destroying their supplies. Lt. Day met the returning troops with a small detachment and aided in their defense along the trail where some reported that Chief Kamiakin continued in pursuit.[13]

Lt. Slaughter learned of Haller's mauling while crossing the Cascades and returned to Puget Sound without engaging the Indians. Five of Haller's men died and another seventeen were wounded during the engagement. Indian losses are believed to have been fewer. The Battle of Toppenish Creek proved significant because Army and civilian leaders realized that defeating the tribes would require significantly more time and preparation.[14]

The Wiyáwiikt clan was divided in prospects for the future. Kamiakin, flush with confidence after the victory, said to Owhi: "If we had not fought, they would have kept coming, but we have driven them away."

According to Owhi's son, Lokout, the elder chief replied in fatalistic terms: "There will be more coming, for there are many of them. You do not need to talk that way to me now. I am going to fight, and be killed by the soldiers." Owhi also blamed Kamiakin for further inflaming the hostilities of his son, Qualchan, against the Whites.[15]

News of Haller's defeat shocked the White citizenry and a chorus of complaints arose demanding swift retribution. Chief Kamiakin became a principal focus of their wrath. Some tribal leaders also blamed him for difficulties arising out of the treaties. The frustrations, suspicions, and hostilities of both Whites and some Indians, and awareness that the soldiers would return, were cast against him. For these reasons and because of continued factionalism within the Wiyáwiikt family, his high stature among the Yakamas began to wane.

Agent Olney chose to advocate confrontation over further attempts at diplomacy. In doing so, he contributed to Stevens' and Oregon Governor George Curry's decisions permitting volunteer forces to launch winter campaigns across the interior. But it was far from clear which of the various Indian leaders east of the Columbia had sanctioned the recent violence. Inaccurate accusations would invite tragedy in future months.

Writing from the Walla Walla Valley a week after Haller's defeat, Olney informed Curry of "the most alarming state of affairs as to the friendly relations heretofore existing between the Americans and Walla Wallas, Palouses, Umatillas, and Cayuses. I am doing all in my power to check the gathering storm; but I fear nothing but a large military force will do any good.… The regular [Army] force now in the country I do not consider sufficient for the protection of the settlers and the chastisement of the Indians. One thousand volunteers should be raised immediately.… These Indians must be taught our power. The winter is the very time to do it."[16]

To combat this perceived rising threat east of the Cascades, Major Rains organized his forces at Ft. Dalles, and joined Olney in calling upon the territories of Oregon and Washington to recruit mounted volunteers. Governor Curry and Acting Governor Mason requested help from their constituents to defeat the Indians, who had "appeared in arms to murder our citizens in defiance of the power of the United States." Volunteers were needed, the governors proclaimed, to protect lives and "meet and subdue the foe."

Civilian fears were heightened by rumors from Ft. Vancouver that emissaries from Kamiakin in October had sought fighters at White Salmon from among the Klickitats and Teninos. The message "Let all come and join the Yakimas in war!" reached Chief Umtuch of the Taitnapams and Chief White Swan near Ft. Vancouver and they agreed to meet Kamiakin. Two days after these chiefs began to move eastward, however, soldiers from the nearby fort intercepted them near present-day Battleground and a brief melee ensued. Clad in a black coat and hat, Chief Umtuch was mistaken for a soldier by some of his warriors and accidentally killed when he rode toward them. The other Indians were then led back to the fort, where they remained many months under the watchful eye of military officials.[17]

In an atmosphere of war fever and glory seeking, the governors received an overwhelming response to their plea for volunteers. Meanwhile, some sixty White fugitives from the upper country had hastily sought refuge at The Dalles by late October. West of the Cascades, hundreds of young men from both sides of the Columbia assembled in a frontier array of slouch hats, corduroy coats, and butternut hickory and homespun wool shirts to answer their "country's call to arms." While the Washington Volunteers mainly remained west of the mountains, nearly five hundred Oregon Volunteers assembled at The Dalles under a fiery militia "colonel," James Nesmith, and were amply provisioned with buckshot, bar lead, and rifle powder. These companies were largely comprised of French Prairie Métis and young men from the Willamette Valley farming districts who had come west with their parents over the Oregon Trail.

By heritage and résumé, some represented the entire course of America's Westward Movement. Antoine Revais's late father, Francois, was Lewis and Clark's "Old Revay," while famed "mountain man" Joe Meek lately had served as the territorial federal marshal and presided at the hanging of the five Cayuses blamed for the Whitman Massacre. The volunteers were to be under the authority of the Army, but, in fact, the governors granted them independent command under appointed "officers." The hardy, wild volunteers operated with the Army when it suited their purposes and were far less scrupulous in their conduct in the field. "Extermination of the Indians" became their "order of the day" and little effort on the part of many officers was taken to restrain them.

Write to the Soldiers

While some of the younger warriors celebrated in the aftermath of Haller's defeat, Kamiakin soberly considered the soldiers' likely response. He strained for a resolution to prevent tragedies in what seemed an irrepressible conflict. Once again he sought out Father Pandosy. However, instead of presenting questions for the priest or government negotiators, Kamiakin plainly stated his cause, the Indians' perception of recent events, and the case for establishing an enduring peace.

The unvarnished epistle was dictated to Father Pandosy on October 6, shortly after the Toppenish Creek fight, and was kept at St. Joseph's for later presentation to the Army. Kamiakin's words reveal the frustrations of a leader who had earnestly striven to protect his people while granting accommodation to the Americans. He confessed in passionate tones both the limitations of his position as well as the ultimate pledge of his life in what he deemed the tribes' "common cause"—to safeguard the Indians' "nationality and country."

Write to the soldiers and tell them we are quiet, friends to the Americans, that we were not thinking of war at all, but the manner in which the governor has talked to us among the Cayuses has irritated us and made us decide that a general war will not end except with the complete extermination of all Indians or all Americans.

If the Governor had said to us, my children, I am asking you a parcel of land in each tribe for the Americans, but the land and your country is always yours, we would then have given with good will what he would have asked us and we would have lived with you as brothers. But he has taken us in small groups and thrown us out of our native country, into a strange land among a people who is our enemy (for between us we are enemies) in a place where our people do not even have enough to eat for themselves.

Then we said, now we know perfectly the heart of the Americans. For a long time, they hanged us without knowing if we are right or wrong, but they have never killed or hanged one American, though there is no place where Americans have not killed Indians. We are therefore as dogs. They tell us that our ancestors had no horses nor cattle, nor corn nor seeds nor instruments to garden, that we have received all of these riches from the Americans; that the country was already full of us and at the same time the Americans chase us from our native land, as if the Americans would tell us: "We have sent you all things so you could multiply them until my people arrive: then my people will find something to eat when they arrive." You Americans want, therefore, to make us die of famine little by little. It is better for us to die at one blow. It is you, Governor, who has wanted war, by these words: "The country will be ours—all tribes, all nations, and you will go to a designated place and leave your land."

Our heart was torn when you pronounced these words. You have fired the first shot. Our heart is broken. There is only one breath left in us; we did not have the strength to answer. Then we took common cause with our enemies to defend all together our nationality and our country.

However the war was not going to start so soon, but the Americans who were going to the mines have fired on some Indians because they did not want to give them their women and we have taken the measure to defend ourselves.

After that came Mr. Bolon, who strongly insulted us, threatened us with death when announcing to us that he was going back to the Dalles from where he would send soldiers to destroy us. Nevertheless, we had let him pass quietly, but after having thought of what he had just told us we went to join him. We were without arms and without any idea to kill him but as he went on talking to us with much harshness and threatened us with soldiers, we have seized him and we have killed him, so that we can say, it is not we who have started war, but we have only defended ourselves.

If the soldiers and Americans after reading this letter and learning about the motives which bring us to fight, want to retire and treat us in a friendly way, we will consent to put down our arms and to grant them a parcel of land from each different tribe, as long as they do not force us to be exiled from our native country. Otherwise, we are resolved to be cut down and if we lose the men who keep the camp in which are the wives and our children we will kill them rather than see them fall into the hands of the Americans to make them their playthings. For we have hearts and self-respect.

Write this, Father Pandosy, to the soldiers and the Americans so that they can give you an answer and let us know what they think. If they do not answer, it is because they want war; we are at this moment 1,050 men assembled. Some only will go to battle, but as soon as the war is begun the news will spread among all our nations and in a few days we will be more than 10,000. If peace is wanted, we will consent to it, but it must be written to us so we may know about it.[18]

The letter cites several causes that precipitated the conflict. Kamiakin mentioned that Americans had been hanging Indians "for a long time" without always providing the grounds for such extreme measures. Indeed, such had been the case four decades earlier, when the crass Astorian fur trader John Clarke stunned the villages at *Palus* in 1813 by hanging a Palouse for stealing a silver goblet. Kamiakin also charged Governor Stevens with highhandedness, treating the elder chiefs of the proud and ancient Plateau peoples as if they were naïve children. Instead of acknowledging that the land had always belonged to the Indians, Stevens announced, "the country will be ours."

His negotiations involved designating reservations—"places where our people do not even have enough to eat"—rather than dealing with the fundamental issue of tribal sovereignty. Even as the reserves were established, Stevens refused to appreciate, or chose to ignore, the tribes' need to range widely across the Plateau and into the mountains for their livelihood. Many of Kamiakin's people, for example, journeyed every year to The Dalles to catch a year's supply of salmon, which along with roots was their most important staple. Neither The Dalles nor Kettle Falls was within a proposed reservation, as well as many other locations of both sacred and practical significance.

Kamiakin's specific mention of the Whites' treatment of Indian females as "playthings" is almost certainly a reference to the rapine assault the previous summer, although that inci-

dent by a miner might not have been an isolated one. Kamiakin, with five wives and a nearly grown daughter, would not tolerate the prospect of such crimes.

For all these reasons, Kamiakin felt he had no choice but to defiantly oppose the soldiers even to the point of being "entirely cut down," preferring death "at one blow." His hope of summoning thousands of Indians against the invaders likely was wishful thinking, but probably alluded to his dream of a Plateau Indian confederacy to which he was strongly committed. He deplored the killings on both sides, and despaired of the present circumstances. His heart was "torn" and "broken," terms expressing profound inner turmoil. The letter is both a plea for understanding and a declaration of resolve. Kamiakin would soon learn, however, that other chiefs did not share his convictions, and that the volunteers coming to oppose him had no interest in further understanding.

Rains and Nesmith Expeditions

After several weeks of fevered preparations, Major Rains' command, including Lt. Phil Sheridan and other officers, left Ft. Dalles on October 30 for the Yakama country with some 350 regulars and two companies of Washington and Oregon militia, followed soon afterward by Nesmith's Oregon Volunteers, for a total force of about 700 men. By November 8, the soldiers reached the Yakima River as they engaged in skirmishes with Indians.

Volunteer William C. Painter's journal for that week listed a series of incidents against the Indians and depredations of their property: "Some Indians scalped" (November 9), "Returned…with 40 head of horses and 14 head of cattle and two scalps" (November 10). Sporadic skirmishing occurred as the Whites marched upriver through Union Gap, where the brief but indecisive Battle of Two Buttes (*Puxutakyúut*) occurred on November 9.

By the time the troops headed west up Ahtanum Creek toward St. Joseph's Mission, Father Pandosy had fled to St. Paul's Mission near Kettle Falls. When Governor Stevens later issued an edict forbidding the Oblate's return to Yakama country, Pandosy responded in a letter to Bishop de Mazenod: "Such a defense is not surprising on the part of a man who, like a new Pilate, recognizing the Americans as the first authors of the war says, when speaking of the savages, 'I know no cause' and nevertheless when a means of establishing peace is proposed to him, stated, 'Yes, Father, I will make peace, I will make peace with fire and sword, I will make peace when there are no longer any Yakimas!'"[19]

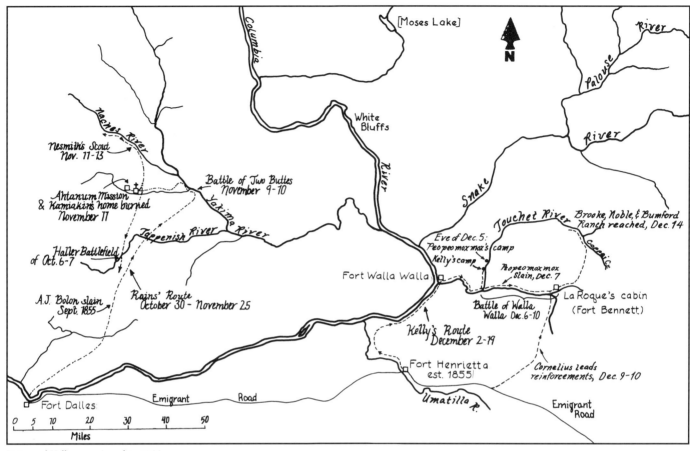

Rains and Kelly campaigns, late 1855.
From Trafzer & Scheuerman, Renegade Tribe *(WSU Press, 1986)*

The settlers' bias against Catholics became especially apparent when they found a half-keg of gunpowder buried in the garden, which the volunteers offered as treasonous evidence of Oblate support for the Indians. Consequently, "wild excitement ensued." On November 14, according to Lt. Sheridan, the volunteers made a mad dash for the mission and priests' home, tearing up the gardens and setting the buildings on fire, burning them "to the ground before the officers in camp became aware of the disgraceful plundering in which their men were engaged."

Cutmouth John pranced around clad in vestments looted from Father Pandosy's home. Despite the fracas, Major Haller managed to rescue the Yakama dictionary and five-chapter grammar, account books, and "a great many pictures, crucifixes, etc." But Nesmith felt that Pandosy's malfeasance was revealed in his men's discoveries—he reported to Oregon Governor Curry that it was "a matter of uncertainty whether *Gospel* or *Gunpowder* was his principal stock in trade."[20]

Kamiakin's letter was found on a table in Pandosy's quarters and given to Major Rains before the premises were put to the torch. The volunteers also destroyed a nearby cabin, winter food stores, and other provisions used by Kamiakin's family. In a cavalier disregard for the conventions of diplomacy, Rains spewed forth an insulting written reply to Kamiakin that only exacerbated the volatile situation: "You know that you murdered white men going to the mines who had done you no injury, and you murder all persons, though no white man has trespassed upon your lands.... Your foul deeds were seen by the eye of the Great Spirit, who saw Cain when he killed his brother Abel, and cursed him for it. Fugitives and vagabonds shall you also be," Rains arrogantly prophesied, and "all that remain of you, upon the face of the earth, as well as all who aid or assist you, until you are gone."

In response to Kamiakin's offer to reconsider a land settlement for the tribes, the major provided an incendiary rejoinder: "We will not be quiet, but war forever until not a Yakima breathes in the land he calls his own. The river only will we let retain this name, to show to all people that here the Yakimas once lived."[21]

The soldiers had come for war, not peace. Proceeding north but unable to find any Indians in the vicinity, since most had fled to the high country or across the Columbia despite frigid weather, Rains proceeded to burn the Mission of the Immaculate Conception on Manastash Creek in the Kittitas Valley. The lack of "Indian signs" and heavy snows in the Cascades convinced Rains to return to The Dalles several days later without further engaging the Yakamas.

However, the Oregon Volunteers under Nesmith set up camp in the Walla Walla Valley, which served as a base of operations to raid Indian camps throughout the winter. The volunteers, of course, were caught up in the "great excitement and alarm" sweeping across the Northwest, fearing that the tribes would "combine and come down at once upon the settlements." They failed to accept Kamiakin's olive branch, and instead proceeded to further antagonize Indians east of the Columbia River, who might have remained neutral if not further disturbed or attacked. Father Chirouse reported in November: "The whole country is on fire—slaughter, murder, and war is all that is heard of."[22]

A second force of volunteers entered the theater in late fall under James Kelly and began operations south of the Snake River in what some called "Kamiakin's War." But they were unable to locate Kamiakin, who in the aftermath of the Nesmith and Rains campaign may have sought sanctuary for his family, as well as those of his brothers Showaway and Skloom, east of the Columbia. Indian Agent Green McCafferty, who had traveled with the volunteers, believed these chiefs were camped with other Yakamas and Klickitats in the Priest Rapids vicinity.

Their influence was being felt throughout the region; reports to Olney from the Walla Walla country indicated "the young men are rather disposed for war, misled by stories forwarded to them by Kymahyuken."[23] Kelly deemed Walla Walla Chief Piupiu Maksmaks as of "hardly less importance than Kamiakin," and blamed him for threatening Whites in the region and for his people plundering and burning Ft. Walla Walla on the Columbia, recently abandoned by the Hudson's Bay Company.

On December 5, 1855, Kelly's force marched up the Touchet River and found the Walla Walla chief's camp. Unaware of the imminent danger, Piupiu Maksmaks approached the soldiers under a flag of truce, but Kelly proceeded to take him hostage while hoping the chief's entire band would scatter or surrender. On December 7, a running and indecisive four-day battle commenced during the command's return to the Walla Walla River, involving Walla Wallas, Cayuses, and Wascos under Chief Stáquthly.

On the first day of the fight, Piupiu Maksmaks was killed by the volunteers after a small number of Indian prisoners allegedly attempted to flee their captors. His body was infamously mutilated. News of Piupiu Maksmaks's fate stung the Wallas Wallas and Cayuses, as well as those tribal leaders who knew of his untiring efforts to steer a peaceful course as the volunteers committed recurrent depredations. Now Tilcoax offered sanctuary to members of Piupiu Maksmaks' band who had fought and fled from Kelly's rampages.[24]

The volunteers' campaigns caused a whirlwind of dispute, wrangling, and bickering among both Indians and Whites. General John Wool, Commander of the Department of the Pacific at the Presido in San Francisco, was outraged by the militias' excesses and expenses. He accurately perceived that Kelly's expedition served only "to unite all the tribes in that region against us." Indeed, among the Nez Perces, proud of their longstanding friendship with the Americans since the arrival of Lewis and Clark, Joseph and Red Wolf began listening to Looking Glass instead of the compliant Lawyer.

Wool felt that the volunteers had acted unjustly against Indians who did not want to fight. They had attacked, he wrote, "without discriminating between enemies and friends." The general was responding to a lengthy late-December letter he received from Stevens, in which the governor strongly recommended that the Army "occupy Fort Walla Walla and the Yakima country, and be ready early in February to take the field."

Wool found Stevens' tone highly presumptuous, and replied in February that the volunteer forces were guilty of "brigand actions," citing the murder and mutilation of Piupiu Maksmaks "after he met them with the flag of truce." The controversy fueled a longstanding animosity between Wool and Stevens, who persisted in supporting the volunteers and blamed Kamiakin for fomenting hostilities. Wool sought to intervene by deploying the recently commissioned Ninth Infantry Regiment from Ft. Monroe, Virginia, to Ft. Vancouver, where they arrived in January 1856.[25]

The political feud between Stevens and Wool played out in the regional and national press, and Oregon's Governor George Curry soon joined the call for Wool's dismissal. Condemnations of Stevens' policies, however, often headlined

Olympia's *Puget Sound Courier,* which characterized the hostilities as "Gov. Stevens' War." The governor was charged with fomenting a "civil war" in the territory by "cheating" the Indians out of their lands through threats and payment of a "nominal price" instead of their true value.

On the other hand, a Stevens' partisan, Editor E.W. Wiley of the capital city's most widely circulated weekly, the *Pioneer and Democrat,* regularly responded to such broadsides in unmistakable terms of party fidelity. Wiley informed his readers that the government's pattern of dealing with Indians on land issues "since the days of Wm. Penn" was to give them "a fair hearing." Wiley characterized criticism of "so much benevolence and liberalism" as "treasonable."[26]

Difference between Us and You

During his further travels and negotiations among the Rockies and Plains tribes following the Walla Walla Council, Stevens had remained nominally informed about the extent of hostilities that had broken out on the Plateau during the fall of 1855. Only when he returned west to the Coeur d'Alene Mission in late November 1855 did he fully learn from Father Ravalli about the recent events in the Yakima Valley and elsewhere. The governor also noted the distinct change in attitude of the previously compliant Coeur d'Alenes and Spokanes. He had hastened along snowy trails due to "the excitement," and held a "stormy" three-day council with Spokan Garry, Sgalgalt, and other tribal leaders, which opened in early December at Antoine Plante's log cabin near his landmark ferry on the Spokane River.[27]

At Stevens' request, Father Joset came from the Colvilles with trader Angus McDonald to help restrain hostile Indian intentions. Accompanying them was Kentucky native Benjamin Franklin Yantis's fourteen-member "Spokane Invincibles," a volunteer force of gold miners wisely departing the country. They joined other Whites in the governor's own "Stevens Guards." Consistent with Kamiakin's views, the northern Indians brandished a warning that soldiers must not cross north of the Snake River, since the tribes had not relinquished claims to their portions of the vast Palouse "garden" between the Snake and Spokane rivers. Furthermore, the Spokane and Coeur d'Alene leaders were firmly opposed to plans earlier voiced by Stevens for them to relocate to the Nez Perce Reservation in return for land payments.

Stevens replied that the matter was open to negotiation and that he only was presenting a proposal, not a demand. The able negotiator used all his powers of persuasion with the Indians to

"win their hearts" through offers of preventing military incursions and a willingness to treat with them for reservations of their own as soon as the present difficulties were resolved.

Garry concluded the proceedings by upbraiding the governor with words the Spokane leader hoped would be heeded: "When you look at those red men, you think you have more heart, more sense, than these poor Indians. I think the difference between us and you Americans is in the clothing—the blood and body are the same. Do you think, because your mother was white and theirs black, that you are higher or better?… [I]f we cut ourselves the blood will be red, and so with the whites it is the same, though their skin is white. I do not think we are poor because we belong to another nation. If you take those Indians…to make a peace, the Indians will do the same to you."

Stevens listened quietly to Garry's oration, then replied: "I do not know where the Spokanes, Colville and Coeur d'Alene would be moved until…they had given me their hearts about it." The governor offered to return at a more "expedient" time to engage in negotiations, and he managed to grudgingly obtain pledges of neutrality from the assembled chiefs.[28]

The governor grew anxious to conclude the council, and obtained fresh horses from the Spokanes to hazard his way to Olympia through Walla Walla lands, where Looking Glass was said to be seeking his capture. On the way south, Stevens also heard rumors from friendly Indians about Kamiakin's inducements for Spokanes to join him along the Columbia River, where the chief's forces threatened the return of the governor's party to Puget Sound. Reaching the Walla Walla Valley, Stevens appointed a French Canadian trapper and trader, George Montour, as a special agent to the Spokanes in order to thwart Kamiakin's efforts to form an alliance with the northern tribes.

Montour soon returned to Plante's home and convened another gathering of Spokane and Coeur d'Alene leaders. Sgalgalt reaffirmed his friendship, and informed Montour that Kamiakin had traveled to the Spokanes earlier that very week with an "impassioned plea," repudiated by the Spokane chief, that the tribes unite in a general uprising to expel the Whites from the region.

Stevens received similar reports from friendly Cayuses, with whom he met during the last week of December 1855 in the Walla Walla Valley. Stickus informed the governor that Kamiakin had sent runners to his people enticing them to fight, but the Cayuse leader had counseled against war. Stevens then mustered his Nez Perce escorts out of service, and directed Virginia native William Craig, a resident of the

Lapwai Valley since 1840 and who was married to a chief's daughter, to take whatever action was necessary in the Nez Perce country to maintain peace.[29]

The governor finally managed to reach the rain-soaked capital on January 19, 1856, where he was hailed with a thirty-eight-gun salute for each state in the Union. He continued to encourage the volunteers' efforts over objections by U.S. Army officials, while also addressing his constituents about the immediate need for decisive action. That month, Stevens delivered a speech in Olympia embracing themes of pragmatism and thralldom. He proclaimed that while Kamiakin did not personally favor the treaties, he had consented to the agreements because "his people all wanted it."

After castigating the Army for its continued restraint, Stevens suggested a hasty renewal of campaigning against the warring tribes in spite of the time of year. He reasoned that a winter war would be to the volunteers' advantage, since the snow on the Columbia Plateau "is but a few inches deep, and lasts but a short time," while the impassable mountain routes would prevent Indian escape. Therefore, "vigorous operations should be made.... The Indians must be struck now. Gloom must give way to sunlight."

He also sought to remind his hearers of the potential benefits of their sacrifices in this critical hour: "Let us never lose sight of the resources, capacities, and natural advantages of this Territory.... Gold, in considerable quantities, has been discovered in the northern part of that interior. There are fine grazing tracts, and rich agricultural vallies, and that interior will fill up when these Indian difficulties are at an end."[30]

Fueled by such rhetoric and political maneuvering, the volunteer campaigns under Kelly and his successor, Thomas Cornelius, continued against the Walla Wallas, Palouses, and Yakamas into the spring of 1856. When not seeking Indians in vain attempts to "give Camiackin a fight," the Oregon

Volunteers devoted considerable time from their base in the Walla Walla Valley to plundering the tribes' horses and cattle for sustenance. When livestock was not available, the militiamen scavenged whatever could be found, consuming prickly pears, badgers, and prairie chickens.

Pandosy's fellow blackrobe among the Umatillas, Father E.C. Chirouse, wrote that the volunteers acted "without discipline, without orders, and similar to the madmen of the [French] revolution.... They have already entirely despoiled of their provisions the inhabitants of the country, the Indians, who have so nobly followed the advice...to remain faithful friends of the Americans."[31]

In early spring 1856, Kamiakin and his allies were being likened by some Whites to the confederacy of Tecumseh. His following included warriors from the Yakama, Palouse, Walla Walla, and other tribes. He had gathered disaffected Indians like so many pebbles from a stream, fashioning a broad mosaic of people inspired to resistance. In February, Kamiakin's forces were committed to number some 500 massing at Priest Rapids, while a force of about 200 Cayuses, Teninos, and Wascos under Stáquthly resided near the lower Palouse River.[32]

Indian leaders certainly were becoming aware of differences in the Army and volunteer commands, but probably were not fully aware of the caustic political and administrative disputes that divided these military forces. In any event, this seemed to matter little when recurrent attacks upon villagers and the murder of a revered tribal elder like Piupiu Maksmaks had taken place. The Whites' rampages had to be stopped. Rather than continue uncoordinated engagements in the field against random strikes by Whites across the southern Plateau, a more strategic plan was decided upon. For six months, the Indians had been fighting defensively. Now they would take the war to the Whites.

Chapter 5

Forests Must Fall

The Wolf Brothers went on,
they traveled faraway
to Rattlesnake's lodge.
"You can kill Salmon Man
with a single bite," they told him.
He thought it over, he told them,
"Why hurt someone
who does not bother me?"
The Wolf Brothers told Rattlesnake
that Salmon had wronged them.

They told him, that is why.
They offered him warm furs
for winter, and other goods.
He agreed to help.
The Wolf Brothers put Rattlesnake
in the front of Salmon's canoe
where it rested by large rocks.
Salmon Man did not see.

Although military and civilian leaders in the Willamette Valley and Puget Sound spoke and wrote extensively in 1855 about their fears of a Plateau tribal alliance, few seemed to note the historic cultural ties between the Yakamas and Puget Sound Indians. Known collectively to the Yakamas as the "Forest Peoples," Puget Sound tribes such as the Nisqually and Snoqualmie had a long tradition of trade and intermarriage with the mid Columbia River peoples.

The earliest documented reference to Owhi appears in the Hudson's Bay Company's Ft. Nisqually journal in 1833. The Yakama chief and his band traveled to trade furs and investigate the White outpost. The journal indicates Owhi remained for some time, and likely visited among coastal bands, since the Wiyáwiikt clan had intermarried with these people. In the 1840s, Owhi and other members of his family continued to visit the fort, and were likely hosted by local tribal leaders, such as Kamiakin's cousin, Chief Leschi.

Owhi's sons and nephews were thoroughly acquainted with the trails over the Cascades. When the adventurer Theodore Winthrop visited the Yakima Valley in 1853, Owhi offered the services of his son to guide him to the coast. By 1855, relations between the Whites and the Puget Sound tribes had grown increasingly strained because of problems arising out of Stevens' coastal treaties and due to isolated murders committed by both sides. Communication between the Yakama and their Nisqually allies certainly occurred in late 1855, as fast riders and swift runners undertook ordeals of endurance to maintain communication between tribal leaders on both sides of the mountains. A snow-warming Chinook wind in January 1856 opened a route across the mountains for the Yakamas to attempt the unexpected.[1]

On January 26, 1856, residents of the pioneer community of Seattle were stunned when a substantial force of Yakamas and Nisquallies attacked the town. Here was further evidence of Kamiakin's expanding "common cause" among tribal people. Friendly Duwamish and other Indians had just sounded the alarm earlier that morning, so most residents barricaded themselves in a blockhouse on high ground near the waterfront. Fortunately for the Whites, the U.S. Navy sloop *Decatur* had been moored in Elliot Bay for several months because of rising threats in the area. The vessel lobbed a devastating shower of cannon shell against the Indian positions along the tree line overlooking the town.

Sporadic exchanges took place throughout the day, before the Indians were forced to withdraw. A couple of settlers were killed and an undetermined number of Indians, though the military reported it inflicted significant casualties among the attackers. Other Whites had died at outlying farmsteads. Qualchan had joined with Leschi to press the assault, but Whites also blamed Kamiakin for fomenting the brazen attack.

After the Seattle fight, one of the leading spirits behind a continuing Indian offensive in the Puget Sound region was Qualchan's uncle, Kanasket, considered by Captain Erasmus Keyes to be "a model Indian patriot," and "the most deadly foe to our race." In the early hours of February 29, an alert picket discerned the figures of several Indians sneaking toward a blockhouse position at Ft. Maloney, near modern-day Puyallup. The picket shot the leader of the war party, who fell paralyzed by a bullet to the spine. Recognized by the soldiers, Kanasket continued to loudly defy them until killed by a shot to the head.

Skirmishes between settlers and Indians continued for several weeks along the White River east of present-day Tacoma, culminating in the Battle of Connell's Prairie on a trail leading toward Naches Pass. Lt. Gilmore Hayes reported that his force of 110 Washington Volunteers met approximately 150 Nisqually and Yakama warriors under Leschi and Qualchan. On March 10, 1856, after fierce fighting throughout the day, the Indians withdrew, marking the turning point in the war west of the Cascades. Deciding that further attacks against superior firepower and fortifications so far from their homeland were unwise, the Yakamas returned east. But panic throughout Puget Sound continued, and was a precursor to other violence along the Columbia.[2]

Fatal Encounters

Among neighboring Plateau tribes, Kamiakin had particularly close personal relations with the Klickitats. He had married Kem-ee-yowah, daughter of the highly influential Chief Tenax, and inherited her other three sisters as wives.

Kamiakin was in frequent contact with his influential father-in-law, whose people had especially suffered from recurrent epidemics and other problems due to their proximity to frontier communities on the Columbia, such as The Cascades settlement.

Kamiakin and other tribal leaders understood the strategic significance of The Cascades, located thirty miles downstream from Ft. Dalles. The place was a vital link in Columbia River navigation, where horse-drawn cars on a wooden tramway provided a portage around the treacherous, impassable rapids, moving freight to steamships docked at Lower and Upper landings. Two log blockhouses offered limited defense for the small White community. Both the Indians and the Whites knew how essential The Cascades settlement was in the military's supply link to the east.

About the time of the Seattle fight, Colonel George Wright, the new commander of the recently formed Ninth Infantry from Ft. Monroe, Virginia, had arrived with his troops at Ft. Vancouver via Panama. The Ninth increased the number of regular soldiers in Oregon and Washington to about 2,000, or about one-fifth of the nation's entire troop strength. Wright relocated the Columbia Department's headquarters inland to Ft. Dalles in March 1856, assigning about 450 men there. Immediately, Wright's command began drilling the troops whenever weather permitted. Wright's experienced officer staff included Lt. Col. Silas Casey, Major Edward J. Steptoe, and Major Robert Garnett.

Workmen soon erected substantial officers' quarters of striking Gothic design, which seemed incongruent against a backdrop of simple frame structures and nearby barren slopes. Wright was a Vermont native, a West Point graduate, and a career soldier, with fighting experience in the Seminole and Mexican wars. He sought to continue General John Wool's peace policy, against the remonstrations of civilian authorities. The colonel believed that goodwill could be regained if the Indians better understood their reservation status, and not listen to the several radical chiefs urging war, such as Kamiakin. Stevens, nevertheless, portrayed Wright as "one who would most assuredly hang" Indians. As the colonel's reputation became known to the tribes, many bands again sought refuge in the mountains.

A common opinion among Whites on Puget Sound was that "the war…was unjustly provoked by the murder…of some 15 or 20 of our citizens." Vitriolic charges continued to be heaped on the Yakamas and Walla Wallas, along with pleas for increased military intervention. Territorial officials and others blamed General Wool for passivity in the face of threats posed by the tribes, which they felt had justified Stevens' call for volunteer troops under his command.[3] Wool and his "pensioners" also were castigated for characterizing the governor's treaties as "unfairly negotiated," and for using such terms as imbecile, insane, and criminal in their assessment of Stevens' actions.

Editor Wiley of the *Pioneer and Democrat* was especially harsh in his allegations against the U.S. Army, and such views likely were held by a majority of his readers. He charged Wool of being in league with the Indians, and accused Kamiakin of "spreading lies to other tribal leaders to incite them to war." According to reports, Kamiakin, Piupiu Maksmaks the Younger, and the Palouse leader Tilcoax were making "extravagant offers" of horses and cattle to enlist more fighters.

This latter claim was not fanciful, as Stevens later learned from Nez Perce leaders. Based on information supplied by an

Oregon volunteer and scout, Absalom Hembree, Kamiakin was believed to be camped with "eight or nine hundred warriors between the Columbia and Snake Rivers." Reportedly, they were soon to join an equal number of Walla Walla, Cayuse, and Palouse Indians gathered at Palouse Crossing.[4] Hembree and coastal Indian agent Richard Lansdale had just returned to Portland after the Oregon Volunteers' winter campaign east of the Cascades. In the third week of January, they had spied a large Indian encampment near the mouth of the Palouse River.

Hembree expected renewed fighting in March when the volunteers and Army moved in separate forays on the Plateau. The Tennessee native shortly rejoined the Oregon Volunteers under Thomas Cornelius. Indeed, on April 10, 1856, Hembree would be killed in a fight with Yakamas in the Satus Creek country. The fatal encounter was described in a report written later that day by Captain Alexander Ankeny

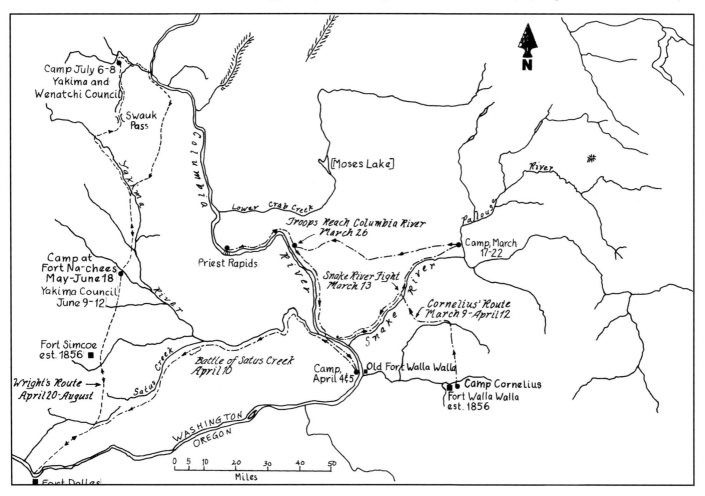

Wright's U.S. Army and Cornelius's Oregon Volunteers campaigns, 1856.
From Trafzer & Scheuerman, Renegade Tribe *(WSU Press, 1986)*

of the Oregon Volunteers' First Regiment. The letter to "Commander in Chief" George Curry, Oregon's governor, stated that Hembree died early in the morning, when a scouting detail was "suddenly surprised and surrounded by the noted Chief Kamiakin and about 150 of his warriors."

Cornelius added that after further fighting, "the notorious Chieftain Kamiakin" was repulsed northward with his forces to a butte, where the fight continued before the Indians withdrew. Cornelius expressed regret "that Kamiakin would not again willingly meet us," but, without adequate provisions, the militia was "in no condition to hunt him down." The volunteers killed and scalped at least three Indians in the locality during this time. [5]

The Cascades Battle

A couple of weeks earlier, in March 1856, Wright had departed Ft. Dalles to scout out the Walla Walla Valley, where he believed the most hostile of the Indians had gathered and where he planned to establish a military post at Wool's directive. As soldiers moved up the Columbia toward the Deschutes River, a messenger from Major Granville O. Haller reached Wright with the alarming news that Indians had attacked at The Cascades, the strategic outpost servicing the portage link between the Upper and Lower landings and a small flotilla of steamboats.

Wright properly surmised that the timing of the raid was not coincidental, since his troops had just set out upstream in the opposite direction that very day. He turned back to hasten to the settlers' aid, later learning that enemy scouts had infiltrated The Dalles to learn of the expedition's plans, and that they communicated this intelligence to the warring factions.

Kamiakin would again be charged with complicity. Wright's Indian sources reported that Kamiakin had persuaded a group of twenty Klickitats under Chief Tow-a-tax, very likely Kamiakin's father-in-law, Tenax, to join a party of thirty Yakamas in riding to The Cascades, striking at "the moment when both steamboats should be there, to burn them, and at the same time make a simultaneous attack on the whole line" to preempt military operations east of the Cascades. [6]

On the morning of March 26, a large party of Indians surprised the settlement on the north side of the river, sending survivors fleeing into a mercantile store operated by the brothers Putnam and Daniel Bradford. The steamers *Mary* and *Wasco* hastily left their moorings and escaped upriver

toward The Dalles. Meanwhile, a friendly Indian canoed down the Columbia to alert the citizens of Portland and the troops at Ft. Vancouver, who quickly formed a relief expedition.

In bitter fighting, the Indians laid siege to the Bradford store and an Army blockhouse, and burned surrounding property. The Whites' situation grew desperate over two days that claimed the lives of nineteen men and one woman, before their rescue by Wright's troops arriving by the steamboats on March 28, and by forty dragoons coming upriver from Ft. Vancouver under Lt. Philip Sheridan.

Faced with a well-armed, superior force, the Indians withdrew and the battle ended, but not before Sheridan had a bullet graze his face and kill a nearby soldier. One of the victims of the battle was a noted Hudson's Bay Company official, James Sinclair, who was returning from Ft. Vancouver toward the HBC's interior posts. Sinclair's death became a factor in the company's decision to develop an all-Canadian trade route from the Kootenays to the Pacific Coast, rather than traveling through the Columbia Basin.

Wright was shocked at the extent of the damage and the loss of civilian lives in the daring strike, but he, Joe Meek, and some others also deplored the barbaric strangling of Klickitat Chief Spencer's wife, father, and several children by Whites seeking revenge. Spencer had been a friend to the soldiers, but Wright seemed powerless to bring those believed responsible to justice. Wright remained in the vicinity for a month, securing the area and waiting for streams feeding the Columbia to retreat from flood stage. He then could directly confront the Yakamas in their own territory. [7]

The Cascades Battle further inflamed tensions between Army and territorial officials in Oregon and Washington, and sparked new diatribes in the regional press. Olympia's Wiley mocked in Jingoistic terms an editorial in San Francisco's *Alta California* suggesting the war was "a natural resistance of the Indians to the encroachments of the Whites upon their hunting and fishing grounds." He wondered again why General Wool had left the settlers to fend for themselves.

In the same month that Wright and Sheridan rescued The Cascades survivors, the *Pioneer and Democrat* offered an altogether prosaic epitaph on the means and ultimate outcome of the conflict: "The Anglo-saxon race will spread—and the forests must fall, and the deserts must grow green and flowery, before and around its advancing footsteps. Its pioneers will be rude and uncultivated men of fierce hearts and strong and steady hands…. The proud and passionate savage will waylay and murder, as they always have, and the revengeful frontiersman will kill…. Unless the pioneers are exemplarily forebearing and forgiving Christian, or unless the savages shall become such in advance of them, neither which condition seems likely to be fulfilled, the collision is absolutely necessary."[8]

Wiley could not abide the impertinence of any civilian sympathy for the Indian cause. But he did concede the apparent tactical superiority of Kamiakin at Wool's expense in an article headlined "Gen. Kamiakin *versus* Gen. Wool." He wrote that "Kamiakin is a better general than Wool," since the Army had been preparing for five months to resolve the situation only to lose the strategic Columbia River depot on the very day that troops headed east. Wiley then ventured to wonder publicly if Portland and Olympia residents could be considered safe, and if these places, too, might be "attacked, taken, sacked, given to flames, and a large number of its citizens murdered."[9]

Such rhetoric in the tense days following the Cascades Battle significantly added public pressure on federal authorities to overrule the Army's objections to Stevens' Indian policy, and accordingly change course.

Parleys and Outbreak

Colonel George Wright eventually resumed his expedition into the interior from The Dalles on April 28, 1856, but the alarming events at The Cascades led to a change in itinerary. He decided to follow the route taken north by Haller's ill-fated command in the previous October. Wright's powerful column of soldiers moved along the old trail east of present-day Goldendale, and on May 4 crossed Toppenish Ridge, which had a fresh dusting of snow. Wright hoped to locate Kamiakin, but only a few Indians were seen in the distance and no clashes occurred. On the following day, the soldiers approached the charred remains of the Ahtanum Mission. Late on the morning of May 5 they were briefly attacked as prairie fires were lit to hinder the troops.

Minor skirmishes continued on the following day as the soldiers left the Yakima River and entered the Naches Valley, where "the Indians appeared in large numbers on the crest of the long range of hills." On May 9, Wright sought to parley with the chiefs—something neither Haller nor Rains had attempted. He succeeded in obtaining a pledge from Indian intermediaries that Kamiakin, Owhi, and Skloom were considering the offer. The soldiers set about fashioning a protective "basket fort" of willow gabions and earth—"Ft.

Na-chess"—about nine miles up the Naches River near modern-day Gleed.[10]

Meanwhile, young Piupiu Maksmaks, the son of the slain Walla Walla chief, apparently arrived around this time in the Indian leaders' camp to challenge the Yakamas: "He did not know what reliance to place on the word of the White chief, who said that his heart was good; that they had been deceived before, and that his father had lost his life." Moreover, the impassioned warrior contended he was now a "poor man," who had given away his horses to fighters from between the lower country to the Colvilles in preparation "for a general war during the summer."

As Wright struggled to understand the dramatic events being reported to him by intermediaries, he concluded that Kamiakin "seems bound to act in accordance" with words of opposition, and that "angry talks" were taking place among the chiefs.

The elder Piupiu Maksmaks had been one of Kamiakin's most trusted mentors. The Walla Walla chief had known the explorer Fremont, the Whitmans and Spaldings, and traders such as Andrew Pambrun, and was long held in highest regard by both Whites and Indians. He had sought the peace road against the objections of others, including Kamiakin. Now the chief was dead, murdered under a flag of truce and his skin flayed for souvenirs. If Kamiakin had doubts about his earlier resolve to defy the White invaders, the circumstances of Piupiu Maksmaks's death and the passionate words of the slain chief's son may have dispelled them.

Wright's and young Piupiu Maksmaks's arrival would mark a turning point in Kamiakin's life and the history of the Yakamas. Indian leaders—harboring conflicting and vacillating viewpoints, facing a seemingly overwhelming military force, and with their peoples' normal seasonal subsistence rounds disrupted, gardens plundered and abandoned, and herds dispersed—struggled again to chart a course for an uncertain future.

Wright pressed for resolution. He sent a message meant for Kamiakin, stating that "no messengers of his will be received by me, unless he is desirous of making peace—that all Indians found approaching my camp will be fired upon." An uneasy calm followed the note's delivery. Then, at evening time, Kamiakin replied through two messengers that the chiefs had "agreed to make peace."

Lokout was present in the Indian camp on the Naches, along with his father Owhi, the Columbia chief Quilte-nenock, Kamiakin, and other leaders who were considering Wright's overtures. According to Lokout, Owhi upbraided

Kamiakin for his inability to formulate an acceptable alternative to accommodation with the Whites. "Maybe you do not know what to say," he exclaimed to Kamiakin. "I have asked you, and I have asked all your people what to say, and you do not know! A long time ago we Indians were all enemies. We used to fight among ourselves, but we have quit that. If those soldiers would make a peace now, and we not have to fight again, it would be well. I have many people, and I do not want them killed; and I do not want to kill the soldiers.... If that captain agrees to my word, we will not fight again."

Quiltenenock concurred with Owhi's sentiments, and it was Lokout who was dispatched to deliver the olive branch to Wright.[11]

The next day, Lokout returned to the soldiers' camp with Owhi, Quiltenenock, and Qualchan. Owhi presented Wright with a white horse and confirmed his pledge. Kamiakin seemed to have fully accepted what he often professed in times past—he claimed no leadership role above that of his elders, Owhi and Teias, or even his brothers, Skloom and Showaway. The other chiefs seemed to seek peace despite the high cost.

For Kamiakin, however, the biting words of Piupiu Maksmaks's son and the memory of the great chief's bitter fate were too compelling. He would leave friends and relatives, his large gardens near the mission, and horse herds pasturing on the Wenas, and return to the land of his father's people east of the Columbia, continuing to resist alongside the Palouses and Walla Wallas. The chief's relocation to the east in late June 1856, beyond reach of soldiers and missionaries, would become known in the frontier literature as the "Kamiakin Outbreak."

Not fully aware of the shifting alliances occurring within the Indian camps, Wright had begun to fear the worse as the days passed by. He wrote to his superiors at department headquarters: "It seems that this country has been selected as the great battle field, where all the Indians east of the Cascades, propose to unite and oppose us," He listed the tribes that had joined "the whole Yakima Nation" in the hills before him—Umatillas, Walla Wallas, Palouses, and others, including Nisquallies from Puget Sound with chiefs Leschi, Nelson, and Kitsap. The colonel noted that Leschi was related to Owhi, and was in frequent communication with Indians on both sides of the Cascades.

Wright's anxieties eased on May 16, however, when "Chief Teias and his people" crossed the river to meet Wright with pledges of friendship, to be followed the next day by Owhi, who expressed "a great wish to stop this war."[12]

Wright also was informed that the "renegade chiefs," Kamiakin and his brothers Skloom and Showaway, no longer were in league with the older Yakama leaders. "I sent word to Ka-m-akin," Wright wrote on June 11, "if he did not come over and join in the treaty, I would pursue him with my troops, and no Indian can remain a chief here in this land that does not make his peace with me."

Wright reported that Kamiakin and his brothers, whom he noted were "properly Palouse Indians," had been near his camp across the Naches River on June 10 and 11, but then traveled eastward "to see some of the Nez Perce chiefs who were engaged with him in getting up this war." Although Wright believed that Kamiakin briefly returned to the Yakima Valley in the middle of the month, subsequent intelligence received by early July indicated the chief had "fled to the Palouse Country."

Encouraged by these events, the colonel became hopeful about prospects for defeating any warriors who remained hostile. He boasted of having "a force sufficient to crush these Indians at once, if I can only bring them to Battle. I shall pursue them, and they must fight or leave the country." He further assumed "a tone of high authority, and Power," noting that "if they all desired peace, they must come to me, and do all that I required of them, that I had a force sufficient to sweep them from the face of the earth." The threat was not idle.[13]

Kamiakin's movements soon after departing the Yakima Valley reveal his considerable efforts to maintain, and even expand, a regional tribal coalition. He had rode northeast to meet with Spokane and Coeur d'Alene leaders in late May, and dispatched Skloom and Showaway to council with the Nez Perces. The brothers spoke with renewed urgency now that Army regulars and the militia were on the move east of the Cascades.

Given the significance of Nez Perce support, Kamiakin might have considered meeting with their principal chiefs himself. However, he had reason to be pessimistic about the prospects of such a mission, given the large tribe's tradition of accommodating Americans and their successful negotiation for retaining a vast mountain and prairie domain during the Walla Walla Council. Furthermore, Lawyer, Timothy, and Spotted Eagle earlier had pledged their protection to Governor Stevens. Kamiakin could ill afford provoking such prominent leaders, which might shake the solidarity of other bands in his alliance. Kamiakin, however, was openly critical of their stance in his councils with the upper tribes.

Meanwhile, Nez Perce agent William Craig pressed Stevens for supplies and ammunition to help keep the Nez Perce loyal, which were sent from The Dalles in June. After Lt. Col. Benjamin F. Shaw's Washington Volunteers moved into the Walla Walla Valley with these provisions, Craig collected them and he personally supervised deliveries to the Nez Perces in July.[14]

After concluding the "Fort Na-chess" parleys, Wright marched his column across the Wenatchee Mountains in early July and camped at the great fishery above the confluence of Icicle Creek and the Wenatchee River. Here, he found Chief Teias and "a large number of Indians with their families." The fishery was the focal point of the vast thirty-six square mile tract, the Wenatshapam Fishery Reservation, which had been negotiated by Kamiakin, Tecolekun, and other chiefs in the Yakima Treaty. Wright also found the irrepressible Father Pandosy here, ministering again to the Yakamas and Wenatchis.

With great regret, the Oblate had fled St. Joseph's in the Ahtanum eight months earlier in advance of Major Rains' marauding soldiers. He had found sanctuary with his Jesuit brothers at St. Paul's Mission near Kettle Falls, but sought means to circumvent Stevens' order forbidding his return to the Yakima Valley. The opportunity came soon after Wright's column had left Ft. Dalles. Indian messengers came to Pandosy asking for advice on whether the tribes should negotiate with the colonel. The intrepid blackrobe told the Indians that Wright could be trusted. When news of this testimonial reached Wright, he invited the priest to serve as interpreter and mediator in deliberations at the fisheries.

Father Pandosy jumped at the opportunity and had raced to the Wenatchee Valley, covering nearly 200 miles on horseback in three days. Highly regarded by both sides, Kamiakin's old friend celebrated Mass daily in the camp to both Indians and Whites. In doing so, he might have been the first Oblate chaplain to the U.S. Army.[15]

Wright assured tribal leaders assembled at the fishery that if they remained beyond the influence of "the refuge chiefs Kamiakin and Owhi," they could peaceably resettle on lands reserved for them in the Yakama and Wenatchee valleys, and fear no harm from the Army or interference from settlers.[16] Wright even recommended to his superiors that the entire area from west of the Columbia to the crest of the Cascades be returned to the tribes. The very idea of this proposal stirred such fervor in Stevens that he immediately wrote Secretary of War Jefferson Davis condemning the notion in the strongest terms.[17]

By mid July, Wright successfully concluded negotiations, due in large part to "the great influence" of Pandosy. The bands gathered their horse herds in an immense train five miles long that lumbered down the Wenatchee to the Columbia, on their return to Yakama country. Wright and Pandosy, and Teias and other Indian leaders, now risked hoping that tranquility might finally return to the land.

Bluecoats and Blackrobes

In an effort to impose military control over the region, and to restrain the rash conduct of the volunteers, General Wool renewed his directive to Wright in 1856 to establish additional U.S. posts in the interior. Wright had received orders from Major W.W. Mackall, the Pacific Department's Assistant Adjutant General, to garrison four companies in the Yakama Valley, and then proceed to the Walla Walla Valley to build another post.

Mackall reaffirmed that "No emigrants or other whites, except the Hudson Bay Company, or persons having ceded rights from the Indians, will be permitted to settle or remain in the Indian country, or on land not ceded by treaty, confirmed by the Senate." An exception was made for miners presently "engaged in collecting gold at the Colville mines," as long as they did not "interfere with the Indians."

As Wright proceeded back to Toppenish Creek in early August, one of his sergeants, a Bavarian native, William Kohlhauff, discovered the "pleasant shade of the oak trees" and "two immense springs" along a western tributary of Toppenish Creek.[18] Wright then ordered Major Robert Garnett to establish Ft. Simcoe at this traditional Yakama wintering grounds, known as *Mulmul* (Mool Mool) for its bubbling springs.

The soldiers at this first American outpost in the upper Columbia region billeted in tents until December, during construction of blockhouses, barracks, and other structures, as well as officers' quarters based on plans drawn-up by Wright's supply clerk, a German immigrant and draftsman named Louis Scholl. His striking designs were derived from a Gothic "villa farmhouse" layout in Andrew Jackson Downing's *Architecture of Country Houses*. These fort homes stood in solemn grandeur in this remote setting. In springtime, the post grounds soon blossomed with added lilacs and rose gardens.

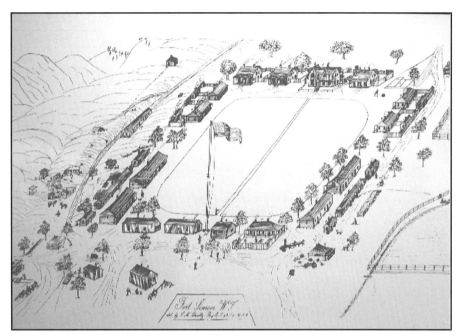

Ft. Simcoe, Washington Territory.

Commanding Officer's house, Ft. Simcoe.
John Clement

Wright also ordered Captain Frederick Dent to construct a wagon road from The Dalles to the new outpost, a distance of some seventy miles. Dent chose a route that generally paralleled the ancient Eel (*Asúm*) Trail, used for centuries by Indians traveling to and from the lower Columbia.

In addition, Wright directed Lt. Col. Steptoe, a recent participant in the Naches foray, to make preparations to proceed east from Ft. Dalles to locate a fort in the troublesome Walla Walla Valley. A Virginia native and West Point graduate, Steptoe had first been ordered west in the summer of 1854 to escort troops toward California. This led to residence for a time among Utah's Mormons when he wintered near Salt Lake City. President Franklin Pierce wanted Steptoe to replace Brigham Young as governor of Utah Territory, but the Army officer refused the offer. Two years later, Steptoe was in the Northwest with the Ninth Infantry, as part of Wool's effort to bolster the Army's presence east of the Cascades.

The militia continued to frustrate the military's peace efforts in the region when a large contingent of Washington Volunteers came east via Naches Pass and other routes. They proceeded to attack Indians in northeast Oregon. Benjamin Shaw's "Grande Ronde Battle" was considered by official Army accounts and by Indian survivors to be a raid upon primarily non-combatants, who had fled the fighting in the Walla Walla Valley to this remote prairie locality in the southeast Blue Mountains.

Shaw reported that, on July 15 and 17, the Washington Volunteers assaulted some 300 Cayuses, Walla Wallas, and Umatillas, with "Tahkin," Stáquthly, Piupiu Maksmaks' son, and a "choice band of Yakima warriors" under Kamiakin, "the ruling spirit of the hostiles."

The militia inflicted heavy casualties and destroyed the camp's stores of "dried beef, tents, some flour, coffee, sugar, and about 100 pounds of ammunition and a great quantity of tools and kitchen furniture," in addition to taking "about 200 horses, most of which were shot." But the incident was described by Colonel Wright, based upon Cayuse eyewitness report, to be an attack on "women, old men and children, with a few of the young men," and without any indication of Kamiakin's presence.[19]

As word spread, Army officials railed again against Stevens and the volunteers' methods, which were "to provoke a continuance of the war and to plunder the Indians of their horses and cattle." The barbaric circumstances of Piupiu Maksmaks's death also were later reported in lurid detail.

Stevens, however, was encouraged by what he perceived to be a civilian militia success. He would later fete Shaw at a dinner in Olympia, where the governor toasted the "brilliant victory of the Grande Ronde," and heralded the action as the "bright spot" of the campaign east of the Cascades. The confident executive now thought his hand as a negotiator was sufficiently strengthened to convene a second Walla Walla Council, to settle outstanding matters with the "great war leader" Kamiakin and other chiefs. The governor planned to speak to leaders of both friendly and hostile bands, "under the sole condition of submission to the government, requiring them to come unarmed and assuring them of safe conduct to, at, and from the council."[20]

Word soon was received that Kamiakin was camped among the Okanogans with his brothers, as well as Owhi and Quiltenenock. (Teias, "the only reliable Yakima," remained in the Kittitas Valley. Leschi and Kitsap also were rumored to be in that locality.) Contrary to allegations trumpeted in the coastal press about renewed Indian attacks, conciliatory words came from the upper country: "They do not intend to fight…, but are on the defensive," and they sought to meet Stevens in order to secure a just peace. But peace to Kamiakin meant recognition of Indian sovereignty north of the Snake River beyond the lands ceded at the Walla Walla Council. To Stevens, reconciliation was defined in terms of the Native people's unconditional surrender.[21]

In preparation for this second Walla Walla Council, Stevens relied heavily on intelligence gleaned from observers in the interior whom he deemed trustworthy. He respected the views of William Craig, a veteran of Sublette's trapper brigades, who had given up the life of a roaming mountain man and now resided with his Indian family among the Nez Perces. Stevens had appointed Craig as a special agent for the Indian Service, and his valued perspectives were passed through Shaw and other militia leaders to the governor.

Stevens also had gained information from acquaintances among the scattered French Canadian settlers in the northeast Plateau, whom Stevens had known since his initial trek west in 1853. Antoine Plante continued to reside with his Spokane wife, several miles east of the falls at an important crossing of the Spokane River. Frontiersman George Montour roamed to the north among the Pend d'Oreilles and Kutenais. Stevens' network of observers in these areas, most of who, ironically, were not of American origin, provided news to the governor throughout the winter and spring of 1856. They reported that the northern tribes were in a high state of anxiety and that diplomacy was urgently needed to avert hostilities.[22]

These views were consistent with information Stevens solicited from another source. One of the governor's most valued correspondents during these months was Father Anthony Ravalli, one of the Jesuit missionaries to the Coeur d'Alenes and neighboring tribes. Beginning in 1848, the Italian blackrobe had been responsible for the design, construction, and interior decoration of the resplendent Sacred Heart Mission. This remote cultured oasis also included a mill, smithy, barns, and fields, situated on the north bank of the Coeur d'Alene River, abut fifteen miles upstream from the lake of the same name.

When Stevens first entered the Northwest in 1853, he found respite here and was deeply impressed with the mission's immense Greek Revival structure—soaring sixty-feet high and framed entirely of hand-hewn timbers joined by mortise and tenon. In spite of the governor's recurrent criticism of the Catholics, who continued to assist tribes east of the Cascades, Stevens occasionally confessed his respect for their record of service and familiarity with tribal leaders, earned through years of effort.

Ravalli endeavored throughout the winter to heal the growing breach between the local tribes and the government. The blackrobe saw evidence of growing solidarity between the Spokanes, Coeur d'Alenes, and other Salish tribes of the upper Interior, who so far had withstood pressures to join with warring Sahaptin groups to the south. Ravalli set upon a vast summer tour to persuade local tribes about the futility of conflict. His words and commanding presence drew pledges of peace from Vincent, Stellam, and Melkapsi of the Coeur d'Alenes, and Polatkin and Sgalgalt of the Spokanes.

But at every turn, Ravalli also heard of Kamiakin's influence to oppose any American advances in the region. Kamiakin had "personally visited most of the tribes," speaking with persuasion and authority. He was "universally credited by the Indians." This renewed Stevens' resentment against the man he held primarily responsible for threatening the governor's grand scheme of development in the Columbia Plateau.[23]

Every Settler Must Leave

The same week that Stevens departed Olympia for the Walla Walla Valley, his steadfast ally in Congress, Territorial Representative J.P. Anderson, hailed the Northwest's "salubrious climate, magnificent forests, broad prairies, and rich valleys" in a House speech that renewed the attack on the Army's deference to protecting Indians and indifference to the governor's agenda. Anderson reminded listeners that the record "proved" how "Kamiakin, head chief of all the tribes and bands," had consented to the Yakima Treaty, but then only to renege in response to such "accidents" as the burning of the Ahtanum Mission. Consequently, volunteer units had to be marshaled causing "great pecuniary distress," reducing many Washington citizens to a state of "absolute want."[24]

Stevens traveled with an escort in early August 1856 and spent little time conferring with military officials as he passed through The Dalles. He had been pleased to learn, however, that in accordance with Wool's earlier directives, Wright was sending Steptoe to the Walla Walla Valley to establish a military post. Stevens departed The Dalles on August 19, accompanied by his young son Hazard, trader Pambrun of the HBC's Ft. Walla Walla, and civilian employees, including herders and men driving thirty wagons.

They arrived in the Walla Walla Valley four days later. Here they met Shaw's volunteers, which soon were reduced to one company of sixty-nine men when most returned to Western Washington. On September 8, stalwart Father Ravalli, who had met recently with Kamiakin, would also arrive. According to expressman John Dunn, who later reported news of the Walla Walla council in Olympia, Kamiakin "had taken advantage of the recent cessation of hostilities," to excite "the Indians to a point of verging on open declaration of war upon the whites."[25]

The governor, disappointed in Kamiakin's reluctance to participate in talks, established camp in the same vicinity on Mill Creek as the previous year's council. Steptoe's five companies of Army regulars arrived on September 5, but bivouacked several miles away. In spite of the governor's repeated pleas for protection, Steptoe intentionally keep his distance from Stevens, which underscored the military's wariness of territorial officialdom. As Steptoe's men scouted out likely places for a new fort, he, too, held councils with the Indians, granting a conciliatory understanding that sharply differed from the governor's views.[26]

Outraged by broken promises after the 1855 Walla Walla Council and by the conduct of the volunteers, Kamiakin remained at a safe distance on the nearby Touchet River, not participating directly in the proceedings. However, as Dunn would later relate from information possibly gleaned from Father Ravalli, Kamiakin said: "It is useless to talk—Gov. Stevens knows my heart already, everyone knows that I am for war." The hostile leader's terms were tersely summarized: No Indians implicated in the deaths of Whites would be surrendered to territorial courts, lands ceded in the treaties were to be returned, and "every settler must leave the country." Scarcely before negotiations got underway, these conditions had muted Stevens' hopes to defuse regional tensions.[27]

Kamiakin's "Outbreak," however, had been less a declaration against White persons, and, instead, was more of a resolution against the imposition of White principles. Kamiakin's bellicose expressions in the "Letter to the Soldiers," left for the Army at the Ahtanum Mission the previous year, were dictated when his blood ran hot in the aftermath of the Haller fight. In the following unstable months, however, he had intervened among his followers with moderation toward White civilians, and would do so again in the months to come, as reliable reports would confirm. Experienced military officers readily dismissed recurrent newspaper accounts claiming Kamiakin's direct participation in the deaths of A.J. Bolon and trespassing miners. The war he sought to wage during this tumultuous period was one of defending sacred places and an ancient way of life from the zealous advocates of conquest and acculturation.

The Second Walla Walla Council

How different from the festive atmosphere that greeted Stevens when he dined with chiefs under the council arbor a year before. On September 11, Stevens opened the proceedings with headmen from the Nez Perce, Walla Walla, Cayuse, Umatilla, Palouse, and other southern Plateau bands, representing an estimated 6,000 Indians. Kamiakin's friend and ally, Quiltenenock of the Columbias, had felt cheated at not being able to represent his people at the 1855 council, when his band's mid Columbia domain was signed away under Kamiakin's mark. He would now seek redress at the second council, but it would prove of no avail.

The governor's rhetoric and inflexibility failed to convince many headmen to abide by the terms of the original treaties. Five Crows as well as the normally compliant Nez Perces contended that White trespassers and the volunteers already had violated the original Walla Walla agreements. Stevens responded in similar fashion as when addressing the Territorial Legislature in January, demanding that any hostiles should be punished for their "perfidy" and "the remainder placed upon reservations."

Stevens noted that the leaders seemed reluctant to speak in Kamiakin's absence and he became increasingly alarmed at the prospect of the Yakama leader's overshadowing proximity, as well as the "unmistakably hostile feeling" of a number of the Indians. Despite the presence of his militia guard and friendly Nez Perce tribesmen, on September 13 Stevens sent an urgent request for protection to Steptoe, encamped several miles away.[28] The governor was stunned when Steptoe refused to move closer to the council, on the basis of Wool's orders not to intercede on Stevens' behalf. On Sunday, September 14, the chagrined governor began relocating his camp closer to Steptoe's.

Some Indian observers now perceived strained relations between the two American factions, but could not understand why there was a rift. Kamiakin, indeed, understood much of the differences between the military regulars and the governor and his civilian volunteers. The chief explained the distinctions to the Indians and sought to exploit the division to his advantage.[29]

In this highly charged atmosphere, while moving their camp to near Steptoe's command, Stevens and Shaw suddenly encountered Kamiakin, Owhi, Qualchan, and a force of some 100 mounted warriors, "making a fine show, accoutered in all the Indian war paraphernalia, riding abreast." The Indians approached within a few hundred yards of the governor's entourage, while trader-interpreter Pambrun cautiously rode forth to meet Kamiakin. Pambrun's horse, however, accidentally stampeded through the Indian ranks after the animal's bridle became dislodged. The mount then reeled back in a sprint to the soldiers. George Montour, Stevens' French Canadian interpreter, proceeded ahead.

Kamiakin motioned as if wishing to shake hands with the governor, but Pambrun thought it might be a ruse to stampede the teamsters' livestock. He advised Stevens against it. The governor announced that he was in a hurry to make camp and Kamiakin could come in and meet him there. Stevens warily continued on, finally reaching Steptoe's position where he treated himself to a bottle of bourbon, perhaps to relieve tension and the discomfort of a perennial hernia. The governor's frustration would grow when Kamiakin did not appear later, and when some Nez Perces reassessed their views. As later reported by Dunn, these headmen demanded that the government "do away with all treaties, give us back our land, let no White man come into our country and there will be peace, if not we will fight."[30]

When Stevens reconvened the council on September 16, Chief Quiltenenock came from Kamiakin and Owhi's camp to present his people's cause. Under the terms of the Yakima Treaty, the Columbia-Sinkiuses were to abandon their Columbia homelands and move southwest to the Yakima Reservation, but the prospect was unacceptable to this proud Half-Sun scion. Stevens now refused to even consider his complaints, and also soon declared an end to the futile council and decided to return to Olympia.

The governor's abrupt action infuriated Quiltenenock, who on September 19 joined Lokout, the quick-tempered Qualchan, and a number of other young warriors in attacking the governor's party shortly after they left Steptoe's camp and had proceeded a few miles down the Walla Walla Valley. The Whites chained their wagons together into a circle along the banks of Russell Creek to protect livestock, but the attack began before all the animals were secured. The governor requested his sizeable Nez Perce entourage to leave the camp, to avoid accidental shootings by the volunteers.

A Nez Perce messenger rode east to Steptoe, who sent a relief detachment and ordered the governor's imperiled

party to rejoin his troops. The wagons proceeded back to the Army's camp as night approached, under intermittent gunfire that mostly missed the harried targets in the blackness. The soldiers' mountain howitzers eventually dispersed the Indians. Stevens was unharmed, but four of Shaw's volunteers were shot, and about as many Indians were killed in the fracas. Lokout sustained two bullet wounds in the fight and a fleeing volunteer also smashed a gunstock into the warrior's forehead. He incredibly survived, but the blow left a substantial depression in his head for the rest of his long life.

The following afternoon, the Stevens party hastened to resume its way toward Ft. Dalles under a strong Army escort led by Steptoe himself. Meanwhile, Kamiakin returned to the Palouse country.[31]

War Parties and Peace Missions

The fiasco left Stevens embittered over the failure of what he considered a reasonable gesture of goodwill. But he had offered no compromises regarding the treaties, and demanded "unconditional submission to the justice and mercy of the government." News of this failed diplomacy was not altogether depressing for citizens on Puget Sound. Branding the previous months' "syrean song of peace" as an "utter illusion," a Wiley editorial opined, "the only method of opening up a way of settlement east of the Cascades, WILL BE BY CONQUEST."[32]

These events had again drawn into stark contrast the aggravating divisions between territorial officials and the Army. Steptoe, along with Wright, shortly returned to the Walla Walla Valley and pledged friendship with Indian leaders, who tarried while observing soldiers wielding axes and whipsaws in constructing a blockhouse for fledgling Ft. Walla Walla.

Steptoe told the Indians: "My mission is pacific. I have come not to fight you, but to live among you.... I trust we shall live together as friends." But a later message to Wright betrayed a resignation to events that Steptoe seemed powerless to change: "In general terms, I may say that in my judgment we are reduced to the necessity of waging a vigorous war, striking the Cayuses at the Grand Ronde, and Kam-i-ah-kin wherever he may be found."[33]

Prospects for a peaceful resolution also seemed remote to Indian leaders. Kamiakin felt rebuffed by the governor at their meeting on Mill Creek; Quiltenenock, wounded in the recent fighting, remained angry at the prospect of not having a reserve in his homeland; and Tilcoax, Piupiu Maksmaks the

Younger, Camaspelo of the Cayuse, and others still opposed even the peacekeeping presence of soldiers.

In October, Steptoe and Wright decided on a site for the fort that afforded good pasturage, near the present-day downtown section of Walla Walla. A final location eventually was selected on a higher terrace to the west in May 1857, seemingly a better defensive position. The Stars and Stripes soon appeared atop an immense flagpole, standing adjacent to two rows of log barracks flanking a broad parade ground, where soldiers regularly drilled within distant sight of passing bands of wary Indians.[34]

In spite of recurrent expressions of hostility from citizens and volunteers, Kamiakin personally took no action against Whites in the Colville mining district or at the Army posts under construction in the Walla Walla and Simcoe valleys. The intrepid trader, Victor Trevit, journeyed through the Palouse during these volatile months, demonstrating that a peaceful traveler need not necessarily fear the legendary chief. In the summer of 1856, 30-year-old Trevit proceeded north to provide provisions to Colville miners.

In September, when returning to The Dalles, Trevit "struck the camp of Kamiakin," and "had a talk." Kamiakin informed the trader that he and other Whites had "permission to pass through his country on peaceable missions—only war parties need fear anything from him or his people."[35] Trevit's encounter, obscure though remarkable, reveals Kamiakin's tolerance for law-abiding Americans east of the Columbia in the tense months of 1856 and 1857.

Others on both sides, however, were less inclined to peacefully resolve differences. Governor Stevens still sought the active intervention of the Army to forcibly move the tribes within the boundaries of his yet unratified treaties, and young firebrands among Kamiakin's Palouse hosts threatened to kill any White trespassers regardless of their intentions. In December 1856, Quiltenenock and a band of marauding Cayuses visited Kamiakin's camp, bringing news of their capture of cattle from the soldiers and their Nez Perce allies.[36] Reflecting on Pandosy and McDonald's words before the fighting began in 1855, Kamiakin surely knew that the consequences of this action could be grave.

Earlier, Indians also had threatened a few Whites, who had ventured to settle in the Touchet or Walla Walla valleys. For example, legendary mountain man turned rancher, Louis Maranguoin (Marengo), fled from his cabin to Henry Chase's claim at present-day Dayton, where the men barricaded the place and cut portholes for rifles. They dug a trench to the

river for water, and endured ten tense days before fleeing to Lapwai. Indians then set fire to the premises.[37]

Stevens returned to Olympia on October 15, only to hear about General Wool's recent order for the Army to seal off the interior from White settlers, with the exception of HBC personnel, people holding "ceded rights" from Indians, and Colville miners. Wool warned: "These will be notified…that if they interfere with the Indians, they will be punished and sent out of the country." If word of this reached Kamiakin, he may have felt that the many challenges he had endured— from both Whites and Indians—in his struggle for tribal sovereignty might yet prove worthwhile.

During the late summer and fall of 1856, Kamiakin likely ranged widely among the Plateau bands, and probably dispatched emissaries to tribes as distant as the Flatheads.[38] He had relatives and friends among the Spokanes, Nez Perces, and Walla Wallas, who bordered his Palouse hosts' extensive homeland. With the withdrawal of the volunteers, along with the Army's new presence at Walla Walla and Simcoe, White depredations had ended. But Kamiakin may have felt this was probably but a respite.

By early winter, the periodic Indian raids on the Army's livestock herds would be blamed on Kamiakin. The soldiers, however, could only offer second-hand evidence of his involvement. During the fragile peace, the Yakama-Palouse chief visited camps at the confluence of Crab and Wilson creeks and other customary gathering places to parley with chiefs, while their families fished and gathered wild foods.[39]

Olympia's *Pioneer and Democrat* reported in August that Kamiakin's warriors, believed to be in the Grande Ronde region with Upper Nez Perces and Cayuses, recently had been joined by Spokanes and other Indians.[40] The Nez Perces' affiliation with Kamiakin raised new fears among many White officials. Since the coming of Lewis and Clark, the Nez Perce had been stalwarts of accommodation. Highly regarded chiefs such as Red Wolf, Lawyer, and Tuekekas (Old Joseph) had defended the Whitmans and Spaldings at risk to their own reputations, and even the wary Looking Glass had sought amiable relations with White traders and officials.

Given their reputation, coupled with a geographical advantage of possessing an ancestral domain more remote from White incursions, the Nez Perces had successfully negotiated for a vast reserve in 1855, extending from well below the Clearwater-Snake confluence up to the crest of the Bitterroots, and from the Salmon, Imnaha, and Wallowa valleys to the Palouse Hills. Stevens allowed these generous borders, partly so that the Nez Perces might influence other Plateau tribes to accept treaty proposals. For these reasons, a number of Nez Perce leaders did not feel inclined to support Kamiakin and neighboring tribes in opposing the Whites. In fact, Nez Perces had disapproved of, or even thwarted, some warring Indian parties from crossing their lands.

But alarm over recent events caused many Nez Perces to reassess their views regarding Stevens' policies toward other Plateau tribes. In 1856, Agent William Craig estimated that two-thirds of the tribe now favored the hostiles, though this fell short of the number actually joining to take up arms. In Stevens' view, Looking Glass only was waiting for "a favorable moment to join bands with Kama-i-akun in a war against the Whites." Indeed, Agent A.H. Robie at The Dalles reported that Kamiakin had sought out Looking Glass and Three Feathers on a visit to Lapwai in February 1857.[41]

Camp at the Crossing

Steadfast peace advocates among the Spokane tribe, such as Stevens' old friend Spokan Garry, may have felt uneasy over Kamiakin's close proximity to their lands. However, a key historian, W.C. Brown, later claimed that Kamiakin's decision to reside on the Palouse River was "on account of fear that his return and affiliation amongst" other bands "might further increase their difficulties with the whites."[42]

That Kamiakin chose to establish his camp adjacent to the point where cession boundaries met should not be discounted as mere coincidence. Few others among the region's tribal leaders might have comprehended more clearly Stevens' complicated delineations of ceded lands in the 1855 treaties. The Walla Walla-Cayuse and especially the Yakima and Nez Perce land cessions trisected the southern Palouse, but lands at Kamiak's Crossing, just to the north, could have been interpreted by Kamiakin as entirely free of American claim. The camp was strategically located where a principal branch of the north-south Spokane Trail struck the river, while another ancient route crossing at this point led north from Penawawa on the Snake to Rock Lake and T'siyiyak's Place east of Sprague Lake.

Kamiakin's personal responsibilities also were increasing, since his immediate family had grown to the size of a small band by 1857. Kamiakin's wives now had four children to care for, including We-yet-que-wit and Yumasepah (these youngsters by Kem-ee-yowah were adolescents). The mothers and their older offspring helped tend the needs of the younger children and elders, who joined Kamiakin after fleeing from the Yakima Valley. Kamiakin's brothers,

Skloom and Showaway, are also believed to have been with him at this time.

Decades later, a friend of the Kamiakin family, W.C. Brown, was informed about the location of this camp site on the northernmost section of the Palouse River, near present-day Matlock Bridge north of Endicott. The place was an ancestral habitation site, shown to Kamiakin by his father, T'siyiyak, and close to rich camas and berry grounds, but normally not used in winter.

In 1856–57, however, Kamiakin and his family and immediate followers wintered here, spending time "cutting fence rails and poles and getting out building materials for fence and cabins." A small outcropping of green and yellow common opal in a bluff above the camp would have provided raw material for the boys to try their hand at fashioning projectile points and tools. Kamiakin, meanwhile, had more strategic measures in mind.[43]

In case soldiers threatened, Kamiakin needed an ample supply of ammunition. He sent envoys to his old friend, Angus McDonald, at Ft. Colvile with an offer of 100 horses for 70 pounds of powder. The Hudson's Bay trader, knowing the high stakes involved in such an exchange, "declined acquiring wealth in that way."

Kamiakin's peregrinations among the northern tribes were necessary in part because of difficulties in procuring sufficient weaponry for a sustained war. Coastal newspapers, of course, charged Kamiakin with the most malevolent endeavors in these travels, recruiting Indians to his "murderous cause" from eastern Oregon to Montana. Because of years of trading with the Hudson's Bay Company, the Spokanes, Kalispels, and Coeur d'Alenes possessed a large number of trade guns and other supplies and equipment.[44]

Kamiakin knew that a disparity in firepower could be significant, since even improved muskets with an effective range of up to 200 yards were no match against new percussion cap rifles that accurately fired Minié balls over twice that distance. Kamiakin also was acquainted with the Army's new Sharps rifle, a single-shot breechloader introduced in the early 1850s. The weapon lacked the range of rifled muskets, but cavalrymen prized its ease of loading and getting off a shot in seconds, whereas recharging a muzzleloader could take half a minute or more. Lt. Saxton of the Stevens survey had demonstrated the Sharps to a group of Indians gathered at the mouth of the Palouse River in 1853, but few had fallen into Indian hands. Many of Kamiakin's Palouse, Yakama, and Walla Walla warriors still used bows and arrows.

Kamiakin and Tilcoax's unsettling near-proximity to the Coeur d'Alenes and Kalispels was noted by the Jesuits Ravalli and Congiato in the summer of 1856. During this period, the missionaries worked tirelessly to keep the northern tribes on peaceful terms with the Whites. Joset confessed, however, that Kamiakin "had won over the richest of the Coeur d'Alenes."[45]

Angus McDonald found his loyalties divided. In spite of his refusal to provide ammunition for warfare, he remained a trusted friend of tribal leaders. He likewise communicated with government officials, such as Isaac Stevens, about the northern bands' interactions with the Yakama-Palouse chief, but he also upbraided the governor for Piupiu Maksmaks' barbaric murder. Such frankness was rather risky for a British citizen residing in American territory and surrounded by restive Indians.[46]

During this time, Kamiakin likely visited the Penawawa Creek village, located in the deep Snake River canyon west of present-day Pullman. This was another of T'siyiyak's favorite camps, where the Kamiakin family had Palouse relatives and the winters were much milder than up on the hills. During this time, Kamiakin likely avoided the main village of *Palus*, located on the main trail between Walla Walla and Colville. This location saw more travel by miners, blackrobes, traders, and soldiers than any other village in the locality. Moreover, the headman at *Palus*, Slowiarchy, seemed ambivalent about the White presence.

On the other hand, the Upper Palouses at *Pinawáwih*, *Alamótín*, and *Wawáwih* were more resolute in their opposition to the Americans. The Washani leader Húsis Kute, and Chief Hahtalekin and his brother Húsis Paween, favored Kamiakin's plan to close ranks in a united front against miners and settlers. Kamiakin was aware of similar divided opinions among the Spokanes and Nez Perces, where prominent leaders differed on whether to join in opposing the Americans. Kamiakin's presence anywhere could become a flashpoint. Camping deep in the labyrinth of Palouse Hills seemed an appropriate neutral location, but also a well situated place for quick communication in all directions.

Chapter 6
Lake of Fire

Salmon Man stepped into the canoe.
He was carrying a bundle
of the Wolf Sister's belongings.
He felt a sharp sting,
the pain of Rattlesnake's bite.
Salmon Man turned around;
he fell onto a flat rock.

A Wolf Brothers drew his bow.
He shot Salmon Man in the head.
The others fell upon him,
cutting with flint knives,
and threw the pieces onto the sand.
That is how a tiny piece
fell in the water, and floated away.

From the start of 1857, a nearly eighteen-month inter-regnum of relative calm prevailed in the Inland Pacific Northwest. Trader John Owen ventured west from his Bitterroot Valley sanctuary in early spring to gather supplies and news on the Columbia. He found reason to hope for peace. In late March, Owen encountered a party of Spokanes in the mountains who reported that the fighting was over. He noted in his journal: "Kamiacin the Yacima chief & head warrior of the Consolidated tribes" had reached an understanding with military leaders.[1]

Indeed, General John Wool's actions had helped forced the dissolution of the territorial militias, and the Army maintained the *status quo* from forts at The Dalles, Simcoe, and Walla Walla. "Special Order No. 87" issued on June 29, 1857, would further formalize the Army's earlier prohibition on settlement east of the Cascades and called for the withdrawal of all Whites from the Columbia Plateau except Hudson's Bay employees and miners in the Ft. Colvile vicinity, and the few possessors of donation land claims, mainly

some retired HBC personnel, largely clustered in the Walla Walla Valley.

Area Indians remained tolerant of the British traders, but recent events had cast a pallor on their presence as well. Company herdsman John Campbell encountered a "pretty hostile camp of Palouses" at Red Wolf's Crossing on the Snake River during an 1857 trek to Colville. Only when his mixed companions attested to Campbell's HBC credentials did he consider himself "safe once more."[2]

In spite of regional tensions and the Army's intervention, Stevens remained resolute in his intention "to get my [rail] line to the Sound." The frustrated but resourceful politician shifted tactics from the territorial to the federal realm in his struggles. At his instigation, the Washington Territorial Legislature incorporated the Northern Pacific Railroad in January 1857. Also that same year, Stevens left the governorship when elected territorial delegate to Congress. After arriving in Washington, D.C., late in 1857, and now among influential friends, the new delegate lobbied for his policies. But congressional consideration of an Indian appropriations bill soon led to spirited criticisms of Stevens' actions.

When New York Representative Whitney informed House members about the Nisqually prisoner Quiemuth's recent murder in Stevens' very own office in Olympia and implied the former governor's complicity with the perpetrators of this notorious tragedy, the new delegate from Washington Territory could hold his peace no longer. Stevens rose to defend his record with impassioned rhetoric, and then set to work assembling a cadre of sympathetic colleagues in political and military circles to discredit opponents.

Earlier, in a January 5, 1857, letter to the *New York Tribune*, Stevens had defended himself from "notoriously false" accusations, and ventured to blame Wool for the circumstances that led to The Cascades massacre. The governor claimed that the presence of territorial volunteers during the previous year in the Walla Walla Valley, now withdrawn by Wool, had protected settlers and friendly Indians alike, and "kept Kamiakin and the other hostile leaders with their followers north of the Snake." Without that deterrent, Stevens reasoned, Kamiakin and others had attacked "substantial and quiet citizens" traveling beyond the Columbia as well as civilians at The Cascades.

Stevens' persistent efforts to discredit General Wool had ultimately prevailed. In March 1857, following excoriating resolutions to the Secretary of War from the territorial legislatures, Wool had been replaced by General Newman S. Clarke. However, the new commander initially sought to continue his predecessor's unpopular "exclusion policy," and directed Colonel Wright to protect Indians and maintain peace with the 1,500 troops garrisoned in the Columbia District.[3]

Saintly Interference

In part, Clarke was reacting to the alarming prospect of clandestine support to the Indian cause from a remote source. Rumors of Mormon influence among the Plateau tribes had circulated since Brigham Young directed followers to establish a northernmost mission in the Salmon River country in the spring of 1855. About the same time that Stevens was negotiating with Kamiakin and other Indian leaders at the first Walla Walla Council, some two dozen Mormon missionaries traveled northward from Salt Lake City to establish Ft. Limhi (Lemhi) near present-day Tendoy, Idaho—a "Mission to the Remnant of the House of Jacob."

Soon after the Walla Walla Council, Eagle of the Light and other Nez Perces visited the colony. Word about Mormon

efforts to convert Indians soon reached the Jesuit missions as well as John Owen in the Bitterroot Valley. Whites in the Northwest had long been suspicious of Mormon intentions, and read far more intrigue into their actions than merely religious interest.

Since the late 1840s, in fact, Oregon residents blamed Mormons for inciting Indians to raid wagon trains and frontier settlements. This rancor contributed to President Buchanan's decision in 1857 to launch a clumsy campaign to wrest control of Utah from Brigham Young by appointing new civil officials. Some 2,500 newly marshaled troops had moved westward to occupy Salt Lake City. Unfounded rumors spread in all directions that Young's disaffected followers intended to enlist Indians in a general war of resistance.

The "Mormon Rebellion" stirred passions throughout the Northwest, with the implications east of the Cascades being especially acute. George Gibbs recorded peculiar news in November 1857 when Klickitat Indians claimed "Choosuklee (Jesus Christ) had recently appeared on the other side of the country," as a precursor of "the whites being sent out of the country." Government officials associated this report with Mormon influence among the Nez Perces and Flatheads.

Writing from Ft. Walla Walla in December 1857, Captain Ralph Kirkham informed an increasingly restive General Clarke: "The Snakes tell our Indians that they are well supplied with ammunition, and that they can get from the Mormons any quantity that they wish." Kamiakin's brother, Skloom, informed Major Robert Garnett at Ft. Simcoe in January that two delegations of Mormons had visited interior tribes with pledges of military support. Although no firm evidence emerged in regard to these allegations, prospects of such involvement contributed to Steptoe's anxieties at Ft. Walla Walla about finding ways to lessen regional tensions.[4]

In addition to raising the alarm about the Mormons in 1857, the territorial press celebrated General Wool's dismissal. The *Pioneer and Democrat*'s Wiley expressed hope in March that his successor might finally use decisive force to secure the region east of the Cascades for settlers. That vast area's only real civilian outpost consisted of a dozen business establishments adjacent to Ft. Dalles, including dry goods and grocery stores, saloons, and livery stables. The steamers *Wasco* and *Mary* had resumed alternate daily runs from Cascade City, although that isolated hamlet had yet to fully recover from the previous year's Indian attack.

This pair of frontier communities hosted an often rough clientele, who could challenge the rules of civility and conduct with one another as well as the Indians. The same issue

"The Battle of Tohotonimme (Pine Creek)," May 17, 1858.
Nona Hengen

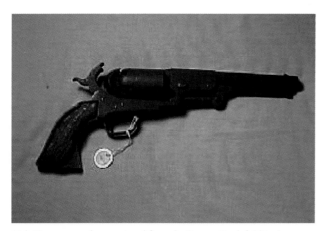

Colt Dragoon revolver, retrieved from the Steptoe Battlefield in the 1890s.
Museum of Arts & Culture, Spokane

Steptoe Battlefield Memorial.
John Clement

"Military Post & City of Walla-Walla, W.T. in 1862…Drawn by G. Sohon."
Mullan Report, 1863

Ft. Walla Walla cemetery.
John Clement

"Colonel Wright's Snake River Crossing."
Nona Hengen

Incident during the 1858 Wright campaign.
Nona Hengen

Springtime, lower Palouse River canyon.
John Clement

Colors of decorated arrows used by Palouse warrior Pahka Pahtahank, son of
Chief Hahtalekin, both killed at the Battle of the Big Hole, August 9, 1877.

Palouse River near Kamiak's Crossing, in autumn colors.
John Clement

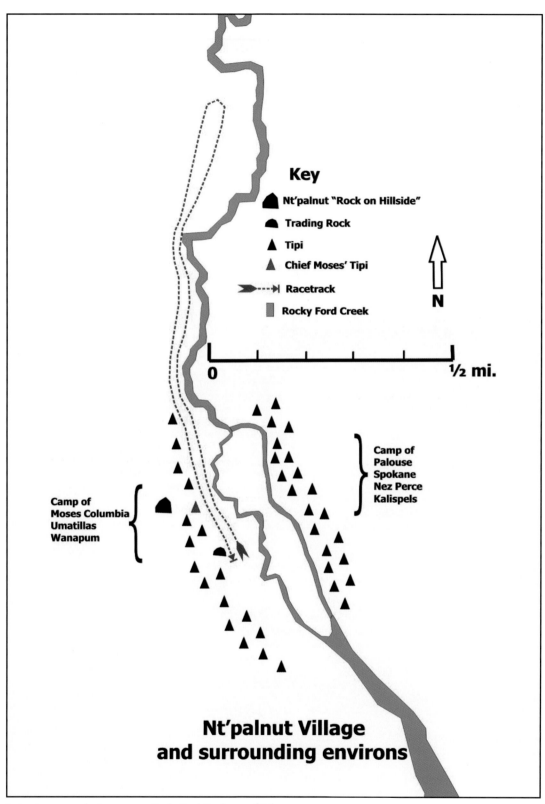

Key

▲ Nt'palnut "Rock on Hillside"

◗ Trading Rock

▲ Tipi

▲ Chief Moses' Tipi

⇢⊩ Racetrack

▌ Rocky Ford Creek

N

0   ½ mi.

Camp of
Palouse
Spokane
Nez Perce
Kalispels

Camp of
Moses Columbia
Umatillas
Wanapum

Nt'palnut Village
and surrounding environs

Springtime root gathering camp on Rocky Ford Creek, east of Ephrata.

Rock Lake.
John Clement

Rock Lake.
Richard D. Scheuerman

Horses in sunset.
John Clement

of Wiley's newspaper reported the arrest at The Dalles of a "notorious outlaw," Jack Hurley, wanted on a California murder charge, and the shooting of a horse-stealing gang leader that moved stock from The Dalles to California.[5] Local residents at The Dalles, therefore, may not have seen anything unusual in the arrival of a haggard traveler in early March, except for the direction of his approach.

Unlikely Emissaries

Frederick White rode toward the settlement from the contested lands to the east, an unlikely emissary from Chief Kamiakin. In late December 1856, the native of Germany had been herding Army cattle and mules on Toppenish Creek below Ft. Simcoe, when he was captured by Skloom's warriors and subsequently spent some weeks in captivity. The hapless immigrant was taken to White Bluffs, and then east of the Columbia to Kamiakin "on Camas Prairie near the Palouse River," where he estimated the chief was camped with "some 500 warriors."

White's account is entirely plausible. A substantial Wanapum village stood on the right bank of the Columbia at a strategic crossing long used by Plateau peoples. In historic times, a White Bluffs Road continued northeast to Ft. Colvile, while other trails fanned out eastward to the Palouse Country through Lind Coulee and over other well-worn routes. In an episode reminiscent of Vic Trevit's earlier encounter with Kamiakin, White was later released unharmed, to carry a message of reconciliation to government officials.

He reported being "treated well," and that Kamiakin "professes friendship and pledged to return cattle, horses, and mules stolen…in Ft. Simcoe Valley belonging to Capt. [Dickinson] Woodruff."

About this time, Army officers ascertained that Kamiakin seemed to be presenting "offers of surrender." Although the chief's renewed overtures for peace were viewed with "great suspicion by the people" on "the Columbia river," even skeptical J.W. Wiley confessed in his newspaper that "further acts of hostility and robbery" had not occurred.[6]

True to their word, Kamiakin and Skloom arranged to have the retrieved animals returned to the fort by Skloom soon after setting young Frederick White free. Captain Woodruff thanked the Yakama leader for White's release and for returning livestock. The Army also was provided with additional details about Agent Bolon's murder. This intelligence, implicating Showaway's son, Mushíil, and several others, was communicated by Major Garnett when at Ft. Dalles in May. It exonerated Kamiakin and Skloom, who had been "very angry" over the news of Bolon's death. At The Dalles, Garnett provided Wright with specific reports about Mushíil, Qualchan, and others killing Whites, but the Army wished to preserve the region's fragile peace and thus took no action.

Members of the territorial legislature, however, pressed for the arrest of the Yakamas complicit in the killings, and many still blamed Kamiakin. Moreover, reports about favorable mining prospects near Ft. Colvile and in Canada regularly appeared in newspapers. From The Dalles, parties of roaming White miners from west of the Cascades and California began venturing northward almost weekly beginning in March. Many camped among the oak copses surrounding Ft. Simcoe, where several officers' wives, including Major Garnett's recent bride, Marianna, were planting flower gardens, arranging a post library of 150 volumes, and conducting evening dinner parties.

Kamiakin likely believed his peace overtures had been rebuffed, and that American officials felt no inclination to negotiate for Indian lands north of the Walla Walla treaty cessions. Whites again were on the move across the interior. Spring issues of the *Pioneer and Democrat* regularly featured stories about recommended routes to the Walla Walla Valley and the Ft. Boise country, and about the progress of a new Naches Road across the Cascades into the Yakima Valley.

In August 1857, the newspaper reprinted an April 17 letter from a Colville miner, who reported "no trouble in passing through the hostile country," but cautioned that the Spokanes and Pend O'reilles could rise up, "if Kamiakin does not make a treaty of peace with the proper government authorities this summer or fall."

Nervous Americans in the Colville Valley laid aside any differences with their British neighbors and set about building defenses around the Hudson's Bay post. However, these concerns did not allay the miner's enthusiasm for the results of their grubstakes. Letters from them in the coastal press elicited further excitement. The placers, usually worked along streams from late July to October when water ran lowest, were heralded as "equal to those of the 'Golden State.'" Enterprising merchants also were tempted to risk heading east with sugar, coffee, salt, and other supplies that sold at luxury item prices.[7]

Two weeks after the delivery of Frederick White's message from Kamiakin, the *Pioneer and Democrat* nevertheless claimed that the Indians "were determined to renew hostilities…on a grander scale," and that "a general outbreak… appears to be inevitable."

A June 1857 *Oregonian* article from the *Tilacum Cumtuxer*, reprinted in Wiley's paper, lampooned Indian leaders under the headline "President Kamiakin's Inauguration," and listed the members of Kamiakin's "cabinet." These included "Looking Glass, Secretary of War," "Chief Justice, Lawyer," "Skloom, Commander in Chief," and also Owhi and Teias. Whites believed to be sympathetic to the Indian cause also were publicly ridiculed, including Victor Trevit, Kamiakin's "Secretary of Foreign Affairs," and "Senate Chaplain—Rev. Mr. Pandozy."

The French and Italian missionaries and British HBC personnel were frequent targets of the territorial press and public perceptions were significantly shaped by such rhetoric. This factor coupled with further misunderstandings on both sides would soon lead Clarke to take action against the tribes.[8]

In May 1857, to better ascertain conditions in the Columbia District given the varying views from officials in the War and Interior departments, Commissioner of Indian Affairs James Denver had authorized an independent assessment. He made arrangements for Special Agent J. Ross Browne of the Treasury Department to visit Oregon and Washington, and make extensive "inquiries respecting the condition of the Indian reservations and to investigate the causes of the Indian war." Browne's subsequent report offered an extensive chronology of American and British settlement, as well as an assessment of congressional action in the Donation and Pre-emption acts and other legislation that encouraged regional development.

Browne provided a candid assessment of American Indian policy, characterizing the entire history of treaty negotiations as one in which "the terms were always dictated and enforced on the one side, whether the other party was satisfied or not," and that "this compulsory process cannot properly be dignified by the title of treaty." Like previous arrangements between the government and tribes, treaties in the Northwest were "forced agreements which the stronger power can violate or reject at pleasure." But Browne really did not quarrel with the federal government's utilitarian approach in making "such regulations respecting the Indians…as it may deem expedient."[9]

He argued with Machiavellian logic: "The question is simply one of public policy. When it becomes necessary to remove the aboriginal races to some more convenient location, they must be removed." Browne criticized the military for not heeding intelligence received as early as April 1853 that Yakamas, Cayuses, and Nez Perces had determined to make war on the Americans, since their leaders had concluded that

their dispossession otherwise was inevitable. Browne identified Kamiakin as the principal leader, "bitter in his animosity," and who "spared no inducements to effect a coalition" among the tribes against "the whole race of Americans within the country."

Browne continued: Since the Army as early as 1853 branded such reports as "alarmist" and refused to suppress recurrent Indian insurrections, the military had failed to provide adequate support to the territorial governors in their endeavors to implement national policy. Therefore, "the treaties were not the cause of the war," nor were the interferences of Hudson's Bay officials, Mormon agitators, or Catholic missionaries.[10]

In Browne's view, the differences between the cultures rendered conflict inevitable. He confessed that his opinions were based on conversations with the region's federal officials and "leading citizens." He made no attempt to speak directly to tribal leaders, or with men such as Frederick White, who had most recently been among the Indians. In Browne's mind, Indian viewpoints, however valorous, were irrelevant to the preeminent interests of frontier America.

Browne enclosed a copy of Father Pandosy's 1853 letter to Mesplié pointing out the likelihood that war was imminent. The blackrobe's letter had opened by invoking Cicero's words in the face of Cataline's conspiracy: "The Senate sees these things and remains immoveable spectators." Browne might have sought to better understand the Indian side if he had considered Manlius's message to the Roman army dispatched against Cataline: "But at power or wealth, for the sake of which wars,…we do not aim; we desire only our liberty, which no honorable man relinquishes but with life."

Mullan's Road and Walla Walla Valley Settlement

During this period, Delegate Stevens addressed Congress on occasion, further vindicating his policies and castigating the Army for not insisting upon the "absolute and unconditional submission" of the Indians. Regarding Wool's "edicts" preventing White settlement east of the Cascades, Stevens branded the general a "dictator of the country." Wright's 1856 foray into Yakama country and maladroit offering of gifts also was "greatly to be deplored." The "long delays," "talking and not fighting," gave "safe conduct to the murderers." Even worse in Stevens' view, Wright's failure to apprehend Kamiakin gave him "the whole field of the interior," which the chief secured "by threats, lies, and promises" to area tribes.

Stevens continued his railing against Kamiakin. At the first Walla Walla Treaty Council, "Kam-i-a-y-kan was the last man I saw; and that chief parted from me in the most cordial manner, expressing the utmost satisfaction at the results of the treaty." In the same speech, Stevens reported that A.J. Bolon's killing was "by order of Kamiyakan." This charge was never espoused by Indians or Army officials, of course, who were familiar with the circumstances of the agent's death. Stevens' rhetoric characterizing Bolon as "much beloved by the Indians" strained credulity, as did his description of trespassing miners all being "men of sobriety, men of character."[11]

Stevens was responding in part to his frustration over congressional rejection of his proposed northern transcontinental railroad in favor of a more central route. But the irrepressible promoter then lobbied strongly for constructing a military road from Ft. Walla Walla to Ft. Benton on the Missouri River. An appropriation for the "Northern Overland Road" was quickly forthcoming. Lt. John Mullan (1830–1909), who had served as one of Stevens' most capable topographers during the railroad surveys and who now was in Washington, D.C., was named chief engineer for the work in late 1857. Mullan soon returned to the Pacific Northwest.

In spite of effusive newspaper accounts celebrating the anticipated "large population…soon to be attracted to" the Columbia Plateau, the uncertain tribal situation in the interior stalled the road work. Mullan waited impatiently for things to change. Coastal residents, aware of ranching and farming possibilities east of the Cascades, warmed to the prospect of settling on broad swaths of productive land along Mullan's intended route. Press accounts described the Bitterroot Valley as a place "capable of grazing immense bands of stock of all kinds," while the Palouse was "a rich, fertile, and productive area that needs but the proper means and measures…to be turned into public and private benefit."

Writing from the Colville locality in November 1857, Indian Agent B.F. Yantis added to a chorus of assurances that travel to the gold fields now was "perfectly safe for Americans in any number," and that "with the exception of Kamiakin, all the principal chiefs" of the Spokane, Colville, Yakama, Palouse, and other tribes expressed "in strongest terms their friendship." But the Indians' abiding desire for peace was not necessarily synonymous with accepting an unrestrained surge of additional Whites crossing their lands north of the Snake River. Knowledgeable White officials, too, did not share Yantis's cheery sentiments.[12]

Stevens' insistence that road building should commence as soon as possible in 1858 aroused the ire of both military officials and Indian leaders. In making preparations, Mullan was dispatched to Ft. Dalles, where on May 15, 1858, Colonel Wright flatly informed him that "no probability" existed for work on the route that year. The ambitious road builder was ordered to remain at the fort, and later would be attached to campaigning troops. Wright condemned the effort as a dangerous provocation. "In fact," he stated, "the proposed opening of the road through the Indian country was a primary cause" of renewed tensions in the spring of 1858.

Stevens continued his facile maneuverings in Congress, publishing circulars widely distributed in the East that informed prospective immigrants about opportunities in Washington Territory. In the Northwest, public attention also increasingly focused on the advantages of the fertile Walla Walla Valley, which was situated outside of any reservation boundaries and already had attracted a small enclave of French Canadian and American ranchers by the mid 1850s.

In March 1853, for example, John Noble and Lloyd Brooke, civilian quartermaster clerks at Ft. Vancouver, had joined New York native George Bumford in a substantial cattle ranching partnership near the old Whitman Mission. The men also filed half-section donation land claims on the Touchet River, but were forced out after hostilities commenced. Noble later noted in disgust that the volunteers vandalized their property.[13]

In early 1858, new mineral strikes on Canada's Fraser River and in the Colville Valley inflamed the Plateau's tenuous situation anew. Increased streams of miners again ventured across the Cascades passes or more frequently came up the Columbia to The Dalles, and then formed into sizeable brigades for protection before proceeding north across contested lands to the gold fields. Relations between Indians and Americans at the scattered gold camps remained tense.

In that troubled spring, tough-minded George Blenkinsop came to assist veteran trader Angus McDonald at Ft. Colvile. Hudson's Bay personnel and Jesuit missionaries continued to tread in relative safety between both worlds, but occasional American officials in the region, such as John Owen, were wary of Indian intentions. Isolated provocations finally occurred. Two French Canadians headed to the strikes were killed in the Palouse country in the spring, and on the night of April 12, 1858, Palouse Indians raided livestock near Ft. Walla Walla.

Chief Tilcoax, whose legendary horse herds had ranged across hundreds of square miles from the Walla Walla Valley to north of the Snake River, harbored ill-will against the Whites ever since the days of the Cayuse War. He now was being blamed for the recent trouble. His influence among the disaffected Snake River bands "rivaled that of the great Kamiakin." The Palouse chief had been advocating war for months, as he watched Steptoe's garrison at Ft. Walla Walla grow in strength.[14] Tilcoax felt that Americans were responsible for epidemics that had stricken his people, and the only way to prevent it was to drive Whites from the region. Father Joseph Joset, the Swiss-born Jesuit among the Coeur d'Alenes, believed that Tilcoax, not Kamiakin, now was most active in fomenting armed resistance among the region's Indians, and that he "had bribed the Spokanes, and some Kalispels to continue hostilities."[15]

Kamiakin passed warning to the northern tribes that troops might soon move in their direction and threaten the uneasy peace. But the chief also felt that retaining the stalemate must be reluctantly chosen over direct provocations, in order to prevent the Americans from taking over the north. A Coeur d'Alene Indian related Kamiakin's views to a government courier, probably expressman W.H. Pearson, who credited Father Joset and the Jesuits for preventing more "hostile feeling towards *los Americanos*."[16] In early May, as the Chinook Wind Brothers came again out of the southwest to chase leaden clouds, headmen like Kamiakin surely hoped that the months of reprieve were not just a lull before a storm.

The Steptoe Disaster

In an effort "to stop this thieving" of Army livestock by demonstrating a show of strength, particularly among the Palouses, and to respond to miners' petitioning for troops at Colville, Lt. Col. Edward Steptoe departed Ft. Walla Walla on May 6 with five companies of 152 enlisted men, five officers, two howitzers, several dozen packers, and a contingent of Nez Perce scouts. The fort was left in charge of Major William Grier, who donned civilian clothes, suggesting a leisurely pace and little prospect of trouble.

On approaching Red Wolf's Crossing on the Snake River, the column of mounted soldiers scattered a small band of Palouses. Some may have fled northward with the disturbing news about the Army's unexpected advance. Here at Alpowa Creek, Steptoe procured the services of Nez Perce scouts from Timothy's band, since a mixed-blood guide procured at Ft. Walla Walla had lost his nerve and refused to continue. This substitution was ill-boding as it presented an opportunity for the Nez Perces to make trouble for their Indian rivals to the north.

Most of Steptoe's soldiers were insufficiently armed and ammunition was limited. The dragoons, especially, had left behind their sabers and carried only pistols and short-range musketoons. The actions of Steptoe's ally, Chief Timothy of the Nez Perces, helped inflame tribes to the north. He sent envoys to tell opposing bands to fear for their horses and lives. Timothy had feuded with Tilcoax and spoiled for a fight with the abrasive Palouse leader. But Timothy most likely also directed the Nez Perce guides to remain silent about this dispute when around soldiers. Timothy may have known that Tilcoax was among the bands camping along the *Smakodl* (South Palouse Fork), where many gathered each spring to dig roots in Paradise Valley. Thus, instead of heading north along the Colville Trail through the central Palouse, Steptoe would be guided on a well-worn trail in the eastern Palouse to the *Smakodl* vicinity.

The locality essentially would be terra incognita to Steptoe and his men, who would have to rely on the Nez Perce guides for direction. Father Joset, who was trusted by leaders on both sides, later commented that the colonel's decision to confront Tilcoax "would explain the whole puzzle" of why the soldiers used a more eastern route, rather than taking the more direct Colville Trail from Ft. Walla Walla. The choice of this peculiar itinerary would prove fateful.[17]

The column proceeded toward the Snake-Clearwater junction and then turned north through the dips and swells of the eastern Palouse Hills, little known to Whites. Timothy rode ahead of the column with his scouts, and, as anticipated, came upon Tilcoax near present-day Moscow, possibly at the prominent campsite known as *Táthinma* (Fawn Place), where area tribes gathered in the spring to dig roots, socialize, and race horses. Here, the Nez Perce leader defiantly challenged the Palouse chief, saying, "Telxawey, very soon your wives, your horses, and your goods shall be ours." Or, according to Father DeSmet, "Telgawêê, soon we will go and divide your spoils."

With the soldiers approaching from a distance on the afternoon of May 8, the camp immediately scattered. Tilcoax moved north to inform other bands of the Army's march. However, when he finally encountered a group of skeptical Coeur d'Alenes, likely those with Vincent camped near modern-day Oakesdale, the canny Palouse translated Timothy's remarks in altered terms: "*Coeur d'Alenes*, soon we will go and divide your spoils." Vincent then rode further north to confer with Seltice, who was hosting an annual spring feast of camas, barbecued beef, and dried fruit at his camp in the Spokane Valley.

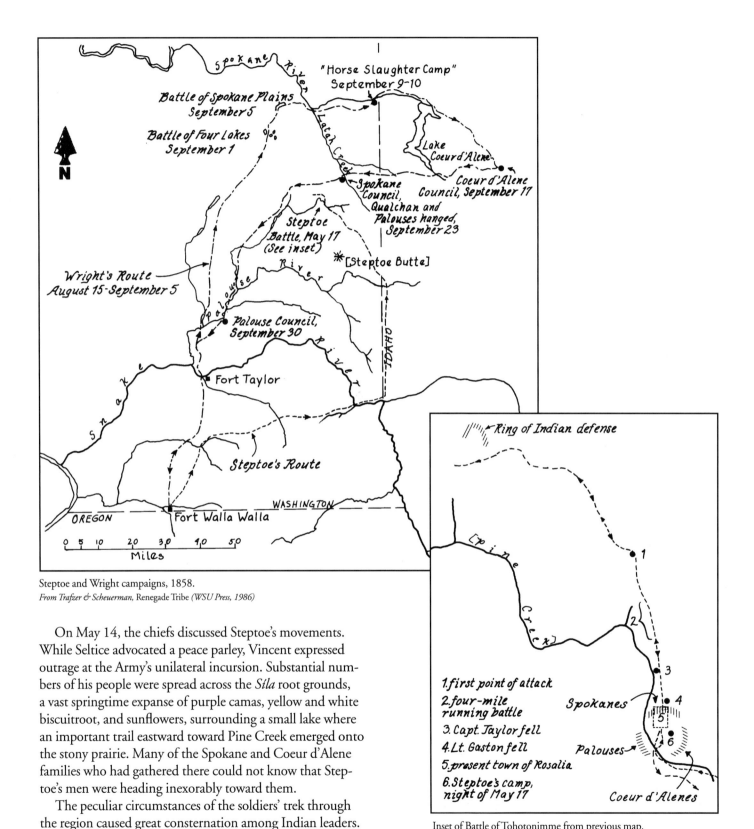

Steptoe and Wright campaigns, 1858.
From Trafzer & Scheuerman, Renegade Tribe *(WSU Press, 1986)*

Map labels (main map):

"Horse Slaughter Camp"
September 9-10

Spokane River

Battle of Spokane Plains
September 5

Battle of Four Lakes
September 1

Latah Creek

Lake Coeur d'Alene

Coeur d'Alene
Council, September 17

Spokane Council,
Qualchan and
Palouses hanged,
September 23

Steptoe Battle, May 17
(See inset)

✻ [Steptoe Butte]

Wright's Route
August 15-September 5

Palouse River

Palouse Council,
September 30

IDAHO

Fort Taylor

Snake River

Steptoe's Route

WASHINGTON

OREGON   Fort Walla Walla

0 5 10   20   30   40   50
Miles

Inset labels:

///// Ring of Indian defense

Pine Creek

1
2
3
4
5
6

1. first point of attack
2. four-mile running battle
3. Capt. Taylor fell
4. Lt. Gaston fell
5. present town of Rosalia
6. Steptoe's camp, night of May 17

Spokanes

Palouses

Coeur d'Alenes

Inset of Battle of Tohotonimme from previous map.
From Trafzer & Scheuerman, Renegade Tribe *(WSU Press, 1986)*

On May 14, the chiefs discussed Steptoe's movements. While Seltice advocated a peace parley, Vincent expressed outrage at the Army's unilateral incursion. Substantial numbers of his people were spread across the *Síla* root grounds, a vast springtime expanse of purple camas, yellow and white biscuitroot, and sunflowers, surrounding a small lake where an important trail eastward toward Pine Creek emerged onto the stony prairie. Many of the Spokane and Coeur d'Alene families who had gathered there could not know that Steptoe's men were heading inexorably toward them.

The peculiar circumstances of the soldiers' trek through the region caused great consternation among Indian leaders. Scouts exaggerated Steptoe's forces at "four hundred men,

Chief Timothy of the Nez Perces.
WSU Libraries

morning, he dispatched a Nez Perce messenger back to Ft. Walla Walla with news of factors influencing his mission. By now, he received intelligence about belligerent Palouses and Spokanes in the distance ahead, and wrote: "They say that they will fight; I daresay they will, but I hope we shall be able to give them a good drubbing," since peace could not be established in the region "until some of these people are overhauled."

The letter bore no real indication of alarm, though Grier at Ft. Walla Walla immediately forwarded it to department headquarters in San Francisco. About the same time, Coeur d'Alene couriers from Vincent raced north to find Father Joseph Joset on May 15 at the Sacred Heart Mission, bringing an urgent appeal for his immediate intervention on their behalf. The blackrobe mounted his horse and sped off "in an instant."[19]

Joset had long counseled the Coeur d'Alenes to avoid fighting the Whites. "I had always repeated to our Indians: 'Have no fear. If the troops cross the river, it can only be against the Palooses or the whisky sellers at Colville.'" But Tilcoax would respond by chiding other Indian leaders, saying they were "very brave in words," but acted "like cowards."

The blackrobes recorded further evidence of Timothy's subterfuge in these highly charged days as Steptoe's troops advanced toward upper Pine Creek on May 15. (Steptoe identified the stream as the "Ingossomen," likely from the Coeur d'Alene word *Hngwsumn*, or "Rope Making Place." The name probably derives from *gwes*, for Indian hemp fiber.[20]) Timothy apparently dispatched envoys in several directions to continue carrying intimidating messages. On May 16, Father Joset quickly headed toward the large Indian encampment of *Síla*, near Stubblefield Lake, in an urgent attempt to prevent confrontation or hostilities. He learned that one of Timothy's scouts also had reached Kamiakin's band, which apparently was in Coeur d'Alene country for spring root-digging. The messenger repeated the infuriating claim about taking Indians' wives and children, while adding that these words came from "the chief of the soldiers" himself.[21]

Kamiakin likely was stunned by the soldiers' approach, and, even if suspicious of the validity of Nez Perce words, their claims could not be ignored. By spring 1858, Kamiakin had reason to hope that a new era of peace had emerged. The boundaries of the ceded lands and reservations delineated in the 1855 Walla Walla Treaty Council lay substantially south of Kamiakin's principal Palouse River camp and the villages of his Coeur d'Alene and Spokane neighbors. Stevens could have his iron road, and General Clarke's troops at Ft. Walla

all carrying rifles, and…four large guns.…This is no sign of peace! Steptoe is coming for war!" But throughout the day, Steptoe continued northwesterly at a leisurely pace along the ancient thoroughfare, apparently unaware of Timothy's confrontation, Tilcoax's scheming, or Vincent's response.[18]

Steptoe camped on the evening of May 14 at a Palouse River ford, east of present-day Palouse. On the following

Walla and Ft. Simcoe could defend it and keep the peace in the ceded areas. Kamiakin personally had not participated in raids upon these soldiers or their livestock. To be sure, the recurrent appearance of miners crossing Indian lands north of the Snake was an annoyance and cause for vigilance. But Kamiakin had demonstrated tolerance in recent encounters with Whites, such as Trevit and others. Now, hearing alarms and threats, Kamiakin rode to investigate, likely armed with his buffalo country musket.

After spending the night of Saturday, May 15, along Pine Creek near modern-day Rosalia, the soldiers rose early to tend their horses and again formed a long column, which along with the two howitzers and pack train spread out for nearly a mile. Steptoe veered northwest from Pine Creek, to follow a prominent trail leading northwest through the bunchgrass hills along Sanders Creek and directly toward *Síla*. About 11 a.m., the soldiers reached a point within a mile of the vast inter-tribal "Kamas Prairie," where the village with numerous buffalo-hide tipis and horses was clustered near a fringe of trees.

The soldiers were dumbfounded by the sudden appearance of Indians, "armed, painted, and defiant," swarming on the hilltops before them. Steptoe likely had no idea he was almost upon the village spread out near the lakeshore. Charles Winder, an Infantry captain, raised his field glass, seeing some seventy warriors in the distance, but "in a few seconds as if by magic," their strength grew to "some 800, and in half an hour from 1,000 to 1,200," including Coeur d'Alenes, Spokanes, Palouses with Tilcoax, and some Kalispels and Kettles. A small band of Yakamas under Qualchan also likely was present—the prominent Spokane war chief, Polatkin, was Qualchan's father-in-law. Kamiakin and Spokane Garry probably had not yet arrived.

Both forces warily approached each other before Steptoe's column halted about 300 feet from the Indians' position. Seeking a peaceful resolution to the growing stand-off, Chief Vincent of the Coeur d'Alenes and Spokane Chief Sgalgalt warily rode out to meet Steptoe. A soldier later wrote that the large numbers of Indians "painted in the most fantastic and savage style" made for an "awesome sight." Many were decorated in brilliant colors, and they were armed with guns, lances, and bows and arrows. Some wore headdresses such as those of Plains tribes, while others donned headpieces of buffalo horns, eagle feathers, and the dried hides of animals and birds.[22]

Thus began the first of three remarkable "interviews" over the next eighteen hours between Indian leaders and Steptoe.

Vincent and Sgalgalt demanded an explanation for the soldier's trespass across their lands. They found the colonel's professed peaceful intentions at odds with his bringing so many armed men with howitzers and the threats communicated by the Nez Perces. The colonel's brash request for Indian help to ford the Spokane River was flatly refused. He now was left with few alternatives in the face of Vincent's demand that the soldiers turn back. While the consultation continued, warriors and troopers exchanged taunts. One Indian rode close enough to Sgt. Michael Kenny, a devout Catholic, to notice the rosary he wore. The Indian shouted to the anxious sergeant that he would not need it much longer.

Soldiers viewing the armed array on the hilltops likely prayed or cursed, and readied their arms. Many of Steptoe's recruits were young, whose only military experience had been marching on parade grounds, shooting on firing ranges, and in peaceful field maneuvers. Few had seen real battle.

During the parley and for the rest of that tense afternoon, no shots were fired, since Steptoe agreed that circumstances justified "a retrograde movement" and because the Catholics among the Coeur d'Alenes opposed fighting on the Sabbath. Steptoe, however, rather than ordering an immediate return on the trail they had come by, which would have placated some of the chiefs, instead struck out southwest toward water, crossing several swales before establishing a redoubt about two miles away on a high rocky ledge overlooking Sanders Creek. The Indians, meanwhile, responded by harassing the command's right flank with yells and feigned charges. The soldiers remained mounted until nightfall, listening to unsettling war songs and harangues coming from the nearby hills.

Tribal leaders were angered that Steptoe's response was not compliant enough. Kamiakin eventually arrived to participate in a dramatic council of chiefs that Sunday. Like Vincent, he seems to have advised constraint. But other leaders, aroused by soldiers so close to the Indian encampment, did not. The tempestuous Tilcoax rose to challenge those stepping back from the brink of what could be a great victory—the moment was at hand to inflict on the soldiers what had been done to Indians by Kelly and Shaw.

Questions over Steptoe's reasons for coming revealed deep divisions between war and peace factions among the Spokanes and Coeur d'Alenes. Peacemakers, such as the Spokanes' Sgalgalt, opposed his fellow tribesman, Chief Polatkin, while Vincent urged consideration of Father Joset's long-standing counsel in avoiding antagonisms with the Army. Vincent pressed for reconciliation, but the Coeur d'Alene leader found his pleas drowned out by voices calling for action. He may have come to the conclusion that further reasoning with the hostility-inclined chiefs was futile.

In a subsequent conversation with Father DeSmet, Kamiakin confessed to being "at last drawn into the contest" following a stormy counsel. His tireless efforts to form a coalition of the tribes, indeed, had seemingly come to fruition, and the soldiers appeared to be peacefully turning back. But Tilcoax, using fiery rhetoric in advocating an attack, "upbraided" Kamiakin before the others for voicing caution at the moment of triumph. The Palouse headman stirred restive younger warriors to take decisive action. At this juncture, according to Joset, Tilcoax "had just what he wanted," and "did his utmost to raise enemies against the Whites." Taunts and past grievances held sway.

When Joset finally arrived at *Sila* late on Sunday, May 16, he met a disheartened Vincent, who was expecting the worst. In spite of an exhausting ride from the mission, the priest set out to reason with the warring chiefs. He found that many already had scattered to assemble their forces. He rode east to a Coeur d'Alene camp to provide counsel, and eventually rested from the long day's travel and tense diplomacy.

Vincent decided to risk another visit to the soldiers in a last attempt to avert disaster. Toward evening, he bravely rode to Steptoe's camp and offered a sober assessment of the situation. Lt. David Gregg, present at this second parley, recalled that Vincent urged Steptoe to withdraw as soon as possible. Orders then circulated among the men and around 2 a.m. the soldiers broke camp. They began heading east through the darkness, where they struck their previous trail in about three miles.[23]

Battle at Tohotonimme

After a fretful night, Father Joset set out at dawn on Monday, May 17, to meet with Steptoe. Escorted by several Indians and riding pell-mell, the priest arrived at the redoubt, only to find it deserted. The emissaries then followed the soldiers' trail east and met up with Steptoe's column moving back toward Pine Creek. Joset made his way past exhausted troopers to find the colonel.

After courteous introductions, Steptoe emphasized the pacific nature of his expedition. While Joset considered the colonel's explanation implausible, he offered to arrange another meeting with tribal leaders to defuse the situation. With increasing numbers of Indians now appearing on the hilltops around them, Steptoe sensed the growing danger. He

said he would refuse to halt to parley, but consented to confer while riding down the trail.

Joset then rode off in a desperate attempt to summon tribal leaders. Steptoe no doubt was shaken by the series of events that brought his command into such unexpected peril. To Sgt. Kenny, Steptoe appeared "like a man in a coma," which suggests that the colonel's medical condition also may have contributed to his discomposure. For months, Steptoe had suffered from periodic bouts of hemiplegia, caused by small strokes rendering partial paralysis to the right side of his body. The affliction greatly interfered with his ability to rest, and may well have been exacerbated by the strain of the current confrontation (the disease ultimately claimed his life in 1865). But the black-haired colonel was a Southern aristocrat and seasoned officer, who had distinguished himself under fire in the Mexican War. Not one to cower in the face of adversity, he kept his wits and pressed ahead toward the canyon bottom of Pine Creek.[24]

Father Joset succeeded in returning to the column, but only with Vincent and several lesser Coeur d'Alene headmen. After a congenial meeting with the colonel during a pause in the retreat, all seemed "fully satisfied" and preparations began for the soldiers to continue down the trail. As the conference was concluding, however, a heated argument broke out between Levi, one of Steptoe's Nez Perce scouts, and Chief Vincent. Levi struck the Coeur d'Alene leader on the shoulder with a quirt and challenged, "Proud man, why do you not fire?"

Vincent glaringly replied that the Nez Perce should be "ashamed of having struck your relative." This provocation now offered further evidence to the soldiers' growing realization that Timothy's scouts were scheming to make trouble. Vincent stoically endured the offense in the presence of the priest. They turned back to report to other tribal leaders that the crisis had passed, and Joset rode on about a dozen miles to *Sila* to reassure people there.[25]

According to official Army report, the fighting commenced at about 7 a.m. when the soldiers reached Pine Creek and began fording the stream. Chief Seltice later related that five Palouses rode with Qualchan, who "ran his horse down to the moving column and fired twice into the column at close range. Then the bugle sounded, and the troops quickly turned and fired."

According to Coeur d'Alene tradition, one of the Palouses survived a head wound sustained in the first volley. He took the name Húsis Kute, or "Bald Head," from this event. Joset identified about a dozen young Coeur d'Alenes led by Stellam, Peenchi, and Melkapsi in the first wave of the attack. He reported that the soldiers held their fire for several minutes after the Indians commenced shooting, but when pressured by an increasing number of warriors, Steptoe's men returned fire and three Coeur d'Alene fighters fell. One of them was the popular headman, Victor, a brother-in-law of Chief Vincent. This exchange then brought other Indians into the fight.[26]

"The battle became continuous" as the troopers climbed up a ravine to the east, led by Steptoe for a short distance. The colonel then turned right up a hill where Lt. David Gregg advanced with a group of his men. They rode to the top, only to see Indians forming on the next hill to the southeast ahead of the column. Steptoe formed a temporary defensive position on the hilltop, momentarily waiting for his withdrawing troops, who now found themselves "warmly engaged with 500 Indians" delivering a "constant and raking fire."

Capt. O.H.P. Taylor and Lt. William Gaston were dispatched on the left and right respectively for the "dangerous duty of flanking the column" up the hillside. Both of these West Pointers bravely exposed themselves to gunfire when directing their troops to the top of the hill, where Steptoe paused and was directing howitzer fire at warriors clustered near some pines in the distance. Gaston then saw that the Indians were gaining the higher ground on the next hill to the south. With his men, he sped down from his previous position to again press uphill, to prevent the enemy from forming above them. At this juncture, a party of Coeur d'Alenes saw an opportunity to cut off Gaston and his men from the main column. They charged down the ravine dividing the slopes and opened fire. Comprehending the situation, Gaston reeled back to attack, while Taylor charged down from the main column in a combined attempt to crush the warriors in a pinchers movement.

The most savage fighting of the battle ensued in this place where Gaston first fell, followed moments later by Taylor. In the melee of such close fighting, cavalryman Victor DeMoy, a French veteran of the Crimean War, screamed for a saber and also sustained mortal wounds. This action momentarily scattered the Indians and enabled Steptoe's command to continue south one mile further to a long ridge overlooking Pine Creek at present-day Rosalia. The soldiers hastily formed a broad defensive ring to avoid annihilation.

The fighting continued "with unabated activity" for the rest of the afternoon. The huddled soldiers twice repulsed significant Indian assaults. Soldiers armed with rifles fumbled amidst flying lead and arrows to bite off the end of a paper cartridge, drop the powder and ball down the barrel, ram in a wad, and fit a copper cap over the breach nipple. Some recruits packed new Colt revolvers, which were more effective in close range encounters than cumbersome single-shot muzzleloader pistols or the wide-mouth musketoon, the short-range carbine carried by the two companies of dragoons.

By nightfall, the situation clearly was desperate. The spirits of exhausted young soldiers faltered amidst "the howling of Indians, the groans of the dying, and the whistling of balls and arrows." Steptoe discussed their grave circumstances with the other officers, finding none "doubted that we would be overwhelmed…in the morning." It was decided to attempt an escape under the cover of a moonless night, back along the trail by which they had come north. Soldiers strapped wounded men to horses, discarded unneeded baggage, and hastily buried their fallen comrades and the howitzers. They slipped off the hill before midnight, between the glowing fires of the Coeur d'Alene and Palouse camps, perhaps fortuitously aided by some intentional oversight of Vincent's Coeur d'Alenes.

Proceeding south, the hushed soldiers may have soon seen the murky silhouette of *Yáamuštas*, "Elk's Abode"—the butte that one day would bear their colonel's name. By dawn on May 18, Steptoe's men reached the Palouse River. They now had diverted to a different route south. At 10 p.m. that night, after proceeding down Sklassams Creek (Steptoe Canyon), the soldiers crossed the Snake River with Nez Perce help at Red Wolf's Crossing. They soon straggled wearily back to Ft. Walla Walla.

News of the battle reached Joset at *Síla* later on the day of the fighting. The priest predicted certain and severe retribution. The following morning, he witnessed the grim evidence of what he had labored so hard to prevent. Indians arrived carrying the body of Zachary, another one of Chief Vincent's brothers-in-law, killed with the other two Coeur d'Alenes at the outset of the fighting. Joset tended to Zachary's burial at *Síla*, before heading back to the mission where other casualties would be interred.[27]

Although seven of Steptoe's men were killed and thirteen others wounded in what some historians call the "Steptoe Disaster," the command had managed to escape at night and prevent much higher casualties. Estimates of Indian losses were in the range of about a dozen killed, including the Coeur d'Alene headman Victor, and at least twice as many wounded. The loose Indian alliance was defiant and victorious, and now, by Father DeSmet's account, had grown beyond the Yakamas, Spokanes, Palouses, and Coeur d'Alenes to include Kalispels, Flatheads, Okanogans, and Kettles.

The ignominy of Steptoe's withdrawal sent a shudder through the coastal settlements and registered as far away as the nation's capital. General Clarke felt he had no alternative but to act decisively. He specifically mentioned Chief Kamiakin as a principal antagonist (though it now is clear that other chiefs, such as Tilcoax, played a more significant role in the opening of the Steptoe hostilities).[28]

At the time of the Steptoe battle, a Hudson's Bay brigade of seventy-five pack animals, led by George Montour and others, as well as sixty-five animals led by Major Owen's small party, unwittingly had ventured from The Dalles toward Ft. Colvile. They learned about the Army's defeat from a Nez Perce Indian while camped east of the Columbia's White Bluffs. They spent a wearying week of hasty travel northward, only to find "500 or 600 Indians gathering outside the post to celebrate the victory over Steptoe."

Spirited war dances lasted through the night. Charles Frush, an American camped at the fort with Bitterroot trader John Owen, observed many warriors, "some painted half red and half black, and some daubed all over with white mud… and then spotted with red. All were armed with Hudson Bay guns, rifles, or with bows and arrows, and were drumming and singing." Owen and Frush attempted a discrete nighttime departure toward Owen's post, but a group of alert warriors spied their train and lassoed seven or eight horses before allowing the men to continue eastward.[29]

Isaac Stevens, now serving as territorial delegate in Congress, found reason for his vindication. News of the Steptoe defeat "made a great sensation" in Washington, D.C., while the August and September issues of *Harper's Magazine* turned the Northwest's "imminent danger of a general outbreak" into national news. Stevens mused that his remonstrations about the Army's reluctance to forthrightly intervene on the behalf of miners and settlers might finally bring fruition. Meanwhile, Stevens pressed Congress for ratification of the Walla Walla treaties.

The long absence of any skillful new diplomatic initiatives in the Northwest, however, would further embroil both sides in conflict, and the seemingly intractable antagonisms between civilian and military officials compounded the situation. In hindsight, had Wool's view prevailed longer, perhaps a more reasonable period of transition might have emerged, facilitating peaceful change for the regions' tribes.[30]

Packmaster Tom Beall claimed Kamiakin took part in the fighting on May 17, but perhaps the most relevant word in this regard was Joset's report to Father Nicholas Congiato in June. The priest, who had considerable communications with both the Indian leaders and Steptoe, made no direct reference to Kamiakin's presence. He begged his administrative superior, however, not to abandon the work at Sacred Heart, lest the Coeur d'Alenes be delivered "to the conceit of Kamiakin," resulting "I think," in "a universal war throughout the whole country." Meanwhile, reports in the coastal newspapers blamed the "unfortunate disaster" on "the cunning treachery of Kamiakin."

While Tilcoax exalted in the battle's aftermath, Vincent brooded. Father Joset demanded to know why Vincent and his people attacked the soldiers after they began withdrawing. Vincent confessed, "all the fault is on our side." Joset responded with the dire observation that the Americans "would never keep quiet until they got a fearful revenge."

In regard to the Indians, Father DeSmet later wondered if "any thinking man" would have acted differently under similar circumstances. Had "it been a white people, would the magistrates, with no other resources than words, have been able to control the uprising?" The Jesuit missionary heard the Indians ask rhetorically: "Did we go to hunt for the Federal soldiers? Was it not their bands who came upon us, when we had not done a thing?"[31]

Mission of Peace

In the wake of Steptoe's defeat, Joset traveled feverishly among the Coeur d'Alenes and Spokanes in an attempt to restore peace. He rebuked chiefs for starting the fight "without provocation" after the soldiers began retreating, and found it shameful "that Christians should have behaved that way." Vincent and Garry were shaken by the prospect of a Jesuit withdrawal from the region. They pledged to make amends, while blaming Kamiakin, Qualchan, and Tilcoax for problems with packers and soldiers since 1855.[32]

Joset realized it was imperative to personally contact military authorities at Ft. Walla Walla and Ft. Vancouver to avert further bloodshed. He had other personal concerns as well. His presence among the Coeur d'Alenes during the Steptoe battle likely gave soldiers reason to suspect his complicity in the attack. The charge was groundless, but many Americans held doubts about Jesuit and Oblate intentions.

Joset set out on his dangerous mission, crossing often rough and disputed terrain, first to St. Paul's near Ft. Colvile, then hastily down the Colville Road to the Spokanes, and on to Ft. Walla Walla. Steptoe, however, warmly received Joset. The priest's thorough reporting and sincere expressions of goodwill also won the admiration of skeptical Captain

Thomas Jordan at Ft. Dalles, whom Joset met several days later. At Ft. Vancouver in June, the weary priest received a warmer reception than he might have expected. General Clarke considered the Northwest's Jesuits to be "reverenced and enlightened," who should be treated "at any time in a conciliatory manner."

But Clarke now strongly advocated war. In June, he conferred with Wright and Steptoe at Ft. Dalles, formulating strategy for a complete military victory. The Army's terms for restoring peace included the return of Steptoe's abandoned horses and equipment, and the surrender of those warriors responsible for precipitating the attack. When Kamiakin, Vincent, and Garry received word about this, they agreed to send whatever property might be salvaged, but bristled at the temerity of Clarke's insistence on Indian prisoners. The matter stirred disturbing memories of the fate befalling the Cayuses charged with the Whitman killings a decade earlier.

"We cannot turn over our people," Kamiakin is said to have replied to Clarke's emissary, Father Congiato. "We don't want another 'Whitman Trial,' where all five Cayuses were hung by an angry jury, and one was finished off by the executioner's ax." Kamiakin acknowledged that the Army's likely response would be to take to the field with "a thousand well-equipped men and much better guns than we have, but we can still fight."[33]

Soon after Clarke had arrived at Ft. Dalles, he learned disturbing details of yet another fatal encounter, this time along the Columbia. In May, a large group of miners led by Mortimer Robertson left the The Dalles en route to new strikes in Canada's Fraser River district. Chief Owhi helped ferry the men and their provisions across the Yakima River. The brigade continued northward across the Wenatchee Mountains and proceeded down Peshastin Creek, where Robertson's eye saw color in the fine gravels of the clear stream. Robertson divulged his discovery only to two others, and they agreed to continue with the brigade in order not to draw attention to the find.

When they reached an Indian camp on the lower Wenatchee River, the miners were confronted by Quiltenenock, still smarting from Stevens' rebuff at the second Walla Walla Council. The chief warned them against crossing the river and proceeding north, but the Whites pressed on. Soon after the miners reached the Wenatchee's mouth, shooting broke out, claiming the life of one miner as well as Chief Tecolekun of the Wenatchi. The Whites fled south along the Columbia pursued by Quiltenenock, who was killed by a miner hiding behind a rock at a crossing near the mouth of

Squilchuck Creek. The miners raced southward toward Ft. Simcoe.

Qualchan was seriously wounded in another confrontation near present-day Beverly that also claimed another miner. Two days later, the beleaguered survivors straggled into Ft. Simcoe and shared news of the attack with Major Garnett, who blamed Owhi, Qualchan, and Skloom for having "no just provocation for their conduct."[34] Garnett learned that at least ten miners had been killed in incidents like this.

At Ft. Vancouver on June 26, when Joset and diocesan priest Rev. J.B.A. Brouillet had met with General Clarke, news of Steptoe's defeat and the miners' Columbia River fights was arousing great alarm. Joset presented the peculiar circumstances of the Steptoe episode, noting the role of the soldiers' abrupt and disturbing appearance, and the fact that there were hostile influences from other groups angering the northern tribes. Clarke respected Joset's views and his record among the Coeur d'Alenes, but demanded that the tribe agree to allow soldiers and Whites to cross tribal lands and to surrender the Indians who attacked Steptoe. He announced his intention to "make war" on the hostiles, specifically naming Kamiakin as a principal target.[35]

As Joset returned up the Columbia along with his superior, Father Nicholas Congiato, the Jesuits found themselves among large numbers of miners undeterred by the hazards revealed in recent events. Buoyed by Clarke's bold statements for conquest now being reported in newspapers, the gold seekers pressed on by steamers from Vancouver to Ft. Dalles to proceed overland across the dry mid Columbia prairies to the mining districts. When Joset and Congiato finally arrived at Sacred Heart Mission on July 16, they were shocked to learn that the tribal resolve for peace was gone. Chief Vincent and several dozen other warriors were virtually alone in their fidelity to not take up arms.

The Army's demand for the tribes to surrender up the warriors precipitating the Steptoe fight was entirely unacceptable to the northern Indians. The priests learned that, during their absence, Kamiakin, Owhi, and Tilcoax offered horses and pledges of mutual support to Coeur d'Alene and other warriors. Congiato informed Clarke by letter that Kamiakin "has been living, and still lives" in the upper country and was most responsible for Indian resistance. In attempting to overcome the bellicose mood, the two harried blackrobes rode throughout Coeur d'Alene and Spokane country in late summer, counseling with Indian leaders. They dismissed Kamiakin's Yakamas and the Palouses as being beyond the pale of any fruitful diplomacy.

Indeed, the camps of Kamiakin, Tilcoax, and their people were situated far from the reach of missions and trading posts; thus there was little opportunity for priests or traders to meet and parley with them. Furthermore, the hostile bands felt the moment had come to challenge Father Pandosy's dire prophecy. They knew all too well the likely fate of any accused Indians turned over to soldiers. Indian fighters had been hung after the Cascades fight in 1856, and just months before in February 1858, Kamiakin's cousin, the Nisqually Chief Leschi, met a similar fate at Ft. Steilacoom.

Kamiakin may well have received word of Leschi's recent execution, since his cousin had been imprisoned for months following arrest for allegedly killing a soldier in time of war. The trial of the Nisqually chief resulted in a hung jury, but civilian authorities orchestrated an appeal overturning the court's decision. Kamiakin's own fatalistic thoughts may have been similar to Leschi's words spoken at the trial: "I went to war because I believed that the Indian had been wronged by the white men, and I did everything in my power to beat the Boston soldiers, but, for lack of numbers, supplies and ammunition, I have failed."[36]

Kamiakin and Tilcoax's scouts south of the Snake River informed the chiefs about new troop deployments at Ft. Dalles and Ft. Walla Walla. Like Owhi and Qualchan countering the new flood of miners crossing Yakama lands, Kamiakin prepared for battle in the east. Great swaths of grasslands were set afire south of the Snake River to deprive the Army's livestock of forage. Kamiakin's band also rounded up their horses, joining them with the vast herds of Tilcoax and other Indians, and headed them north. Kamiakin sequestered the women and children, but his beloved warrior wife, Colestah, vowed to fight at his side. Her aged mother tied the young woman's hair into tight braids and helped prepare her battle dress as death clothes. News of the Army's advance came in the second week of August.[37]

The Wright Campaign

The sting of the Steptoe defeat was a national embarrassment for the military. General Newman Clarke, commander of the Army of the Pacific, directed a torrent of men and supplies to the Columbia Department during the summer of 1858, as thorough preparations were made for striking into the heartland of the disputed region. On July 4, he issued orders to Colonel Wright for a "complete submission" of the warring tribes, causing a dramatic change from Wright's previous strategy for dealing with Indians. Known to his men as a

stern but even-handed taskmaster, the 54-year-old officer had commanded the Ninth Infantry from Ft. Dalles since 1856. The colonel's peace initiatives in the Yakima Valley now stood discredited, and he felt that Steptoe's defeat represented a personal affront by Indian leaders to his authority, as well as a breach of trust.

By August, about 2,200 men were deployed in the Northwest, with 1,000 of these assigned to Wright, who would be the principal architect of a grand pincers movement across the Columbia Plateau. The operation called for Major Robert Garnett, a Virginian, former West Point instructor, and now the commander at Ft. Simcoe, to lead 300 men north toward the confluence of the Columbia and Okanogan rivers. Garnett aimed to punish the Indians harassing miners, and at the same time force hostiles eastward to face Wright's larger force.

While Garnett marched north from the Yakima Valley, Wright planned to strike northeast across the Columbia Basin to the Coeur d'Alene Mission, then northwest to Ft. Colvile, and finally down to the confluence of the Spokane and Columbia rivers, where he expected to encounter warriors fleeing Garnett. The staff officers' greatest concern was that the Indians might conduct wide ranging guerrilla operations and avoid mass confrontations. As Oregon and Washington Indian Superintendent James Nesmith observed, a substantial military force "is always adroitly eluded" in such scenarios, "while an inferior and weak [command]…is invariably defeated." Due to the strident tone of political leaders in Olympia and Washington, D.C., and given the enormous expenditures needed to field the operation—especially in the face of the Army's preoccupation with the Mormon confrontation—Clarke demanded definitive results from his field commanders.[38]

Thus, throughout the summer of 1858, troops and equipment had moved up the Columbia River and through The Dalles to Ft. Walla Walla and Ft. Simcoe. During the last week of July, Wright arrived at Ft. Walla Walla to make final preparations. Major Garnett proceeded north from Ft. Dalles to Yakama country, and departed Ft. Simcoe on August 10 with four companies of 300 regulars, some mounted and the others on foot, and 50 packers and herders. He intended to follow Wright's route taken two years earlier to the Wenatchi country.

At this time, Owhi and Teias were camped with their wives and children on the east side of the Columbia near the mouth of the Wenatchee River. The group included Sanclow with her warrior husband and brothers, Quetalican (Moses), Lokout, and Lesh-hi-hite (*Lišxayxit*), plus Teias with his son and daughter-in-law, Tom-teah-kuin and Hana-yah-kla-ka. Qualchan was recovering from injury sustained in the late June conflict with miners that claimed the lives of his brother Quiltenenock and Chief Tecolekun. Garnett planned to continue up the Columbia River to the ruins of the HBC's Ft. Okanogan and move east to the Spokane River.

News of the approaching invaders preceded their arrival. Owhi and Teias made a scouting trip across the border into Canada where they were offered safe haven in the future. Upon their return, however, younger family members prevailed upon them to remain in the Plateau. The Star Brother chiefs soon followed their sons across the Waterville Plateau and continued east to camp near the mouth of the Spokane River. They planned to join Kamiakin and the other patriot chiefs, whose people were massing in Spokane and Palouse country to meet Wright's forces.[39]

Wright's advance party left Ft. Walla Walla on August 7 to secure the Snake River crossing near the mouth of the Tucannon. Here, they fashioned alder bastion posts and gathered basalt to build Ft. Taylor. The post was named in honor of slain Captain Taylor, whose body still layed on the Steptoe battlefield. On the forthcoming expedition, the soldiers hoped to retrieve the captain's body and the remains of other fallen comrades. Meanwhile, light skirmishes occurred with some warriors in the area.

This forward guard soon was followed by the main force, which altogether would include some 700 well-armed troops and Army support personnel, plus 30 uniformed Nez Perce scouts, civilian packers driving 800 horses, mules, and cattle, five weeks of provisions, and "a very wholesome respect for the Indians who had so thoroughly defeated Steptoe's command."[40]

In the torrid heat, the long column of infantry and mounted troopers marched through charred grass stubble, recently torched by Indians in a "lake of fire." From Ft. Taylor on the Snake River, the soldiers crossed north to the nearby mouth of the Palouse River on August 25. The Indians usually residing at *Palus* had moved out of harm's way, with the Tilcoax, Paween, and Poyahkin families driving their vast herds to relative security in the Coeur d'Alene Mountains.

Plains Aflame

The measured pace of Wright's grand cavalcade gave Kamiakin and other Indian leaders ample time to plot strategy. Many had grown overconfident after their victories against Haller and Steptoe, whose professional forces were repulsed

by warrior courage and Indian belief in guardian spirits, invoked by song and sacred relics carried in leather medicine bundles. Wright feared his adversaries might "resort to guerilla warfare…and endeavor by every means…to embarrass and cripple our operations."

The loose Indian confederation that Kamiakin and Tilcoax sought to sustain over the objections of the Jesuits and peace chiefs included an impressive number of experienced fighters, although virtually every tribe other than the Palouses remained split into hostile and neutral factions. But the circumstances now were significantly different from Steptoe's lack of preparedness and unexpected intrusion. Wright commanded a much larger force and his soldiers had superior weaponry—including several hundred new long-range rifled muskets, additional .54 caliber Harpers Ferry rifles that were a reliable standard issue, perhaps several dozen of the novel Sharps carbines, and a mountain howitzer battery. Whereas McDonald at Ft. Colvile, now succeeded by George Blenkinsop, had turned a deaf ear to Kamiakin's pleas for ammunition, HBC personnel at Ft. Vancouver had been doing a booming business all summer, meeting the needs of Wright's forces, and earned a commendation from the American Secretary of War for the valued support.[41]

Wright's command pressed beyond the Snake River through the western Palouse scablands—rocky, wild scenery interrupted periodically by fantastic basaltic crenellations and patches of open prairie and grassy bottoms. Great plumes of dust trailed behind in the hot summer air. On August 30, the column marched eighteen miles to the Fishtrap Lake vicinity. No sooner were they settled into camp than Nez Perce scouts returned with word of approaching warriors. Wright immediately prepared to ride forward with dragoons as shots were exchanged in the distance. Soldiers advanced north for about three miles, but did little more that disperse what was likely a scouting party.[42]

On September 1, Wright's command finally emerged onto broad prairie land, where the opposing forces finally met in the Battle of Four Lakes. The Indians assembled amid scattered pines and bunchgrass flats between Granite and Willow lakes. The soldiers' thrusts led directly into this position between a "bald butte" to the east, later named Wrights Hill, and Riddle Hill to the west. Kamiakin likely knew that the dragoons advancing in the lead were led by Nez Perce scouts. Kamiakin's Palouses and Yakamas occupied the center, directly facing Wright's line of march, while Qualchan's warriors formed to his right. Spokanes under Polatkin and other chiefs rode near the Yakamas to the north. The Coeur d'Alenes under Stellam assembled beyond the Army's right flank.

Both sides cautiously approached, until the soldiers opened a withering fire at several hundred yards with firearms the Indians had not faced in the Steptoe fight. These weapons had a longer range than the warrior's HBC trade guns. Indian ranks were torn by the soldiers' improved weaponry, as warriors slowly fell back in spite of Qualchan and Kamiakin's appeals to stand their ground. Indian resistance, however, held for some three hours before the warriors finally had to scatter in turmoil. Lt. Lawrence Kip observed that the bands had met "the long range rifles now first used by our troops."[43]

The companies led by Taylor and Gaston in the Steptoe fight were "burning for revenge," and rushed headlong into the Indians with swords and pistols. Some warriors were overrun, shot down, or clubbed, as the sound of Native war songs added to the clamor. "It was a race for life, as the flying warriors streamed out of the glens and ravines and over the open plain, and took refuge in the clumps of woods." One Yakama warrior later reported witnessing "utter confusion" in the din and shove of battle.

The soldiers returning to Wright's camp saw a macabre scene—scattered "in all directions" were Indian casualties, estimated to be between forty and fifty, along with "muskets, quivers, bows and arrows, blankets, robes, etc." Riderless Indian ponies roamed about. The warring bands had sought refuge among pines beyond the lakes, before fleeing further north. They did not regroup to challenge the soldiers again that day.

For several days, Kamiakin and the other leaders discussed their circumstances in tense councils, while tending to their wounded and anxiously awaiting Wright's next move. Disagreements erupted between those arguing for peace and those remaining intransigent, such as Kamiakin, who sought to renew the fighting in spite of the soldiers' overwhelming firepower. Kamiakin suggested night attacks to counter the enemy's superior weaponry. But other leaders opposed this tactic, which they were unaccustomed to, as being too risky. During this fateful period in early September, Donati's Comet flared portentously in the night sky—the two tailing trails of the fiery traveler curved ominously like a scimitar. Perhaps the Star Brothers were falling, with the rest of the Indian world.[44]

On September 5, the fighting bands had sufficiently regrouped a half-dozen miles northwest of Four Lakes to challenge the soldiers again at the Battle of Spokane Plains. This proved to be the decisive action of the Wright campaign and a defining moment in the region's primal clash of cul-

tures. Indians set the dry prairie-grass on fire south of Deep Creek to confuse Wright's advancing column, which was slithering forward as if possessed by the Rattlesnake spirit. Smoke billowed up, a final exhalation of Native freedom, but the soldiers held their ranks and marched toward the mayhem, watching "the enemy collecting in large bodies" to the east. Wright estimated their number at five to seven hundred.

Warriors also rode parallel to the soldiers' line of march, massing in larger enclaves as they rode north. Wright halted on a slight rise overlooking a bluff of "rocky ravines & canons," about two miles north of present-day Airway Heights, where the Indians took positions among the scattered pines. The colonel ordered Lt. James White's howitzer to the front, and also called for the main pack train to come forward. To protect his livestock, Wright placed three companies of troops on both flanks and the rear, with Mullan's Nez Perces at the head. In launching the attack in front, Wright dispatched in close semi-circle formation companies G, E, A, and K. Captain C.S. Winder's E Company formed directly behind White's artillery piece. Prairie fires threatened to engulf the soldiers as shooting "now became brisk on both sides."[45]

Again Kamiakin and Qualchan led the Palouses and Yakamas at the Indians' center left and right, respectively. Stellam's Coeur d'Alenes took the right flank and Spokanes under Garry and Sgalgalt formed on the left. As rifles barked and the howitzer began thundering, Indians from the north dashed "down a hill five hundred feet high and with a slope of forty-five degrees, at the most headlong speed," in "feats of horsemanship...never seen equalled." They rushed forward to join other warriors attempting to contain the soldiers' horseshoe formation.

Nevertheless, Wright sounded the advance. The forward companies under Winder, Ransom, Tyler, and Ord began moving through the cindered prairie directly against the Indians. As the soldiers noted: "The enemy was braver and bolder than Indian enemies usually are," only leaving "the field from the most dire necessity."[46]

Again the Indians faced a deadly fusillade of rifle and artillery fire. Wright estimated that some eight howitzer shells exploded amidst Indian positions, as the warriors stubbornly gave ground northeast toward the Spokane River. At one point, when soldiers turned to maneuver the howitzer into a better position, a group of warriors swept forward in brazen, desperate heroics to silence the hellish weapon. The gun's defenders immediately spun the cannon around and fired directly into the attackers, forcing them to spread in all directions.

Battle of Spokane Plains, by eyewitness Gustavus Sohon.
WSU Libraries

Gustavus Sohon

Two topographers, John Mullan and Theodore Kolecki, along with the interpreter/artist Gustavus Sohon, were assigned to Wright's command to render graphic portrayals of events, the only visual documentation done in any of the regional Indian campaigns of this period.

Sohon's striking perspective on the Battle of Spokane Plains was rendered from the relative security of the main pack train. At the center of Sohon's sketch, seven men, likely Wright with his senior staff, aides, and messengers, confidently sit on horseback atop a slight rise flanked by a line of infantry on each side. In front of them, a long line of skirmishers, with a company of dragoons also moving on the left, advance toward billowing smoke and a cluster of mounted warriors in the distance.

When some warriors sought to regroup on a small prairie to the southeast of the main column's slow advance, Wright dispatched Major William Grier with companies I, C, and M to disperse them in close combat. The Indians slowly gave ground in the fight, moving "from cover to cover, from behind the trees and rocks, and through the ravines and canons, til the woods for more than four miles, which lately seemed perfectly alive with their yelling and shouting, were entirely cleared."[47]

Kamiakin and his wife Colestah, who was clad in battle dress with a scarlet headscarf, fought together until a cannon shell shattered a tree over their heads. According to family accounts, a falling branch struck Kamiakin, knocking him from his horse and likely breaking his shoulder. Colestah was unharmed. The injured chief was taken to the distant safety of the family's camp at the mouth of the Spokane River. Lt. George Dandy, whose company attacked Indian positions in the pines and rocks below Deep Creek, recalled that the howitzer commanded by Lt. James White of the Third Artillery fired the shot that almost claimed the chief's life. According to Dandy, "one of his shells tore a limb from a large tree under which some Indians were grouped; among whom… was the great chief Kamiakin of the Yakima tribe, who was seriously hurt."

Seven hours of the soldiers' unremitting onslaught pushed the Indians back seven miles to the Spokane River, where Wright encamped atop a steep western bluff of the river, one or two miles below the mouth of Latah Creek. The soldiers were "entirely exhausted," but Wright commended the "zeal, energy, and perseverance" they displayed throughout "this protracted battle."[48]

column had swung around Lake Coeur d'Alene to upper Latah Creek, Wright hoped to encounter Kamiakin and other Indian leaders, whom he still considered a threat to an enduring peace. On September 22, upon reaching an ancient crossing of Latah Creek, Wright established camp, hoping to entice the chiefs still at large to parley. The colonel dispatched Spokan Garry and Big Star to specifically find Kamiakin, said to be in the vicinity with Tilcoax, with the message, "if he did not surrender himself, he…would hunt him down until he captured him, and then put him to death."

Lt. Kip characterized Kamiakin as being "for years the most powerful chief among all these tribes…. He is the head chief of the Yakimas, his mother having been a Yakima, and his father a Pelouze. This gave him great influence with both these tribes, and by his talents he has acquired authority with all the northern Indian nations. He seems to occupy the same position with them that Tecumpsah formerly did with our [mid West] tribes…. With more far-reaching wisdom than the rest, he probably saw that this surrender of their lands and intrusion of the white men, would be the final step in destroying the nation."

Catch and Kill

The Battle of Spokane Plains had ended disastrously for the Indians. After a three-day respite on the Spokane River in today's Ft. George Wright locality, the soldiers continued east up the Spokane Valley, destroying Indian food caches and overtaking a herd of nearly a thousand Indian horses near today's Washington-Idaho state line. The soldiers were ordered to shoot most of them. Recollections of the ominous pall of death over this place would long weigh heavily in the memory of both Indian and White passers-by.

Wright continued eastward, forcing terms upon the Coeur d'Alenes at the Cataldo Mission, but not exacting any executions of warriors, though demanding some hostages. After the Army

"Camp on the Spokane river Sept 6th. 1858," by Sohon. Following the drawn-out Spokane Plains fight, Wright's soldiers bivouacked in today's Ft. George Wright district of Spokane.
WSU Libraries

The lieutenant likely intoned Wright's special interest in Kamiakin's capture when further observing that he was "the moving spirit in arraying all these tribes against us this season, and bringing on this open warfare." Given the seriousness of the Army's allegations against Kamiakin, Kip did not find it unusual that the chief would not accept the offer from Wright to come and parley. Meanwhile at this camp, Wright imposed the same terms on the Spokanes as the Coeur d'Alenes.[49]

Owhi, perhaps hoping to pacify the soldiers in this fateful campaign, decided to surrender, although the chief's farewell to his relatives presaged dire consequences. His niece, who witnessed the scene as a little girl, later remembered: "He took his children in his tepee and kissed them; also his cousins and all his people." She continued: "And he kissed me. Owhi, the war chief of the Yakamas, kissed me goodbye."[50]

About sunset on September 23, Owhi cautiously rode his white war horse into Wright's camp to discuss peace terms. The aged Yakama leader shortly was seized and shackled. Veteran packmaster Tom Beall, who conferred with Wright that evening, related that the colonel's intention was to imprison Owhi, as well as Kamiakin, at the Presidio in San Francisco for two or three years and then permit their return to the Northwest. If this was the case, Wright did not inform Owhi of the plan. Beall found the celebrated Yakama chief to be a man of "mild, kind disposition" in spite of his circumstances, but who probably concluded he was being held for execution.

Although Wright claimed that the messengers he sent out demanded the surrender of Qualchan and Kamiakin, the courier who found Qualchan said that the soldier chief wished to speak of peace. Kamiakin's recent injuries may have prevented his going, but Qualchan, still recovering from the serious wound inflicted in the fight with miners, approached Wright's lethal trap on the morning after Owhi's capture.

This was around the time that a detachment of soldiers left camp to retrieve the remains of fallen comrades at the Steptoe battlefield. Qualchan rode a bay horse into Wright's camp, accompanied by his wife, Whistalks, and a young rider, possibly Lokout or Lesh-hi-hite. According to Kip: "With the utmost boldness they rode directly up to Colonel Wright's tent.… Captain Keyes, thinking he might meditate some desperate act, placed himself on his right, a little in the rear, with his eye fixed on Qualchien's rifle, ready to spring upon him on the slightest demonstration."

After a few words with the visitor, Wright ordered the warrior seized and disarmed—he also was carrying a pistol—although the effort required all the strength of several soldiers. In fifteen minutes, as Wright very briefly stated in a later report, Qualchan was hung, as were some Palouses who Wright seized around this time. Captain E.D. Keyes, who had faced Qualchan in fights on Puget Sound and in the present campaign, offered commentary on the legendary warrior's execution and *miyawaxpamáma* heritage not found in Wright's short laconic reference to the incident. "He was still young, not over twenty-five years of age, and his physical constitution was apparently perfect," Keyes observed. "Seemingly his renown as a prince and warrior gave to his life a charm and value he was unwilling to surrender."[51]

Whistalks defiantly flung Qualchan's beaded medicine lance at Wright's tent and rode back to the Spokane River camp to report the fateful encounter. The quiet stream would now be named "Hangman Creek."

On September 30, returning toward Ft. Walla Walla, Wright hastily called a "Palouse Council" at the mouth of Willow Creek on the Palouse River. Here, he ordered several more Indians to be hanged. The colonel threatened to "annihilate the whole nation" of Palouses should they make any further trouble.

The column then crossed the Snake River at *Palus*, and not long after, when fording the Tucannon River near present-day Starbuck, Owhi's horse sprinted ahead. He was fired upon and wounded by his guard, Lt. Michael Morgan. A mounted soldier immediately raced after him and felled Owhi with a bullet to the head at close range. The aged chief languished for about an hour before expiring. Some of the scouts broke apart his grizzly claw necklace and distributed these tokens of authority that Yemowit had bestowed upon the chief years before. Lesh-hi-hite later became the only family beneficiary of one of the sacred talismans.

Wright's war making had relied on applying overwhelming force as well as a focused assault on tribal leadership. He combined these objectives against the tribes to obtain unconditional surrender, seizing warring chiefs for confinement or execution, and destroying herds and food caches. Horrific memories of these events left a deep impression with each retelling in Indian camps during the coming winter's deprivations, and for years to come.[52]

Reports from the Columbia Department and General Clarke concerning Wright's campaign soon reached General-in-Chief Winfield Scott in New York. On November 12, 1858, Scott noted the "unqualified submission" of the tribes and "subjugation of the whole alliance." A month later, Secretary of War John Floyd added that the Indians "sued abjectly for peace," and those guilty of "murder and rapine,…the immediate cause of the recent hostilities, were surrendered, tried, and executed." Floyd announced the establishment of a "permanent peace" and commended Wright and the men of his command.

In the aftermath of Wright's campaign, Father Joset of the Coeur d'Alene Mission explained how the delicate balance of power between the Indians and Whites had shifted dramatically. "The volunteer expeditions had exasperated the Indians, without inspiring them with any dread; but by the able manner in which the colonel made the most of his resources, he completely rid [them] of any desire to measure themselves with the American troops."[53]

The Indian confederacy was destroyed and Wright sought out tribal headmen to secure an enduring peace. Indian leaders whom he felt were a threat or could not be trusted had been executed or arrested. Those deemed reliable or necessary to maintain tribal stability were ordered directly, in harsh terms, to break any ties with Kamiakin, Tilcoax, or other exiled chiefs.

Wright's policy of executing captives, particularly those seized under the pretense of entering negotiations, strikes many today as a particularly reprehensible aspect of the campaign. The warriors had felt the soldiers' fury in battle and commonly assumed that Wright, from his position of strength, now would demand peace in council with Indian leaders. Mary Owhi Moses claimed that her brother, Qualchan, entered Wright's camp under a flag of truce after receiving an invitation to parley. He would not have gone under any other conditions.

Historian and jurist W.C. Brown later made a thorough study of the circumstances: "Among all peoples, an invitation to come into an enemy camp for a parley invariably implies absolute immunity from arrest or harm while...to do otherwise is by immutable law always an act of treachery." Indeed, Qualchan entered the soldiers' camp "relying on that universally accepted rule."[54]

The Native American community today still harbors bitter feelings about these events, acerbated over the years when Northwest communities named streets and facilities in honor of Colonel Wright. Furthermore, efforts persist even today to use the name "Hangman" for Latah Creek, an appellation that remains offensive to many in Indian country. Sanclow (Mary Owhi Moses) characterized Wright's methods as using any approach, fair or unfair, "to catch and kill all our good fighters."

In shock from the defeats inflicted by the Army and by Wright's summary brutality, the Wiyáwiikt clan scattered in several directions. Numerous family members remained

Garnett's Campaign

At the time of Wright's advance across the Palouse, Major Robert Garnett's 300 soldiers and 50 packers from Ft. Simcoe proceeded north between the Columbia and the Cascades, also dispensing some harsh summary retribution. Indian informants identified 25 warriors responsible for attacking miners in the previous months.

Of these, one was shot in the confusion of a mounted detachment's predawn assault on an Indian camp on the Yakima River above the Kittitas Valley, and nine others were seized and executed by firing squad, at the captured Yakima River camp and later in the Wenatchi country. The other 15 accused warriors successfully evaded infantry and cavalry sweeps by hiding out in the Cascades or the upper Columbia country, and by heading toward Canada or the Rockies and Plains.

The Army, too, suffered a couple of casualties. A lieutenant was fatally shot, perhaps inadvertently by his men, during the attack on the Indian village, the only sizeable skirmish of Garnett's campaign. A private was ambushed when straggling behind a main column north of Ft. Okanogan.

By September 15, Garnett received word that Wright's superior weaponry had broken the back of major Indian resistance at Four Lakes. The guerilla warfare that senior officers feared never materialized.

separated for years to come. Kamiakin and Skloom hastened eastward to the Bitterroots, while Sanclow rode northwest with her husband Moses and his band to the Columbia River.

In the months ahead, soldiers and Indian scouts in the Yakima Valley were dispatched to seize or kill those implicated in the deaths of Bolon, Matisse, and Eaton. They wounded and captured Kamiakin's nephew, Mushíil, at his camp near the confluence of Toppenish Creek and the Yakima River. He died shortly afterward. Two of his accomplices in the Bolon murder were hanged at Ft. Simcoe.

Due to the war-induced hard times, Chief Teias and Tomteah-kuin journeyed to British Columbia for provisions, but were intercepted on their return in the Nespelem Valley by tribal soldiers from Ft. Simcoe who executed the chief's son. Chief Saluskin fled with his family from the Yakima Valley to the Moses Lake area, where they remained for several years before venturing back to their homeland. Others vanished from the region, never to return.[55]

Civil War Era Forts and Fights

Wright's victory and the ending of Indian sovereignty opened a new era of opportunity for American settlers, long waiting to claim lands in the vast intermontane region. In the spring of 1859, the Army established Harney Depot, fourteen miles southeast of the old HBC fort at Kettle Falls. The new post, soon known as Ft. Colville, was commanded by Major Pickney Lugenbeel and served as a base of operations for the U.S.-Canadian Boundary Survey. Lugenbeel reported that Indians in the area remained surly, but miners faced little risk of Indian reprisal.

In 1860, however, rich gold strikes in the Salmon River district on the Nez Perce Reservation significantly shifted the flow of White miners coming east of the Cascades. In June, the hamlet of Lewiston suddenly sprang up at the confluence of the Snake and Clearwater rivers, several miles north of T'siyiyak's original home of *Hasúutin*. This ushered in an era of steamboat traffic up the Snake River to service miners and merchants in the surging boomtown of false fronts and canvas roofs. Two years later, the Army established Ft. Lapwai, several miles east of Lewiston, in a vain attempt to forestall conflicts between the Nez Perces and a remarkably diverse population of wealth seekers from both the West and East coasts, Scandinavia, Western Europe, Latin America, and elsewhere.

The outbreak of the Civil War, however, temporarily slackened the onslaught. During the seething national conflagration of 1861–65, Colonel Wright, Isaac Stevens, and many of their fellow comrades-in-arms during the Indian wars period would not survive or come through unscathed. While serving as a Union commander at the Second Battle of Bull Run,

Lt. David Gregg

In 1908, the last living officer from the Steptoe campaign, David Gregg, corresponded from the East with Garfield historian Benjamin Manring: "On my visits to West Point I do not fail to go to the Cadets Cemetery where repose the remains of so many distinguished soldiers and stand by the graves of Captain Taylor and Lieut. Gaston where is brought to memory the thrilling events of that fateful 17th of May 1858."

Brigadier General Stevens was killed on September 1, 1862, leading a charge at Chantilly. (His son, Hazard, who had observed Kamiakin at the Walla Walla Council, survived a serious wound incurred in the same battle. Years later, he returned to Washington where he and P.B. Van Trump made the first recorded ascent of Mt. Rainier.)

In July 1861, President Lincoln appointed George McClellan to lead the Army of the Potomac, the U.S. military's top field command. Though credited with fine organizational skills, the same pattern of indecision noted by Stevens eventually led to his reassignment in late 1862.

Colonel Wright remained in the West, assuming command of the Department of the Pacific in October 1861. He perished along with his wife and numerous passengers when the *Brother Jonathan* sank near Crescent City, California, in July 1865.

Many of the officers who served in the Columbia Basin in the 1850s later became generals on both sides during the Civil War, including Union commanders E.O.C. Ord, George Crook, and Frederick Dent, who served on General Grant's staff. Charles Winder, a Confederate brigadier general, fell at Cedar Mountain. William Pender, who earned Wright's special praise at the Spokane Plains battle, died at Gettysburg in 1863 while leading a Confederate charge against the Federals on Seminary Ridge. Brigadier General James Archer, who had served in the Yakima Valley, was captured by Union forces at the same battle, and released from a POW camp in 1864, broken in health.

Johnson K. Duncan, one of Stevens' most valued topographers in the railway surveys, commanded Mississippi River defenses as a Confederate general, while Lt. Christopher Augur, who served with Rains against Kamiakin in 1855, was a major general and responsible for apprehending the Lincoln assassination conspirators.

Several of these veterans eventually were laid to rest in the West Point cemetery, a short distance from the graves of William Gaston and O.H.P. Taylor, casualties of Steptoe's fateful foray.[56] Steptoe himself, despairing over the 1858 defeat and his prolonged illness, resigned his commission in 1861. He retired to his native Lynchburg, Virginia, and died in 1865 without seeing action during the Civil War.

Robert Garnett, the Ft. Simcoe commander, capably served as adjutant general to General Lee. But Garnett had experienced personal tragedy before joining the Confederacy. Upon returning toward Ft. Simcoe in late September 1858 after leading the Okanogan campaign, Garnett heard the tragic news of his wife Marianna's recent death from fever, and that their infant son, Arthur, desperately clung to life. The child died within hours of Garnett's return. During the Civil War, Garnett was one of the first Confederate generals to fall.

Major Nathan Olney, Kamiakin's friend-turned-adversary, who served as both Indian agent and a soldier in the volunteers, was seriously wounded in the 1860s when an arrowhead lodged in his skull during a fight with Indians in Oregon. The projectile could not be removed, but Olney eventually resumed responsibilities in the Indian Service at Ft. Simcoe. While riding a horse near the fort in September 1866, he was thrown off and struck his head, dying instantly. Olney is buried just east of the parade grounds in one of only two burials still marked at the fort.

Chapter 7
Home in the Hills

When Rattlesnake and the Wolf Brothers
had killed Salmon Man,
they decided to travel back upriver.
The brothers were jealous
if anyone else was interested,
and wanted their sister.

She did much of the work.
She worked around their camp.
Rattlesnake had killed Salmon Man,
and did not return to his lodge.
He found a cave on a rocky cliff,
high above the river.
This became his home.

For several decades, Wolf Necklace ("Tilcoax
the Younger") refused to leave his father's
Palouse homeland where he tended vast herds
of horses in the livestock business.
WSU Libraries

*I*n the fall of 1858, while most Yakamas and Palouses
sought a return to normalcy on the Columbia Plateau,
those with Kamiakin and Tilcoax fled into the Bitterroot
Mountains. Tilcoax and some followers continued on to the
Great Plains, while Kamiakin, Skloom, Lokout, and others of
their fugitive band moved northward in Montana and toward
Canada. They arrived in the Pend d'Oreille country, but the
local Indians refused to help them, fearing punishment for
harboring hostiles. The outcasts remained despite the cold
reception, until some Indians stole one of their horses. The
disconsolate band then moved on to the Kutenais, north
of Flathead Lake. The Kutenais also were cool to the exiles,
refusing to allow them to settle there.[1]

Lacking horses, shelter, and food, Kamiakin's destitute
band, including his wives and children, and his brother,
Skloom, was "in a very hungry situation." In the meantime,
Father DeSmet speculated that Tilcoax, the "prime mover
in all the late wars," had fled to the Plains of Montana and
lived "among the Buffalo Nez Perces." According to family
accounts, he died there of natural causes in the early 1860s.[2]

From the Kutenai
country along the
U.S.-Canada border,
the refugees next traveled
a hundred miles south
to St. Ignatius Mis-
sion in the southern
Flathead Valley. Here,
the exiles met Father
Adrian Hoecken and
Chief Alexander of
the Kalispels, both of whom turned their backs on the band.
Hoecken knew of the troubles on the Plateau, and feared that
the Americans' anti-Catholic sentiment might extend to his
mission. Chief Alexander also wanted nothing to do with
Kamiakin. They ordered him to leave in spite of the desperate
situation of the women and children.

They continued farther south, toward the Bitterroot Valley
and the homeland of Chief Victor, a courageous and generous Flathead leader. They found sanctuary for the winter in

the Bitterroot Valley near today's Darby, Montana. None of the mountain tribes, however, wanted Kamiakin to remain in the region, because they feared White reprisals. Indeed, Kamiakin was an outcast and his people had no home.

Perhaps for the first time in his life, Kamiakin felt engulfed by despair. Long ago, T'siyiyak's Palouse relatives had spoken of an elder who remembered three days of cataclysm, when great billowing clouds of gray followed a shuddering peal of thunder from the southwest. The coolness of the day turned hot as the skies fell to earth in wafts of dry, foul-smelling snow. Since that time, dreams of doom had visited Plateau prophets. They told their people that changes brought by newcomers soon would cause the world to "fall to pieces."[3]

Entire Hopelessness

Such dire warnings had peculiar similarities in the doctrines of the Protestant missionaries, such as Samuel Parker and William Gray, whom Kamiakin befriended upon their arrival in the region years earlier. These stern men had opposed the teachings of the blackrobes, and preached a message of cataclysm, culminating in confrontation between the forces of good and evil. This great contest would vindicate their righteous beliefs, and usher in a thousand years of blessings for Christians throughout America and the world.

Kamiakin had not professed belief in the millenarian pessimism of Parker and Gray or other prophets of doom. Yet the cruel realities that so recently and disastrously disoriented his world must have led him to reconsider all he had learned from tribal elders and the blackrobes, such as Pandosy. Here, beneath the snow-capped peaks of the Northern Rockies, he seemed to exist in another dimension, with little hope of restoring any semblance of his former life. Kamiakin played over in his mind the tragic sequence of recent events. He knew there could have been no restraining Qualchan and Tilcoax's fervent passions. But others, such as Owhi and Skloom, had been persuaded to take up arms in great measure because of Kamiakin. Initially, he had no way of knowing about Owhi's sorrowful death, but likely assumed the worst, given Qualchan's fate.

Skloom shivered nearby in their make-shift camp, where the tiny remnant of the once proud Star Brother chiefs clung to survival—aliens in a hostile landscape. Now, Kamiakin's demoralized band was forced to live not far from the Crows, a Plains tribe facing the restrictions of reservation life in Montana. Following their eventual confinement, these proud Plains people came to have an expression for their former life

of freedom on wild landscapes fashioned by the Great Mystery: *"Back when there was time."*

Kamiakin groped for answers. Near their camp, the local Salish's sacred Big Horn's Medicine Tree offered evidence of another trial. For generations, the massive ponderosa pine towering above the river bank had been an object of reverence and offerings. A bighorn sheep's skull was embedded in the tree near its base, witness to a legendary role in the past. During the Animal People time, Bighorn Sheep charged the trunk, betraying to Coyote that he was a threat to the existence of The People, who soon would be coming. As the fearsome creature struggled to free its horns, Coyote slew the beast and announced: "In time this tree will be a place to leave offerings, thanks, and prayers for well-being and good fortune." In Kamiakin's day, gifts of colored beads, cloth, and feathers adorned the trunk and his family likely contributed their own offerings.[4]

Through the strength of his guardian spirit and the God in whose name he had baptized his children, Kamiakin awaited his fate with dignity, trusting in powers beyond his own as he moved through the vortex of a changing world, from ancient to modern. He would not despair over prophecies about the end of time, either born in titanic Cascades volcanism or the interpretations of Holy Writ. As another expatriate, Father Pandosy, had taught: "Even if grace was the only thing we had, we would have everything,…and this invisible grace will sustain." Kamiakin's meditations turned to themes of deliverance as he sought anew to safeguard his children's future. Hope unexpectedly came to the forlorn band's wintry mountain camp from a voice Kamiakin found familiar and trustworthy.

In late winter 1859, the Jesuit pathfinder, Father Pierre Jean DeSmet, entered Kamiakin's camp on horseback, surely lifting the chief's spirits with his characteristic grin and a hearty greeting. Writing from the Sacred Heart Mission soon after the war, DeSmet had proposed to the newly appointed Columbia Department commander, William S. Harney, that the general offer an olive branch to the refugee chiefs, including Kamiakin. Harney had made a thorough study of events in the long conflict and realized that responsibility rested on all sides—civilian and military, as well as Indian. Moreover, without hereditary chiefs of standing, such as Kamiakin, conditions among the Plateau tribes were in ferment and far from placid. Harney then sought to meet with a delegation of leaders, designated by his own advisors, of persons deeply experienced in regional Indian affairs. DeSmet joined in recommending a reconsideration of Kamiakin's status and

Tespaloos Kamiakin (1858–1933), born during the final year of the Plateau wars.
WSU Libraries

Harney had consented in a letter written on New Year's Day, 1859.[5]

With usual fortitude and perseverance, DeSmet ventured forth with Father Joset into the Bitterroot Mountains in February, finally learning from other Indians in hiding where Kamiakin was sequestered. DeSmet, while being hospitably received by various Indians, including Palouses, lamented their "state of entire hopelessness" during his long arduous journeying. Nevertheless, DeSmet was additionally shocked by the sight of Kamiakin's camp, where the chief and his followers resided in appalling conditions, destitute of adequate food and shelter in the brunt of severe weather.

"The sight of Kamiakin's children, poverty, and misery in which I found them, drew abundant tears from my eyes," the missionary wrote in his report to military authorities. "Kamiakin, the once powerful chieftain, who possessed thousands of cattle, has lost all, and is now reduced to abject poverty." But the exiles warmly welcomed the weary blackrobe. Kamiakin offered to counsel with DeSmet.[6]

Military and Agency Overtures

Into the spring, DeSmet conducted visits to Kamiakin's austere camp in the Bitterroot country. Kamiakin and Skloom listened to the blackrobe and responded "with greatest apparent earnestness," but were divided over whether or not to risk returning to their homeland. Kamiakin declared he "never was a murderer, and, whenever he could, he restrained his people against all violent attacks on Whites passing through the country." He conveyed to DeSmet that the Indians wanted "the path of peace."

The peripatetic priest concluded that if Kamiakin were "allowed to return…to his country, it will have the happiest and most salutary effect among the Indian tribes."[7]

After weeks of discussions with DeSmet and among themselves, Kamiakin and others agreed to return and meet with government officials. On the eve of their April 16

departure, Flathead Agent and trader John Owen falsely insinuated to DeSmet that he had been delegated by the commissioner of Indian affairs to bring in the chiefs. With horses eventually supplied by Spokan Garry—Kamiakin's mounts were in too poor condition—a delegation consisting of Kamiakin, DeSmet, Owen, the Kalispel chiefs Victor and Alexander, Red Feather of the Flatheads, and others crossed the Bitterroots to the Spokane Valley, reaching Ft. Walla Walla on May 13, 1859.[8]

After arriving at the post, DeSmet shortly left for Ft. Vancouver to meet with General Harney and the chiefs remained with John Owen. Kamiakin, while in camp with the other Indian leaders at Ft. Walla Walla, learned of Owen's meddling and disputes. Rumors also spread that local Whites planned to hang Kamiakin.

Indeed, Walla Walla and The Dalles were rough and tumble frontier towns, where even White newcomers often were at risk. In 1860, an Englishman, Charles Wilson, writing with some hyperbole, found Walla Walla inhabited by "miners, gamblers, loafers & rowdies of the very worst description," while the "new El Dorado" of The Dalles was a place of nighttime "free fights," where "everyone draws a revolver and shoots away as hard as he can, on which occasions there is generally a large loss of life." The rambunctious river settlement was "a most strange place and a very motley crowd live in it; American officers, trappers in their buckskin, regular wild men of the plains who…obey no laws but their own inclinations, Jewish pedlars…hard featured Yankees…wagon teamsters, muleteers, Canadian voyageurs…all jumbled up together, with a sprinkling of Indians on their wild horses galloping about."

Shortly, Kamiakin disappeared. Major Lugenbeel at the Army's newly established Harney Depot in the Colville country reported: "Kamiakin was scared away from Walla Walla by Timothy and other Nez Perce chiefs." Memories of the fates of Piupiu Maksmaks and Owhi after agreeing to council with Whites also may have influenced Kamiakin's thinking. To Harney's great disappointment, Kamiakin had quietly slipped away. When the general and DeSmet learned the circumstances of his departure, neither held the chief to blame. Harney heaped scorn upon Agent Owen's "officious interference."[9]

In light of the "prejudice and ill will felt toward" Kamiakin by "many misinformed and evil disposed persons," recently appointed Yakama Indian Agent Richard Lansdale at Ft. Simcoe appealed to Commissioner Edward Geary to provide for the chief's protection. Landsdale also advised that officials insist he not "remain more than a few hours in any of the settlements, lest injury might befall him." But Lansdale also expressed optimism that Kamiakin would be returning to his people in the Yakima Valley in August.[10]

Skloom, whose health was nearly broken from the recurrent travesties of war and exile, also may have returned west at this time. He was living in the Yakima Valley the following year, as was Showaway, whose son, Mushíil, was killed in 1859 in retribution for Agent Bolon's murder. Kamiakin, however, rejoined his huddled band under cold skies in Montana, residing on the Bitterroot and Clark Fork rivers, before moving north to hunt in remote regions of the Canadian borderlands. They resided in make-shift camps, where the women dried meat and tanned hides for tipis, clothing, and moccasins.

The hunters likely noticed that the buffalo herds were noticeably diminished since the days of "going to buffalo," in the time of Wiyáwiikt and Sulkstalkscosum. Was the great denizen of the Plains that so recently thundered in herds of millions also destined for oblivion? Surely Kamiakin pondered the Indians' plight, shared with this living expression of his spirit power. Would his people also be reduced to *kow-tol-iks*, "bones scattered about"?

For many months, the prospect of harm to himself and his family probably dissuaded Kamiakin from returning to his homeland. The Kamiakins chose to remain in the mountains, but, by the summer of 1860, they did move to the Lake Coeur d'Alene vicinity, where Indians had been allies during the recent conflict and where trusting relationships were reestablished with Catholic missionaries. Throughout their mountain exile, Kamiakin's band remained unbothered by the Army or territorial militia. No expeditions had pursued them, so they had gradually drifted westward. But Kamiakin's initial effort to reestablish a horse herd was dashed when a member of Garry's band, learning of the chief's return, stole some thirty head including a stallion.[11]

Kamiakin likely did not hold Garry responsible for the actions of others. His longtime friend had fought alongside him against the Army, and the Spokanes faced similar challenges in the wake of the growing American presence. Both men visited Ft. Colvile in mid July 1861. Garry did not conceal his antipathies to Americans in the presence of trader McDonald. Charles Wilson, an eloquent British diarist assigned to the international boundary commission survey, was residing in the area that summer. He noted that Garry had "a prominent part in the late Indian war with the Americans & hates them…with some reason, for all his immense bands of horses & cattle were killed by them & he has been reduced from opulency for an Indian to perfect beggary."

Wilson also was struck by the arrival of "Kamiakin, the great war chief…the heart & soul of the last war against the Americans & a finer looking fellow & more graceful rider I never saw." To the 24-year-old Englishman, the legendary leader about whom the traders whispered did not resemble a vanquished foe. Kamiakin looked "very formidable," and approached the enclave in "war costume & fully armed," yet no incidents took place.

Meanwhile, four companies of U.S. infantry were assigned just fourteen miles to the southeast at the new Army depot, with the duty of protecting and supporting boundary commission workers to the north. The surveyors labored for months, cutting a twenty-foot swath through the thick forests along the 49th parallel and setting stone monuments indicating the border between Canada and the United States. News of this joint U.S.-British venture may have finally put to rest any lingering hope in Kamiakin's mind that international negotiations might have ceded lands north of the Columbia to the more amendable British.[12]

Kamiakin had no direct contact with any government officials until the summer of 1860, when he met Richard Lansdale from the Yakima Agency. Lansdale sought out Kamiakin, asking him to assume "the chieftainship of the confederated tribes," as stipulated by the Yakima Treaty of 1855. The chief would receive "a full amnesty" and liberal benefits, including a home, farm, and an annual $500 stipend. Lansdale needed firm Indian leadership to bring order to the new reservation. In the spring, he had launched an ambitious plan to show Indians the benefits of agriculture by setting out 300 fruit trees near the agency, planting grain fields, and reintroducing cattle from Oregon. The irony of the proposal may have raised the chief's eyebrows, as Kamiakin advocated agrarian pursuits years earlier. Kamiakin refused Lansdale's offer and said his band did not recognize the treaty.

The disappointed Lansdale returned to the reservation and did not press the matter further with Kamiakin. The Klickitat leader Spencer was then appointed to serve as chief until a tribal election could be held. In 1861, reservation voters selected White Swan (Joe Stwire) as head chief. Meanwhile, W.B. Gosnell soon replaced Lansdale after charges of fraud were filed against the latter. The new agent encountered a host of problems in the absence of stronger tribal leadership and because of recurrent government delays in delivering annuities and supplies.

The situation grew worse under the incompetence of Gosnell's successor, Ashley Bancroft (brother of historian Hubert H. Bancroft), which led to threats of resignation from agency schoolteacher James Wilbur and physician S.H. Roberts. A force to be reckoned with, Wilbur steadfastly sought honest means to introduce Indian youths to modernity through general education and religious instruction. Standing well over six feet tall and weighing some 300 pounds, the burly frontier teacher personally carried complaints to the Lincoln Administration in Washington, D.C., which led to Bancroft's dismissal and Wilbur's assignment as agent in 1864.[13]

Kamiakin had been periodically apprised about "the condition of affairs" in his yet troubled Yakama homeland through his first wife, Sunk-hay-ee, daughter of Chief Teias, who appears to have occasionally visited the reservation to tend to her ailing father and also visit with her sister and brother-in-law, Josephine and James Yemowit. Meanwhile, Skloom had returned to reside in the valley, before dying of natural causes at his camp near the Cascade mill on February 1, 1861. (According to Splawn, his remains were later reburied near Toppenish Creek in the vicinity of Ft. Simcoe.)

During Gosnell's tenure as agent, he had spoken with Sunk-hay-ee about a renewed offer for Kamiakin to return and even live at his old home on the Ahtanum. The resolute chief, however, refused to reside on any reservation. The exchange, however, provided the agent with insights into the chief's circumstances. "The character of Kamiakin is, I am afraid, not generally understood. Though he went to war with the whites, yet his whole course was marked by a nobleness of mind that would have graced the General of a civilized nation—he never harmed the women and children of settlers, or waylaid the lone traveler, but has been in many instances their protector."

The leading advocate for Native sovereignty was derided by many Indians for his actions in causing the war and the subsequent complete submission of the tribes. But Gosnell knew the naysayers would be wise to recognize that, in spite of ultimate battlefield defeat, Kamiakin's stature alone at the Walla Walla Council had been influential, if not the decisive factor, in Stevens' decision to set aside lands for the region's largest Indian reservations at that time.[14]

Return to the Crossing

Assurances by Ft. Simcoe officials that they sought to maintain peace encouraged Kamiakin. He also received similar messages from Father DeSmet and Spokan Garry. Some tribesmen, however, expressed their concerns over the prospect of Kamiakin's return. At a council attended by Spokane and Coeur d'Alene leaders, where "arguments waxed warm,"

Kil-mo-see, possibly Slowiarchy, headman at *Palus*, rose to Kamiakin's defense: "He has done no more than what we did in fighting for our country, except that he refused to surrender, which is to his credit. He was my friend all through the war. Now I will be his. He will go with me to my home. If the soldiers want him, they will know where to find him. I and my tribe will be responsible, not you."[15]

Buoyed by such expressions, Kamiakin returned to the land of his Palouse father to raise his family and live in peace. Like the other chiefs, Kamiakin understood that conditions were fundamentally different. The seasonal rounds and tribal interactions that had guided their peoples' lives for centuries were now shifting. They could not hope that the vast prairies and forest lands would remain beyond American exploitation. Yet, in 1860, not a single permanent American resident lived between the Snake River and the Colville Valley. Not for long, however, as settlement across these broad areas would become the focus of what British surveyor Wilson characterized as the "wonderful wandering mania of the Anglo-Saxon race."

The Kamiakins could have moved to *Palus*, but instead the chief chose to settle again at sheltered and remote "Kamiak's Crossing" along the Palouse River. Here, family members searched in vain for enormous hemp *wápas* bags, which before hostilities in 1858 had been filled with provisions and belongings, and then cached. Nearly two years of mountain exile and wandering had taken an emotional toll on everyone—now they could not find their buried dried foods, beaded buckskin finery, and other treasured heirlooms, which either had been looted, despoiled by animals, or lay hidden under resurgent prairie grass and vegetation. The men and older boys soon turned their attention to setting up lodges and corrals, while the women gathered roots and berries and mended clothing.[16]

Earlier, in July 1859, topographer Theodore Kolecki and two companions assigned to John Mullan's road building project rode past this strategic location on the Palouse River. Mullan had dispatched them east from the Union Flat Creek-Palouse River confluence vicinity to explore several potential routes across the central Palouse. Meanwhile, Mullan continued northeast to "Sil-sil-cep-pow-vetsin," or Rock Creek, at Hole-in-the-Ground. The term Mullan used for Rock Creek likely was derived from a Coeur d'Alene name, *Slslpsp'uɫtsn*, or "Foam Swirling on the Water."[17] The surveyor marveled at the spectacular clarity of the prairie sky at night, rendering moons of Jupiter and Saturn visible without the aid of a telescope.

As Kolecki had proceeded east, he recorded, in his microscopic handwriting, a dramatic deepening of the Palouse River canyon, where rocky bluffs four to five hundred feet high shielded Kamiak's Crossing. Adjacent bottomlands were "extremely fertile, covered with tall grass, cottonwood groves, and wild currant bushes." The threesome continued several more miles upstream through "increasingly beautiful scenery," to stay overnight at the main Spokane (Kentuck) Trail crossing, where they encountered a friendly but unidentified camp of Indians.

On July 8, the three men decided to climb Steptoe Butte, enabling Kolecki to pen the first account of an ascent of the "steep and rocky cone" they called Pyramid Peak. By the setting sun's last rays, the surveyors viewed the vast countryside, from the Blue Mountains to the Bitterroots, describing the Palouse Hills as a vast "rolling prairie, very much resembling a stormy sea."[18]

Kamiakin, of course, had developed a love for gardening before the war, and now found great pleasure again in raising corn, potatoes, and other vegetables near the crossing. His family fished, hunted, gathered roots and berries, collected wood, and tended livestock. They established their summer camp along the south side of the Palouse River, on a broad flat situated a short distance downstream from the ford. Here, Kamiakin's sons fashioned a race course, where they rode the finest horses from a family herd they endeavored to restore. Like the meanderings of the region's free-flowing rivers, however, Kamiakin's family could not be fixed in any single place throughout the year. They again followed a seasonal round in accordance with ancient patterns, but leading to some new destinations.

Annual spring trips led northwest to the stony environs of T'siyiyak's Place to gather nutritious bitterroot, and continued east to the black earth prairies along upper Rock and Latah creeks to dig camas. During one of these treks to *Ni'lukhwaqw* in 1862, Colestah gave birth to her first child, a son, Tomeo. The Kamiakins joined others in fishing along the lower Spokane River and at Latah Creek, amidst the sweet pungency of blossoming riparian flora. In autumn, family members often ventured south to gather berries and hunt along the Snake River and in the foothills of the Blue Mountains.[19]

As in bygone days, Kamiakin instructed his sons after they killed their first game of the season to offer prayers of thanksgiving; first sharing their bounty with others before taking for themselves. Stalking fleet-footed creatures among the pines and grasses required patience and skill. The story of a boy's first success was told and retold in detail around the campfire,

along with expressions of the people's oneness with nature and its bounty. At their Palouse camp, the women might tend to the weeklong process of *elum-kshtsh* ("smoking yellow")—splitting, treating, and smoking the hides of deer and elk. The men and boys treated and preserved the pelts of smaller fur-bearing animals such as marten and otter.

As winter approached, they moved camp about a half-mile upstream, to a small knoll overlooking the northeast side of the river.[20] The first pioneers settling in the vicinity—Joseph DeLong, and the families of Missouri natives John and Preston Matlock, who sought a new start after the Civil War—came to know the locale as *Kumtux*, Chinook jargon for "Place of Understanding."

From high bluffs surrounding Kamiakin's camp, the sacred summit of *Yáamuštas* (Elk's Abode) was clearly visible far to the east. (The Sahaptin term literally refers to mule deer, but in myth it also is associated with Elk.) The lone promontory known to Whites as Pyramid Peak, and later Steptoe Butte, had long been a "power mountain" to Native peoples. Kamiakin directed his children to its rocky summit for their spirit quests, where seekers found many-colored stone offerings of exquisite beauty.

According to Palouse lore, the butte provided sanctuary to Elk and the Wolf Sister, married in the time of the Animal People. But her ravenous Wolf Brothers sought to kill their new brother-in-law for eloping with a member of their family. At a later time, an Indian prophet told the people that *Náami Piap* was sending a great flood because they had neglected to honor sacred ways. They were told to flee to the summit to escape the deluge and those heeding his counsel were saved. Perhaps Kamiakin's children heard these and other stories from ancient *walsa'kwit* lore, accompanied by wistful music from one of the family's heirloom instruments, including a foot-long copper flute, and another one of five holes made from an eagle's legbone.[21]

Kamiakin also honored Christian ways, which he had learned when Pandosy and the blackrobes settled among his people. He knew of the blackrobes' feast-days and holy rites, which had been impossible for the chief to observe during the recent chaotic times. He wished for his children to follow the Catholic faith. From the early 1860s, he periodically took his family to upper Hangman Creek prairie, visited by Father Joset and other priests from Sacred Heart. The Jesuit's main mission stood east of Lake Coeur d'Alene, but Kamiakin was reluctant to venture to a place standing alongside Mullan's new thoroughfare.

He preferred to visit the priests at the verdant *Ni'lukhwaqw* root grounds, about two miles west of present-day Tensed, where area Indians had long gathered in June and July to dig camas and race horses. On these annual spring treks to gather roots, the family sometimes visited Qualchan's hillock gravesite, overlooking the quiet stream named by some for his tragic fate. As the women lay strips of colored cloth and lupine blossoms to honor the warrior's memory, Kamiakin would tell the story of Qualchan's sacrifice to the children.

They also dug bitterroot at T'siyiyak's Place east of Sprague Lake, where the children's grandfather lay buried. The occasion often prompted Kamiakin to narrate his father's fabled exploits to the children. Such memorials also offered opportunity to impart important spiritual lessons. They came to understand that, however keen the sense of loss, upon the release of an elder's spirit the surrounding trees, bushes, and flowers offered a sacred and joyful song of welcome from the Earth Mother to a person's mortal remains.[22]

During the last week of November 1861, Kamiakin joined in the celebration of St. Andrew's Feast and the first day of Advent by having his five youngest children baptized, since administering this rite previously was impossible after the family left the Ahtanum. Perhaps Kamiakin drew some assurance from Joset's message about the heroic struggles of St. Andrew, Christ's first apostle, who would not bend to the brutalities of the Roman authorities. One by one, his four youngest sons and newborn daughter, Kiatana, were baptized that day, probably with the oldest Kamiakin son We-yet-que-wit—Joset's "Xavier Chamayakan"—serving as godfather. As other children were born, they, too, would be presented for baptism.

On July 13, 1866, at the baptism of another Kamiakin infant son at *Ni'lukhwaqw*, Father Joseph Caruana named the boy Andrew, possibly in honor of the great saint. About 1867, Wal-luts-pum gave birth to her fourth and last son, Sk'olumkee—later known to Whites as "Snake River Kamiakin." The popularity of the upper Latah Creek spring-time camas grounds led the Coeur d'Alene priests to erect a log chapel there by 1874, on a prairie swale near the tree line overlooking the vast meadow.[23]

As Kamiakin's band slowly recovered and their lives stabilized, fierce Indian-White clashes persisted south of the Blue

Sohon's 1855 sketch of the Tenino chief, Stáquthly, known to Whites as Stockwhitely.
Washington State Historical Society

Mountains in eastern Oregon, where Paiute and Snake raids on pioneer outposts led to a long series of campaigns by troops coming from The Dalles and Ft. Walla Walla. The Army recruited numerous Indian scouts from the Plateau tribes, who were traditional adversaries of the warring bands. In May 1864, Kamiakin's old ally, Stáquthly of the Teninos, was killed when fighting Paiutes near Canyon City.

In that same year, while Kamiakin resided at the river crossing, Agent Bancroft dispatched "two reliable Indians," Tuichalt and Minote, from the Yakima Agency on a three-week trip to offer Kamiakin and his people blankets, provisions, and "a lot of other goods" worth $150. They left May 9, carrying the agent's pledge that should Kamiakin be "faithful to the interests of the Ind. Dept.," he would receive a house, farm, and $500 annual salary. Kamiakin kindly received this delegation, as he did all such overtures, but refused to accept gifts from the government representatives.[24]

However, the appointment of Rev. James Wilbur, schoolteacher and Methodist pastor, as Yakima agent in 1864 brought an end to official proposals to Kamiakin. "Father" Wilbur sought to break up the Indians' adherence to the "old ways," represented by the legendary chief. Consequently, Wilbur promoted Methodist converts as leaders, such as Chief White Swan.

In January 1865, frontier packers Tom Beall and Bob Emery left Lewiston, risking a winter trek through deep snow to deliver much needed supplies to the Spokane Valley. The pair traveled with two Indian guides who led them down the Snake River to *Alamótín*. They then took a trail north to the Palouse River, finding "Kamiaken's camp." Beall noted "about eight or ten Indians" remained with Kamiakin at a time when most of the area's non-reservation Indians sought warmer climes and winter fellowship in villages along the Snake River. Before continuing north to the Rock Lake area where they struck the Mullan Road, Beall most likely did not divulge his role as one of Qualchan's executioners under Colonel Wright.[25]

Relocation to Rock Lake

About 1865, Kamiakin and his youngest wife, Colestah, had a child whom they named Tomomolow. The birth of this boy caused great rejoicing in Kamiakin's camp, as the infant was another son by the chief's warrior-woman wife. In the months that followed, Tomomolow grew in strength, but the mother's health failed. Revered as a medicine woman and healer, Colestah seemed powerless to cure herself. Kamiakin's favorite wife—who delighted the children by transforming huckleberries into glass beads, and the woman who fought alongside the chief in the Four Lakes and Spokane Plains battles—soon died, and was buried at the river camp.

Kamiakin grieved deeply, withdrawing into himself and refusing to eat or talk. Only Yumasepah, the second-oldest daughter with delicate features and intense eyes, could comfort him. The older sons encouraged their father to resettle north at another ancestral camp on Rock Lake, where they hoped to escape the sorrow of Colestah's passing. The brothers also wished to avoid the increasing number of White travelers on the Palouse Trail, who used the nearby ford during their forays in the region.

Kamiakin finally consented. The family moved to the western edge of a broad flat on the southeast shore of Rock Lake near the creek outlet. The new camp, nestled among scattered pines, became known as Kamiak's Hollow, an extension of the broader Kamiak's Flat. (An insequent canyon stream to the southeast was later named Kamiacan Creek by Whites.) Kamiakin directed his sons to fell trees nearby to build a log home, in which his substantial family resided during the warm summer months. The winter camp was located a short distance east up the canyon to afford better protection from inclement winds.[26]

Life for the Columbia Plateau peoples had seen periodic alteration ever since Kamiakin heard reports of Lewis and Clark's arrival, but now the rate of cultural change was accelerating. Before the 1860s, only traders consistently traversed through the hills, "an immense tract of splendid country." After Wright's campaign, however, additional Whites eyed the region. John Mullan and numerous others recognized the fertility of the Palouse soil and speculated about the day when it would be cultivated.

In 1858, Lt. Lawrence Kip wrote prophetically: "The time is not far distant when settlers will begin to occupy it, and the farmer will discover that he can reap his harvest…without danger from their former savage foe." Such was the essence of America's philosophy of Manifest Destiny—to expand from shore to shore, and to spread White American culture.[27]

Still, a few years would pass before significant numbers of settlers moved on to lands north of the Snake River to raise livestock and crops. Meanwhile, Indian agents did not converge on the dispersed Indian camps, nor order an immediate removal to reservations. That would come after the American Civil War, when a new wave of Blue and Gray veterans and their families began claiming homesteads and started farming the rich Palouse soil.

The Kamiakins' first years at Rock Lake were relatively pleasant, except for the abiding concern about future White encroachment north of the Snake. Once again the family experienced nature's rhythms, seasonally gathering roots and berries, and catching salmon on the Snake and Columbia. They planted sizeable gardens of corn, beans, and potatoes near the lake and maintained a small herd of black beef cattle and milk cows. The men hunted abundant deer and small game in the surrounding bunchgrass coulees, which blossomed each spring with delicate pale green rein orchids and mauve mariposa lilies, along with sunflowers, larkspur, hyacinth, and blue swaths of camas. Red-winged blackbirds inhabited the shoreline willows, arriving to nest several weeks earlier than their more aggressive yellow-headed cousins, who gave out similar songs of guttural prattle.

Family members fished for trout in Rock Lake, a long body of water noted for its prodigious depth, thus called *Tax'líit* and *Limek' Kúus* (Deep Water). A favorite fishing place was along the transparent brook feeding into the lake from the north, and at a small waterfall farther upstream. Along the stony ledges at these sites, they speared ample quantities of *xúlxul* throughout the year, while eagles sometimes swooped down to join in the catch. According to tribal lore, a giant water creature (*Papúumus*) lived in the lake and once devoured a canoe carrying three Indian women. The tale seemed to explain the sudden swirls of wind and waves that often assail those venturing upon the water, and may suggest why White settlers later called it Spectre Lake.

The mysteries of the place did not deter Kamiakin from taking morning baths in the pristine waters. The legend of the lake was one of many stories Kamiakin shared with his daughters and sons. Although the children's mothers were native Sahaptin speakers, Kamiakin's upbringing had allowed him to know both Sahaptin and Interior Salish dialects. This fact, and the Rock Lake camp's close proximity to the Spokane and Coeur d'Alene country, led to the children being fluent in both languages.[28]

Cavalcades and Cowboys

Kamiakin's love of sharing tales about Coyote, Salmon Man, and Blue Jay contrasted with his stoic response to inquiries from his children about the war years. The questions they sometimes posed to their elders could prompt a dark brooding in their father and reduce their mothers' happy talk to silent sobs. Yumasepah and We-yet-que-wit had been old enough to experience deprivations firsthand during the war and mountain exile. Whatever private thoughts and disappointments Kamiakin harbored, the other children might well have imagined what they were and shared them. When the family camped with other bands, the children heard curses hurled against their father in the drunken rages of other men. They also were aware of recurrent threats made by some Whites, who still held the chief responsible for the killing of miners in the Yakima Valley and Palouse Hills.

The oldest son, We-yet-que-wit or "Young Kamiakin," began regularly accompanying his father, providing personal protection when the chief ventured into the countryside beyond Rock Lake. Kamiakin's abiding concern for his family's well-being restricted his movements—he never again traveled to Oregon and Montana, or places that were beyond close proximity to his wives and children. During the chief's infrequent appearances in frontier settlements, such as at Sprague and Spokane Falls, Kamiakin rode in a cavalcade of a half-dozen or more young men, and sometimes carried a large horse pistol in a beaded holster, hanging from the saddle of his blue dun stallion.[29]

On a rain swept day in 1865, two White strangers on horseback approached the Rock Lake camp. Andrew Splawn and Willis Thorp, young ranch hands returning to the Kittitas Valley after a cattle drive, had veered off the main road, becoming lost in the western Palouse. Thorp was ill after the wet night. They met an aged Indian, who agreed to guide them eighteen miles west to get supplies at the hamlet of Sprague.

"On our way we talked and found him very interesting," Splawn recalled in a history and memoir he later published about life on the Northwest frontier. "But when we happened to say that we were going to Yakima, his eyes flashed fire, he seemed to take on new life." The guide now "wanted to know all about the white settlements and all the prominent Indians we knew, saying that they were his friends and that he had once lived above the mission on the Ahtanum."

The cowboys remained unaware of their guide's identity until the storekeeper at Sprague greeted Kamiakin by name. Splawn was dumbfounded: "I quickly asked if he had once been chief of the Yakimas."

Splawn continued: "For a moment he was silent: then, with proud mien, he stood erect and said, 'Yes.' Once, he said, his horses could be counted by the thousands and his

cattle grazed many hills. He had fought for his country until his warriors were all dead or had left him…. 'There is no more war,' he said. 'I wish to live in peace until the Great Spirit calls me to take the long trail….' And he rode off, head bowed."

The two young men were struck by the aura of one who had greatly suffered. This peculiar incident contributed to Splawn's decision many years later to write a substantial history of the Yakama Indians in *Ka-Mi-Akin: The Last Hero of the Yakimas* (1917), based on Splawn's own experiences and extensive oral accounts from Indians. Kamiakin's resolve to live in peace while overlooking the bitterness of past indignities and mistakes was similarly reflected in a newspaper article published several years later, characterizing the chief's plight as a "voluntary exile" in which he sought "to live in peace with all the world."[30]

Regional Indians traditionally traveled about a great deal locally. From Rock Lake, Kamiakin ventured each year to the Spokane Valley and the Coeur d'Alene root grounds, where the chief and some several dozen of his followers frequently camped among towering pines. On one occasion when the family was with a band of Nez Perces at *Tekam*, the "Falls" of the Spokane River, Kamiakin freed Askolumkee, or Atween, the family slave. Askolumkee then joined other bands, and subsequently took part in the 1877 Nez Perce War.[31]

In May 1870, Kamiakin's band joined Spokanes, Coeur d'Alenes, and others on Latah Creek to discuss matters of mutual interest concerning the growing number of Whites in the region. Some traders sold bad liquor to Indians, and rustlers stole Indian horses and cattle. White ranchers were preempting the choicest grazing lands and watering holes, and some were denying Indians access to them. The government also reneged on some promises, particularly a guarantee to compensate Indians for improvements on properties they lost, and in preventing White activities from encroaching on Indian-occupied lands. Outraged at events accumulating over a decade, some younger men advocated armed revolt. Tribal elders, veterans of the fighting against Wright, opposed outright hostilities, frequently weeping when younger people spoke of war.[32]

Shortly after the council, Indians met with Farmer-in-Charge George Harvey of the recently established Colville Indian Agency. Harvey ostensibly summoned the Indians to hear their concerns, but in truth, to tender their favor. When they met Harvey at *Tceliyutum*, the agent denounced Industrial Instructor W.P. Winans at the agency. During the council, Harvey asked the Indian leaders to sign a petition asking

Superintendent of Indian Affairs Samuel Ross to appoint Harvey as the sole agent of the Colville Reservation.

According to a report by Winans, Harvey told the Indians: "The Whites have been abusing you. They will drive you to the mountain tops. They will make slaves of you, use you like horses and cattle, make you pull your own plows. This land is your land, and you are being robbed of it."[33]

About this time, Kamiakin's favored young son by Colestah drowned in Latah Creek. Tomomolow was entrusted to wife Hos-ke-la-pum, who had taken the boy to swim in the stream that settlers were calling Hangman Creek. While playing in the water, his sister pushed him. The boy perished in the current, a grim reminder of another death along Latah Creek years earlier. Kamiakin temporarily banished Hos-ke-la-pum, though she soon returned and gave birth to the chief's last son, Piupiu K'ownot ("Bird of the Morning"), born in 1870. Kamiakin delighted in the presence of the boy, soon presenting him for baptism at Sacred Heart where he was given the English name "Peter."[34]

Agent Winans' Blankets

Harvey's fiery oratory had moved some Indian leaders to sign his petition (the Palouses, however, refused). A number of the non-treaty Indians tried to use the situation to their advantage and were "anxious to negotiate a treaty," establishing a separate reserve for themselves. Chiefs Seltice, Tonasket, and Garry all signed the petition in hoping to secure their own separate reservation through Harvey's influence. But Kamiakin and the Palouses refused to go along. They chose to avoid embroilment in an internal administrative fight within the Office of Indian Affairs. Harvey's attempts to rally Indians for his support failed; William Park Winans received the appointment.

In the fall of 1870, Winans set out to "make a tour of observation" among the Indians. Harvey's earlier counciling, however, clearly had born bitter fruit, since many Indians received the

new agent with indifference. McDonald, who still tended waning Ft. Colvile, had added to Winans' anxieties when telling the agent, "indications point strongly to an Indian war."

During one of the councils, Indians refused to recognize Winans, and the agent was "annoyed and hindered in every possible way." Finding most of the chiefs insolent, Winans solicited Superintendent T.J. McKenny's assistance to secure the intervention of "Kam-i-ac-um, the leading spirit in the last Indian war." McKenny, in turn, referred the matter to the secretaries of Interior and War in Washington, D.C.[35]

Winans was authorized to offer Kamiakin an unconditional gift of 350 blankets and other supplies, as "dues withheld him by other Superintendents," and he also had McKenny's pledge that Kamiakin "could do as he pleased, live where it suited him best so long as he remained peaceable." Winans took wagons carrying twenty bales of blankets to the chief's Rock Lake camp in November 1870. Kamiakin was hospitable, but again refused to accept any gifts, fearing that government agents might claim he sold his lands.

Kamiakin told Winans: "I do not want to hurt the Superintendent's feelings but I cannot receive them. When all the Indians around here…receive presents and should there be any left, I will think about it."

Winans, seeing the sparse conditions at Rock Lake, tried to reason with the chief: "Other Indians have nothing to do with this matter." Since Kamiakin had been named head

Ft. Colvile in about 1863. Following U.S.-British negotiations, the Hudson's Bay Company finally abandoned the post in 1871, ending forty-six years of occupation.
WSU Libraries (Alexander Gardner 97-005)

chief of the Yakamas, he was entitled to such gifts. But the chief was unyielding.

"He listened silently to all I had to say," Winans later recalled, and then rose to extend his left arm while pointing with his right hand to the ragged sleeve of his gray woolen shirt. "I cannot receive them," he said with finality. "I am a poor man but I would rather have the Government indebted to me than to be indebted to the Government."[36]

During the conversation, when discussing provisions in the 1855 Walla Walla Treaty, Winans learned that Kamiakin had "concluded that he and his people had been deceived, lied to, and tricked in that treaty by the white men, who were rapidly coming on from the East…and taking their country."

Winans informed the chief of McKenny's orders for the delivery of blankets, telling him to "give them to whomever you please."

Kamiakin replied: "No! Neither I or my people will care for or use [them].… I will not receive them."

But the chief, in seeking conciliation, concluded by telling Winans, "I have a good heart to all white men. I am always pleased to see the Agents. I advised the Indians in council last summer not to make war. This is not the first time I have refused presents. I do not refuse them now to offend you."

Kamiakin and the agent parted friends. Winans left Rock Lake impressed with Kamiakin and his band's resilient resolve "to be independent of the government."[37]

Kamiakin's many relatives and other Indians continued to seek the venerated chief's counsel at his remote home. The Indian Service still believed that Kamiakin should take "no secondary part in any arrangements" for additional res-

ervations sought by Moses' Columbias and Spokan Garry's people. Tribal leaders, such as Garry and Andrew Seltice, periodically visited Rock Lake where they consulted with Kamiakin over matters concerning families and relatives, problems with White encroachment, and other issues. Kamiakin expressed high regard for the Spokanes and others who fought by his side in the late 1850s.

On special occasions, family members again wore their finery, which had been exquisitely crafted by the women. The wives wore necklaces of glass and copper beads with shell, deer hoof, bear bone, and eagle claw pendants. Kamiakin donned a red wool robe, with profusely beaded buffalo hide panels sewn with sinew, and further decorated with weasel tails, small copper bells, and colored feathers of forest birds. The chief's customary welcome to old friends opened with a solemn pipe-smoking ceremony, followed by feasting and deliberations. In this way, he kept keenly abreast of developments within Indian communities in all directions.[38]

Traveling between the Yakima Valley and the Coeur d'Alene Mission in the spring of 1873, Father Caruana visited the Rock Lake camp, where he would be asked to later pass greetings from "old Kamaiàkin Yakama Chief" to Father DeSmet. The blackrobe found Kamiakin "very old but stout," while also noting that the chief, and Moses too, had high regard for the Catholic missionaries. Caruana reported that Moses spurned the efforts of Protestants, such as Rev. Wilbur, still laboring among the Yakamas in the early 1870s. Whatever Kamiakin's views were regarding denominational disputes, he apparently did not voice them to the young Jesuit.[39]

Chapter 8
Deceived and Deserted

Rain fell for five days and five nights.
The little piece of Salmon Man
that fell during his death struggle
was carried down the river.
Life soon moved inside.
A smolt grew and began to swim.

Faraway it went and became stronger,
faraway beyond the mountains.
Young Chinook grew in the ocean.
One day he was ready to return home.
He brought the warm air
of the great waters.

hen the Civil War commenced with Abraham Lincoln's inauguration in 1861, Washington Territory had a population of approximately 12,000. (Many tribal peoples living along the lower Snake and Columbia rivers, however, frequently spurned the efforts of 19th century federal census takers, preventing an accurate counting of their numbers.) Not a single White settler resided in the vast undulating prairie north of the Snake River until 1862, when George Pangburn squatted on unsurveyed land not far from modern-day Endicott. The choice bottomland of Union Flat and Rebel Flat would draw the first settlers.

The nearby Palouses and these Whites lived in peace, as would a number of other early settlers and Indians who developed a mutual respect as neighbors. This was the case with Joseph DeLong, coming to Union Flat Creek in 1867. He soon moved to the Kamiak's Crossing vicinity, around the time Kamiakin's band relocated to Rock Lake where the chief would maintain cordial relations with DeLong and other Whites in the area.[1]

The growth of transportation routes across the Palouse in the 1860s greatly stimulated pioneer movement into the region. Previously, Whites followed timeworn Indian trails, but after the Indian wars, Lt. John Mullan surveyed the newly authorized military road linking Ft. Walla Walla with Ft. Benton, the upper terminus of steamboat traffic on the Missouri River. On the Columbia, the first "upriver" sternwheeler to operate above Celilo Falls was the *Colonel Wright*, launched in October 1858 at the mouth of the Deschutes and named for the Ninth Infantry commander. The 101-foot-long, shallow-draft vessel began its celebrated tenure by regularly hauling freight to the Army's Wallula depot. Packtrains then moved supplies to Ft. Walla Walla.

In the spring of 1860, high runoff enabled the *Colonel Wright* to venture over the treacherous rapids of the lower Snake to *Palus*, inaugurating Palouse Landing as a connection to the overland route to Ft. Colville. Later, captains Leonard White and Ephraim Baughman guided the *Colonel Wright* farther up the Snake to the Clearwater vicinity, where the new boomtown of Lewiston sprang up to serve the Idaho gold rush. At numerous places along the Snake, "the sound of the steam whistle and the pounding of the engines naturally attracted the attention of the Indians who flocked to the waters' edge to gaze on the wonderful fire-boat."[2] In the early 1860s, additional sternwheelers soon followed in the *Colonel Wright's* wake.

But not all Indians remaining on the Snake were pleased by the novelty of steam power. And some attempted to "retard" and "obstruct" Mullan's road building expeditions northeast toward the Bitterroots. Others such as Chief Slowiarchy, however, assisted the survey parties. The Palouse leader personally guided Gustavus Sohon in the summer of 1859, when surveys began in the Palouse country. Sohon proceeded to the timbered *Tatuna* highlands near present-day Moscow, before going farther north to chart a route in the Coeur d'Alene country.

Another survey party under topographical engineer P.M. Engle investigated the Snake River area. From the abandoned ruins of Ft. Taylor, Engle investigated upstream to the villages of the Upper Palouses. In this locality, he was surprised to find the Palouses and Nez Perces cultivating seven large farms, "amounting to from 300 to 400 acres." The Indians planted along the river banks and on some islands in the river. "Besides wheat and corn," Engle noted, "they raise vegetables of different kinds, and gain sufficient crops to encourage them in their labors." Although Engle judged the soil in the Snake canyon to be gravelly and sandy, he noted that "the plateaus on both banks produce fine grass, offering magnificent pasture grounds."[3]

Pioneer Trails and Outposts

Mullan's main survey group moved north from Ft. Walla Walla to the Snake River. One man was lost in fording the Snake, but the party continued working northeast through the Palouse Hills, meeting no Indians until crossing the Spokane Trail in the north. However, the Palouse Indians knew that soldiers were on their lands, planning to open a road. But the surveyors encountered no real difficulties.

In their reports, Sohon and Engle noted the fertility of the rolling bunchgrass hills, once grazed by vast herds of Indian horses. Mullan wrote: "The soil is mostly a black loam and will doubtless produce cereals and vegetables," and predicted it was "not at all improbable that the grazier and agriculturalist will find at no distant day tracts of land that will amply repay their reclamation."[4] Indeed, news of the fertile soil soon attracted Whites, who settled on Indian lands, in time gradually pushing most Palouses onto reservations.

As the Mullan Road's initial route was cleared in 1860, gold discoveries occurred in the Idaho mountains, and shortly thereafter in Montana in 1862. Mullan's route extended from the lower Palouse River northeast across the hills. After 1861, it crossed the Spokane River at Antoine Plante's ferry in the Spokane Valley, continuing north of Lake Coeur d'Alene to the Cataldo Mission, thus avoiding flooding hazards of the St. Joe watershed to the south.

Numerous fortune seekers soon were passing through the Palouse country. Several roadhouses as well as ferries were established along the trails to accommodate travelers. In 1859, Edward Massey had begun operating the "Palouse Ferry" (called Lyons Ferry after 1872), situated a mile below *Palus* where the Colville Road crossed the Snake. Ferry traffic became brisk in the early 1860s, with soldiers and civilians using the popular route. Palouse Landing also became a principal destination for sternwheelers of the Oregon Steam Navigation Company, which commanded a unified transportation system on the Columbia and Snake rivers from Portland. In 1864, Kellogg's Ferry began operating three miles above *Palus* near the mouth of the Tucannon, and a year later Taksas (later Texas) Ferry was established four miles upstream. Derivation of the name came from the Palouse word for the neighboring village, *Téksaspa*. Additional ferries would be established in the 1870s on other new roads near the Palouse villages of *Pinawáwih*, *Alamótín*, and *Wawáwih*, and at Central Ferry.[5]

In 1861, Canadian immigrant William Newman built a cabin near the head of Sprague Lake, at the junction of a branch of the White Bluffs Road from the Columbia and the Colville Road. His way-station served freighters, mail riders, and others. In 1865, Henry Wind opened another roadhouse farther south on the Colville Trail at present-day Benge on lower Cow Creek.

The first settler in the Palouse Hills, the aforementioned George Pangburn, claimed land in 1862 along lower Union Flat Creek south of present-day Endicott, near camas grounds frequented by Palouses. He established a small orchard, raised hogs, and planted small plots of wheat, corn, and oats. As other scattered farmers and ranchers arrived in the 1860s and early 1870s, Indian and White relations generally were friendly, but conflicts occasionally arose over ownership of unbranded livestock. In an effort to prevent these disputes, most Palouses eventually branded their animals. The Kamiakins used an "S" on the right jaw or shoulder of a horse; the Paweens a simple plus sign "+"; and the Poyahkins, a horizontal quarter moon. Among the Lower Palouses, Harlish Washomake (Wolf Necklace) skillfully revived herds noteworthy of those of his father, Tilcoax, and branded them with an open box "☐". The Jim family used a modified letter "J."[6]

Many of the White packers, miners, and soldiers traveling on Mullan's road and other newly developed routes recognized the region's agricultural potential. Increasing numbers of them would return to the Palouse Hills to establish farms and ranches alongside other new immigrants. The Homestead Act of 1862 offered free land to those settling on and "improving" claims on the public domain. Adult citizens could file for up to 160 acres, although lands "improved" by Indians were exempt from staking by homesteaders. Under the terms of the 1855 Walla Walla treaties, Indians were not required to remove to reservations until the government had paid them for their cabins, corrals, and fencing. With the government failing to compensate the Palouses, many Indians chose to remain on their traditional lands, ignoring pressures to relocate to reservations.

Chains, Rods, and Stakes

The first White settler in the Rock Lake locality, New York native John Eaton, homesteaded about two miles northwest of Kamiakin's summer camp locality in 1870. He had overlanded as a young man to Oregon City in 1853 following the path of his older brothers, Charles and Nathaniel, who came west ten years earlier with immigrants led by Marcus Whitman. The Eaton brothers settled in the Nisqually Valley, but service in the territorial militia acquainted John with settlement opportunities east of the Cascades.

His older brother Charles remained in the Yelm area and was married to Jennie Leschi, daughter of Chief Leschi and his Yakama wife, Slo-let-sa. For this reason, John Eaton and Kamiakin's relationship was more than simply an incidental acquaintance. Both were related to Jennie Eaton, and both had lost family members during the war years.

After operating the Kentuck Ferry near the mouth of the Palouse River in 1868–69, where he likely met the chief's sons, John Eaton established a large cattle operation northwest of Kamiakin's Rock Lake camp. Perhaps influenced by their peculiar family ties, along with the changes of passing years, the chief developed an interaction with this American in ways not allowed to others. The two became friends. Eaton often stopped to visit and deliver supplies to the Kamiakin family after periodic trips to the nearest trading centers at Spokane Falls and Walla Walla.[7]

By the 1870s, pioneer families crossing the Plains to the fabled Willamette Valley and the Puget Sound country were disappointed to find "all that land taken up," but many "heard there was still plenty of good land in the Palouse country." As early as 1872, Washington's territorial surveyor general, L.P. Beach, recorded: "During the last two years the Palouse country has been rapidly settling up, and those who first located in that section, for the purpose of grazing stock, have found that the soil produces abundance of all grains and vegetables."

Beach personally supervised surveys in the Palouse region, as teams of workers bearing measuring chains, rods, stakes, and brass optical instruments set claim boundary grids across the bunchgrass hills. Many local Indians, of course, realized the implications of the platting, but were powerless to oppose it. Yet, the terrain did not surrender to this taming easily—it took Beach's survey teams several years to complete the task amongst the tumbled landscape. Settlers already residing on land could now legitimize their "squatter's rights" with completion of the survey in the mid 1870s. Newcomers also could file claims on other parts of the public domain not held by "squatters," or they could plan to purchase Northern Pacific Railroad acreage for $2.50 per acre.[8]

Henry Villard, a robust, handsomely mustached Bavarian, would eventually transform Isaac Stevens' dream of a northern transcontinental railroad into reality. In April 1874, he had journeyed from Germany to the United States as the representative of several prominent European banking firms that were heavily invested in tycoon Ben Holladay's waning Oregon and California Railroad. After reaching Portland in July, Villard became enamored with the region's beauty and economic potential.

Within seven years, Villard rose to the presidency of the Northern Pacific Railroad. The company had long planned to exploit the valuable natural resources and economic opportunities of the Pacific Northwest. Villard devoted special attention to encouraging agriculture and commerce in the Palouse country. He organized a Northern Pacific subsidiary, the Oregon Improvement Company, largely to develop 150,000 acres of railroad land grants in the Palouse Hills.

As part of a congressional incentive in 1864 to encourage the building of the railway, the Northern Pacific had been granted all odd-numbered sections in an eighty-mile swath along the proposed route in Dakota, Montana, Idaho, and Washington territories. There were some exclusions—for instance, the Northern Pacific could not take sections within established Indian reservations. When the Northern Pacific finally was completed in 1881–83, however, the company's holdings cut a wide swath across Eastern Washington without regard for non-reservation Indians, such as the Palouses. The eighty-mile zone affected every township in Spokane County, and in Whitman County northwest of Colfax. As early as 1872, Indian Agent John A. Simms had talked to the Palouses about the advantages of the yet to be built Northern Pacific Railroad, and urged the Indians to relocate to reservations or face eviction. As on other American frontiers, White demands for removal of the Indians sometimes grew strident.

In the 1870s, rumors about the coming of the Northern Pacific had additionally stimulated White settlement. In October 1870, James Perkins, Hezekiah Hollingworth, and Anderson Cox established the first sawmill in the Palouse region near the forks of the Palouse River at present-day Colfax. The place was known to the Coeur d'Alenes as *Hnch'laqhemn* ("Canyon"), while Sahaptin speakers identified a fishing campsite here as *Tinatpolmat*, a name also applied to the river's South Fork, which abounded with trout and whitefish. The new enterprise stimulated local settlement, with farms soon sprouting in the locality. In 1872, Whites raised over 60,000 bushels of wheat in Whitman County. The Portland *Oregonian*, however, lamented: "This amount will not do any more than supply the settlers with seed for this year and yet, strange to relate, they have no thriving [flour]mill between the Snake and Spokane Rivers."

Nevertheless, Whitman County had become "dotted all over with the improvement of energetic farmers and some of the land was already in a high state of cultivation." In 1873, Joseph W. Davenport arrived from the Willamette Valley to construct a flour mill in Colfax—local farmers responded warmly by pledging to process 5,000 bushels of wheat. Kamiakin and his sons also were raising small tracts of wheat, which they cut, threshed, and winnowed by hand, and sold to local newcomers.

Farmers continued to demand completion of the long anticipated northern transcontinental railroad to carry wheat and other produce to markets.[9] As more acres were cultivated each year, other commercial interests responded by expanding steamboat navigation on the Snake River. The relative isolation of the Palouse region had hindered farmers from reaching outside markets. Now, however, the locations of former Palouse villages on the Snake River took on new meaning as the Oregon Steam Navigation Company established landings at or near these places. In 1876, businessmen built shipping facilities at Almota for hauling out grain and fruit, and to bring in freight, enabling farmers in the Palouse

to export nearly 10,000 bushels of wheat from this port to Portland. One report noted that "four threshers, three sulky plows, three reapers, three headers, 15 wagons and 100 tons of produce were unloaded there." The following year, officials constructed other shipping warehouses near the Palouse village sites of *Wawáwih* and *Pinawáwih*.

The volume of river traffic increased significantly by 1877. Steamboat captain Henry Spalding (son of Nez Perce missionary Henry H. Spalding) reported that farmers shipped 1,000 tons of produce from Almota. The Palouse country, once synonymous with bunchgrass and wild horses, was rapidly becoming a haven for prospering farmers and orchardists, while its First Peoples clung to shrinking outposts in their former domain.

Rock Lake Turmoil

Advancing White settlement inevitably caused strained relations with the increasingly outnumbered Native population. In the 1870s, regional newspapers reported several disputes between Whites and Indians, as stockmen and farmers filled up "the country between the Snake and Spokane Rivers." One incident involving the Kamiakin family occurred when a rancher sought passage for his livestock to get water at the south shore of Rock Lake, since massive basalt cliffs prevented accessibility along both sides of the lake. The southeast shoreline provided for the best watering spot, but the Kamiakins had used this place as their principal summer camp for years. They willingly shared their water rights with local Whites, but refused to move their homes or permit cattle to trample their gardens and fields. Resentment erupted into open confrontation.

In August 1872, the rancher and his sons stormed into Kamiakin's camp, pillaging crops and threatening harm if the Indians refused to move. Kamiakin avoided further difficulty by resettling his family on a stony flat nearby. In early September, the old chief, "determined not to give it up without an effort," sent one of his sons to find Agent Winans at Colville to intervene on their behalf. Preoccupied with agency matters and the grain harvest, Winans sent an assistant, S.F. Sherwood, to investigate.

Sherwood learned that the small band had justifiable cause for concern. The Whites planned to file claims on property long occupied by Kamiakin "and his fathers." The rancher reasoned that the Indians had no legal right to lands off the reservation, and he wanted them to relocate.

Winans reported the matter to Robert H. Milroy, the regional Superintendent of Indian Affairs, who responded that the Kamiakins had surrendered their right to a tribal claim on the reservation, had lived in the Rock Lake vicinity for over five years, and therefore held a *de facto* claim to the property, based on 1866 revisions to the Homestead Act. Moreover, Kamiakin had "been faithful to his promise of peace."

At this time, Beach's survey teams had yet to reach the Rock Lake area, and would not for two more years, which currently made legal entry by anyone impossible. Milroy, a former Civil War general, used bluster and his position as superintendent to recommend "the amplest protection" to Kamiakin and his sons by the military, since civil protection in this remote locality was "insufficient." Milroy directed John A. Simms, the new agent at Colville, to inform Kamiakin that his claim would be recognized by the government. Local livestock raisers were ordered to accept the Kamiakins' presence, and they reluctantly did so. Despite a resolution of these difficulties, the incident clouded the small bands' situation as White intrusion continued to grow.[10]

In spite of such brutish behavior directed against him and his family, Kamiakin in his last years continued to exert considerable influence to ameliorate disputes involving others. In 1874, Bayless Thorp had relocated with his family from the Kittitas Valley to the western Palouse, but Indians drove off his stock and burned his barn and hay supply. Thorp rode to the old chief's camp at Rock Lake to appeal for help, much as his brother, Willis, had done when riding into the Indian camp with A.J. Splawn nearly a decade earlier. Kamiakin determined that Thorp was unjustly victimized and interceded on the rancher's behalf. The guilty were punished and the harassment ceased.[11]

Expanding Alliances

During this time, some of Kamiakin's adult offspring, who had spent their adolescence at the remote family camp on Rock Lake, sought closer ties to the Palouses living at the ancient village sites along the Snake River. Kamiakin remained adamant in his refusal to leave Rock Lake, but did not prevent his older sons and daughters from residing elsewhere. We-yet-que-wit married the daughter of Chief Húsis Moxmox of *Palus*, and oversaw the Kamiakin family horse herds that spent much of the year grazing in the sheltered coulees of the lower Palouse River district. As befitting prominent young men even after the war period, he took more than

1864 Tintype.
WSU Libraries (McWhorter Collection)

The man in this striking tintype, dated 1864 and likely taken in a Walla Walla studio, initially was identified as "Chief Kamiakin," but the inscription was altered to "Junior Kamiakin." Kiatana Kamiakin believed the picture was of her older brother, We-yet-que-wit (b. 1840?), in about his mid 20s at the time. He wears a feathered hairpiece and is clad in ceremonial dress embellished with strips of white ermine, long dangling buckskin shoulder fringes, and a large beaded gorget worn over a patterned shirt. The man in the tintype, indeed, bears a resemblance to and exudes the strong self-confidence revealed in Kamiakin's own portrait, drawn by Gustavus Sohon at the 1855 Walla Walla Council.[12]

one wife. He also married Tallas Koltsenshin, a Coeur d'Alene whose grandfather had been killed at the Steptoe Battle.

We-yet-que-wit's sister, Yumasepah, married Peopeo-hi-yi-toman, a Nez Perce relative of Chief Joseph. Yumasepah occasionally visited Walla Walla, where the presence of one noted for being from such a celebrated family was sometimes reported in local newspapers.

Also, the marriages of sons by his wife Wal-luts-pum suggest familial connections that had been formed by the influential leader in the past. Their son T'siyiyak, named for Kamiakin's father, married Ni-ka-not, the highly esteemed daughter of Chief Slowiarchy at *Palus*. Lukash married Chief Moses' daughter, Sinsinq't.

This alliance of the Kamiakin and Moses clans was especially significant for both families. The mantle of leadership among the Columbia-Sinkiuse tribe had been capably carried by Moses after the death of his elder brother, Quilte-nenock, in an 1858 fight with miners. According to agency officials, Moses' exploits during the battles of the late 1850s had earned him a reputation for having a "charmed life," and possessing "more influence than any other chief" in the mid Columbia region. Sinsinq't was Moses daughter by the delicate Quo-mo-lah, favored daughter of Chief Owhi (Quo-mo-lah had died in the 1860s about the same time Kamiakin lost his beloved Colestah).

Kamiakin's daughter by wife Hos-ke-la-pum, Kiatana, would marry Ben Owhi, grandson of the legendary Chief Owhi. Hos-ke-la-pum also bore Kamiakin his youngest son, Piupiu K'ownot ("Bird of the Morning"), about 1870. Later known as Cleveland Kamiakin, he would become prominent in 20th century tribal affairs.

Kamiakin and wife Colestah's son Tomeo, noted for his wisdom and safe-guarding of family history, would marry Ot-wes-on-my, granddaughter of the Palouse Chief Húsis Paween, whose horses had ran with the Tilcoax herd that was slaughtered by Wright.[13]

Chief Moses, himself married to one of Kamiakin's cousins, impressed Kamiakin above most everyone else because of his solidarity with the Yakama-Palouse leader during the most difficult episodes of the war, and his cleverness in dealing with Whites. Although Moses was young enough to be Kamiakin's son, the vener-

Yumasepah (1845–1920).
WSU Libraries (L.V. McWhorter Collection)

able chief also admired Moses' generosity toward others and the protection he offered to his people in the face of struggles similar to his own.

As Kamiakin approached his last years, however, he realized his family could not indefinitely live among the Whites at Rock Lake or return to the Palouse River camp, where an ill-tempered settler from North Carolina resided and slept with a shotgun. White families were streaming to the region in unprecedented numbers and more confrontation was inevitable. Kamiakin, however, knew his presence on any reservation would be unsettling to many Indians and agency officials. He personally could never break free of his old homeland anyway. After Winans had visited Kamiakin in 1870, he noted that the chief felt "deceived by the United States," and "deserted." But Kamiakin believed his family's destiny could be different—they need not inherit his tragic predicament and plans must be laid for their future.

Established in 1872, the Colville Indian Reservation embraced a vast area northwest of the Columbia River and east of the Okanogan River. The reserve bordered Kamiakin's favorite fishery at Kettle Falls. The ancient root grounds situated in the dry coulees adjacent to the reservation offered fewer prospects for White settlement. Furthermore, agents Simms and Sherwood had proven their trustworthiness, unlike some other officials Kamiakin had known over the years. Also, Catholics supervised worship and education while still showing tolerance for the old ways. Thus, there were several reasons why family members should move north after he was gone. "Move to the Colville Reservation," Kamiakin advised his children.

He realized, given his daughters' marriages, that this might not be possible for them. (In fact, his daughter Yam'naneek by his first wife Sunk-hay-ee went to Yakama country where she had spent her childhood, and Yumasepah, married to a Nez Perce, also may have lived among that tribe for some time.) But his sons and their wives would either remain in the Palouse villages or join with Moses. The assurance surely brought Kamiakin some consolation in his last years.[14]

Conflicts over land use, such as the Kamia-kins experienced at Rock Lake, occurred elsewhere in the Palouse during this time. In May 1873, for example, a number of farmers in Paradise Valley near Moscow armed themselves in anticipation of the arrival of a band of Palouses, who frequented the ancient root grounds on the border between Washington and Idaho. During the previous spring, the Indians had journeyed "into the valley with their stock and entered…fields for the purpose of digging camas. When ordered out they refused, and pistols were drawn by the Indians and shooting seemed imminent. But the timely arrival of settlers with rifles held them in check." The editor of Lewiston's *Idaho Signal* wrote, it was "high time that the settlers should know whether they have any rights that are not subject to the arrogance of these Indians."

Whites considered the Indians trespassers, who should be prevented from entering lands owned by others. On the other hand, Chief Hahtalekin's band of Upper Palouses had often visited these traditional root grounds. Meanwhile, some pioneer residents allowed their hogs to destroy camas fields, while others plowed under vast areas of roots. In 1873, when the Palouses decided not to dig in Paradise Valley, Whites feared that they were plotting an uprising—minor hysteria gripped the locality when the Indians failed to appear. A militia mobilized, a blockhouse was built, and petitions were sent to the governor asking for arms and ammunition. Agent Sherwood was again dispatched. He assured Whites that the Indians had no hostile intentions, but were digging camas elsewhere. The agent's words allayed fears and prevented a broader panic.

During the third week of September 1874, surveyor Edson Briggs finally appeared at Rock Lake to complete a series of township plats, which finally would allow local residents to obtain legal title to property. His surveyor's wagon lumbered along the ancient trails criss-crossing through the vicinity, from which his party measured and marked section corners.

Briggs' mapped the location of the William Hendersons, who had erected a substantial home about a mile south of the lake. A two-story Gothic structure dating from 1872 and architecturally elaborate compared to typical Palouse frontier buildings, it still stands today as one of the region's oldest houses. A short distance away, the Kamiakins' cabin likely stood deserted, as the family probably was hunting game and gathering berries in the high country at the time.

A contemporary description of another typical cabin gives an idea of what Briggs might have seen inside—a stone fireplace, split timber table, stools, bedsteads, tallow candles, and pitch pine splinters for kindling and nightlight. Perhaps the women's coiled Klickitat baskets were clustered in a corner,

while a steamer trunk and parfleche, *shaptákay*, safeguarded the family's treasured regalia, catlinite pipe, copper flute, Colestah's red beads, and other articles not usually carried on the annual treks during *tiyám*.

The following year, Palouse farmers harvested a bumper crop and the news attracted still more immigrants. Filings were soon made by newcomers on the recently surveyed quarter-mile sections (160 acres) throughout the Rock Lake vicinity. The Kamiakins may have considered applying for Indian homesteads. However, the sons might have objected to the area's isolation from other Indian enclaves, or perhaps they simply lacked capable intermediaries to complete the documentation. For whatever reason, the Kamiakins never did file an Indian homestead claim at Rock Lake.[15]

Through his Coeur d'Alene friends, Seltice and Vincent, and itinerant priests such as Father Caruana, Kamiakin kept abreast of the contentious negotiations for a Coeur d'Alene Reservation. In 1867, President Andrew Johnson signed an executive order designating a 250,000 acre reserve south of Lake Coeur d'Alene, but the chiefs balked at such a meager reservation compared to the vast territory they were expected to surrender. In 1873, further deliberations between tribal elders and treaty commissioners led to a new agreement, extending the boundaries and encompassing a portion of Lake Coeur d'Alene. Traditional lands east of the lake, however, including the Sacred Heart Mission, were excluded from the agreement.

In February 1877, most Coeur d'Alenes reluctantly began acting on recommendations from Joset and Diomedi to relocate their homes and the mission forty miles southwest to the more isolated, yet fertile, environs of *Ni'lukhwaqw*. Here, they could establish a farming community and avoid conflicts with immigrants and other travelers along the Mullan Road. Kamiakin's longtime friend, Andrew Seltice, undertook the arduous trek, with ox teams pulling two-wheeled carts and sleighs with massive fir runners, carrying their people's belongings.

The Seltice family settled on prime land near *Tkwe'nkwe'nmi'wes* ("Clasping at the Waist"), the Coeur d'Alene word for the present-day Tekoa locality at the confluence of Hangman and Nest creeks. The buffalo hunter Andrew Youmas had relocated earlier from his camp at today's Oakesdale to land adjacent to the Catholic log mission at *Ni'lukhwaqw*, where the Kamiakins often visited in June. Several years later, a magnificent frame structure replaced the log chapel here, and boys' and girls' boarding schools were completed, where the thriving Indian community of De Smet appeared.[16]

Sweeps of Wild Rose

In July 1876, Kamiakin became ill. His health then further deteriorated during the fall and winter while they continued to reside at Rock Lake. His hair turned almost white, he lost considerable weight, and was bedridden for weeks. John Eaton periodically looked in on his neighbor and hoped in vain that the kidney medicine he shared might spark a recovery. The two men, who long ago raised arms in battle against each other's people, had overcome substantial cultural biases to become close friends.[17]

The relationship likely gave Kamiakin pause to think of others whose influence had been for better or for worse. He would remember two of his closest brother-friends, Qualchan and Quiltenenock, who perished in the war for which many still held Kamiakin responsible. Was the Squilchuk rock cairn still standing in Wenatchi country to mark where the Columbia chief fell in battle? On the other hand, no such marker attracted Whites to Qualchan's serene gravesite; the circumstances of his death had been violation enough.[18]

Kamiakin surely thought of old adversaries, such as Governor Stevens and Colonel Wright, who had both died not long after the 1855–58 war that claimed brave men and women on both sides. Stevens and Wright had fashioned a new world fraught with unprecedented challenges for Indian people. Kamiakin must have thought how mysterious it was that his own life had been spared these many years. He was grateful for the blackrobes, who had helped his family and others through the transition. Father De Smet, too, had been gone several years now. Beloved Pandosy, now expelled beyond the border to King George's Country, had been the Yakamas' erstwhile advocate—was he still ministering to Indians in the Okanagon Valley? Trader McDonald would likely know, but Kamiakin had not shared wine with the old Scotsman in years.[19]

The wives kept the younger children isolated from the aged and ill chieftain. In April 1877, Kamiakin's condition worsened. He awoke one day and told his family, "I always have dreamed and seen things and could read people's minds. Now I know there is a heaven. I can see it." He finally summoned the family, asking for a priest from the Sacred Heart Mission at De Smet. Father Caruana came and baptized the dying man, giving him the name Matthew. The following day, the legendary chieftain passed away.

The grief stricken women made preparations for the customary *patkwawsa*, or "body wrapping." Their sons dug a grave in the stony soil of the family's burial ground overlooking the lake, and traditionally cleansed it with sweeps of wild rose sprigs. Kamiakin's body was dressed in his finest clothes, and then ceremoniously wrapped in fine buckskin and other emblems of personal significance. The body was placed in a simple wood coffin constructed by John Eaton and Thomas May. Both ranchers had long been family friends, and they, along with Jack McElroy, another Kamiakin friend, accompanied the wives and children to the burial site.

Sorrowful wails from the women pierced the wind as Kamiakin's body was lowered into the ground next to the graves of his late sons, Skees and Tomomolow, and other relatives in the *yáwatash* on a stony ledge above the lake. Perhaps Tomomolow's mother, Colestah—Kamikian's beloved—also had been reburied there.

Here, in the heart of the Palouse country, the mourners returned the chief to the bosom of his earth mother, where *wawiyúk's* plaintive murmurs may have offered a melancholy requiem. The passing of one of the Northwest's great chiefs went unheralded by the general public or the Indian office. Word of Kamiakin's death, however, spread throughout the Indian community, and his family made the customary extensive arrangements to hold a grand memorial gathering. About a month after Kamiakin's death, friends and relatives from the region's reservations made the long trek to Rock Lake, where they gathered with non-reservation Indians to commemorate the legendary leader's passing.[20]

Many of Kamiakin's personal possessions were distributed to men and women, who, over the years, had treated the chief with the deference due a man of his stature. Colorful beadwork, finely knotted sallee bags, and red catlinite pipes, as well as practical items such as blankets, iron *kapin* root diggers, and butcher knives, were given away on such occasions. Perhaps the family parted with some of the buckskin clothing decorated with red beads that Colestah had deftly fashioned for her husband.

In accordance with the old ways, a presiding elder may have ceremoniously called out the chief's name three times. *K'amáyakun!*—first to commemorate deeds of valor and sacrifice in life. *K'amáyakun!*—as a blessing upon personal belongings now to be freely distributed. And finally, *K'amáyakun!*—rendered to solemnly surrender a revered name never to be spoken aloud again in months or even years of mourning, until bestowed by elders upon a deserving youth to perpetuate the name and its power.

Kiatana recalled that the feasting at Rock Lake lasted for several days before the crowd dispersed. Soon, only the widows remained with their sons and daughters at the ancient lakeshore camp. Each day they could look toward the sunrise and see where Kamiakin slept beneath a low basalt bluff, still decorated with purple lupine and other mementos left by the mourners. And each day they likely wondered how long they would stay.[21]

Following the war and their exile in Montana, Kamiakin's band attempted to live in accommodation with Whites. The chief had said: "There is no more war. I wish to live in peace until the Great Spirit calls me to take the long trail. I have lived to see Wa-tum-nah's words fulfilled." According to A.J. Splawn, the chief referred to a prophecy delivered to Kamiakin's father by an aged Yakama medicine man, who predicted that T'siyiyak's first-born son would lead the people in a valiant but futile effort against the Whites. The prophecy had come true, but no one could have envisioned the final indignity that would be committed against the patriot chief.[22]

No Rest in Death

About a year later, Kamiakin's remains were desecrated. In April 1878, while on a fossil-hunting tour on the Columbia Plateau, 28-year-old Charles H. Sternberg learned about the famous chief's burial after stopping at the Henderson ranch. Local resident Jack McElroy happened to be passing by that very day and saw men with packhorses, who said they were "exploring for fossils." He heard one make a curious remark, "Wouldn't the old chief's head look good on the shelves of the Smithsonian Institution?"

Many years later, McElroy still remembered the encounter and related the incident to a Walla Walla area historian, Harry Painter. McElroy, however, could not recall the identities of the passersby. But details about the sacrilege committed at Kamiakin's grave would be revealed later.[23]

The main "fossil" hunter, Charles Sternberg, was a passionate self-taught scientist in the employ of Professor Edward D. Cope, a prominent Philadelphia paleontologist who later served as curator of the University of Pennsylvania Museum of Anthropology and the American Museum of Natural History in Washington, D.C. Sternberg's older brother, George, had served as an Army surgeon at Ft. Harker, Kansas, and in 1867 his parents and siblings, including young Charles, settled on the Kansas frontier. Charles Sternberg's youthful explorations of Cretaceous sandstone deposits led to a lifelong study of paleontology. He became a key figure in the 19th century "fossil wars" between Edward Cope and a professional rival, Yale University's O.C. Marsh.

Accompanied by Joe Huff and Jacob Wortman, other Cope protégés, Charles Sternberg disinterred Kamiakin's body and took the head, carrying it away in a sack reportedly to "make certain measurements." The Indians did not learn of the ghoulish deed for some time, until family members returned to visit the grave. They saw it had been opened and found the body decapitated. The sons' outrage was beyond bearing. Some threatened retaliation against local Whites, but Eaton eventually managed to calm them down. He explained that others in the vicinity, such as himself, also deplored this reprehensible act.

The family had a holy man supervise the re-internment of Kamiakin's bones, and possibly those of other family members, on the other side of the lake. Here the chief's body could rest in the bosom of his motherland. In the strongest terms, the brothers commanded all family members present that under no circumstances should they divulge the location of their father's second burial.[24]

Details of the crime went unsolved for seven decades, until Judge W.C. Brown of Okanogan, a writer focusing on regional Indian history, learned the gruesome details from Roland Huff, a son of one of Sternberg's assistants. Huff was serving as supervisor of the Colville National Forest in 1948 when Brown asked him about Indian burials in the area. (Sternberg had died only five years earlier.) Huff recalled his father's tale of the episode.

Judge Brown, an acquaintance of Kamiakin's sons, then made further inquiries into the matter, learning that Sternberg had worked for the eminent paleontologist Edward Cope from about 1876 to 1879. To corroborate Huff's story, Brown obtained Sternberg's 1909 memoir, *The Life of a Fossil Hunter*, and found that the collector's account of western travels in the spring of 1878 coincided with Roland Huff's information. Sternberg's popular writings and reports in professional journals had earned him a reputation as one of the nation's foremost scientists of his day.

But Sternberg's account of his Northwest travels contained numerous racial epithets regarding Native peoples. He called them "expectant beggars" and "treacherous redskins," who sometimes frustrated his access across their lands. These references, not uncommon in frontier literature, nonetheless suggest an attitude consistent with Forest Supervisor Huff's allegations. For example, in 1877 when Charles Sternberg and his brother, George Sternberg, sought lodging near Klamath, Oregon, they came to a river where an Indian tended a toll bridge. "But as American citizens we had paid taxes to help pay for that bridge," Sternberg protested, "so we refused to pay toll for the use of our own property, and rode across in spite of the threats hurled against us."

That night they found a vacant house "a short distance from a large Indian town" where "death ceremonies" for a local chief were being conducted. George Sternberg went to observe the "incantations" and "death music," while Charles tended to other priorities. Charles sought to prevent any "thieving Indians" from pilfering their belongings, so he remained to sleep in the shack.[25]

The brothers then headed north to Ft. Walla Walla where George served as post surgeon. Charles then continued northeast into the Palouse country with assistants Wortman and Huff to spend the winter of 1877–78 seeking fossils along Pine Creek. At the time, some of the country's largest mammoth skeletons were being unearthed in the Rosalia vicinity. Sternberg likely wanted a piece of the action to interest his benefactors.

He wrote that the three of them "camped on Pine Creek, Washington, exploring the swamps in the neighborhood and fighting against water to secure specimens." The confluence of Pine and Rock creeks is situated a half-mile above the head of Rock Lake in Hole-in-the-Ground Canyon. Kamiakin's winter camp was located in the lower canyon of a Rock Creek tributary, several miles south, which still bears the name Kamiacan or Kamiache Creek. Since members of the Kamiakin family likely were still living in the vicinity, the party worked at night to conceal their crime.

Library at the Museum of Archaeology and Anthropology, University of Pennsylvania.

"We took a boat and rowed to the grave after midnight," Forest Supervisor Huff wrote quoting his father, and used "a light while we dug down to the body." Roland Huff also remembered that his father advised, "I should not say anything about this as there could be trouble about it."

Supervisor Huff related other recollections of his father in a letter to Judge Brown, mentioning that Sternberg's party then traveled south, possibly via Washtucna Lake, to Ft. Walla Walla. On April 23, 1878, the three men headed for the John Day fossil beds in northeast Oregon, where they collected for several weeks in spite of warnings about an uprising among the Indians. Sternberg

found comfort in his fourteen-pound Sharps rifle, claiming it was the best weapon he ever owned.

Inquiries Worldwide

Over the years, family members, agency representatives, and historians made numerous inquiries to museum officials regarding the whereabouts of Kamiakin's skull. Upon learning of Sternberg's contacts in Pennsylvania and Washington, D.C., Judge Brown wrote to the Philadelphia Museum of Natural History and the Smithsonian Museum of Natural History, where spectacular dinosaur skeletons unearthed by Sternberg are still on display. No record of any human remains sent by Sternberg was located.

Yakima Valley resident and celebrated Nez Perce and Yakama historian, L.V. McWhorter, also had sought justice in the matter on behalf of the Kamiakins. He likewise wrote to the Smithsonian as well as to the Army Medical Museum, two institutions known to have amassed relics taken from Indian graves across the country. McWhorter's efforts also were in vain. Subsequent investigations by family members and others into collections associated with Cope and Sternberg at the University of Pennsylvania's Museum of Archaeology and Anthropology, the Canadian Museum of Civilizations in Ottawa, and the Sternberg Museum of Natural History at Ft. Hays, Kansas, likewise yielded nothing.[26]

Because Sternberg throughout his long career collected specimens for others to study, Kamiakin's skull may have been acquired by a private collector. A number of Army medical officers on the western frontier are known to have kept collections of Indian remains. Through his Army surgeon brother, Charles Sternberg might have sold or given Kamiakin's skull to another post doctor or a curiosity seeker. Disposition of the chief's skull is further complicated by the possibility that Sternberg included it in shipments of specimens to foreign destinations. In the 19th century, European museums hotly competed for the remarkable fossils of prehistoric creatures found in North America, and had a special interest in Native American cultures as well. For this reason, some of Sternberg's collections

Native American Graves Protection and Repatriation Act (1990)

In the 19th and much of the 20th centuries, Native burial items and human remains numbering in the tens of thousands were collected and stored by museums and other research repositories across the United States. Numerous private citizens also held similar items in their homes.

In 1990, at the urging of politically-involved Indians and other persons sympathetic to the return of cultural collections to the tribes, Congress passed the Native American Graves Protection and Repatriation Act (NAGPRA). This far-sighted amelioration requires agencies and institutions receiving federal funding to return burial items and human remains to their respective peoples. Where the cultural affinity of objects can be established, they can be claimed by that respective tribe. Many thousands of cultural materials now continue to be returned to tribal peoples.

But even with the successes of NAGPRA, disputes can occur. An example is the controversial disposition of Kennewick Man, a 9,300-year-old skeleton found in 1996 along the Columbia shoreline and therefore under federal jurisdiction. Many scientists interested in the early peopling of the Americas have found means to hold these extremely rare human remains in a laboratory, with the theory that they predate area Native tribes.

It is important to note, too, that NAGPRA only pertains to federally owned and supported institutions, and not to private collections, for instance. But at the federal level, at least, a major step was started to make amends. Despite NAGPRA's passage years ago, many people in the general population unfortunately remain unaware of the sensitivity of this issue to Native peoples.

reside at the British Museum in London, the Museum of Natural History in Paris, the Sneckenberg Museum in Frankfurt, and Berlin's Museum of Natural History.[27]

Several obscure references suggest Kamiakin's skull might not have even left the area. In the early 1900s, two Inland Northwest curio collectors boasted that each owned Kamiakin's skull, but the provenance of their claims has been lost.[28]

Although well over a century past, this cruel affront to the dignity of the Kamiakin family and the tribes remains an open wound. Indian sanctity for the dead is profound. The desecration of Kamiakin's body, and the graves and bodies

of Chief Moses, Old Joseph, and hundreds of other Indians throughout the region by amateur and professional collectors, are matters of deep personal insult. To people of many cultural backgrounds, the recent disposition of *Tiičáminsh Uytpamá Natítayt*, the Ancient One ("Kennewick Man") and Snake River burial excavations indicate that many scientists and government officials have sought means to hold Indian remains in laboratories despite federal provisions. To this day—because of the experiences of the Kamiakins and other families like them—public indifference in such cases is incomprehensible to many in the Indian community.

Chapter 9
Salmon Out of Water

Young Chinook became strong
and made a bow and arrows;
carried them toward the mountains.
He knew his father had been killed.
He swam past Celilo and found
the familiar waters of Pik'úunen.

Sometimes he walked along the shore,
and then returned to the water.
He came to the lodge of Old Lady Spider
and saw her spinning in the corner.
"What are you doing there?"
"Just making clothes," she said.

*I*n the final months of Kamiakin's life, tensions between Indians and Whites again led to open warfare. Confrontation had resurged in the Umatilla area and especially in the Nez Perce country south of the Snake River, which threatened to engulf the Palouse region as well. Many headmen such as Kamiakin realized the futility of armed resistance, however, as it would only inflict more misery upon elders, women, and children and offer little prospect of benefit.

Through Kamiakin's father, T'siyiyak, the family had many relatives among the Nez Perce bands, as did many of the Upper Palouses who shared a borderland with the large tribe. These relationships grew and were strengthened by Kamiakin's children, who married Nez Perce and Palouse spouses. Yumasepah had married Whistling Bird, a Palouse-Nez Perce from *Wawáwih*, who was a close relative of Joseph, the highly regarded chief of the Wallowa Nez Perce. Joseph's father, Tuekekas, had been born at *Wawáwih*, and considerable interchange took place between both peoples at this popular fishing and council grounds.

Characteristic of the fluid inter-personal relationships among the Plateau peoples, Kamiakin's own Wiyáwiikt clan of the Yakamas also had close connections with the Nez

Perces. A grandson of the martyred Chief Owhi—a young man later known to Whites as Ben Owhi (Awhi)—eventually married Kamiakin's daughter, Kiatana.

When a young man, Owhi nursed a strong resentment toward area settlers. Members of his family lived at *Palus*, Wallula, and in the Kittitas Valley, and sometimes quarreled with Whites in those areas. Like other young men growing impatient with their elders' advice to accept accommodation, Owhi sought an opportunity to avenge his grandfather's death. About this time, another young man from *Palus*, Chief Slowiarchy's grandson, Pahka Lawash-hachit (Five Shades), joined the non-treaty Nez Perce out of similar frustrations.

Past killings of headmen and continued dispersals caused by White advances on ancestral lands had disrupted the traditional bonds that formerly provided direction for some Indian adolescents. Owhi recalled: In consequence of the "murder of all my relatives" during the wars of the 1850s, "I had no place to stay." Like a number of others of his generation in these times, young Owhi wandered between the Umatilla area and the Yakima Valley. He later lamented about not having grandparents to tell him "how to be a good man." Mindful of his ancestors' hunting and trading exploits on

Wallowa Lake, Oregon.
WSU Libraries (Emil Kopac 70-0225)

the Plains, Owhi journeyed across the Rockies in 1876 to hunt buffalo in the Milk River district west of the Bears Paw Mountains and along the Yellowstone River.[1]

During the 1870s, settlers throughout the Inland Northwest were perplexed at seeing numerous parties of Indians traveling to visit widespread villages from the Columbia to the Bitterroots. From spring to fall, they also rode on horseback to root and berry grounds and to hunting and fishing areas long favored by their ancestors. To many Whites, the Indians had been defeated in the recent wars, and as signatories to the Stevens' treaties, should be confined to reservations in Washington, Oregon, and Idaho.

However, a number of headmen, such as Húsis Paween, Hahtalekin, and Poyahkin of the Upper Palouses, felt little obligation to accept the treaty provisions because they had not been present at the Walla Walla Council. Moreover, at the villages of *Pinawáwih* and *Wawáwih*, their livelihood was substantially based on maintaining vast horse herds in the

hills, for which the Palouse region had become famous. They also understood that pledges were made in the treaties to compensate Indians for improvements and personal property in ceded areas, yet little resolution had been forthcoming.

The Thief Treaty of 1863

Húsis Kute, a venerated Dreamer or *tewat* of the Upper Palouses, was a veteran of the fight against Steptoe in 1858. His name, Bald Head, derived from a near fatal gunshot wound received during the battle. A revered orator, he adhered to the traditional Washani religion. He believed, in accordance to treaty provisions, that his people should be able to travel unmolested throughout ancestral lands to their customary gathering, fishing, and hunting camps. In the 1870s, the Dreamer grew angry with new White settlements disrupting his people's winter villages at the mouths of Penawawa, Almota, and Wawawai creeks. Moreover, rustlers periodically attempted to raid the Indians' herds on the unfenced grassy bluffs from *Palus* to Lewiston.[2]

For similar reasons, Húsis Kute and the band's civil leader, Chief Hahtalekin, had much in common with the Idaho and Oregon "non-treaty" Nez Perces, led by Looking Glass (the Younger), White Bird, Toohoolhoolzote, and Joseph. Of course, many Upper Palouses, such as the Paween and Poyahkin families, had intermarried with the Nez Perces, and the relationship with the Looking Glass band was particularly close.

These non-treaty Nez Perce groups resided in localities promised to them by the Nez Perce Treaty of 1855. After the early 1860s gold strikes in the Idaho mountains, however, pressure from White miners, settlers, and political and business leaders eventually prevailed upon the U.S. government to force a renegotiation of the 1855 treaty. After decades of uncommon service—aiding the Corps of Discovery in 1805–6, defending the Spaldings during the Cayuse War, and furnishing scouts for the devastating Wright campaign—the Nez Perces' reward for accommodation was an ultimatum to surrender approximately 90 percent of the recently ratified 1855 reservation.

A new 1863 treaty compelled the tribe to surrender land for about eight cents an acre. Generally, those bands retaining their homes within the reduced reservation signed the document; in total number, they were a slight majority of the tribe. But most residing in the ceded localities, who would be required to move to the Clearwater reservation, refused to accept what they called the "Thief Treaty." They remained on their disputed homelands, and the controversy simmered for another thirteen years

Finally in 1876, the Secretary of the Interior directed government officials to remove the non-treaty Indians to the reservation. In November, Nez Perce Agent John Monteith convened a council at Lapwai to make arrangements for relocating the bands. Five commissioners appointed to negotiate an agreement, including General Oliver Howard, met in council with Indian leaders at the Nez Perce Agency. The chiefs, however, were in no mood to move. Joseph expressed this conviction, saying: "The Creator, when he made the land, made no marks, no lines of division or separation on them." The earth was "too sacred…to be sold for silver or gold…. We love the land; it is our home."

Several of the commission members from the East left in frustration, blaming Indian intransigence on the religious influences of Washani priests, such as Húsis Kute, and an elderly Nez Perce spiritual leader, Toohoolhoolzote. The commissioners recommended to the Interior Secretary that such individuals immediately be forced on to the agencies or, in the event of non-compliance, be exiled to Indian Territory.[3]

In January 1877, Monteith received orders to move the non-treaty bands to the reservation "in a reasonable time," which he defined as by April 1. Soldiers at Ft. Lapwai were at the agency's disposal. The chiefs, having a need to consult with all their people and to move their herds across streams swelled by the springtime runoff, urgently requested a second meeting with Monteith and Howard, which was granted at Lapwai for the first week of May.

Húsis Kute, Hahtalekin, and the Nez Perce leaders again attended, witnessing more of Howard's stormy exchanges with Joseph and Toohoolhoolzote. When the latter asked rhetorically, "What person pretends to divide the land, and put me on it?" the one-armed general exclaimed, "I am the man! I stand here for the President, and there is no spirit good or bad that will hinder me." After threatening the immediate arrest of the assembled Indian leaders, the chiefs with great reluctance consented to relocate. "We were like deer," Joseph later explained; "they were like grizzly bears."[4] The Palouses were to be given lands near the agency along with other non-treaty bands.

The Nez Perce War

Howard offered some compromise on the timetable, giving the bands thirty-five days, until June 15, to complete the relocation. Hahtalekin and Húsis Kute were particularly dismayed at the short time allowed for the Palouses to gather up their vast, wide-spread Snake River horse herds. As June approached, it became obvious that summoning all the families, many of whom were digging camas across the northern Palouse region, and rounding up all the livestock would be impossible tasks.

On June 14, three restive youths of Joseph's Wallowa band killed four settlers on the Salmon River in retaliation for the murder of one of the young warriors' father. All four victims were known to have acted hostilely toward Indians, but the news of their deaths stunned Joseph when he heard it the following day. Joseph advised a meeting with Howard to explain the situation; he felt the rest of his band should not be held accountable. But the chief's counsel was spurned by a number of younger braves, whose patience with their elders' peace talk had worn thin.[5]

Now emboldened, sixteen members of White Bird's band and one Wallowa attacked other Salmon River miners and

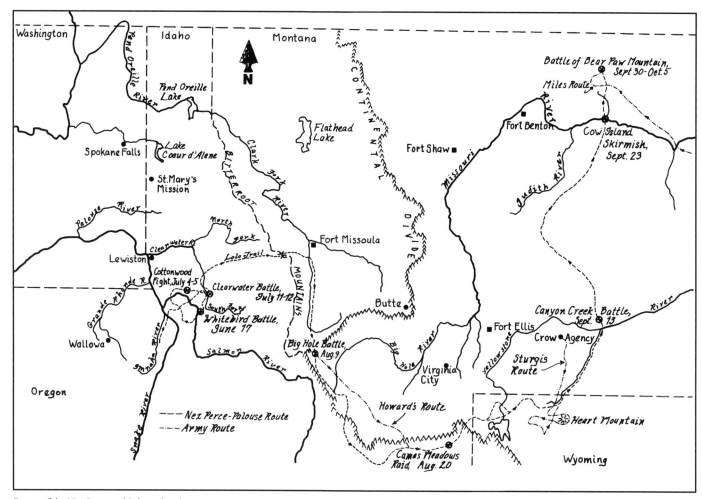

Route of the Nez Perce and Palouse bands, 1877.
From Trafzer & Scheuerman, Renegade Tribe *(WSU Press, 1986)*

ranchers. Joseph, oblivious of these latest depredations, led his people to join White Bird in White Bird Canyon, where both leaders hoped to resolve the sudden turn of events by talking with General Howard. Whites fleeing in panic pleaded for protection from Ft. Lapwai, and two companies of cavalry were dispatched to White Bird Canyon on June 17. Ignoring a flag of truce sent by the chiefs, one of the volunteers accompanying the soldiers fired on the Indians, opening a brief but violent exchange that left thirty-four soldiers dead while the Indians suffered only two wounded. With no real alternative, Joseph, too, had joined the revolt.

On July 1, a group of soldiers and trigger-happy Mount Idaho volunteers fired on Looking Glass's village along the South Fork of the Clearwater, an incident not countenanced by Howard. After the unprovoked attack, about a dozen Palouse families under Hahtalekin joined the non-treaty Nez Perce.

Looking Glass previously had kept his people out of the fighting and urged peace with the Army. He was residing within the new reservation boundaries near present-day Kooskia when Captain Stephen Whipple's cavalry attacked the village.

Whipple's senseless action that morning drove the Palouses into alliance with the Nez Perce war chief, along with Joseph and White Bird's people. Later in July, after fighting the Army to a draw in the Battle of the Clearwater, the united non-treaty bands sought escape from the soldiers, fleeing to Weippe Prairie and over the Lolo Trail toward Montana.

By the first week of July 1877, Owhi and two Nez Perce traveling companions, the warrior Hahsilatah (Hahartselatokit) and his younger brother Itseyiyi Shamkin, had spent many months hunting buffalo and avoiding hostile camps of Plains Indians. Upon reaching the confluence of the Big Horn and Little Big Horn rivers, the trio encountered a Crow party, serving as Army scouts in seeking Sitting Bull's camp of warring Sioux. Owhi and his Nez Perce friends remained with the Crows for a time, until an Army officer informed them about the outbreak of hostilities a couple of weeks earlier in Idaho.

The news soured the trio's relationship with the Crows and the Army. Hahsilatah advised that they avoid harm's way and return to Owhi's homeland via Missoula. Flathead Indian Agent Duncan McDonald, son of Angus McDonald and his Nez Perce wife, Catherine, gave the young men sanctuary in the Bitterroot Valley for a time, until word reached them of the Army's pursuit of the Nez Perces over Lolo Pass.

"I thought I would go and join and keep my old mind," Owhi reasoned, "to fight and die like my folks did." The threesome then left their camp near St. Mary's Mission and on the following day encountered the large column of Nez Perces and Palouses. They learned of the battles west of the mountains and victories over the soldiers.[6]

In spite of his youth, Owhi was invited to participate in the chiefs' council due to his recent experiences on the Plains. The bands had just completed a difficult crossing of the Bitterroots, and now sought respite and safe passage for their families among Montana tribes. Owhi advised heading north through the Bitterroot Valley and Flathead Salish lands in order to avoid hostile encounters. Looking Glass, the war chief, demurred. His old friends, the Crows, controlled routes off to the southeast near the Plains, where the Nez Perces could hunt buffalo and recover from hard traveling.

It was a fateful choice, as was Owhi's decision to join his Nez Perce and Palouse kinsmen. At daybreak on August 9, just days after Owhi had met the fleeing column, the Army attacked at dawn. In the Battle of the Big Hole, the first to fall in the savage fighting was the Palouse chief Hahtalekin, shot to death when he went out to tend the horses. The battle also claimed his son, the warrior Pahka Pahtahank.[7] After finally fighting off the Army, but with severe losses, the Nez Perces and Palouses continued east—in a long march across Idaho and Montana, through Yellowstone National Park, and north on the Great Plains, never receiving succor from the Crows that Looking Glass expected.

Altogether, the heroic but doomed trek of more than 700 men, women, and children, including vast numbers of

horses, lasted 3½ months and extended across 1,200 miles of rugged terrain with at least a dozen battles and skirmishes. A majority of the remaining Nez Perces finally were captured after the Battle of Bears Paw Mountains near Canada in early October 1877.

However, perhaps more than 200 Indian men, women, and children managed to slip away and escape to Canada to join Sitting Bull's self-exiled Sioux. Some retreated into the Montana Rockies, including the noted warriors Yellow Wolf and Ko-san-yum. After wandering along the borderlands for a year, both eventually surrendered and were sent to Oklahoma in 1878. (Ko-san-yum, also known as Luke Wilson, later married Chief Kamiakin's granddaughter by Yumasepah, Ta-lats Ton-my.) Another who managed to cross into Canada, remaining with the Sioux, was the cripple Askolumkee, or No Feet, the former Kamiakin family slave.

Joseph and Húsis Kute were among the few leaders to survive until the end of the war. The 431 forlorn prisoners captured at the Bears Paw, including Owhi and the Palouse remnant, were sent to Ft. Leavenworth in Indian Territory, eventually known to the exiles as *Eekish Pah*, the Hot Place. They were transferred to the Quapaw Agency, and finally to the Ponca reserve near present-day Tonkawa, Oklahoma, where Húsis Kute and Joseph had sought a better location on the dry Plains.

The trauma of exile, change in climate and diet, and related factors wrought a terrible toll. Nearly a third of them died from malaria and other afflictions, mostly children and the elderly. "The climate killed many of us," Yellow Wolf later recalled. "All the newborn babies died, and many of the old people too. It was the climate. Everything so different from our old homes. No mountains, no springs, no clear running rivers.… We were always lonely for our old-time homes."

Some of the older children, including Húsis Kute's son, attended the Carlisle School in Pennsylvania. Owhi compared conditions in Oklahoma to being "in a penitentiary." The warriors "who had fought the most had to do the hardest work." They cut and hauled wood and tended to other labor, "six days a week…summer and winter."[8]

Return from *Eekish Pah*

In January 1879, Joseph had journeyed to Washington, D.C., delivering an impassioned speech in Lincoln Hall to a large audience of congressmen, cabinet officials, and other political leaders. He recounted the injustices done to his people, and cited specific agreements abrogated by the government that led to the war. He spoke of the Army's favorable surrender terms offered at the Bears Paw Mountains that the government later reneged. The listeners were moved by Joseph's oratory, and congressional intervention eventually enabled the Nez Perce and Palouse exiles to return to the Pacific Northwest in 1885.

Of the captives who arrived at Ft. Leavenworth in 1877, only 268 now survived. (In an incredible feat, the Palouse warrior Pahka Lawash-hachit, Five Shades, had managed to escape confinement and journeyed back to his homeland.) Under the leadership of Joseph and Húsis Kute, the refugees boarded a train in late May 1885 bound for the Northwest. On May 27, they arrived at Wallula Junction and were divided into two groups. Húsis Kute, who had participated in Christian worship services while in Indian Territory, led a group of 118 to the Nez Perce Reservation, while the remaining 150, including Owhi, were directed to the Colville Reservation along with Joseph and Yellow Bull. The latter contingent went northward in mule-drawn Army wagons to sprawling Ft. Spokane. Established five years earlier, this outpost of a couple dozen buildings stood on a broad terrace of bunchgrass and towering pines near the confluence of the Columbia and Spokane rivers.[9]

The Indians remained near the fort for a long stay, while preparations were made for their arrival on the Colville Reservation. If the bewildered newcomers, weary from their extensive traveling, expected a cordial reception back in more familiar surroundings, they were mistaken. A Spokane newspaper denounced their presence under the headline "Unwelcome Immigrants." "These thieves and murderers are now being sent to the Colville Valley," the paper declaimed. "Must we now offer, as an additional attraction to this region to settlers and miners, the fact that they will have these blood-stained demons for neighbors?"

Meanwhile, extra troops were sent to ensure their safe passage to the Colville Reservation, "on account of intense feeling against their return by people of Washington and Idaho."[10] The behavior of some soldiers at the fort was despicable, as they leered at the younger women and threatened harm. Eventually, Joseph asked the officers to intervene. The Indians were permitted to camp north of the river on reservation land for the winter, while preparations were made by agency officials for their move to the Nespelem Valley. Promised government provisions failed to arrive, thus Joseph's people faced deprivation. In November, fort commander Lt. Col. J.S. Fletcher ordered that they be issued full Army rations in order to survive the winter.[11]

Sixteen-year-old Henry Covington, son of the legendary regional frontiersman Virginia Bill Covington who operated the post canteen, sympathized with the Indians' sorrowful plight, noting "the dejected attitude of the displaced people." Young Covington was deeply moved by the elders' "silent weeping." He thought they were dreaming of their own childhoods, while knowing that the little ones fearfully clustered around them would face a troubled future.[12]

Others, such as Dr. George Kuykendall, agency physician at Ft. Simcoe, who knew first-hand of the Indians' plight, offered prescient views that contrasted with prevailing sentiments among many Whites. "What would we do if some alien race of interlopers should come into our country, take and appropriate our lands, drive out our families, and sacrilegiously turn the bones of our fathers and mothers out of their graves and trample them underfoot?... When I have heard of the 'Indian outrages' on our people I have often thought in many cases it was only a part of the price of our own injustice and perfidy."[13]

Indians such as Húsis Kute, who had adopted some aspects of Christianity, soon found antagonism directed against them by other Protestant Nez Perces at Lapwai. A number of the latter Nez Perces were disaffected because reservation lands were to be allotted to the newcomers. Consequently, Húsis Kute was resettled with his old friends and other "recalcitrants" on the Colville Reservation to live among Palouse and Nez Perce traditionalists.

But the legendary Dreamer never forgot his old home. Húsis Kute remained a feared holy man to his last days and asked to be buried in an obscure graveyard on Cache Creek in the southeast corner of the reservation. The peculiar location affords a vista that opens toward the ancestral Palouse country. As the only surviving non-treaty Palouse chief and 1877 war veteran living on the Colville Reservation around the turn of the century, Húsis Kute was the likely subject of artist E.A. Burbank's striking portrait, "The Palouse Chief Hush-Low, a medicine man." (During E.A. Burbank's long life, 1858–1949, he became nationally renowned for painting and sketching over 1,200 portraits from 125 tribes. In 1899, he also prepared images of Lukash Kamiakin's daughter, Sinsinq't, and Chief Joseph.)[14]

Pushed to the Periphery

The return of the exiles occurred at a time when railroad lines were expanding across the region. As their train slowly lumbered toward Wallula, the weary travelers saw that much had changed during their eight-year absence. At the time of the 1877 war, the only functioning railroad in the region was Dorsey Baker's famously named "Rawhide Railroad," supposedly because hides were attached to cover the route's wooden rails, though in actuality iron straps were used. Baker's narrow gauge line ran between Wallula and Walla Walla.

Construction on the main line of the Northern Pacific Railroad across the Columbia Plateau occurred from 1879 to 1881, connecting to Portland. Shortly, work began on several spurs snaking across the region, carrying the land's burgeoning agricultural produce to faraway markets. Farming extended from fertile river bottoms up into the broad Palouse Hills. Settlers now were well aware of the remarkable fertility of the higher steppes, which were no more susceptible to frost than most low lying areas.

Settlers filed for homesteads or purchased land from the Northern Pacific. Land speculators also invested in the region, buying up large tracts and selling smaller parcels to individuals. Many farmers viewed the remaining Palouse Indians as obstacles in the way of civilization and progress. A number of Whites wanted the few remaining Indians removed to reservations, a demand that increased each year in proportion to White population growth. Washington Territory's voters had the ear of territorial and national politicians, who supported Indian removal; they pressured agents on the Nez Perce and Yakama reservations to attempt to force the Palouses to relocate.

The completion of the Northern Pacific's transcontinental line across the Great Plains and Rocky Mountains in 1883 inaugurated ever increasing immigration to the Palouse country. Word of the region's legendary soil spread across the United States and to Europe. In some reports, the Palouse was heralded for possessing "a soil richer than any other portion of the Pacific Coast." Such stories spawned an array of colorful railroad-sponsored promotional brochures and other booster literature that attracted thousands of additional immigrants to U.S. land offices. The Northern Pacific also owned about 150,000 acres in the Palouse, selling parcels to colonists from Europe and from other sections of the United States.

In 1879, the district land office at Colfax had filed the most land claims of any district in the nation. In one month alone, the office registered claims for 711 farms, totaling 144,207 acres. Within ten years, Whites owned virtually all the arable land in the Palouse country. At the start of the 1880s, about 350 Indians lived in the Palouse region, while the White population in Whitman County alone numbered over 7,000. Year after year, the remaining Palouses found themselves pushed to the periphery of their ancestral lands. During annual treks to traditional root grounds and other subsistence areas, they encountered increasing fences and White-owned livestock herds.[15]

In June 1877, mutual distrust resulting from the Nez Perce outbreak had added to the stress, pushing peaceable Indians almost to the breaking point. That month, the *Walla Walla Statesman* reported on wartime restrictions that prevented Indians from visiting traditional fishing, gathering, and hunting grounds, and thus they were deprived of food. In comments rather uncharacteristic of most frontier newspapers, the editor opined that the "government has failed to provide." The consequences, he predicted, were especially disturbing in an area long known for its bounty: "Famine looms." Most Indians, however, managed to eke out an existence by traveling to more remote areas, until salmon runs offered prospects of deliverance.

With Kamiakin's death in 1877, members of his band looked increasingly to their kinsman, Chief Moses, for guidance during these months of renewed turmoil. Moses always admired the great patriot-chief and had sought his wisdom. Moses, however, had been born about 1829 and belonged to a younger generation. He knew that the course of events would not allow him to live out his years in unrestrained exile as Kamiakin had done. Like Kamiakin's sons, he longed to roam freely across the Columbia's Big Bend region, where his wife, Chief Owhi's daughter Sanclow (Mary Moses), could point in virtually any direction and recount some memorable event of their family experiences.

But with thousands of soldiers pursuing the warring Nez Perces and Palouses, the specter of famine, plus the growing lure of some semblance of security in reservation life, Moses' consideration of his people's fate was shifting. He had parleyed with General Howard at Priest Rapids in June, on the eve of the Nez Perce War. Both sought peaceful resolution despite some tough talk. Howard's resolve and his recounting of earlier Indian struggles against the Army sobered Moses, the Palouses, and the Wanapums gathered at the council.[16]

Hearts that Do Not Feel

One by one, most of the non-reservation chiefs came to the realization that their people must relocate. As difficult as the discussions had been with Howard and other White officials, Moses knew that convincing some of his people, especially the younger firebrands, would be particularly challenging. The sudden outbreak of violence in the Nez Perce country had only interrupted Howard's hope for Indian removal as a means of preventing similar difficulties along the middle Columbia. While many Indians cheered the news of the outbreak, Moses knew it meant only a brief respite, delaying an inevitable outcome for his people.

On March 11, 1878, he rose to address "a large council" in the heart of the Wiyáwiikt clan's ancient homeland—the Kittitas Valley. His message was very different from the diplomatic parrying and brash public statements for which the "wily chieftain" was known and respected by Indians and Whites. This time his words were delivered in the measured tones of a heavy heart:

Chief Moses.
WSU Libraries (L.V. McWhorter Collection)

We have asked them to give us peace, and let our old men and old women rest in these lands that belonged to the great chief of our fathers. We have asked them to let our young men and young women go free, to fish where they will, to hunt where they can. We have asked them to take away their soldiers, their agents and their traders.... We have asked them to let us have our own religion, our own preachers and our own places to meet the Great Spirit, to talk with him in our own way in our own belief....

The Great White Father and the Great White Chief have ears but they do not hear the poor Indians' cry for help. They have hearts but do not feel the Indians' pain. They have fine clothes and big houses, and they do not care for our torn blankets and lodges.... They hear the cry of the other colors, but cannot hear us. Their hearts have turned to stone, their eyes look blood, their hands are very cold. What can we do? The White men are as many as the leaves on yonder trees..., the Indians are as few as the leaves on one tree.... If we go to war we will all be shot down like dogs; if we stay off the reservation we will all starve and die, like salmon out of water.[17]

Moses' audience, which included scores of non-reservation Indians such as the younger Kamiakins, listened intently. Moses had fought alongside Kamiakin, Owhi, and Qualchan in the wars against the Army and volunteers, which resulted in defeat for the late patriot chiefs. His pleas had been considered by the Great White chiefs—President Hayes and

General Howard. Many of his listeners still could not bring themselves to accept Moses' disheartening conclusion, but most soon would. Agents on the Yakama and Nez Perce reservations were pressuring their superiors for the removal of all non-reservation Indians east of the Cascades. The small roving bands of Palouse and Columbia-Sinkiuse Indians were of particular interest to these agents. They viewed them as heathens who would benefit from Christian influences found on the reservations.

General Howard and Umatilla Indian Agent John McBean arranged for a delegation of chiefs, including Moses, Chief Homily of the Walla Wallas, and the Cayuse Chief Hiachenie, to visit Washington, D.C., in the spring of 1879. Though White settlement in the drier Big Bend district of Moses' homeland was still fairly sparse, the chief sought secure reservation rights for his people before an inevitable White influx made the prospect impossible.

Meanwhile, settlers flooding into the Walla Walla Valley and the Palouse had created a desperate situation for Indians still living in those areas. Homily's people were impoverished, forced from traditional gathering localities. He pled for a separate reservation for his people and the Palouses along the Snake River, but government authorities would hear nothing of it. Homily and Hiachenie were told to move their people to the Umatilla Reservation or face further problems.

Moses' appeal for a Columbia Reservation, however, was another matter. With Howard's support, Moses argued that a reserve in an area of his preference would not infringe upon White interests. In fact, by attracting many non-reservation bands from across the region, it would defuse recurrent confrontations elsewhere. At this time, Moses and the Kamiakins likely knew of Indian families to the south feeling further dispossessed of their homes, after hostilities and pressures were directed against them by marauding Bannocks and Paiutes in Oregon's 1878 Bannock War.

In the late summer of 1878, a band of Palouse and Umatilla families from Wallula and the lower Snake gathered their belongings and moved north. Chuweah, Tatshama,

Wata-stoma-kolick (Charlie Simpson), and others rode to the isolated environs of Foster Creek on the Columbia, north of Moses Coulee. Still skittish about moving across the river into the Colville Reservation, they remained here, wandering over the Waterville Plateau until eventually moving north at Moses' invitation. Tatshama made his home along the Columbia River opposite Belvedere, while others from his group eventually settled near Nespelem.[18]

In the spring of 1879, when Moses and the delegation of chiefs journeyed to Washington, D.C., they met with Interior Secretary Carl Schurz and Indian Affairs Commissioner E.A. Hayt. These officials suggested a reserve be set aside in the sparsely settled region west of the Colville Reservation—from the Okanogan River to the crest of the Cascades. The plan satisfied the Columbia chief, who also met President Rutherford B. Hayes in the White House library. Moses thanked the president for giving "all the country I wanted."[19]

Moses and his fellow chiefs returned to Washington Territory bearing silver medals embossed with President Grant's image (those with Hayes' likeness were unavailable). At Wallula on May 15, they met with General Howard, Governor Elisha Ferry, and Colville Agent Simms to make arrangements for grand councils held in the frontier communities of Wenatchee and Spokane Falls. These meetings would inform non-reservation Indian leaders about the terms of the new agreement, and encourage them to relocate to the newly established Columbia, or Moses, Reservation.[20]

"Kamiakin Brothers."
WSU Libraries (L.V. McWhorter Collection)

The great gathering on Wenatchee Flat near Moses birthplace began on May 29. Its conclusion was followed by celebratory horse racing. Moses and other dignitaries then followed the Columbia River north to the vicinity of the new reserve and continued east to Spokane Falls. Following a brief tour to Ft. Coeur d'Alene (later Ft. Sherman) on the north shore of the lake, the council congregated on Saturday, June 15, among the pines on the eastern outskirts of the bustling hamlet at Spokane Falls. Attending were Spokan Garry of the Middle Spokanes, Lot of the Lower Spokanes, and other Indian leaders. Noting the conspicuous absence of some other Indian notables, including "Young Kamiakin" (We-yet-que-wit), Howard suggested postponing the meeting for a day, only to elicit Moses' peculiar objection to the devout general's intention to conduct business on the Sabbath.

Howard may have been influenced by Spokan Garry's evident coldness to Moses. Howard, though, felt that Garry had received preferential treatment, in spite of the Columbia chief's special opportunistic relationship with the Whites. Howard delivered an open air sermon, hoping enjoinders to peace and goodwill might improve the council's climate. "Young Kamiakin," the late chief's oldest son, finally arrived at 10 a.m. on Monday.

Upon his coming, Governor Ferry offered opening remarks, followed by Howard lauding the recent achievements of Moses' trip to Washington, D.C. "We are very anxious to have all the Indians who are off the reservation to go on it." Or, if Indians preferred it, "take up land as white people do," under provisions of the Indian Homestead Act.

Garry, Young Kamiakin, and others seemed little impressed by the official words, or the fancy new Eastern clothes donned by Moses for the occasion. Although Umatilla Agency interpreter John McBean attended, Young Kamiakin likely deferred to the literate Spokane Garry to express his people's views. "Those men in Washington keep making laws against the Indians, and keep our hearts disturbed all the time." Like Moses, Garry's Middle Spokanes wanted a reserve of reasonable size in their own homeland. He upbraided the Americans for offering just quarter-section homestead plots when "the Indians were always here."

The Christian Garry also invoked geographic and spiritual justifications for his convictions: "The Great Spirit put us here, and put the English, Scotch, Welsh, Irish, and Dutch, each on their own land.... The Great Spirit put the law over us both here and the first law we had was a good one.... The first law was the natural law of the earth." Howard read belligerence in the words of "growling Spokane Garry," in spite of the chief's reminder that he kept his people peaceful during the recent Nez Perce War.[21]

For the past year, the territorial Indian superintendent had considered creating a Spokane Reservation in the Tshimakain Creek district, east of the Colville Reservation—despite objections from citizens contending that "the rapid influx of immigration makes a change in the Indian status inevitable," and that enough land already was set aside for the tribes. Chief Lot and the Lower Spokanes, though on good terms with Moses, still opposed relocation from their homeland. They had become overwhelmingly Protestant following years of contact with Rev. Henry Cowley at the tribe's Tshimikain Mission. Most refused to move to a reservation under Catholic jurisdiction.

Ferry and Howard, however, had come to inform Indian leaders about recent decisions, not to entertain new proposals for still more reserves (although a reservation eventually was established in Lower Spokane country in 1881). Leaders such as Garry and Young Kamiakin were left to accept what was offered. "If the Great Father will not give me land," Garry threatened, "I will not go to another reservation, but will stay here until the whites push me out, and out, and out, until there is no more out left."

Young Kamiakin's brash heart likely stirred with such rhetoric, but he surely understood when listening to the council exchanges that the Americans favored Moses. Moreover, when viewing the commercial bustle nearby—where James Glover's new mill at the falls supplied lumber for buildings here and throughout the region—perhaps the Kamiakins would be better off in a place where "natural law" prevailed. For his part, Young Kamiakin could find solidarity among his relatives at *Palus*, perhaps finding means through the support of men such as Howard to establish Indian homesteads there.[22]

As the 1879 Moses Reservation was surveyed, objections from miners, settlers, and territorial officials eventually altered the boundaries, taking off a 15-mile-wide strip along the Canadian border. Nevertheless, Moses remained buoyed by the prospects of his people's own reserve, and he invited non-reservation Umatillas, Palouses, and others to relocate there. Moses moved with his band to the Okanogan Valley in 1879, but found his presence opposed by miners and ranchers, who were unwilling to be evicted.

Moses and his people roamed on and off the reservation for several years, until government officials, not wishing to become embroiled in another conflict, offered to purchase the recently designated but relatively little used Columbia Reservation. A $150,000 payment to the tribe, a guarantee of lands in severalty on the Colville Reservation, and an annual $1,000 annuity for the chief eventually prevailed upon Moses to accept the new provisions, approved by Congress on July 4, 1884, in the "Moses Agreement."

The following year, Moses led his band to the Nespelem Valley on the Colville Reservation. They camped near the families of several longtime area residents, including Nespelem George and Nespelem Frank, who were rather disconcerted by the sudden appearance of so many new arrivals in their quiet valley.[23]

Chapter 10

Travois on the Trail

Young Chinook continued upriver.
He heard a noise and found
Coyote sitting on a rock.
He was splitting kamooki [Indian hemp].
"What are you making?"

Coyote said, "I'm making a net
to catch lots of fish
when they pass by here."
Young Chinook remembered
to avoid that place.
And he kept on going
along the river.

Kamiakin family members continued to reside at Rock Lake and at *Palus* after the chief's passing in 1877. His four widowed sister-wives maintained busy households tending the younger children, such as Piupiu K'ownot and Sk'olumkee, and followed the old trails to customary root and berry grounds and to fishing sites. A schoolteacher visiting White families at Rock Lake in June 1878 encountered "a company of Indians…driving a band of cayuse ponies," who may well have been the chief's sons still tending their substantial herds.[1]

In time, the Kamiakins adjusted their seasonal travel patterns to the changing realities of life in the region. The seasonal springtime root grounds to the east were being rapidly claimed and fenced-in by farmers, which also complicated travel to the autumn berry picking areas in the Bitterroot foothills. Like other non-reservation families in the Palouse, the Kamiakins shifted toward more westward destinations during their seasonal journeys. They gathered camas and bitterroot along with their Moses' relatives in the drier Big Bend lowlands, and they participated in deer drives up the coulees to the north. Grand tribal gatherings still were held each

year at places like *Nt'palnwt* ("Rock on the Hillside"), at the ancient Rocky Ford Creek crossing between Moses Lake and the tiny frontier settlement of Ephrata.[2]

A main north-south trail crossed the stream at this site, where large encampments of Plateau tribes had gathered for generations and continued to do so into the 20th century. The Kamiakins joined their Palouse, Nez Perce, and Spokane relatives and friends, camping on the creek's east side. The Columbia-Sinkiuses, Yakamas, and Umatillas occupied the west bank. An enormous race track was located near Moses' camp on the west, where Kamiakin's sons competed, as their Grandfather T'siyiyak had, for piles of valued buffalo hides, bags of root flour, and other prized items wagered on the outcome.

Before moving on to the Snake or Columbia salmon fisheries, the Kamiakins also fished at Moses Lake, or gathered sage hen eggs and hunted migratory fowl nesting there in profuse numbers each spring. Here Kamiakin's son, T'siyiyak, later would die while camped in the vicinity, leaving two sons and a daughter to grieve the unexpected loss. The girl, Ka-mosh-nite—named for Kamiakin's mother—eventually married Hay-hay-tah (Smith L. George), and the couple chose to remain at *Palus* where they were among its last residents.[3]

The Palouse Reserve

Because of the older sons' marriages into non-reservation Palouse-Nez Perce families and the successful filing of Indian land claims by these relatives, the extended family began spending more time along the Snake River. With Kamiakin now gone, the wives and children sought solidarity and fellowship. Tespaloos came to frequently reside at *Palus*, marrying Me-a-tu-kin-ma, sister of Waughaskie (Chief Bones), the Cayuse refugee who would be one of the last permanent residents at the ancient village. Perhaps around the time of the 1879 Spokane Council, Young Kamiakin (We-yet-que-yet), the son-in-law of Chief Húsis Moxmox, also relocated to *Palus*, where he and his brothers maintained the family's substantial horse herds.[4]

The Palouses gradually developed a high regard for a prominent Snake River rancher, George Hunter, consulting with him about land policies. Hunter had served as a volunteer during the Yakima and Nez Perce wars, but after making his home near Grange City, he became a friend of Chief Big Thunder and the *Palus* residents. At the outbreak of the 1878 Bannock-Paiute hostilities in Idaho and Oregon, General Howard held a council with the villagers. Hunter served as interpreter and both men learned of the Indians' desire to remain in the locality, taking up lands in severalty. Howard encouraged them to do so. Big Thunder later asked Hunter "to go with him and others of the tribe to find the 'corner' and 'lines' and generally assist them in locating and entering their lands in severalty at the local land office in Colfax."

About 1884, Hunter traveled with Big Thunder and Chief Bones to Colfax, helping them file claims on their ancestral lands.[5] John Pettyjohn, a Touchet Valley pioneer of 1859, and Dan Lyons also joined with Hunter as unofficial spokesmen for the Indians and advocates for the Indian homesteads. This

Kah-yee-wach Kamiakin (Pete Bones) near Palouse Falls, 1914.
Washington State Historical Society (Roger Chute S1991.51.2.454)

role strained their relations with some of their White neighbors. With the help of these three White men, the Kamiakin brothers We-yet-que-yet and T'siyiyak, their crippled nephew Kah-yee-wach (Pete Bones), We-yet-que-wit's father-in-law Chief Húsis Moxmox, Yosyóos Tulikecíin (Sam Fisher), and other Palouses filed for Indian homestead sites.

By carefully arranging the entries on unsettled lands, Pettyjohn, Lyons, and Hunter helped the Palouses claim quarter-sections totaling some 1,600 contiguous acres along the lower Palouse River, from its mouth up to Palouse Falls. Although the canyon area was semi-arid and rocky, it was the sacred landscape of the Palouse people's origin. Now they held legal title, preventing occupation by settlers.[6]

Young Sk'olumkee ("Snake River Kamiakin") assumed new responsibilities in managing the Kamiakin family's vast remuda. The family's herds never approached the numbers owned before the war, but their distinct "S" brand was seen on scores of animals grazing in the western Palouse. Sk'olumkee's reticent ways and slight hunchback belied his knowledge and wisdom, often unknown to those who might find his silence and appearance somewhat peculiar. Throughout his youth, Sk'olumkee spent weeks on end tending the family herds on the bunchgrass prairies. He came to be utterly self-reliant, subsisting at length in any season by his wits and nature's provision, even in the desolate sand hills and coulees of the lower Palouse River country. Sk'olumkee came to prefer solitude in open spaces and the companionship of the horses and other animals who understood his whispers. In time, he excelled at horsemanship, becoming renowned for his deft skills at taming animals that most others found unmanageable.

The Kamiakins' wayfaring brother often appeared after an extended absence, only to mysteriously vanish again. But Sk'olumkee seemed to have an uncanny sense of coming when needed—to encourage a sick child, or mending gear for managing livestock. He comprehended messages in the howls of coyotes and knew of dire warnings. In this way, he kept herds in shielded coulees and other safe havens when the fearsome weather-changer sent prairie storms. Sk'olumkee also was among the first to hear the colorful *wawshukla* announcing spring's arrival—such long anticipated news by northern orioles generally proved far more important than the meadowlark and magpie gossip he also comprehended.

Sk'olumkee eventually married Pemalks Skumsit (Shumkin). Although the couple remained childless, Sk'olumkee's many nieces and nephews looked forward to periodic visits with their beloved trickster uncle. Sk'olumkee delighted in the children's company, keeping them entertained with storytelling and by such antics as pretending to hide tiny creatures inside his head.[7]

Long Trail North

After the government's confirmation of the "Moses Agreement" in 1884, Chief Moses and many friends and relatives among the Moses-Columbias, as well as some Yakamas, began residing on the Colville Reservation. Yakama-Entiat leader David Nanamkin, a grandson of Chief Owhi, decided to join Moses about 1885. A number of Yakamas with familial ties to other reservations also sought to relocate at this time in response to the harsh tactics applied by Yakima Agent Robert Milroy, who was separating Indian parents from their children. Milroy zealously carried on the boarding school program introduced by Rev. James Wilbur at Ft. Simcoe in the 1860s.

Milroy assumed his responsibilities with implacable zeal, believing that "Indian children can learn and absorb nothing from their ignorant parents but barbarism. Hence the vast importance of detaching them from their parents as soon as they reach school age." Children were rounded up by Milroy's Indian police to attend the agency boarding school, where they were given English names and uniforms, forbidden to speak in their Native tongue, and made to tend vast gardens of cabbages and potatoes. Parents who objected were to be "punished by fine, or imprisonment and labor."[8]

Chuweah, Tatshama, and other Palouse-Umatilla families, who had fled the Bannock troubles in the late 1870s, also joined Moses. The chief likewise had long encouraged the Kamiakins to do so. By the middle 1880s, the Columbia chief's personal household had grown to include the families of his two surviving wives, Sanclow and Peotsenmy, as well as four of his sisters and brothers. In addition, he had adopted the family of Qualchan's orphaned son, Sokula, and his niece, Quanspeetsah, mother of Weashuit (Peter Dan Moses). Moses had been especially pleased when Sinsinq't, his favored daughter by the late Quo-mo-lah, married Chief Kamiakin's son, Lukash. The marriage had occurred in about 1882 and further strengthened the ties between two of the region's most prominent chieftain clans. A child was born to the couple a year or two later, Nellie, on whom the chief doted.[9]

With Lukash now a member of Moses' clan, the Kamiakin band was giving further consideration to the rather dreaded prospect of relocating to the Colville Reservation. Many Palouses, however, still stubbornly wished to cling to slivers of ancient homeland in the sagebrush flats and rocky bluffs along the Snake River. The Kamiakin brothers well knew that the shrinking number of villagers at such places as *Palus, Pinawáwih*, and *Wawáwi* included elders determined to live out their days in familiar surroundings.

Chief Kamiakin, however, had impressed upon his children the importance of planning for future generations. Most of his sons and daughters now were raising young families of their own, and prospects for a viable future along the river were doubtful.[10] Indeed, the Kamiakins and other Palouses were grateful to their White friends for helping to secure legal title to *Palus* vicinity lands—men such as local rancher George Hunter, Major J.W. MacMurray of the U.S. Army on special assignment to provide property rights assistance, and others. But many Indians realized that the relentless press of new settlers all around them, the incessant roadway traffic at nearby Palouse Crossing, and the almost daily whistle blasts of passing Snake River sternwheelers were ushering forth still further assaults on old ways.

Conflicts with some testy teamsters and other Whites regularly passing by the village were commonplace. Abused Indians had little recourse for justice from wrongdoing. Perhaps some specific incident prompted the brothers to make a final break from the places where their Grandfather T'siyiyak won legendary horse races, and where Kamiakin taught them to hunt and shared the *walsa'kwit* of Coyote, Salmon Man, and the Wolf Brothers.

Kamiakin had advised his sons to think of the children and accept reservation life. Most would do so within a decade of the chief's passing. When asked of this final uprooting, occurring about 1885, Tomeo Kamiakin laconically replied: "A-pas-teen-na came to Moses and told them they would come." The proud remnant of the Kamiakin clan packed buffalo robes, large *wapas* hemp string bags laden with roots, cooking utensils, hunting and fishing gear, and other belongings onto travois, and moved their substantial horse and cattle herds on the long trail north to a new life. Tespaloos, Tomeo, Sk'olumkee, Piupiu K'ownot, and other family members joined Lukash on the Colville Reservation, although the Kamiakins were not listed in an agency census until the following decade.

Tespaloos's wife, Me-a-tu-kin-ma—daughter of the Cayuse exiles Waughaskie and Me-a-tat at *Palus*—faced divided

Tomeo Kamiakin, 1905.
Colville Confederated Tribes

obligations to her husband and elderly parents. She grieved over having to choose which path to take, but eventually decided to remain in the adopted land of her parents and care for them. Tespaloos, however, chose to relocate with his brothers to Nespelem, where he remarried. He served as the clan's principal spokesman in agency affairs for over two decades, while also making periodic visits to relatives on the Snake River. His son, Mul-mul-kin, later joined him on the reservation, assuming the name Sam Tespaloos.

Kah-yee-wach (Pete Bones), a skilled horseman in spite of infirmities, remained at *Palus*. Eventually, Sam and Helen Fisher along with Pete Bones would be the last members of the band to seasonally reside at the village.[11]

The Nespelem Community

With Colville Agent Benjamin Moore's assistance, Tomeo, Sk'olumkee, and Tespaloos established homes on the outskirts of tiny Nespelem along a sage-covered flat near the first falls of the river, where a sawmill and flume were built. Joseph's winter camp also was located along the west bank of the river about a quarter-mile further south, flanked by Yellow Wolf and Two Moons. Nespelem had emerged as a supply center for regional mining activity, as well as for local Indian families, and by the mid 1890s boasted a hotel operated by Henry Steele, C.M. Hinman's blacksmith shop, and a general store.

Dr. Edward Latham, who arrived at Nespelem in January 1890 to serve as agency doctor, described the environs in favorable terms: "There is a full half section of beautiful level land located at the base of the mountain, so situated that the sun shines upon it from the time it rises until it sets; and on the side of the mountain, five or six hundred feet above, there gushes forth the finest spring of clear, cold water that I have ever seen.… Here, with little expense, could be made a paradise. There are no mosquitoes, and during the day the wind comes up the valley from the Columbia, and at night it reverses and comes down the valley from the mountains."

Latham served the reservation community for many years and gained the trust of many local residents including Tomeo Kamiakin. When his children were struck by smallpox, Tomeo consented to have his house fumigated and assisted in Latham's "strong medicine" to aid recovery.[12]

The Kamiakins formed part of an extended enclave of Palouses and their Moses-Columbia, Yakama, and Nez Perce relatives. Agent Moore subsequently arranged quarter-section allotments for the Kamiakins and others in outlying localities, although family members chose to spend most of the year in homes near town. Sk'olumkee remained friendly to all, but, somewhat aloofly, soon chose to live on an allotment several miles north near the shore of a small lake. Tomeo was allotted land along Little Nespelem Creek, about one mile east of the new agency headquarters, and later established a home there. Chief Kamiakin's daughter Kiatana (Lucy) now was married to the Nez Perce-Palouse War veteran Ben Owhi, and Yumasepah soon married Peopeo-hy-yi-toman, a close relative of Chief Joseph. A daughter, Sophie (Atwice), was born to the latter couple in 1889; she later became a prominent Kamiakin family historian.[13]

During the time of resettlement, tragedy struck the family. While returning home with his family from a trip to Spokane Falls, Lukash Kamiakin was attacked north of Wilbur by a disreputable Okanogan whiskey peddler named Puckmiakin. The renegade murdered Kamiakin with an axe in the presence of Sinsinq't and little Nellie, who remembered her father's dying screams for the rest of her life. Puckmiakin escaped from the melee, but some years later was killed near the mouth of the Okanogan River for his complicity in other crimes.

E.S. Curtis portrait of Kamiakin's daughter, Kiatana "Lucy" Owhi.
Tanya N. Tomeo

During the winter of 1886–87, We-yet-que-yit ("Young Kamiakin"), still residing at *Palus*, was killed in a horse fall near Washtucna. Chief Kamiakin's eldest son was buried in the sandy, windswept cemetery at *Palus*, overlooking the Snake River.[14] His grief-stricken widow, Tallas (Theresa), soon returned with their daughter to her Koltsenshin family on the Coeur d'Alene Reservation, where the young girl was raised as Ellen (Helen) Chumayakan.

These various developments were likely factors influencing members of the T'siyiyak (Williams) Kamiakin family to also move to the Colville Reservation in 1888. A daughter, Alalumti, born that year at Nespelem to Nez Perce War veterans Koots-koots Tsom-ya-whet (Little Man Chief) and Iatotkikt would eventually marry T'siyiyak Kamiakin's oldest son, Te-meh-yew-te-toot, or Charley Williams. He would serve as the Palouse band's last traditional chief on the Colville Reservation until his death in 1969.[15]

The arrival of members of the Kamiakin and Moses bands on the reservation stirred some opposition from the San Poils

and Nespelems. The latter naturally resented the government's decision to relocate numerous non-reservation families and Joseph's Nez Perces on traditional San Poil and Nespelem lands. Other newcomers included people from the Wenatchi bands, some closely related to the Kamiakins, who had been driven from their scenic homeland by an influx of settlers and railroad builders.

The Wenatchi were mindful of the promise made to Kamiakin and Tecolekun in the 1855 Yakama Treaty for the establishment of a 36-square-mile Wenatshapam Fishery Reservation. The recently platted town site of Leavenworth, however, stood on these lands, and years of neglect by the Indian Service had jeopardized the reserve's formal designation. The situation was compounded by fraudulent maneuverings in 1893 and 1894 by Agent Lewis T. Erwin, who had been dispatched to resolve the issue. Erwin persuaded the Yakamas, who held the treaty rights, that the Wenatchis favored selling the reserve. This deception led to an agreement with the tribe to accept a payment of $20,000 to extinguish title to lands never properly surveyed. Many of the Kamiakins' Wenatchi relatives fiercely protested the sale, but were forced to relocate or take isolated allotments on marginal lands not already claimed by Whites. Most of them reluctantly moved to the Colville Reservation.[16]

New Rounds, Old Trails

In time, the Kamiakins meshed their lives with those of other Indians on the reservation, living out most of their days far from the winding rivers and rolling hills of the Palouse country. Elijah Williams, nephew of famed Nez Perce warrior Yellow Wolf, remembered how his family often joined in activities with the Tespaloos, Tomeo, and Cleveland Kamiakin families, cutting firewood on nearby pine covered slopes, drying salmon and venison outside their houses, and traveling to root and berry grounds. They hunted in the Grand Coulee and Waterville Plateau localities in April and May, while the women dug bitterroot and wild carrots. Camas and wild onions abounded in the prairie districts east of Soap Lake, Almira, and beyond Wilson Creek. In June and July, they often converged with hundreds of other Indian families at Kettle Falls for the annual Chinook salmon run. In late summer and fall, many gathered to collect chokecherries, serviceberries, and elderberries in the Grand Coulee area and around Willow Lake.[17]

During periodic treks between the Colville and Nez Perce reservations, Kamiakin family members also visited relatives in their old homeland. The ancient trails they took now often were graded in long stretches for modern-day traffic. Traveling on horseback between Nespelem and Lapwai took at least a week. Long processions of riders forded the Columbia at Moses Crossing (Barry) or three miles downstream at Seaton's Ferry near the mouth of Spring Canyon. Often traveling in groups of more than a hundred, they camped near pioneer hamlets emerging at *Telahats* (Wilbur), *Sumki-Ilpilp* (Harrington), and *Elatsaywitsun* (Sprague) before reaching the Kamiakins' old home at the foot of Rock Lake (*Tax'liit*). Following respite near the lakeshore and visits to nearby family gravesites, they continued on to camp near St. John, Colfax, Pullman, and Lewiston. Ben Owhi also recalled a pilgrimage with Moses to Qualchan's execution and burial site near the Kentuck Trail Ford, where the men paid homage to their martyred relative.[18]

Tomeo Kamiakin became a skilled builder and blacksmith. He assisted his brothers, sisters, and others on the reservation in constructing houses and barns with lumber provided by Joseph Bousaka's sawmill, where Tomeo and Ben Owhi were employed by the agency to work as sawyers and teamsters. At the turn of the century, Tespaloos continued to serve as a principal spokesman for the Kamiakin band, and in time his role in agency matters would be assumed by his son, Sam Tespaloos. The Kamiakins also eventually were represented by Cleveland and Charlie Wilpocken, Chief Kamiakin's nephew. Sk'olumkee and Pemalks continued to live in their simple home several miles north of Nespelem, usually coming to town only once a week by buggy or wagon to pick up supplies.[19]

Sk'olumkee, the Kamiakin brother most Whites knew as "Snake River Kamiakin," never lost his special way with animals. He could sleep in his hack coming back from Nespelem or Coulee City and his horses invariably knew the way home, arriving to a warm welcome by Sk'olumkee's black dogs. A roadway mishap near Steamboat Rock eventually damaged the buggy beyond repair. The couple spent their later years traveling back and forth to Nespelem on foot. Sk'olumkee rarely spoke in English, and all animals seemed to comprehend his Native tongue. Some folks thought he took better care of his livestock than of himself.

Visitors seldom knocked on the door of the couple's remote home, but if they did, they usually did not remain long, in spite of the pleasing aroma of Sk'olumkee's special blend of kinnickinic and tobacco—the place was bereft of table, chairs, bed, or furniture of any kind. The old couple slept in blankets on the floor. The only objects on the unpainted walls were dried roots and other provisions hung from nails.[20]

For many years, the Kamiakin and Moses families frequently joined members of the Joseph band and other Indians as honored guests in Fourth of July parades at Wilbur, Coulee City, Soap Lake, or other communities. After the turn of the century, week-long pow-wows also were held annually on a broad flat near the Nespelem Agency. As many as sixty tipis stood in a vast circle, not far from a rodeo arena. A pole-framed pavilion was used for daytime ceremonial dances, and for stick-game gambling lasting far into the night. In preparing for these festive affairs, family members of all ages worked for weeks readying their heirloom finery and other exquisitely-beaded costumes and equestrian regalia. They also cut tipi poles and evergreen limbs to shade the pow-wow pavilion, and gathered ample traditional foods for feasting and sale to spectators.

In time, area newspapers came to describe these grand gatherings as "the most colorful and spectacular scenes to be found anywhere," with "many of the costumes made new" each year for events attended by as many as 1,500 people. In later years, Cleveland Kamiakin and Willie Red Star Andrews often were noted as the event's "general managers," whose intention was to enable "the younger Indians to remember and carry on their old traditions." Event organizers Joe Redthunder, Tom Andrews, Elijah Williams, and others often congregated at Cleveland's home on Nespelem's outskirts to plan pow-wow activities, and for *Wáashat* services in the adjacent longhouse.[21]

The Paween and *Palus* Bands

In the 1880s, the Kamiakins' Paween and Poyahkin relatives in the *Pinawáwih* and *Wawáwih* localities weighed difficult choices regarding their future. Chief Húsis Paween had dispatched his nephews, Wayayentutpik and namesake Húsis Paween (Tom Paween), to consult with Moses, who favorably received them. As with the Tilcoax-Wolf family further down the Snake, however, the Paweens' situation was complicated by their desire to maintain large horse herds ranging along the river and to participate in the livestock trade. But several factors conspired early in the next decade to force a decision.

In 1890–91, a regional smallpox epidemic drove more Snake River Indians to reservations. Among those dying in

Village of *Palus* and the Union Pacific's Joso Bridge (completed 1912).
Yakima Valley Museum (C. Relander Collection

about 1890, was Húsis Paween himself, who recently had come to the reluctant conclusion that his family should move with their herd to the Colville Reservation. Before he could act, the "hi-yu fire" exacted a merciless toll, especially among the children. A band member, Ah-kis-kis, reported in April 1891 the recent loss of his own son along with seventeen other children. Parents and elders were left in mourning and despair.[22] One of the outbreaks began after several Palouse women washed clothing belonging to Dayton residents—the townspeople themselves also would suffer from the epidemic. Smallpox, as well as deprivations, drove many to reservations where the Indian bureau provided limited relief.[23]

Even the forces of nature seemed displeased, since the camas harvest and salmon runs were far below normal levels in 1891. The few families stubbornly clinging to their ancient homes from *Alamótin* to *Pinawáwih* faced the pain of separation from relatives, who either had died or moved away. Though Indians grew corn and melons, White settlers claimed the choicest lands along the river, planting vast acreages of orchards and gardens. Heavy snows in late 1893 led to flooding that scattered the remaining Indian horse herds for a time.

These circumstances finally led the Paweens and Poyahkins, including the Jim Billy Andrews family, to move to Nespelem in 1892 and 1893. Nevertheless, family members did return seasonally for some years to work as farm laborers in the Dayton and Touchet districts, and then returned back to Nespelem, or in some cases to the Nez Perce Reservation.

For similar reasons, Chief Tilcoax's son, Wolf Necklace (Peter Wolf), moved a substantial part of his massive herd

to the Colville Reservation in 1893. He also sold some 3,000 head in Ephrata after a celebrated round-up led by his nephew Harry Jim with 34 riders.[24] The rapid influx of so many horses on the bunchgrass prairies in the Nespelem Valley invariably led to conflicts over ownership.

Although most of the stock was rounded up for branding before heading north, disputes arose over inheritance because of recent marital alliances. Soon after Chief Húsis Paween's death, his widow, Teek-ton-nay, had married Wolf Necklace and combined a portion of the herd bearing the Paween's "+" brand with Tilcoax family livestock. About the same time, Húsis Paween's brother, Tenoo Paween, married Alalumti (Alilintai), the daughter of Chief Poyahkin, who also claimed a portion of her late father's substantial herd. Agreements resolving this confusion eventually were brokered after Ben Owhi and Chief Moses met with family members on behalf of newly appointed Agency Farmer John Mires, who welcomed the assistance of these experienced and trusted negotiators.[25]

Over time, close family ties were forged on the reservation between the Kamiakins and Paweens, as several marriages bound these prominent clans together. Tom Paween's sister, Ot-wes-on-my, would soon marry Tomeo Kamiakin, while his daughters Alalumt'i became Cleveland's wife and U-pa-pi later married Harry Owhi, son of Ben Owhi and Kiatana (Lucy) Kamiakin.[26]

At the turn of the century, about seventy-five Indians remained at *Palus*, including remnants of bands once led by Hahtalekin, Big Thunder, and Húsis Moxmox. These Palouses continued "to cling tenaciously to this barren spot where their children were born and their mothers and fathers have died." Events had moved rapidly in their lives, but they had "not changed their minds" about staying. However, they seemed powerless to stop removal actions attempted by the government.

Yakima Agent Lewis Irwin had visited *Palus* in the spring of 1897 to assess the situation. He reported that the Indians cultivated ten acres, but subsisted mostly on fish. Their root grounds were mostly destroyed by the plow, and the Indians were having difficulty eking out a living by fishing due to the intense commercial salmon harvesting and cannery operations on the lower Columbia, depleting the upriver runs. Though the agent wrote about the Palouses with respect, fines of his mind. When Andrew grew older, he asked tribal elders about the removal, but found "they never wanted to talk about it much." The memory was too painful for them to discuss, even to the younger members of their own families. George recalled that when the elders were asked about the event, men and women grew silent and often wept.[28]

Adding to the sorrows of these times was the passing of two of the region's most prominent Indian leaders, who had guided their people through an era of unprecedented change. In March 1899, Chief Moses died of complications from kidney disease and old age. Chief Joseph succumbed in September 1904, with Dr. Latham penning a "broken heart" as the legendary Nez Perce leader's cause of death. Nez Perce War veterans La-cot-to-hiak-teen (Albert Waters) and Ee-lah-wee-mah (David Williams), who had witnessed his mother's death at the Big Hole, succeeded Joseph in leading the Colville Nez Perce. Among the Kamiakin brothers and sisters, too, Indians throughout the region recognized a new

Pete Bones (1895–1954), one of the last members of the band residing at *Palus*.
Washington State Historical Society (Roger Chute S1991.51.2.528)

House periodically occupied by Pete Bones, 1950.
Washington State Historical Society (Roger Chute S1991.51.2.528.1)

he recommended to the commissioner "that they be forcibly removed to the Nez Perce, Umatilla, or Yakama Reservations." Other Indian agents and many White settlers agreed with Irwin's suggestion.[27] The Indian bureau eventually acted upon this recommendation.

In the spring of 1905, a steamboat arrived at *Palus* carrying soldiers with orders to take the Indians aboard, along with their belongings. Most families complied. After boarding, they congregated at the stern, intensely gazing toward their abandoned homes and the graves of loved ones. As the steamer picked up speed, they watched Standing Rock passing from view. They stood quietly until loosing sight of the village.

One Palouse Indian, a small boy at the time, recalled the entire scene, "like a vision of the way things were." Andrew George remembered the removal as a dream outside the con-

generation of respected *miyawaxpamáma* walking the trail with them into the 20th century.[29]

Only a small number of Indian families remained on the lower Snake River in 1910. Stories were told at this time about Palouses being forced off farmers' property at gunpoint. Within two decades, most of them, too, would move to reservations.

New tragedy sometimes befell the remaining stalwarts. In early spring 1914, for example, a group of five Palouses were traveling along the Palouse River about a mile above Rock

Creek when they were caught in a sudden and ferocious March blizzard. A large barn stood nearby, but the group sought refuge in a small cove near the river. By daybreak three had frozen to death. The rancher who rescued the two survivors found that the adults had huddled together over a boy, protecting him. The lad, who barely survived the ordeal, was young Carter Slouthier, a nephew of Sam Fisher. Carter was then adopted by Fisher and his wife, Helen. Though the Fishers were allotted reservation property, they continued to live seasonally at *Palus*.[30]

Agency, Church, and School

In 1912–13, when the Colville Agency was relocated from Ft. Spokane to Nespelem, a burst of boomtown excitement occurred. Agent John Webster's initial staff included a government farmer, doctor, and a matron fieldworker, who visited homes in the area to teach home economics. Land speculators sold town lots to White investors at premium prices, as another general store, a bank, blacksmith and livery shops, and other businesses appeared along Nespelem's several streets.

Sophie Kamiakin (Atwice).

The Friedlander offspring—Emily, George, and Lucy, the grandchildren of Lukash Kamiakin—had the rare privilege of an upbringing guided by their remarkable elder, Mary Owhi Moses. After the deaths of Lukash Kamiakin and his wife Sinsinq't in the 1880s, Mary helped raise the couple's young daughter, Nellie, as her own child. When Nellie grew to maturity, she married Louis Friedlander, the son of post trader J. Herman Friedlander at Camp Chelan. Mary Moses helped tend their new household as a grandmother, and shared her extensive personal knowledge of Owhi and Kamiakin's past with the Friedlander children, as well as their young cousins, such as Mary Kamiakin's daughter Sophie.

Mary Moses matter-of-factly related chilling accounts about the Indians' flight from Wright's soldiers in the late 1850s. She also told tender tales, about Moses and Kamiakin's devotion to their wives in times of cruel deprivation, and the leaders' respect for each other. Despite Mary Moses' rather humble presence and simple ways, family and friends perceived in her the dignified bearing of one whose ancestors were of another realm. As stars twinkled brightly over the small farmstead near Nespelem, Mary often reminisced about

things of past times, when she was known as Sanclow. Sometimes she took the children outside to reacquaint them with their celebrated stellar ancestor, the Evening Star.

The new generation of Indian youths were living in a world both ancient and modern, and sometimes were puzzled by the contrast. Sophie and her sister, Ta-lats Ton-my, often visited James Davis's dry goods store to pick up supplies needed by their mother, Mary, the eldest surviving daughter of Chief Kamiakin. Mr. Davis's gramophone display fascinated young Sophie, but her hopes to acquire one were dashed during a subsequent visit to the store with her mother. "No," she scolded Sophie, "some of those singers might be dead and 'ghost' you."[31]

In the 20th century's first decade, many Colville and Spokane reservation youth were sent to the government's Ft. Spokane Indian Boarding School, which opened in April 1900 after troops at the post were redeployed for the Spanish-American War or to newly established Ft. George Wright west of Spokane. Tom Billy Andrews, a native of the Almota-Penawawa area, attended the Ft. Spokane school for three years beginning in 1901. He remembered that conditions were severe. For months at a time, the children remained at the school, not visiting their faraway homes. They were forced to conform to new rules for speech and dress. "I had hair, long hair almost down to my throat," recalled Andrews, "and then they cut my hair. I almost cried."[32]

The children surrendered their mellifluous names for English ones and were strictly forbidden to converse in their Native languages during classes, under penalty of corporal punishment or even confinement in the post's brick stockade. Educational programs were based on the government's "Rules for Indian Schools," formulated in 1890: "A regular and efficient system of industrial training must be part of the work of each school. At least half of the time of each boy and girl should be devoted thereto—the work to be of such character that they may be able to apply the knowledge and experience gained, in the locality where they may be expected to reside after leaving school."

In the case of one lonesome and resourceful Yakama boy desperate to rejoin his family, not even iron bars in a window overcame his determination to return home. A school matron and seamstress, Frances LeBret, remembered that the morning after the youth was locked up for trying to run away, a staff member found the cell bars sufficiently bent for the boy to escape.

Indian police sent in pursuit eventually caught up with him near the base of a steep cliff. "But the fleet-footed boy had made up his mind that he was not going back to school." Bravely, "he started clambering up the rock cliff which was almost straight up. The men just stood and watched him, almost afraid to breathe, for it seemed that any moment he would fall to the sharp rocks below. Up and up he went, until he reached the top and quickly disappeared, still running."

A likely fate awaiting such truants when reaching home was seizure by the authorities and a return to the school under stricter supervision. Chief Joseph and other tribal leaders pressed for the opening of more local day schools on the reservation as an alternative to the boarding arrangements. Agent Albert Anderson, in the meantime, threatened to arrest parents not complying with the regulations regarding compulsory attendance. Enrollment declined substantially toward the end of the decade, however, as more reservation day

schools were organized. The fort school eventually discontinued operation in 1914.[33]

Nespelem's first Indian day school had opened in 1890, and by 1911 five others were operating on the Colville Reservation. The Moses and Kamiakin relatives were advocates of Indian education, as being necessary for their people to manage their own affairs unfettered by government interference and even malfeasance. (More than one Colville agent was dismissed on criminal charges, including the fraudulent redeeming of annuity checks.)

Many of the younger Kamiakin children, including Arthur and Teddy Tomeo, Annie Cleveland, Ta-lats Ton-my, and Sophie, attended the Indian day school in town. Meanwhile, the Friedlander youths boarded under modest terms at the St. Mary's Mission School, founded by Father Etienne de Rougé S.J., near Omak about 1890. About a hundred children attended St. Mary's in 1910. As was common at Indian boarding schools, the boys donned gray uniforms and caps, while the girls were required to wear dresses and hats. Part of the instructional experience required girls to learn cooking,

Colville Indian Reservation school girls.
WSU Libraries (Avery Collection 80-009)

Tom Billy Andrews, Sam Tespaloos, and Herman Friedlander, c. 1910s.
Colville Confederated Tribes

Greek studies. Classes were strictly segregated by gender. The "commercial courses" included painting, music, photography, taxidermy, and carpentry. Emily and Isabel Friedlander recalled that while English was used for instruction, the missionary teachers insisted that they sing and pray in their Native language whenever Indian elders were present.

By 1915, St. Mary's expanded into "a wonderful institution of many buildings," including the main school, dormitories, chapel, natural history museum, theatre, manual training center, and staff residences, plus barns, outbuildings, surrounding alfalfa and wheat fields, and orchards, where the Friedlander children joined others in picking apples, cherries, and pears in season.

Meanwhile in Nespelem, a parish priest, Father Edward Grivna S.J., established the Church of the Sacred Heart in the fall of 1915, the same year that a Methodist Episcopal church also was built in the community. In keeping with Chief Kamiakin's affiliation, a number of the family attended Sacred Heart, where special family gatherings followed Easter, Christmas, and the Feast of Corpus Christi services.[35]

sewing, and nursing skills, while the boys tended vine crops and extensive corn, tomato, and melon gardens and learned animal husbandry skills.[34]

Though St. Mary's curriculum focused on the manual arts, Father de Rougé, a French scholastic, also emphasized religious studies and academic coursework, including Latin and

WSC Nespelem Art Colony, 1938, with Willie Red Star Andrews in the middle and Anne Harder kneeling to his right.
From J.J. Creighton, Indian Summers *(WSU Press, 2000)*

Chapter 11
Artists and Authors

*Young Chinook reached
his father's old home.
He stepped ashore and
onto Sandpiper's nest.
He broke Sandpiper's leg.
"Tell me where the Wolf Brothers live;
I will fix your leg."*

*Sandpiper told him
and warned of Rattlesnake
living in a high canyon cave.
Young Chinook fashioned a leg
from a twig for Sandpiper.
He traveled a long time
and saw Rattlesnake's home.*

By the beginning of the 20th century, Chief Kamiakin's descendants had married into other Yakama, Moses-Columbia, Nez Perce, and Coeur d'Alene families, which cast them from their heartland to an archipelago of Inland Northwest reservations. Many carried with them the chief's sentiments about living in peace with others and not drawing attention to bygone antagonisms. For this reason, some of the grandchildren discontinued using the chief's family name.[1] They still shared a justifiable pride in their special heritage, however, even as critical depictions of Chief Kamiakin recurrently appeared in Northwest historical literature.

Hazard Stevens' 1901 biography of his father, *The Life of Isaac Ingalls Stevens*, for example, portrayed Kamiakin in inflammatory terms for his intransigence at the 1855 treaty and subsequent hostile actions. Although the younger Stevens offered valuable first-hand observations, since he had accompanied the governor on the treaty-making circuit, he frequently omitted any alternative interpretations and evidence that might cast doubt on his father's reputation and decisions.

A number of other writers expressed similar views detrimental to the reputation of Kamiakin and other Plateau Indian leaders. An 1889 history of the Pacific Northwest accused Kamiakin of being "the wily chieftain and conspirator," who masterminded "the murders of the miners near Colvile, which were committed to provoke hostilities,…the occasion of Colonel Steptoe making a northern expedition towards the Spokane country." Kamiakin "united" the "malcontents" for war.[2]

Some other scholars, however, soon recognized the unfair partiality of such accounts, and several popular histories followed with details about the war years primarily drawn from government documents. In 1912, historian Benjamin F. Manring added to the Kamiakin storyline in his book, *Conquest of the Coeur d'Alenes, Spokanes, and Palouses*. Manring had come west with his family in 1878 and lived the better part of his life in Whitman County, serving as a schoolteacher, county treasurer, and Garfield town mayor.

Much of what Manring reported put Kamiakin's reputation into a more positive light, but some misconception still persisted regarding the chief's involvement in the wars. The Yakama-Palouse leader, Manring wrote, "more than any other of his race, was responsible for the hostility with which the Indians greeted Colonel Steptoe on his northern march, and for the acts of outlawry and murder which preceded that event."

More recent research has shown that Chief Tilcoax actually played a larger role in the Steptoe affair than Kamiakin, who may have arrived after the Indian's initial confrontation with the soldiers. Historians started reconsidering the broadly critical generalities of earlier writers, and Manring himself tempered his views later in life.

In 1941, he joined Sk'olumkee Kamiakin at Rock Lake in an attempt to locate Chief Kamiakin's grave. The opportunity to speak with one of Kamiakin's sons gave Manring new insights into the struggles faced by the famed Yakama-Palouse leader, and led to a new depiction of the chief as the "Tecumseh of the West," or the "Yakima Hannibal." Walla Walla historian William Lyman, too, characterized the struggle in classical terms, opining that "Qualchan seems to have been the Achilles of the tribe, as Kamiakin was their Agamemnon."[3]

The Chieftain Portrait Medallions

In the years after the Kamiakin, Moses, and Joseph peoples had moved to the Colville Reservation, they participated in a remarkable chapter in American art history, which memorialized their leaders in stunning works on canvas and in bronze. The peculiar collaboration began in the summer of 1891, when representatives of Portland's ambitious Industrial Exposition wrote to various Northwest Indian agency officials, requesting a delegation of Plateau Indians to participate in public presentations on Indian culture.

The proposal was approved by the commissioner of Indian affairs, who permitted Moses, Joseph, Lot of the Spokanes, and others to travel to Portland, where they were joined by a similar group of old friends from the Umatilla Reservation, including Young Chief and No Shirt. The party was accompanied by the Colville Agency's interpreter, S.F. Sherwood, and the Umatilla agent, Col. John Crawford. Upon their arrival, a welcoming committee feted the visitors in an impressive reception, and the Indians' speeches and ceremonial dances drew the exposition's largest crowds.

During their stay in Portland, Moses and Joseph met an old acquaintance, Lt. C.E.S. Wood, a former member of General Howard's staff during the Nez Perce War. Wood had become a friend of both chiefs through his years of service in the region. He had been a key figure in pressing military and political authorities in Washington, D.C., to allow the Nez Perce and Palouse exiles to return from Oklahoma. In 1889, during a visit by Joseph to the nation's capital that Wood helped organize, both men met the artist Olin L. Warner, who sculpted a life-size bust of the Nez Perce chief. Deeply impressed with Joseph's moral and physical presence, Warner sought to study the Columbia Plateau people as part of an ambitious plan to commemorate their leaders with a series of bas-relief medallions. The gathering of chiefs at Portland in October 1891 offered a splendid opportunity to pursue this endeavor.[4]

Among artistic circles in the late 19th century, Connecticut native Olin Warner (1844–96) was a leading figure along with Auguste Saint-Gaudens in a national debate between those supporting a European model emphasizing simpler, freer forms that expressed the power of the human spirit, as juxtaposed to others calling for fidelity to American formality and realism in sculpture. During his prodigious studies in France, Warner had mastered bas-relief techniques and returned to the United States with his unique vision, fusing classical styles with realism. While pondering ideal themes to portray in this synthesis, Warner had been introduced to Wood and his Native American friends.

At the Portland exposition, Warner patiently modeled from life the likenesses of Moses, Lot, and others, including "Sabina," a daughter of Cayuse Chief Kash Kash. Warner found his guests willing, if somewhat indifferent, to oblige his interests by visiting make-shift studios at the exposition and a nearby railroad car, where he formed half to two-thirds life-size profiles in clay. From these models, he later fashioned smaller bas-relief busts in the style of European Renaissance medals. His efforts led to the casting of a limited series of bronze "portrait medallions" in New York City, acquired by prominent patrons and art museums across the country.

A special reward for his ideas occurred when he was commissioned to design the monumental main-entry doors to the Library of Congress. Warner's theme for the first of the three bronze doors, each weighing over a ton, was the oral tradition, with images representing Imagination and Memory. A Columbia Plateau Indian orator serves as the splendid centerpiece.

Warner's work strongly influenced Seattle's leading sculptor of the early 20th century, James A. Wehn (1882–1973), who likely learned about the medallions from two University of Washington history professors, Edmond Meany and C.B. Bagley. In 1907, when only in his mid 20s, Wehn won a coveted commission to sculpt a bronze statue of Chief Seattle for downtown Seattle. A bust of the chief was unveiled in Pioneer Square in 1909, and a full-bodied statue was dedicated at Tilikum Place in 1912.

Wehn established the University of Washington's sculpture department in 1919, where his association with Meany and Bagley led to a deep interest in regional Native American and pioneer history. In the 1920s, he embarked on a goal similar to Warner's efforts, creating commemorative medallions of Chief Kamiakin and other prominent Northwest Indian leaders based on Gustavus Sohon's sketches from the 1855 Walla Walla Council. These works by Wehn became part of the permanent art collections at the Washington State Historical Society in Tacoma and the University of Washington, Seattle.[5]

Last Hero and the Nespelem Art Colony

Similar trends transforming American painting contributed to dramatic depictions of Kamiakin's sons, daughters, and relatives during this period. Seeking a distinct style devoid of formalities, painters such as the Midwest's renowned Grant Wood (1891–1942) sought to express the primitive strength of American subject matter. Many like him found inspiration in the "various, rich land abounding in painting material" of the mid and far west. They sought to celebrate the dynamic mix of restless change and an ancient past in these regions with rich palettes of orange ocher, olive green, and other earth tones—shades of dawn and dusk, land and sky, likewise used by generations of Indians to decorate arrows, sallie bags, and imbricated cedar-root baskets.

In 1924, the gifted young artist-scholar Worth Griffin was deeply influenced by such currents of Western Regionalism when moving from Chicago to Pullman to teach fine arts at Washington State College. During his early years at WSC, Griffin became acquainted with the area's Native American heritage through discussions with history professor Herman J. Deutsch and retired college president Enoch O. Bryan. In the course of these conversations, Griffin's mentors advised him to read frontiersman-historian A.J. Splawn's 1917 memoir, *Ka-Mi-Akin: The Last Hero of the Yakimas*. The account written by Splawn (1845–1917) was both controversial and revolutionary. His stories meandered richly like a Tree of Life tapestry, weaving in and out of myriad personal and family connections and to notable figures in the Yakima Valley's Indian and pioneer past.

Splawn's deeper characterization of Kamiakin was derived from both written records and firsthand accounts from the chief's contemporaries and family members. Splawn first met Tomeo Kamiakin in 1907 at a Yakama memorial gathering in Toppenish. The chance encounter represented "unusual good luck and inspiration" in regard to the ambitious book project that Splawn contemplated. He invited Tomeo to his ranch near Yakima, where they spent hours talking about Chief Kamiakin's life. In this intimate private setting, Tomeo shared important details about Kamiakin's earlier years that were never before disclosed beyond family confines. Tomeo offered to introduce his appreciative host to other relatives at Nespelem.[6]

Worth Griffin, inspired by Splawn's book and encouraged by Pullman colleagues, met Colville Reservation leaders and jointly established WSC's Nespelem Art Colony, opening in June 1937. It was modeled after other established art colonies across the country at the time, including at Taos Pueblo and Santa Fe, New Mexico. The project had the full support of WSC President E.O. Holland, a strong patron of the arts. Over the next five summers, a talented group of faculty, students, public school teachers, and freelancers gathered at Nespelem, creating an extensive visual record of Nespelem's residents and daily life on the reservation.[7]

Among Griffin's and graduate assistant Glenn West's most gifted protégés was a ranchers' daughter, Anne Maybelle Harder. The parents of this free spirited and talented young woman, Jacob and Annine Harder, had established a livestock operation headquartered along Cow Creek east of Ritzville. By the 1930s, it had grown into the largest contiguous ranch in the region covering well over 100,000 acres. A major Indian route extended along Cow Creek between Sprague Lake and the Palouse River. Consequently, the Harders became well acquainted with numerous Indian families, who sometimes camped in groups of nearly 200 on the property when traveling between the Snake and Columbia rivers and the reservations.

Anne Harder developed a deep personal interest and abiding friendships with many Palouse Indian families, and sought to study Native American artistic motifs seen on traditional baskets and bags. Although she had graduated from WSC in 1931 and pursued graduate studies in art at the University of Washington in Seattle, Harder remained fully involved in her family's affairs and substantial business interests. When she learned of Griffin's plans in 1937, she jumped at an invitation to sign on for the first two-month stint as a charter member of the art colony.[8]

Purpose of the Colony— The Northwest remains America's last frontier but already the Indians and Pioneers who gave it a unique tradition have been pushed into a remote background. Only in a few places can they yet be found. The project of a summer Art Colony in the Northwest was conceived to give students the opportunity of studying the most interesting of Native material where it yet exists in its original setting.... Out of this should grow a vivid, individual expression.... Representative types of at least six distinct tribes reside in or near the town. During the July Indian festival it becomes the Mecca of Indian peoples from the entire Northwest. Native dances, games, customs, and manners are to be seen in gala profusion and unqualified authenticity.... Many of the teachers did intensified research in Indian design and found that Indian art embodies most of the creative ideals of the modern school.

Under Griffin's tutelage, Harder worked with a more daring palette, including alizarin crimson, cadmium yellow, and ultramarine blue. With bold Fechin-like strokes, she created more than twenty individual portraits of the Kamiakins and others, as well as numerous sketches of everyday life on the Colville Reservation. A number of students boarded with few amenities in the town's tiny hotel or other rented housing, but others, including Harder, ventured to stay in private homes, swim in Owhi Lake, and spent long hours with members of the Kamiakin family and others whose ancestral home had been the Palouse country.

In a history of the art colony (published in 2000), author J.J. Creighton described the artists' rigorous full-time weekly routine, which included three days for portraiture, often conducted in the Nespelem High School gymnasium, and two days for landscapes. Weekend sketching often was done in the nearby Grand Coulee Dam area. Representatives from the reservation's numerous bands were depicted in various clothing, from work shirts and broad-rimmed felt hats, to ceremonial war bonnets, beaded headbands, porcupine roaches, and fringed buckskin shirts and dresses. They generally were paid three to five dollars for a full day's sitting.

Kamiakin family members painted by Griffin, Harder, and other artists included Cleveland Kamiakin, Lucy Kamiakin Owhi (Kiatana), and Sk'olumkee's wife, Pemalks. Other popular subjects for sitting included Nez Perces who had married into the Kamiakin family. Among these were 1877 war survivors Willie Red Star Andrews and Robert Johnson.

Since Griffin's work at the colony and in earlier years was sponsored by the college, much of it remains at the WSU Museum of Art, while Harder's paintings are located variously in private hands and in the collections of the Spokane Museum of Arts and Culture and the Smithsonian. Other important works done by the colony artists are owned by the Colville Confederated Tribes and the Washington State Historical Society, or remain in private hands.[9]

Beaded Martingales and Stick Games

In the early decades of the 20th century, the Kamiakins frequently served in ceremonial roles at intertribal pow-wows and summer rodeos held annually on the Colville, Yakama, and Spokane reservations and in neighboring communities such as Wilbur and Coulee City. In many of these colorful events, Tomeo and Cleveland led parade processions along with relatives from the Moses clan, riding on horses magnificently adorned in beaded martingales and other regalia passed down for generations. The families stayed for days in great "circle" encampments, where they danced, gambled, and competed in rodeos.

These events appealed to the tribes' sense for maintaining the ancient tradition of seasonal travel and gathering together to socialize and celebrate. For generations, Plateau peoples had met around the summer solstice to gather roots and early berries, and to ceremonially recognize *Náami Piap* for this annual blessing. Now in modern times, participation in reservation pow-wows and rodeos had emerged, in part, from this heritage. In the Northwest, these events frequently commenced in late June and early July to coincide with the Fourth of July celebration, and were a time of pause before late summertime grain harvesting and livestock round-ups.[10]

On a number of Northwest reservations, however, dancers were assessed entry fees for competitions and non-Indian visitors were charged for admission. Cleveland Kamiakin

Kamiakin-Moses family gathering at the Wilbur Fair, c. 1913; (l. to r.) Louie (Pe'el) Pierre, Ida Williams (Desautel), Alalumti (Susie Chief) Williams holding Walter, Edward Williams, Willie Red Star Andrews, unidentified boy, Hattie (Paween) Andrews holding Albert(?), unidentified man (W.C. Brown?), Mary (Kamiakin) George holding Frank(?), Catherine Moses, Peter Dan Moses, Smith L. George, and Charley (Kamiakin) Williams.
MSCUA, University of Washington

disapproved of this as a "commercialization" of Indian tradition. For many years, the Kamiakins, Willie Red Star Andrews, and Joe Moses handled arrangements for the Nespelem pow-wow. In the 1940s, when younger organizers moved ahead with plans to introduce fees and cash prizes, Cleveland announced that his family would not participate. The venerable Yakama-Palouse leader felt ceremonial dances revealed "deep beauty, spiritual guidance, consolation and disciplinary power" to everyone present, and would help foster wider appreciation for "the beliefs of their forefathers" among non-reservation visitors. The chief's intransigence on the issue and the prospect of his absence led others to abandon the new recommendations.

Frank George characterized the annual encampment ceremonies as "songs and dances conceived by the counselors of old," that communicated "a harmony of Nature never equaled anywhere." To Tsiyiyak Kamiakin's grandson, their heirloom regalia was far more than just festive costumes—it "brought back many memories to those who recognize the finery on display."[11]

As old prejudices from the conflicts of former days faded in the 20th century, the Kamiakin family elders on the reservation now were treated with the respect befitting descendants of their Star Brother ancestor. However, objections did periodically arise regarding horse racing and stick game gambling, which certain Indians active in reservation churches condemned as indolent practices. In the early decades of the 20th century, Chief Kamiakin's four surviving sons participated in these events, sometimes to the consternation of agency and mission officials.

Yet many members of the Kamiakin clan, such as Tomeo and Cleveland, retained their father's adaptable synthesis of cultural and religious beliefs. They regularly gathered for ancient Washani First Roots and First Salmon ceremonies in the Nespelem Longhouse, where the Creator's blessings throughout nature were honored with sacred dancing to seven drums. But many in the family also were active in local Catholic fellowship, and Tomeo's son, Arthur Tomeo, helped establish the indigenous Full

Cleveland Kamiakin leading Wilbur parade.
Daryll Barr Collection

Gospel Shaker Church. Resident priests and pastors always were welcomed at Kamiakin family ceremonies. While Tomeo and Cleveland preferred to speak in Sahaptin even when outsiders attended, their gifts of family heirlooms to White religious leaders reflected high personal regards.[12]

Brown and McWhorter, Ruby and Brown

Tomeo Kamiakin formed a special friendship with Judge William Compton Brown of Okanogan, who sought to accurately record Chief Kamiakin's remarkable saga during the war years. The jurist knew of prejudicial attitudes toward the Kamiakins, but he concluded from his reading of history and acquaintance with Tomeo that the legendary chief's story needed to be fairly told. Brown's long endeavor eventually led to *The Indian Side of the Story*, published in 1961, though the book was substantially based on interviews conducted years earlier with Tomeo Kamiakin, Mary Owhi Moses, Alalumt'i Paween, and other family members.

In October 1928, W.C. Brown and Tomeo had conducted an extensive tour of the ancestral Palouse camps, where the judge learned important details about the Kamiakins during and after the war. Brown's involvement was timely. The story of the chief and his family in the 1850s–1870s had seemed relegated to oblivion, since memories and questions about those times often were too painful to discuss, even within family circles.[13]

Brown and historian L.V. McWhorter of Yakima also spoke to Tomeo about establishing a monument in his father's memory at Rock Lake. (McWhorter noted that "Kamiakin's Gardens" had been commemorated by the Yakima Pioneer Association near Tampico on June 30, 1918, in a ceremony attended by

Isaac Stevens' aged son, Hazard, and A.J. Splawn.[14]) Tomeo opposed the idea for some years, but McWhorter noted in the fall of 1930 that he finally consented to "the enterprise," suggesting the stone be placed at the bridge on the southern end of the lake.

As early as the 1890s, Yakama Agent Jay Lynch had made inquiries about erecting a marker in Chief Kamiakin's honor at Rock Lake. When Lynch and his wife traveled to the Palouse, however, he learned that the chief's grave had been desecrated; family members were not inclined to cooperate with him in the matter. When Brown and McWhorter revisited the idea, they contacted Rev. H.M. Painter in April 1925. Painter shared their interest and was a Cheney resident, living not far from the lake. But little progress was forthcoming.

McWhorter turned to Professor Edmond Meany and the Washington State Historical Society, an organization active with local pioneer associations in erecting commemorative markers. In Eastern Washington, monuments were erected at Kamiakin's Gardens, the Four Lakes and Spokane Plains battlefields, Qualchan's execution site, and places where the Mullan Road crossed area highways. However, the 1929 Depression struck before work began in earnest. With the passing of Tomeo in 1936 and McWhorter in 1944, the project again was forgotten. Few visitors today passing by Rock Lake, Lyon's Ferry State Park on the Snake River, or the Matlock Bridge on the Palouse River are aware of the special significance of these places in Northwest history.[15]

Many relatives, friends, and public officials looked to Tomeo as the family historian, and he willingly shared stories about the Kamiakin family's heritage with both Indians and Whites whom he

Tomeo and Ot-wes-on-my (Paween) Kamiakin, with one of their sons on horseback, Nespelem.
Colville Confederated Tribes

Kamiak Butte.
John Clement

Steptoe Butte—*Yáamuštas*, "Elk's Abode."
John Clement

Lower Snake River.
John Clement

Autumn sunset from Kamiak Butte.
John Clement

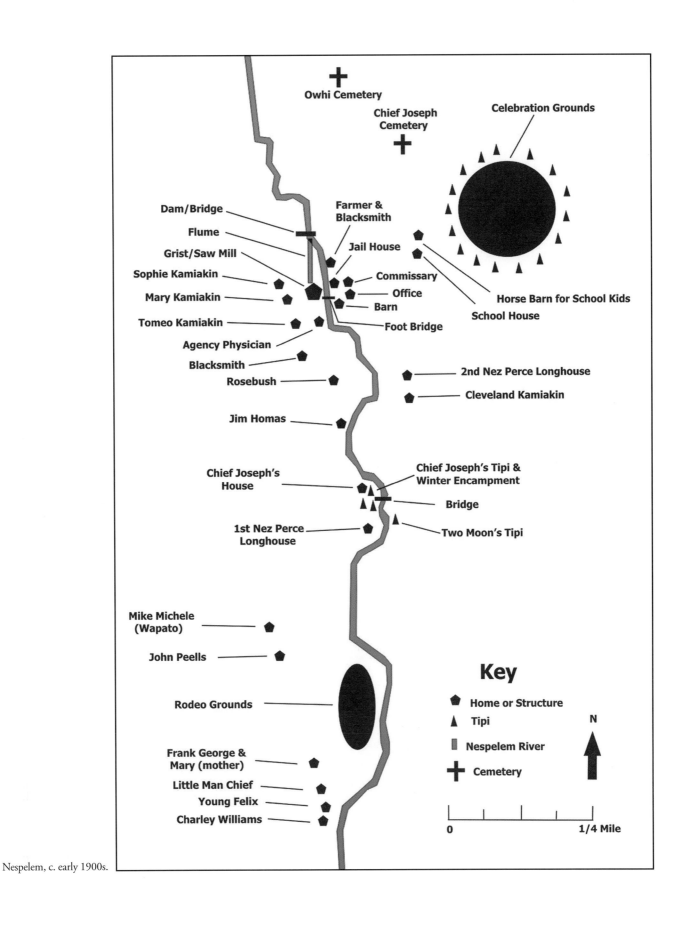

Owhi Cemetery

Chief Joseph Cemetery

Celebration Grounds

Dam/Bridge

Farmer & Blacksmith

Flume

Jail House

Grist/Saw Mill

Commissary

Sophie Kamiakin

Office

Mary Kamiakin

Barn

Horse Barn for School Kids

Tomeo Kamiakin

Foot Bridge

School House

Agency Physician

Blacksmith

2nd Nez Perce Longhouse

Rosebush

Cleveland Kamiakin

Jim Homas

Chief Joseph's House

Chief Joseph's Tipi & Winter Encampment

Bridge

1st Nez Perce Longhouse

Two Moon's Tipi

Mike Michele (Wapato)

John Peells

Rodeo Grounds

Key

Home or Structure

Tipi

N

Nespelem River

Cemetery

0   1/4 Mile

Frank George & Mary (mother)

Little Man Chief

Young Felix

Charley Williams

Nespelem, c. early 1900s.

Ot-wes-on-my (Paween) Kamiakin's cornhusk bag with eight-sided star motif, c. 1930.
John Clement

Chief Kamiakin bas-relief by James Wehn (1882–1973).
Washington State Historical Society, Tacoma

At Nespelem, c. 1935—standing (l. to r.) John Grant, Sidney Pacohtas, Charles Johnson, George Nanamkin, Arthur Tomeo Kamiakin, Peter Dan Moses, Elijah Williams, George Friedlander, Billy Charley, Willard George, Moses George, and Charles Abbott; kneeling (l. to r.) Cato Tomeo and Ned Cleveland.
Robert Eddy Collection

Anne Harder's portrait of Sk'olumkee Kamiakin's wife, Pemalks.
From J.J. Creighton, Indian Summers *(WSU Press, 2000)*

Cleveland Kamiakin, depicted by Worth D. Griffin of the Fine Arts Department, Washington State College.
WSU Museum of Art (37.1.12)

Worth Griffin, principal founder of the Nespelem Art Colony, painted this portrait of Chief Kamiakin daughter, Lucy Kamiakin Owhi (Kiatana).
WSU Museum of Art (37.1.24)

Agnes Andrews, by Worth Griffin.
WSU Museum of Art (37.1.1)

Dedication of monument to Chief Moses' sister, Sinsinq't, overlooking the Columbia at the mouth of Moses Coulee, June 2, 1957. Left to right: Nellie Moses Friedlander, George Friedlander, Cleveland Kamiakin, Billie Curlew, Harry Nanamkin, Peter Dan Moses, and Jim James.
Robert Eddy Collection

Eastern Washington sunset.
John Clement

Wallula Gap, Columbia River.
John Clement

found trustworthy. Some elders could see a resemblance between Tomeo's easy smile and strikingly handsome features and the same attributes in his illustrious father.

The Kamiakin women also served as invaluable keepers of the family's dramatic story in the difficult time of transition to reservation life. Kiatana shared important details regarding Chief Kamiakin's last years with author L.V. McWhorter. Though not published by McWhorter, Kiatana's information nevertheless was preserved in the writer's prodigious collection of letters and documents relating to the Nez Perces and Columbia Plateau Indians that he bequeathed to Washington State University.

Tespaloos died on the reservation in 1933; Tomeo suffered a debilitating stroke two years later and died in February 1936. The following decade witnessed the passing of Kiatana in 1946 and Sk'olumkee in 1949, leaving only Cleveland as the last direct living link to the patriot chief. When the older Kamiakin brothers had become too aged to actively participate in reservation political and business affairs, their youngest brother, Cleveland, had assumed a more active role and often was consulted in family and agency matters.

Problems with tribal enrollment and individual allotments had emerged after 1920 when the same person might claim title to property on various reservations. These complications arose because of extended families relationships, the frequent changing of names common in the Indian community, and the recurrent relocating by individuals between reservations. Cleveland possessed a capacious memory and intimate knowledge of the complex relationships in the Kamiakin, Moses, Joseph, and Yakama bands, and was frequently asked to provide testimony for pending enrollment and probate cases, where applicants were provided resolution in a fair hearing. He also kept abreast of events within his extended family through frequent visits to other reservation communities throughout the Northwest. He looked forward to periodic trips to the Yakama Reservation where he was feted by a host of relatives, including the families of Alec Shawaway and Louis Sohappy, descendants of Chief Kamiakin's brothers Showaway and Skloom.[16]

"Old Mary" Moses (Sanclow), the daughter of Chief Owhi and wife of Chief Moses, who had helped tend Kamiakin's battle wounds, was frequently feted at the grand

Mary Moses, wife of Chief Moses, daughter of Owhi.
WSU Libraries (W.C. Brown Collection)

pow-wows held throughout the region even into her final years. According to family accounts, Sanclow reportedly lived to the remarkable age of 118 before passing away in 1938. Because the parents of Nellie Moses (Friedlander)—Lukash and Sinsinq't Kamiakin—both had died in the 1880s, Mary Moses helped raise Nellie and later often cared for her children by Louis Friedlander—including Emily (Peone), Lucy (Covington), and George Friedlander. From their earliest youth, the Friedlander children committed to memory many stories related by Mary and their Kamiakin aunts and uncles about the clan's special heritage, and the efforts made by Owhi, Kamiakin, Moses, and others to provide a secure future for their descendants. The Friedlanders safeguarded this special knowledge throughout their lifetimes.

In June 1957, Nellie Friedlander gathered with Cleveland Kamiakin and other family members to dedicate a monument in the memory of her mother at one of the family's ancestral campsites overlooking the Columbia River at the mouth of Moses Coulee. Included among several White guests were Wenatchee Valley College professor John A. Brown, and Dr. Robert Ruby, a physician and historian who had established a medical practice in Moses Lake after relocating from the Pine Ridge Reservation in 1955. These two

Emily Friedlander (Peone), c. 1935.
WSU Libraries (W.C. Brown Collection)

colleagues established a close relationship with tribal elders that led to an extensive series of oral histories recorded with Nellie Friedlander, Emily Peone, George Friedlander, Alex Covington, Peter Dan Moses, and others between 1957 and 1963. This work significantly contributed to preserving little-known events in the lives of Chief Kamiakin and his relatives, and formed the basis of Ruby and Brown's critically acclaimed volumes for the University of Oklahoma's Civilization of the American Indian series.[17]

Pillars of the Sky

During Washington's territorial centennial—1953—one of America's most celebrated Western writers, Henry W. Allen, published an historical novel, *To Follow a Flag*. The book was the popular California author's fifth in a career that brought several dozen to print and eight to film. The 1953 release, issued under the pen name Will Henry, was one of Allen's few works with a Pacific Northwest setting. Moreover, the book purports to tell in characteristic Fifties bravado the "powerful story" of the "first U.S. Dragoons—156 foolhardy officers and fearful men…going to show the flag to mighty Kamiakin, the war chief of the bloody Palouse Rebellion."

From the opening lines and a detailed two-page orientation, "War Department Map of Military Road from Ft. Wallowa on the Columbia to Colville Gold District, 1858–1862," drawn by "Capt. J. Mullins," the reader readily recognizes John Mullan's cartography and a fictionalized account of the Steptoe Battle as related through the experiences of Lt. Col. Edson Stedloe, Sgt. Emmett Bell, ill-fated West Pointer Wilcey Gaxton, love interest Calla Lee Rainsford, and a cast of Indian leaders and advocates who retain their actual names—Kamiakin, Timothy, Lawyer, Victor, Joset, and others.

Although often lauded for his historical accuracy and descriptive, poetic prose, Allen presents Kamiakin as the story's principal antagonist responsible for raiding a wagon train destined for the mines on the Colville Road north of Sprague Lake. Stedloe's foray north of the Snake River is in response to the attack and intelligence about the location of Kamiakin's "war camp" on the "Otayoose River" (Rock

Creek). The main characters are presented in ways that allow for Allen's signature in-depth characterizations, which strengthen the telling as ambiguities emerge involving such matters as the Army's true intentions and Bell's alcoholism.

Throughout the first half of the book, Kamiakin is known only through such soldiers' fearful scorn as a "hostile messiah," "great raider," "brainy fox," and "complete renegade." When the soldiers finally meet the restive forces of the Yakama, Palouse, Spokane, and Coeur d'Alene "Northwest Federation" on Ingossomen Creek, Chief Kamiakin finally appears on horseback, dramatically approaching the colonel clad in "cartwheel warbonnet" and "three-point blanket." After insults are traded, the attack ensues, including a last stand by Stedloe's command on "Pyramid Peak," perhaps contributing to the persistent erroneous notion that some of the fighting actually took place on Steptoe Butte.

Despite the sentimentality and generalizations apparent in Allen's depictions of Kamiakin, Timothy, and other Indian leaders, *To Follow a Flag* (published since 1956 as *Pillars of the Sky*) represented a break from typical early 20th century literary characterizations of Native Americans as implacably hostile to peaceful White settlers attempting to defend themselves. Allen's Stedloe is culpable for spurning advice to head directly north on the Colville Road and avoid Kamiakin's forces, and a remarkable exchange among the soldiers suggests the actions of the miners represent a "white conspiracy to defraud" the tribes.

Such scenes based on Allen's novel were effectively incorporated into Sam Rolfe's screenplay adaptation, released in October 1956 by Universal-International as *Pillars of the Sky*. (The film opened as *The Tomahawk and the Cross* in Great Britain.) The movie starred popular character actor Michael Ansara as Chief Kamiakin, and Jeff Chandler as Sgt. Emmett Bell. Harold Lipstein's lush color cinematography focused on the Wallowa Mountains and the LaGrande, Oregon, area where most of the filming took place. A *New York Times* review praised the film's "compassion and cynicism," and noted the significance of its balanced presentation of Indian and White views evident in the portrayals by Ansara and Chandler. It played in small-town theaters throughout the Inland Pacific Northwest before passing into cinematic arcanum.[18]

Chapter 12
Rivers Rise

Young Chinook made his way
up the rocky slope.
He saw Rattlesnake
sunning himself nearby.
Young Chinook aimed an arrow.
Rattlesnake pleaded for his life.
"Don't hurt me, Nephew;
I know why you have come."

"I have power you need
to defeat the Wolf Brothers."
Young Chinook put down his bow.
Rattlesnake kept his word.
He took out some of his teeth
for Young Chinook
to put into his mouth.

*T*he Kamiakins and many Colville and Yakama elders of the 1920s and 1930s had long viewed the allotment policy as a violation of traditional values and an incursion on treaty rights. Indeed, the General Allotment (Dawes) Act of 1887 had been devised by federal policy makers to advance assimilation and to placate paternalistic Indian agency bureaucrats, zealous Christians, and land hungry Whites. The law brought disaster to reservations across the country by 1920, not the least because a patent to an individual Indian land allotment could not be issued for twenty-five years pending the award of "certificates of competency" by local agency officials.

In 1921, BIA Commissioner Charles Burke's annual report outlined the government's long-term intentions: "The general course of treaties, agreements, and legislation has been in line with the purpose of reserving definite areas of land as tribal estates and of allotting therefrom as rapidly as possible freeholds in severalty, with the aim of inducing by this transfer of tribal to individual holdings a departure from the old communal traits and customs to self-dependant conditions and

to a democratic conception of the civilization with which the Indian must be assimilated if he is to survive."[1]

Chief Kamiakin's sons and daughters took allotments after the 1880s when relocating to the Colville Reservation, but the family's horses ranged freely with other herds throughout the Nespelem Valley and on the unfenced prairie lands to the east. Under the terms of the 1887 Dawes Act, individual Indians were to be allocated 40, 80, or 160 acres, depending on the condition of the land and its intended use—for habitation only, for farming, or for grazing respectively. But provisions and adjustments in the law eventually permitted agents through various means to disperse unallotted tracts to non-Indians. Within two decades, property maps of Northwest and other reservations across the nation exhibited checkerboard ownership patterns, including lands lost to outsiders, despite the original federal treaty promises to hold them in trust for the future benefit of the tribes.

Assimilation advocates also lobbied for the 1924 Indian Citizenship (Snyder) Act, bestowing citizenship on all Indians born in the United States, since nearly one-third of all American Indians were still considered legal aliens. (Indians previously had gained citizenship through marriage, military service, successfully acquiring final title to allotments, and by other special legal measures.) With the Snyder Act, a number of Kamiakin family members acquired citizenship. Many reservation residents, however, considered the franchise irrelevant, if not deleterious, to their wellbeing. "Do not tell me to become a citizen by the white law!" Kamiakin kinsman Chief Sluskin told listeners at his home near Yakima.

As a boy he had tended the family's horses at the Walla Walla Treaty Council and witnessed firsthand the decline in fortunes of his people since that time. "I was brought here by a great power," he explained. "We own the fish, deer, berries, and roots. The whole earth was created with the law of light and darkness. Laws were made with the earth and we keep them on our minds.... I was here first, before the white man and a great Indian. How is it now? The white man said, 'You better become a citizen.' To me this is not right. I think in asking this, my rights are being taken away."[2]

Our Fathers Told Us

Since the total acreages on the Colville, Yakama, and most other reserves substantially exceeded the amount of property allotted to individual tribal members, the additional lands were to be held in federal trust and managed for the benefit of the tribes. In 1906, however, Congress passed the Burke Act authorizing fee patent conversion, or unrestricted purchase, of Indian allotments by others.

On the Colville Reservation—already diminished by the government's expropriation of the Northern Half in 1892—the Burke Act threatened to further reduce the viability of the tribe. On the Yakama Reservation, the act resulted in the alienation (or private acquisition) of vast acreage for the platting of three non-Indian agricultural communities—Wapato, Toppenish, and Parker. The 1906 act was rescinded in 1934 and 1935, but not before thousands of acres on the Yakama, Colville, Coeur d'Alene, and other reservations were claimed by White developers or leased at substantial discounts to stock raisers and outside timber and mining interests.

Between 1887 and 1911, tribal lands nationally were reduced by 53 percent as White farmers, ranchers, and entrepreneurs resorted to every legal means authorized by the Dawes Act, Burke Act, and similar legislation to acquire reservation property. This alarming trend fueled the tribal leaders' longstanding determination to seek redress for the surrender

of ancestral territories in the Stevens' Treaties at a fraction of their value. Moreover, the Colville tribes had never received proper consideration for the expropriation of vast aboriginal areas north of the Yakama and Nez Perce cessions.

When Congress approved legislation in 1925 authorizing litigation of these claims against the federal government, President Calvin Coolidge failed to sign the bill into law, citing expiration of the general statute of limitations in cases of such archaic origin. The administration's curt dismissal of matters of such consequence—long pressed by the Kamiakin brothers, James Bernard of the Colvilles, and Jim James of the San Poils—prompted an immediate response. The case had implications for Indians throughout the Pacific Northwest. Tribal leaders from the Colville Reservation joined others in a council held in Spokane in late October 1925. The representatives composed an expansive letter detailing their historic relationship with the land and government officials, and the injustices later arising out of the treaties signed by Chief Kamiakin and other Indian leaders in 1855:

> Our fathers taught us...to be kind to one another, to be friends upon our lands and to have strong hearts. Their words were true and like to the light. We are telling you the truth. Now you will understand.... We will tell you of our fathers. Our fathers were great in the days gone by, and their past will last forever and ever. Our fathers did not have books. Our fathers did not need books. The Indian did not write down his words on paper, and then place his words on a shelf to be covered with dust, forgotten and unknown to his children. The Indian wrote his words, his promises in his memory; in his children's memory, and in the memory of his children's children. Our fathers lived here in happiness. They had hearts that were strong; they regarded them the same as a mountain.... Our fathers allowed the white man to come as our fathers were good and kind to everyone.
>
> Our fathers' roads were straight no matter where they went; their roads were always open never closed; and their words were true. The White Man has brought a change in this, our country. Since our fathers' time even the rocks and trees that our fathers were accustomed to have disappeared. You have killed off or destroyed all that we used for food.... You have done this without asking us, and you have taken away our country by force, against our will.... You have done away with our beautiful land that long ago we roamed over, free as a bird....
>
> We are now told that you, the President, have said that we should have asked you to pay us in that Court before; that our claims are too old—that we have waited too long. We have waited long; we have waited very long. We cannot ask you to pay, only when your Council of Congress says we

may. When did Congress say we could ask? Our fathers told us to pay our debts; to pay all our debts. Our fathers did not tell us we need not pay old debts, our fathers told us if they could not pay their debts, then their children must pay them, or our children's children, else we and our children, and our fathers are disgraced. We are broken hearted because we are treated like children. We wait to know about our claims; we have waited very long. We ask you to now treat us as men; to deal with us as men. Do so now. Make glad our hearts; make whole the broken promises of Stevens....

On this land of ours your children have built great towns; over it they have run railroads; from the belly of the earth they have dug our silver, gold, lead and copper. They have cut down and used the great forests that grew on our hills, they have built great dams across our salmon streams and harnessed the lightning to do their work. They have made farms and orchards out of our root fields and our hunting grounds. Your people have multiplied and grown rich on our lands; these lands that you our friend, took from us without our consent; these lands that you have never paid us for....

We have also been told that you have said that our claim is too large. We have never put any price on our lands, or on the rights you took away from us without our consent. All we have asked, all we now ask is that the matter be settled; that you permit your Court of Claims to decide whatever is just.[3]

This boldly lucid appeal to legal obligation, moral sensibility, and spiritual responsibility largely fell on deaf ears in the Coolidge Administration. When similar legislation sponsored by Senator Wesley L. Jones and Representative Samuel B. Hill of Washington passed Congress in June 1926, Coolidge again responded with a pocket veto. Representing the Colville tribes, Attorney Lewis appealed to the federal judiciary on the basis of the Fifth Amendment prohibition against taking private property without fair compensation. Lewis solicited substantial testimony to prove that vast numbers of northern Plateau Indians had resided for extended times in the upper Columbia districts, unaffected by the Stevens treaties. Aged Duncan McDonald, son of Ft. Colvile chief factor Angus McDonald, offered an unbiased first-hand account of how Kettle Falls served as a strategic annual fishing and trading center for vast numbers of Indians.

In April 1929, Attorney Lewis argued the case before the U.S. Supreme Court, but the court eventually ruled against the tribes. The decision confounded tribal leaders, who faced other mounting threats to their people's wellbeing in the wake of cutbacks in Bureau of Indian Affairs (BIA) programs and economic dislocations resulting from the Great Depression. But reservation families had long endured struggles using ancient skills of self-reliance and by adapting to difficult circumstances. The elders told the President their hair "is now gray," and that they had "waited very long" for just compensation. Moreover, in the absence of reconciliation, they would have to carry the message of their fathers that Governor Stevens' promises "are yet broken."

Many who signed the memorandum would not live to see the contribution that their stalwart efforts would make. Two decades later, the federal Indian Claims Commission was created as a judicial forum for tribes to seek restitution for dispossessed lands and decades of bureaucratic neglect.

Grand Coulee Dam

Challenges regarding land tenure matters in the 1930s coincided with a period when Indian livelihoods were enormously impacted by the construction of high dams flooding the Cascades, Kettle Falls, and eventually the Celilo fisheries on the Columbia, which had sustained Native populations for millennia. These massive public works projects were proposed in the federal government's first "308 Report," authored by Major John Butler of the Army Corps of Engineers in 1931. The study led to the construction of Bonneville Dam on the lower Columbia at The Cascades. Thousands of workers labored on the huge structure from 1933 until 1938, when completion formed Lake Bonneville, inundating the tribes' historic Great Cascades fishery.

Tribal governments and White leaders in communities affected by Columbia reservoir flooding were powerless to prevent federal efforts to develop hydroelectric power and irrigate the Columbia Basin. A proposal favored by Spokane civic interests to irrigate the basin through a gravity flow plan using water from the Pend Oreille River allowed for a low dam at Grand Coulee, but Butler's report concluded that building a monumental high dam was the most feasible approach. Work on this project also commenced in 1933 and, along with Bonneville Dam, it was a key component in President Franklin Roosevelt's New Deal to stimulate economic recovery and create public utilities.

The Roosevelt Administration's initial response for the Grand Coulee project favored a low dam, but in 1935 the Bureau of Reclamation authorized a change that nearly doubled the height of the concrete structure to 500 feet. This resulted in a significant extension of the proposed reservoir to the Canadian border and also would block upriver migration of salmon.

Grand Coulee Dam under construction, c. late 1930s.
Museum of Arts & Culture, Spokane

The many Indian families with allotments along the Columbia from Whitestone Creek to Kettle Falls as well as the entire communities of Keller and Inchelium were forced to relocate. Altogether, about 2,250 residents on the Colville and Spokane reservations abandoned their homes, some Indian cemeteries were moved, and roads were relocated from approximately 40,000 acres of affected reservation lands.

The 1933 Federal Power Act required annual government payments to any tribe for the use of its land, which also should have led to appropriate reimbursements for power generation and the loss of wildlife habitat. But limited compensation was forthcoming in the Acquisition of Indian Lands for Grand Coulee Dam Act of 1940. Federal appraisals for the loss of fish and wildlife habitat and property were far less than what tribal officials deemed fair. The government proceeded with condemnation suits, and by 1942 all lands in the reservoir area had been purchased or condemned. Moving

and relocation expenses were not fairly reimbursed, and the tribes were denied any share in power sales revenue when the dam began operating in 1941.

Indian leaders skeptically eyed government efforts to mitigate damage to fish stocks authorized by the Mitchell Act in 1938, which led to extensive trapping and release of salmon in 1939–43 from the Grand Coulee Dam area to the Wenatchee, Entiat, Methow, and Okanogan rivers.[4] As early as 1937, the federal commissioner of fisheries warned of the need for "eternal vigilance in balancing the productive forces of natural growth and replacement against the destructive forces of man's exploitation," and criticized undertaking such complex endeavors on a "trial-and-error basis" as was being demanded by schedules to complete the dams.

His views proved prescient. Well-intended and expensive methods to perpetuate salmon stocks with fish ladders and hatcheries only temporarily interrupted the steady erosion of annual runs from nearly 16 million salmon in the late 19th century. A decade after the completion of the high dams, native salmon runs were less than 3 percent of historic levels, and fishing for migrating salmon had been functionally relegated to non-Indians residing far downstream. (Subsequent hydroelectric development along the Columbia has led to the virtual elimination of sockeye and chum, and the risk of extinction in what was once the world's most abundant salmon fishery).[5]

Many elders living in the affected areas were traumatized by the calamitous change and succumbed to grief. A tribal member expressed the loss in cultural terms: "The river was the central and most powerful element in the religious, social, economic, and ceremonial life of my people. Suddenly, all of this was wiped out. The river was blocked, the land was flooded. The river we had known was destroyed.... The root-digging prairies were cut off. The salmon came no more, and with the disappearance of the salmon, our traditional economy was lost forever."

In testimony before the Washington State Supreme Court, Yakama Chief George Meninick succinctly expressed the profound significance of Indian fishing: "For I say to you that our health is from the fish, our strength is from the fish, and our very life is from the fish."[6]

In 1942, irrigation water diverted by Grand Coulee Dam flowed south into the basin, rather than to Indian farms, while reservation utility rates remained significantly higher than in the nearby town of Coulee Dam and elsewhere in the state. The vibrant salmon runs—of profound religious and cultural significance, and formerly providing over a third of the Indian diet—were entirely extirpated above the dam.

Lucy Covington—in referring to the 1855 treaty negotiated by her great-grandfather, Chief Kamiakin, that guaranteed to the tribes "the right of taking fish at all usual and accustomed places"—found cruelty in the modern means of entirely destroying traditional places. "We had such a beautiful way of life. We were rich. The dam made us poor.... [As] one of our people said, 'The promises made by the government were written in sand and then covered with water, like everything else.'"[7]

Cleveland Kamiakin, c. 1937.
WSU Libraries (L.V. McWhorter Collection)

In June 1940, about 10,000 people gathered at Kettle Falls in a three-day "Ceremony of Tears," mourning the loss of the ancient fishery that had witnessed First Salmon Ceremony blessings for generations. Traditional chiefs and elected tribal leaders addressed the crowd in somber tones, pressing dam-proponent Clarence Dill, a former U.S. senator, to reimburse the loss of the fishery and to provide power revenue sharing guaranteed by the original Federal Power Act. A year later, during the week of July 4, 1941, the last traces of Kettle Falls and old Ft. Colvile disappeared beneath slack water behind Grand Coulee Dam.

In spite of official pledges for proper redress, the revenue-sharing promise was ignored, until after the Colville Tribes sued the federal government in 1952. This action led to four decades of litigation. Congress finally admitted that "the Federal Government did not live up to the commitments made to the tribes." The House Committee on National Resources awarded the Colville Confederated Tribes a one-time payment of $53 million for the loss of wildlife habitat and related damages, and added annual revenue sharing payments for the life of Grand Coulee Dam.[8]

From Chiefs to Tribal Council

By the 1920s, many younger tribal members, some of whom lived off the reservation, and a majority of White ranchers living on the reserve proposed to restrict the customary open range policy. Objections from elders such as Cleveland Kamiakin and Willie Red Star Andrews eventually were overruled, in part because the issue coincided with new policies resulting from the 1934 Indian Reorganization (Wheeler-Howard) Act, the "Indian New Deal." This reformist legislation overturned Dawes Act provisions that had created allotments, and it sought to promote economic and political development on reservations. Other New Deal programs such as the Civilian Conservation Corps employed many Indian men on Northwest reservations in timber harvesting and road building, but BIA policy under Franklin Roosevelt had new political objectives as well.

The "Indian New Deal" aimed to establish tribal self-government, but in doing so, it

Cleveland and Alalumt'i Kamiakin home (right center) and the Nez Perce Longhouse (large structure, further right), Nespelem, c. 1940. *WSU Libraries (W.C. Brown Collection)*

limited the authority of traditional chiefs. Various reservations bands, long maintaining loose confederations under hereditary leaders, now were encouraged to corporate under constitutions authorizing governance by elected "Business Councils" based on district representation rather than tribal affiliation. Several of the proposed changes were opposed by many residents on the Colville Reservation, including the Yakama-Palouse Kamiakins, Willie Andrews of the Nez Perces, and Peter Dan Moses of the Moses-Columbias. They preferred their traditional shared governance among leaders of the reservation's twelve constituent bands, and feared consolidation of power by a single council head who likely would be elected by the largest tribal faction.

But officials of the Bureau of Indian Affairs informed Cleveland Kamiakin and the other chiefs that the reforms were a *fait accompli*, taking effect in spite of an election outcome. Indeed, voting took place on April 6, 1936, with reorganization being defeated by a vote of 562 to 421.[9] Congressional advocates intervened on behalf of the chiefs and directed Commissioner John Collier to validate the election results. But Depression-era economic realities regarding the control of livestock production, weakening ties among

constituent bands, and federal incentives to organize tribes as corporations, combined with relentless bureau influence, induced the majority of reservation voters to adopt the new system in February 1938.

In 1934, a similar proposal to reorganize governance among the Yakamas had been soundly defeated by a vote of 773 to 361, although a decade later the tribe did decide to establish a constitutional form of government with a business council. As with other tribes, the Yakamas' initial skepticism was not so much focused on New Deal intentions as it was on long-held suspicions regarding any federal proposals and pledges in the wake of past experiences.[10]

In the early 1940s, Cleveland Kamiakin began contacting the state's congressional delegation for aid in the face of rumors that reservation Indians might lose property tax exemptions, hunting and fishing rights, and other privileges derived from federal statutes. Controversy arose in part after a proposed Game Code was drafted by agency and Fish and Wildlife Department officials in 1943. It aimed to regulate reservation fishing and hunting after Lake Roosevelt had been formed behind Grand Coulee Dam, flooding traditional hunting and fishing sites.

In a petition to U.S. Congressman Walt Horan during the winter of 1943, Cleveland reminded the legislator of federal obligations: "I always consent[ed] to live the old custom, all the game, fish, berries, and roots, I retain them which was given to me by [the] Treaty [of] 1855…. Our first president of the United States made a proclamation [that] Indians are owners of United States soil, but white farmers can farm and…pay taxes, not Indians…. I pray to the United States government to make a path for [the] younger generation to have all the privileges of wild game, fish, berries, and so on, so [they] can carry on and not forget race and custom. This was laid down, generation after generation and should carry on."

Horan acknowledged Kamiakin's letter, expressing hope that an "equitable assumption of the cost of government" could be found that balanced reservation benefits with agency expenses. But elders such as Cleveland and Willie Red Star Andrews noted that since "the allotment period came, with the limiting lines, corners, and boundaries,…changes in Indian life began to appear; and the Indians since have been continually losing their lands, rights, and heritage."[11]

This issue also may have revived Cleveland's abiding hope, even in the eighth decade of his life, to yet return to his native Palouse country, or at least to clarify title to properties that might still be owned by the Kamiakin, Paween, and other family heirs. In the spring of 1944, Agency Superintendent F.A. Gross noted that Cleveland had been visiting with him "for some time" about the disposition of Indian homesteads filed in the 1880s along the lower Snake River. His older brothers and other residents living at *Palus* had acquired a tract of contiguous property along the entire lower Palouse River Canyon. Others, such as Húsis Paween, had homesteaded near Almota and Penawawa. Family members sought Cleveland's intervention to clarify the legal status and he had met with Gross on their behalf.

Subsequent investigation by county officials in Colfax revealed that several parcels remained under Indian title. Although relocating to these lands proved impractical, the efforts of such elders as Cleveland and Joe Redthunder allowed younger family members to be reacquainted with their ancestral heritage along the Snake and Palouse rivers and to work to retain this legacy.[12]

In 1941–42, while eligible young men enlisted in impressive numbers for service in World War II, older residents were left to deal with federal efforts to ameliorate outstanding Indian land claim issues and also face outside efforts to terminate or reduce area reservations. Like tribal leaders before them, Cleveland and Charley Williams (Te-meh-yew-te-toot), T'siyiyak Kamiakin's son, had long hoped to secure for their people a portion of their former holdings.

Williams also had been born in the Palouse homeland and had relocated to the reservation in about 1888. He later married Alalumti (Susie Chief), whose family was among the Nez Perce exiles in Oklahoma. Williams and Cleveland were close in years and had grown up together, forming a lifetime friendship and devotion to their people's heritage. The two maintained a strong spiritual attachment to the land of their birth. Cleveland still spoke about selling his allotment and returning to Rock Lake to spend his final years. And, for the benefit of future generations, Cleveland and Williams rigorously opposed termination.

Battle Cries, Quiet Heroes

In December 1943, Harry Owhi informed Agency Superintendent Paschal Sherman that Cleveland Kamiakin, Willie Andrews, Peter Dan Moses, and other elders desired to have a veterans' monument erected in Nespelem commemorating the service of "our boys who are fighting and who have already given their lives."

As was the case with many families in Indian country, which had the highest enlistment rate of any ethnic group in America, each one of Charley and Alalumti Williams' sons—Edward, Walter, Clayton, and Abel—volunteered for military service. As in the case of so many others, not all returned. (During World War I, two out of some twenty soldiers from the reservation had been killed.)

Sergeant Abel J. Williams served as a gunner with the 789th Bomber Squadron based out of Rackheath, England. On April 13, 1944, intense anti-aircraft fire near Lechfeld, Germany, shot down his B-24 Liberator, "Katy." Williams' leg was badly broken during the chaos, but he managed to bail out before the bomber went down near the Swiss border. The impact of landing undoubtedly compounded the injury, but he resolved to fight to the last rather than surrender. When German troops began firing at the men, Williams pulled out his .45 revolver and fought back until he was killed. His longtime Colville friend and fellow crew member, Pierre Joseph, survived and remained confined in Stalag 17 until the end of the war.[13]

Harry Owhi's son, Roscoe, joined the Army, like his enlisted cousins, to "follow the path which his great-grandparents made by Chief Kamiakin, Chief Owhi[, and] Chief Joseph." Owhi noted that though the family was not actually related to Joseph, his father, Ben Owhi, had fought alongside the chief in the Nez Perce War. Other local family recruits included Tomeo Kamiakin's son and grandson, Cato and Stanley, and brothers Albert and Isaac Andrews, as well as their relatives Frank Andrews, Phillip Broncheau, and Edward Chief.

Phillip Broncheau, a star athlete and a Nespelem High School graduate, and Inchelium native Earl McClung were assigned to the 506th Parachute Infantry Regiment of the legendary 101st Airborne Division. McClung jumped behind enemy lines on the night of June 3–4, 1944, at Normandy during the massive D-Day operation. (Other soldiers, including young Frank Andrews, eventually in Patton's Third Army, began landing with the infantry at Utah Beach and other sectors, starting just hours later.) The 506th's battle cry was "Currahee," a traditional Cherokee expression for "Stands Alone"—and the name given a mountain in Toccoa, Georgia, where they had been rigorously trained for the fitness needed in paratrooper combat. McClung became a member of Easy Company, later celebrated in the Stephen Ambrose book, *Band of Brothers* (1992) and the HBO ten-part television mini-series (2001). McClung often served as one of the unit's advance scouts.[14]

Broncheau and McClung both fought at the Battle of the Bulge in December 1944, when the last major German offensive of the war surrounded the 101st Division and other units at Bastogne, Belgium. After a five-mile march before dawn on December 19, Broncheau's unit was given the

Phillip Broncheau.

formidable task of holding Noville, located four more miles to the north and then under heavy attack by a superior force of German tanks. During their approach, Broncheau was cut down on the Bourcy Road when the American attack drew intense tank and artillery fire. The paratroopers managed to evacuate Noville later in the day, and were forced back to defensive positions around Bastogne. Broncheau, seriously wounded, was captured. A foot of snow fell in the next two days. Without huts or warming fires, the men endured conditions that military historians likened to Valley Forge.

Sporadic German shelling continued, but sniper fire took an especially heavy toll on the beleaguered Americans. McClung and another part-Indian member of Easy Company, Darrell "Shifty" Powers, were sent with others on perilous missions to take out German sharpshooters. Noville was retaken on January 17 in an assault that helped finally break the German drive, at great cost to both sides. McClung survived the war and was credited by his fellow soldiers for probably killing more of the enemy than anyone else in the battalion.

Broncheau, remembered as a "quiet hero and unafraid," died of his wounds in German captivity on January 19, 1945. He later was buried in Nespelem, a few feet from the grave of his comrade-in-arms, Abel Williams. After the war, memorials to these soldiers and many other Native American veterans were erected on reservations throughout the Pacific Northwest.[15]

Broncheau's Army Rucksack

In 2005, Phillip Broncheau's World War II rucksack was found in the attic of a stone row house scheduled for demolition in the village of Luzery, just north of Bastogne. It contained his photograph, rifle cleaning materials, and an address book listing family members on the Colville, Nez Perce, and Umatilla reservations. In the nearby Recogne War Cemetery, a stone monument crowned with the bronze relief of a chieftain is inscribed: "In Loving Memory of the American Indian Soldiers Fallen for the Liberation of Belgium." A local *Ferme des Bisons* (Bison Farm) features displays recreating the history of the American West.

Chapter 13

The Essence of Life

Young Chinook traveled
to the river's faraway headwaters.
He saw smoke coming up
from the Wolf Brothers' camp.
Their sister cried as she worked.
They only went outside
to drink from the river.

Young Chinook hid in the water.
One by one, he bit them
on the mouth as they came.
Rattlesnake's poison
worked its power.
Before one could howl,
pulled beneath the waters.

During the war years, correspondence from tribal members to agency officials and legislators questioned why matters involving land issues were being deliberated when so many tribal members were serving in the armed forces. Cleveland Kamiakin, Willie Andrews, and Peter Dan Moses also opposed BIA attempts to consolidate the administration of several Northwest reservations into a single agency on the Spokane Reservation.

Congressman Walt Horan, who generally sought to defend the views of his Indian constituents, confessed to being "at a loss to discover" where the rumor originated. Upon contacting BIA officials, however, Horan learned that "in the distant future" the possibility existed "that with certain progressive changes, the overall operation at Nespelem might be closed and the work centered in Spokane."

These responses offered unsettling evidence of a shift in federal Indian policy that would lead to proposals in the following decade to terminate government trust responsibilities in order to promote Indian assimilation.[1]

Termination and the National Congress of American Indians

In addition to recurrent challenges from the BIA and state authorities to limit tribal hunting and fishing rights, regional White business interests looked with renewed interest in postwar Washington to exploit the mineral-rich and timbered, but sparsely settled, slopes along the reservation's northern tier. Tribal elders remembered that a vast 1.5 million acre tract between the Canadian border and the current northern reservation boundary had been sold to the government in 1891 for a dollar an acre, and the controversial agreement was not ratified by the Senate. Nevertheless, these lands were restored to the public domain in 1892 and opened to White settlement in the fall of 1900. (Approximately 52,000 acres were allotted to Indians wishing to remain north of the reservation.)

Now, White-owned timber and mining companies sought new means to develop the unallotted lands on the reservation.

At the same time, some tribal leaders, encouraged by provisions in the 1934 Indian Reorganization Act, explored the possibility of purchasing back unsettled tracts in the reservation's former Northern Half. These conflicting interests were further exacerbated by the depletion of traditional Indian fisheries, wildlife habitat destruction, and the relocating of Indian burials on the upper Columbia River with the construction of Grand Coulee Dam. Local and regional Bureau of Indian Affairs officials, however, seemed to largely turn a deaf ear to the tribe's petitions in these matters.

In November 1944, Frank George joined prominent Northwest Indian leaders Archie Phinney from the Nez Perce Reservation and D'Arcy McNickle, a Cree raised on the Flathead Reservation, and other delegates from thirty tribes, who gathered at the Cosmopolitan Hotel in Denver for the inaugural meeting of the National Congress of American Indians. Like his uncle, Cleveland Kamiakin, George possessed notable leadership traits. While at Haskell College, he earned a reputation as an astute and independent thinker, while honing notable journalistic skills.

George's burley presence exuded resolution and determination, evident in his prominent service as a Colville tribal relations officer and also as a charter member of the Governors' Interstate Indian Council. The GIIC was formed in 1947 by officials from various states, who were increasingly concerned about the erosion of federal oversight in Indian affairs. Native American participants, such as Frank George, worked to advise the nation's governors, who collectively called for equitable settlement of Indian treaties and increased tribal authority for economic self-sufficiency and cultural expression.

In 1951–53, the tenacious Colville leader served as the executive director of the National Congress of American Indians, where his efforts revived the fledgling organization that had essentially operated without a budget since its inception. George used his various state and national platforms to further a wide range of Indian causes, and helped lead the fight with his cousin Lucy Covington and other Colvilles against the federal government's reservation termination policies.

These efforts, however, were met with significant opposition among some other tribal members, especially mixed-bloods and those working in Grand Coulee or off the reservation. These people believed that termination would benefit the majority of members by allowing them to develop individual holdings unfettered by agency regulations and to pursue business interests elsewhere. This viewpoint, however, was not widely shared by Northwest tribes. In meetings on the Colville, Kalispel, and Spokane reservations throughout the late 1940s and 1950s, representatives largely spoke as one voice with Cleveland and other elders against the government's termination proposals.

A Bundle of Sticks

Concurrent with national efforts by Indian leaders to defend against those government policies that threatened Indian rights, Cleveland Kamiakin, Frank George, and other regional leaders from the Spokane, Umatilla, Nez Perce, and other tribes met in Nespelem in 1947, forming what eventually became the Affiliated Tribes of Northwest Indians.

Supported by Colville Agency Superintendent Wade Head, a planning group for the future ATNI had first convened in Nespelem in the summer, and included traditional chiefs from several reservation bands—Cleveland, Willie Red Star Andrews, Peter Dan Moses, and Victor Nicholas. These elders realized that despite the activities of elected tribal councils now endeavoring to formulate policies and programs, the existence of tribal governments themselves was being

---

Pivotal Organizations in Northwest Indian Rights Issues (with founding dates)

National Congress of American Indians (NCAI), 1944

Association on American Indian Affairs (AAIA), 1946

(U.S.) Indian Claims Commission (ICC), 1946

Governors' Interstate Indian Council (GIIC), 1947

Affiliated Tribes of Northwest Indians (ATNI), 1947 and 1953

---

threatened by adverse political forces. It had to be confronted by a united front. The older leaders, Cleveland contended, were prepared to take the fight beyond any one reservation to create a regional or even national response. He may well have recalled the challenges faced by his father in forming an alliance of the region's tribes a century earlier. "We have a great problem," Cleveland reasoned, and "we must retain our chiefs…, our forefathers died for it."

As if launching an ambitious campaign for political office, Cleveland and the others agreed to begin work organizing the November 1947 gathering of Affiliated tribal leaders, while also formulating plans to lobby the state's congressional delegation and influence public opinion through the regional press. The chiefs prevailed upon a friend, Rev. C.A. Burris, Methodist minister at Nespelem, to compose a lengthy article for the *Wenatchee World* to draw attention to the rumored changes in Indian trusteeship. They also visited Wenatchee in July to meet with the newspaper's influential owner-publisher, Rufus Woods, who turned their story into front page news.[2]

Throughout the fall, Cleveland worked with Frank George, Harry Owhi, and Superintendent Head to contact reservation leaders throughout Washington, Oregon, Idaho, and Montana to insure strong participation for the upcoming Affiliated conclave. In response to formal invitations and the substantial personal respect commanded by Cleveland, some 200 delegates assembled in Nespelem, November 18–19, 1947, for the organizational meeting of the eventual Affiliated Tribes of Northwest Indians.

John B. Cleveland, the Colville council chairman, introduced Cleveland Kamiakin, whose opening remarks focused attention on the regional Native people's most imminent threats: "I want to talk about our tribal holdings. This problem is very important. We want to retain our rights as Indians. The white man tells us that the Indian should relinquish his rights on his lands and other property…. I want the government to know that I want to retain all of my rights. We want to retain our Indian way of life. We have our ancient beliefs and traditions, and we should be accorded the right to retain them under the democratic way of life as practiced in this country."

Willie Red Star Andrews and Peter Dan Moses addressed the gathering in a similar tone, as did Skokomish leader George Adams, a skilled orator and a member of the Washington State Legislature. In strident terms, Adams explained how a similar organization had been formed among the Puget Sound tribes in anticipation of legal fights ahead with "the common enemy." He encouraged his listeners to remember

Harry Owhi, c. 1940.
Robert Eddy Collection

the victories won by elders in the treaty negotiations and on the battlefield. Adams spoke about the Indians' peculiar dilemma, struggling "in the modern age" and living for both "tomorrow and yesterday."[3]

Harry Owhi observed: "One reservation alone can't do very much, but together we will do something…to face the bills which are in Congress."

Chief John Moses from the Nez Perce Reservation alluded to tribal divisions that had constrained Indian progress in the past. He advised the delegates: "We must work together for the common interest…. A bundle of sticks bound together cannot be broken. So we must stand bound together."

Another Lapwai delegate raised civil rights issues experienced by most everyone in the audience: "We can't eat in all restaurants or stay in all hotels. The Whites will not hire us, only if they must, then we are the first ones fired." Only a common front could effectively deal with a host of issues ranging from local discrimination to the threat of federal dismantling of treaty obligations: "Our government's promises to us many times are only a scrap of paper. We should get some very able lawyers and fight our cases through the supreme courts."[4]

At the end of the day, Frank George was assigned the task of drafting the new organization's proposed constitution and bylaws, while the other delegates discussed legislative priorities over an evening feast of venison, fresh fruit, and berry pies. As expected, Cleveland Kamiakin, Willie Red Star Andrews, Jim James, and other leaders spoke strongly in favor of affirming treaty rights and facilitating veterans' benefits. Spokane representative Clair Wynecoop also raised the issue of education, arguing passionately about the need to equip "the younger generation" through adequate schools, capable teachers, and child labor reform, providing the tools to confront impending challenges to personal and cultural wellbeing.

Adams' stirring words were strongly commended by Red Star. Raised in the deprived conditions of the Oklahoma exile, he told the assembled elders that "the time of 'getting by' without an education is past. Everyone must be educated in order to compete in all things."

On the following day, November 19, 1947, after further discussion on the draft constitution, Cleveland Kamiakin formally moved for approval, which was unanimously passed with 116 votes. Legislative priorities included BIA accountability, education and business training, healthcare, and greater recognition of Indian contributions during times of war and peace in the modern development of the United States.

National Honor

The Affiliated Tribes of Northwest Indians further benefited from the leadership provided by Yakama tribal representative Alex Saluskin, who would be instrumental in organizing ATNI's annual conferences. His efforts expanded membership in the 1950s to include several dozen tribal governments from six states, combining to oppose termination, promote indigenous education practices, support land claims, and affirm treaty hunting and fishing rights.

Saluskin worked closely with fellow Yakama council member Watson Totus and other ATNI members in vain attempts to halt the building of The Dalles Dam. The structure threatened to flood historic Celilo Falls, which for generations had

been the principal salmon fishery on the lower Columbia. Abraham Showaway and others still lived year-round at The Dalles, where venerable Salmon Chief Tommy Thompson, nephew of Chief Stáquthly, had presided since 1875.

Celilo Falls had taken on even more significance for Indian families with Bonneville Dam's completion in 1938, flooding the Cascades fishery. Showaway recalled family stories passed down from the time of Cayuse Chief Showaway about Kamiakin's refusal to accept gifts at the Walla Walla Council and his affirming of treaty guarantees for Indians to fish at off-reservation sites such as Celilo. Showaway had never conceded the validity of White property claims at Celilo since the 1880s.

A little more than a half-century later, however, the very existence of the fishery was threatened. At hearings convened by the Army Corps of Engineers to consider compensation for the loss of the fishery, Saluskin told officials that the right to fish at Celilo in perpetuity "was the intent and was what persuaded Chief Kamiakin and others to sign the treaty of 1855.… It became common knowledge among the old people that was the intention of the treaty."

Watson Totus, a descendant of Chief Skloom, termed the proposal a "treaty violation" that threatened to "abolish and destroy one of the most historical and scenic natural monuments in the United States." Mindful of his Wiyáwiikt ancestry, the Yakama-Wanapum elder added: "The spirits of my past chiefs cannot plead for justice. I can only pray, save Celilo Falls and all it represents."[5]

The government eventually agreed to compensate the Yakamas with approximately $15 million for the economic loss of Celilo's flooding. The agreement did not specifically consider revoking treaty rights, but a federal mandate authorized dam construction to proceed over the tribes' continued legal objections. When the massive steel gates closed on March 10, 1957, the tumultuous Celilo cascades that had thundered for thousands of years fell silent under slack water within six hours. The massive Lake Celilo reservoir also eliminated spawning areas and inundated traditional burial sites. According to Kamiakin family member Andrew George, the loss of the ancient fishery was beyond measure in both cultural and commercial terms for future generations. Chief Thompson refused to accept any part of the government's settlement, avoided looking at the enormous concrete structure, and died two years later at the age of 102.[6]

Not long after ATNI's founding, Colville Business Council members and the confederated tribes' three hereditary chiefs, Cleveland Kamiakin, Peter Dan Moses, and Jim James, characterized the national trends in Indian affairs and river development as a new "hour of need." They petitioned the state's congressional delegation in October 1948 to "stand by them" in affirming their hard-earned treaty rights. Spurred by recent ATNI initiatives, they presented a disturbing chronicle of federal irresponsibility that had led to "the serious land situation of the Colville Reservation."

The vast six million acre domain of the Colville and Columbia (Moses) reservations, approved decades earlier by presidential proclamations, had been systematically reduced through political maneuverings to just 23 percent of the original area, or approximately 1.4 million acres. However, 60 percent of the remaining reservation lands were still classified as only "temporarily withdrawn" from public entry. Sales of this property could potentially leave the tribes with just 9.5 percent of the acreage originally negotiated.

The Colville leaders' petition expressed the dire situation in more than just quantitative terms: "The Federal Government has failed to discharge fully the obligations it has assumed…through treaty, promise, and agreement, solemnly ratified by the Senate, is a serious reflection upon the national honor.… The tragic consequence of this intended [Allotment Act] reform was the loss of millions of acres of productive land from Indian ownership. This well intended legislation failed in its purpose because Indians were not prepared for the responsibilities of individual ownership or for coping with the competitive white man."

The seven-page memorandum also decried considerations to abolish the Bureau of Indian Affairs and expressed concern about recent developments that were "all in complete disregard of the Government's obligations." (In a published statement earlier in 1948, Cleveland reported that an agency official told him the Colville Reservation "would be discontinued in about ten year's time.") Rather than supporting the current BIA appropriation structure that maintained redundant bureaucracies, the Colvilles pressed for more effective "direct services" at the reservation level, for vital needs such as rangeland and resource lease management to increase tribal revenue, and to prohibit public entry on undisposed lands.[7]

Possession, Heritage, and Hope

In the 1950s, Cleveland Kamiakin attended meetings across the reservation and from Spokane to Wenatchee to press for approval of the Colville Tribal Council plan to expand the reservation by purchasing unoccupied land in the former Northern Half. He urged tribal members to consider the sacrifices made by Kamiakin, Moses, Joseph, and other leaders of bygone times to affirm the treaty rights for which they had so long struggled and to preserve their people's distinct heritage through self-sufficiency. Cleveland continued to press Walt Horan and U.S. senators Warren Magnuson and Harry Cain to support legislation authorizing such land transactions in defiance of BIA opposition, and also to preserve the tribe's hunting and fishing rights and the federal government's trust responsibility.

In May 1950, Kamiakin joined Peter Dan Moses, Jim James, and members of the Colville Business Council in composing a document specifically meant for the White House. They presented the "Truman Scroll" to President Harry Truman during his visit to Grand Coulee Dam on May 11, 1950, for the Second Power House inauguration.

Truman Scroll

A signing ceremony for the Truman Scroll in the Nespelem Council Hall, May 1, 1950—(l. to r.) Cleveland Kamiakin, leader of the Palouse band; Billy Curlew, chief of the Moses-Columbia band; Harry Owhi of the Colville Business Council; Peter Dan Moses who would make the presentation to President Truman on May 11; Victor Nicholas (signing), chief of the Colville band from Ferry County; George Friedlander of the Colville Business Council; and Eddie Yeracostchin, chief of the Nespelem tribe.

The document, signed by 823 members of the Colville tribes, eloquently expressed their commitment to self-reliance and stewardship of natural resources. Many of the ideas, and even some of the wording in the scroll, were similar to portions of the Colvilles' 1925 letter to President Coolidge:

> Our holdings have diminished through the years. This at one time was Indian country. God created this Indian country, and it was like He spread out a big blanket, and He put the Indian on it. The Indians were created here in this country, truly and honestly, and that was the time our rivers started to run. Then God put fish in the rivers, and He put deer and elk in the mountains and buffalo upon the plains, and roots and berries in the field, and made laws through which there came the increase of fish and game. This land was ours, and our strength and our blood was from the fish and the game, the roots and the berries. These are the essence of our life. We were not brought here from a foreign country. We did not come here. We were put here by the Creator.
>
> Our roots are deep and our past is ancient. Our fathers were great in the days gone by, and their past will last forever and ever. Our fathers did not write in books nor did they put their words on paper to be put on a shelf to be covered with dust, forgotten, and unknown to their children. The Indian wrote his words, his promises in his memory; in his children's memory, and in the memory of his children's children. Our fathers allowed the white man to come as our fathers were good and kind to everyone.
>
> Now a great change has been made in this, our country. Much of the things we used as food has been killed off. Our land base has been drastically reduced and we have now reached the point where our way of life may become seriously jeopardized by the uncertain status of the land that we call our home. A home, to all people, is one of their most cherished possessions, and we are no different from others. With all our hearts we are endeavoring to preserve that home. For our old people, to whom it has always been home. For our young people, to whom we desire to give the opportunity for a decent standard of living; and also to the coming generations, to whom we earnestly hope to leave a heritage that they can be proud of.
>
> The ultimate goal of the Colville Indians is to become self-sustaining and we feel that this cannot be done without a secure and definite land base.... [A]ction will reestablish the once proud self-reliance in the Colville Indians and remove all doubt and insecurity. It will give us the needed encouragement to proceed with the development of our own resources. Preservation of the homeland is paramount in the hearts and minds of all people. It is our most precious possession, our heritage, and hope. May the title of our land be clarified to give the present and the generations to come the needed opportunity for progressive self-development.[8]

The scroll's references to words, promises, and memory offer insight into the significance of the oral tradition in Native American culture, in this case with special relevance to Indian treaty rights. During the slow transition from orality to literacy, tribal leaders maintained a clear understanding of key provisions of the Walla Walla treaties, including specific and detailed references to reservation boundaries, participant bands, and signatories.

Moreover, their understandings contributed and added to important interpretations of such treaty terms as right, privilege, and grant that had been variously interpreted in the narrowest sense by many jurists and historians. Cleveland and Jim James endeavored through the Truman Scroll to focus attention on the validity of Indian interpretation of treaty terms as understood through the oral traditions, transmitted to succeeding generations by the principal negotiators such as Chief Kamiakin.[9]

The Meyer Era

After the founding of the ATNI, Cleveland Kamiakin and Jim James helped lead other specific campaigns countering federal-level proposals for terminating reservations, delays in Indian veterans' benefits, and other issues. They encouraged the anti-termination efforts on the Flathead Reservation led by Chief Paul Charlo, grandson of Chief Victor, who alone had risked giving sanctuary to Chief Kamiakin's small band a century earlier. Cleveland also supported Chief Sam Boyd of the Spokanes and Joseph Garry of the Coeur d'Alenes. Garry, a descendant of Spokan Garry, had intimate knowledge of the Kamiakins and held them in high regard. He had been raised on the Coeur d'Alene Reservation, where Helen Chumayakan (Kamiakin), daughter of We-yet-que-yet, was a lifelong friend and relative by marriage. Helen's son, Ray Pierre, served as a tribal chair on the Kalispel Reservation in the 1950s.

Cleveland Kamiakin's greatest challenge in overcoming threats of federal termination was at home in the Colville region, at such place as Nespelem, Keller, and Omak. The octogenarian Cleveland, and his nephew Charley Williams, regularly emerged from their small clapboard homes along Nespelem Creek to help Frank George, Lucy Covington, and other younger leaders turn the tide of local sentiment away from the termination advocates.

The nation's leaders in post-war America, preoccupied with the Red Scare, McCarthyism, and the Cold War, encouraged termination policies and nearly reversed the many Indian affairs reforms occurring after the Indian Reorganization Act of 1934. Dillon S. Meyer's appointment as Commissioner of Indian Affairs in 1950 signaled the change in thinking.

In his former role as director of the War Relocation Authority, Meyer had established West Coast internment camps for Japanese-Americans during World War II. He viewed termination of Indian reservations as the best means to diminish federal paternalism and promote equality of citizenship. Critics characterized his autocratic style as "blundering and dictatorial," but he was consistent with the views of the times and the incoming Eisenhower administration. The Department of Interior and the BIA now advocated the termination of reservations and removal of "all disabilities and limitations specifically applicable to Indians." They found little sympathy in petitions from Indian country seeking expansion of the Colville Reservation; the tribe's eloquent appeal fell on deaf ears.

In his role as executive director of the National Congress of American Indians, Frank George became a leading national spokesman for Indian rights, and his views were strongly influenced by the counsel of his great-uncle and mentor, Cleveland Kamiakin. George rallied reservation and national convention audiences with spirited words about the "pride of Indianhood," and encouraged dignified, activist confrontation of "bigotry, pessimism, and discrimination."

In a 1952 speech to ATNI delegates in Spokane, George reaffirmed Indian resolve for self-reliance in practical terms, while warning against inimical schemes in the name of "emancipation" aimed at the liquidation of longstanding federal treaty obligations. He spoke of the responsibilities of stewardship, and how reclamation, mining, and timber management practices could threaten the blessings of the Creator. The tribes could manage themselves, he reasoned, conducting comprehensive surveys of mineral and forestry resources. Moreover, the tribes should have the right to procure legal counsel without limitations imposed by the BIA's "past dictatorial proclivities," in order to more fairly represent Indian views in state and federal courts, and to more actively pursue settlements through the Indian Claims Commission, created by Congress in 1946 following a major campaign by Indian leaders and their supporters.[10]

Charley Kamiakin Williams, c. 1950.
Daryll Barr Collection

Meanwhile, the passage of House Concurrent Resolution 108 in August 1953, and subsequent termination proposals, repudiated the New Deal's Indian revitalization policies, and threatened to obliterate the principle of limited tribal sovereignty that had guided government relations with Indians since the nation's inception. Cosponsored by Senator Henry Jackson and Wyoming's Representative William Harrison, HCR 108 gave tribes the option to dispose of their lands either by forming a corporation to manage the remaining assets, or by liquidating their assets and distributing the proceeds among tribal members on a blood quantum basis. The plan had the strong support of other influential terminationists, such as Utah's Arthur Watkins, who expressed support in the Cold War rhetoric of "liberation of enslaved peoples" previously confined to "socialist environments."

As further incentive for the Colvilles to approve termination—called "extermination" by leaders such as George— Congress passed Public Law 772 in 1956, which would return 818,000 acres of unallotted reservation lands to the tribe in return for the business council's decision to terminate within five years. The case had further national implications. A clause required the Colvilles to make significant annual payments in lieu of county property taxes, from which reservation Indians had long been exempt.[11]

Well into his eighties, Cleveland continued to take annual trips to see friends and relatives, and to participate in tribal ceremonies on area reservations. In 1953, he visited the Priest Rapids locality where Johnny Buck (Puck Hyah Toot) was determined to continue the Washani legacy of his uncle, the *yánča* Smohalla (c. 1815–1895), formerly the spiritual leader of Indian traditionalists throughout the region. Buck safeguarded the Wanapum teacher's sacred flag and wooden oriole, *Wawšukla,* and presided over longhouse ceremonies on the sagebrush flat at *P'na,* one of the region's last outposts of off-reservation Indian autonomy and ownership.

In the early 1950s, Congress authorized the construction of a dam at nearby Priest Rapids with implications that greatly disturbed Buck and his small band. In the 20th century, their people had continued to roam freely in the area, gathering roots and fishing at the rapids. Since 1942, however, they had been forbidden to utilize the White Bluffs, Wahluke Slope, and adjacent downriver ancestral lands, which during World War II were taken over by the federal government for the Hanford atomic bomb project. Cleveland encouraged Buck's course of action, pressing for a dialogue with the Corps of Engineers and Grant County PUD officials to establish special arrangements for the Wanapums' continued presence in the locality.

Under the leadership of Buck, his sons Rex and Frank, and Robert Tomanawash, a "unique relationship" was established with these agencies to ensure the small band's livelihood. Following condemnation of their properties for the dam's reservoir, the residences and longhouse were relocated on forty acres near Priest Rapids Dam, which was completed in 1961. Eighteen miles upstream, another hydroelectric facility, the Wanapum Dam, started operation in 1963 and featured the Wanapum Heritage Center.

Cleveland also showed a special interest in school activities and other events in the lives of his children, grandchildren, nieces, and nephews. Many of them accompanied him on excursions throughout the region, where he pointed out old family campsites from the Big Bend to the Bitterroot Valley. While going to Toppenish during the summer of 1953, he saw gargantuan excavation equipment digging enormous canals in the first phase of the Columbia Basin Irrigation Project to bring water from Grand Coulee Dam to 120,000 dryland acres. Many sections of the insequent streams and time-worn trails of his youth were being impacted. On the same outing, he ventured east to the Palouse country to visit family gravesites. When stopping at Rock Lake, he wistfully told his companions that it was the last time he would see his ancestral homeland.

On the Snake River at *Palus*, his nephew Pete Bones (Kah-yee-wach) continued to periodically reside in the forlorn remnants of the ancient village. Following the death of Sam Fisher in 1944, he served as the protector of the fenced cemetery where Cleveland's mother and two brothers had been buried amidst dozens of other graves. The windswept place was unattended in the summer of 1953, however, since Bones was convalescing with relatives at Nespelem after suffering a paralyzing stroke the previous September. (He prevailed on his hosts to allow his return to Dayton, however, where he died on August 13, 1954.)

Over the years, Fisher's nephew at Lapwai, Carter Sloutier and his son Gordon Fisher, had periodically checked in on

their relatives and fished with them at *Palus*, but Sloutier also died in 1954. Since Sloutier was closely related to Cleveland's wife, Alalumt'i, young Fisher lived with the Kamiakins in Nespelem and accompanied Cleveland on his far-flung travels, listening attentively to many of the elder's stories and seeking to abide by his counsel—"Always remember who you are, and where you came from." The cemetery at *Palus* was excavated by Washington State University archaeologists in the summer of 1964 due to the construction of Lower Monumental Dam and its reservoir, which would flood the site. The remains of 262 individuals—buried between about 1820 and 1945—were exhumed and eventually repatriated by area tribes in June 2006.

Opposing Termination

In 1955, Frank George was a prime mover in drafting the NCAI's "Point Nine" program, reaffirming many New Deal precepts and underscoring the necessity of preserving the reservation system. A century earlier, warfare followed the Walla Walla Council. Now, George wondered if a new "political war" was coming, undoing Indian rights.

Termination sentiment was strongly rebuffed on the Yakama Reservation by such tribal leaders as Thomas Yallup and Watson Totus, and by Kis-am-x'ay (Annie Billy), the tribe's oldest member. Reckoned to be well over 100 years old, the blind and frail "Grandmother of Grandmothers" made a rare appearance at the annual General Council meeting. She addressed the assembly in the ancient Sahaptin dialect of her native Columbia River village, *Weyounut*, near Plymouth, Washington. Alex Saluskin translated her memories of when Chief Kamiakin led the fight for their homelands—a time when Kis-am-x'ay herself had been wounded by soldiers.

Kis-am-x'ay mourned the loss of sacred lands stretching across *Nch'i-Wána* in a great arc from Umatilla Landing to Pasco. She then turned to matters at hand. "We have come to decide our future. Unless we stand together, united, we will lose the fishing, hunting, and root digging rights that God gave us. When everything was dark so long ago, the Great One who rules over us all said there should be light.... So there was a sun. In the same manner He created the land and the water. Upon the land, animals and then mankind were created and so were roots, water, and timber. These five things held sacred by our people were made in five days.... He blessed each and everything. He blessed the red man as well as the white. He blessed the food and water for the use of both, everlasting.… Only the Creator gave us our lands and the things upon them."

Kis-am-x'ay recalled the Walla Walla Treaty Council where Kamiakin and her uncle had expressed these Indian truths to Governor Stevens. "But the *Suyapos* stood on one side holding their firearms and the *Nahtietee* stood on the other." She urged her listeners to "remember the message" before casting their votes on termination. When they did so, the measure was soundly defeated.[12]

In 1955, at a Walla Walla Treaty Centennial commemoration at the Yakama Agency Headquarters in Toppenish, Thomas Yallup and visiting dignitary Cleveland Kamiakin addressed a large audience in front of a 13-ton block of polished black granite, upon which rested a gleaming white monument bearing an engraved likeness of Chief Kamiakin based on Sohon's portrait. Cleveland paid tribute to the 234 Yakama veterans of the two world wars, whose names appeared beneath his father's depiction on the monolith. He reminded the Assistant Commissioner of Indian Affairs, Thomas Reid, and others in the crowd of Chief Kamiakin's words to Governor Stevens at the conclusion of the treaty council a century earlier: "Perhaps you have spoken straight, that your children will do what is right. Let them do as they have promised."

After paying courtesies to federal and state officials, Yallup likened the challenges faced by "the old treaty chiefs" to his own "heaviness" over recent threats to government treaty obligations. Yallup told his listeners: "Kamiakin…never accepted from the Americans the value of a single grain of wheat without paying for it," and that his final words to Stevens about straight talk and doing right were of special significance to later generations. Yallup then asked, "What more wisdom and foresight could be said in so few words?" He concluded by couching Chief Kamiakin's long-ago statement in sacred terms as "the prayer of the Yakima Nation."[13]

Leaders such Yallup, Frank George, Paschal Sherman, and Joseph Garry stood on speaker platforms across the country, pressing for wider tribal participation in NCAI affairs and strategies to oppose termination. They also sought to inform the non-Indian community about the central role of tribal identity in Native American cultural wellbeing, and how legislation threatening the status of reservations jeopardized that identity.

The efforts of these Northwest leaders led to the hosting of the twelfth convention of the National Congress of Ameri-can Indians in Spokane—in the centennial year of the Walla Walla treaties. The historic three-day gathering convened during the last week of August 1955, within the white stucco walls of the Davenport Hotel. Over 700 delegates representing more than 60 tribes attended. President Joseph Garry guided deliberations concerning a number of issues brought to the assembly floor, and worked with Frank George, NCAI executive director Helen Peterson, and others to focus the organization's efforts in the following year on opposition to termination.

Peterson used the occasion to speak out against more subtle methods used by federal officials to dispose of reservation lands, which tribal leaders had long understood were held in trust. "Driven by sheer poverty, Indians have been 'fee patenting' their individual allotments prepatory to sale," which "then passes from Indian ownership." She echoed the recurrent theme in remarks by George and Garry that the basis of Indian society is "a tribal existence."

No participant at the convention was more feted than Cleveland Kamiakin, still vigorous in his old age and a living expression of cultural pride and the personification of the long-time struggle to maintain rights negotiated by his father a century earlier. As one observer recalled, his mere presence "stood for everything." Cleveland's trademark braids and broad-brimmed hat may have seemed incongruous in the renowned hotel's gilded Hall of Doges. But his dignified bearing and earnest words of encouragement to delegates such as George, Garry, and Alex Saluskin—all his relatives—carried hope that legal efforts might succeed, in a similar legal court as depicted in the Davenport Hotel's recreation of the famous Venetian palace of justice.[14]

The pivotal 1959 U.S. Supreme Court decision in *Williams v. Lee*, although involving a case on the Navaho Reservation in Arizona, was not without influence and consequence for the Northwest. The Supreme Court had long strayed from Chief Justice John Marshall's historic 1832 decision in *Worcester v. Georgia*, recognizing Indian tribes as self-governing "nations" within the United States. In spite of that early ruling, state and local authorities across the country had over time recurrently imposed restrictions on Indian fishing and hunting rights and other matters. Now, *Williams v. Lee* reaffirmed tribal court jurisdiction in tribal civil affairs

Also having bearing was a 1945 case, *Northwest Band of Shoshone Indians v. United States*, in which a Supreme Court majority upheld the federal government's right to not compensate Indians for lands expropriated during the previous century. Although the Supreme Court majority ruled against the tribes, Indians across the country found a spirited voice for their rights in a vigorous dissent filed by Justice William O. Douglas. The Washington State native argued that "Indian title is the right to occupancy based on aboriginal possession," and is "considered as sacred as the fee-simple of the whites." He stated that "to deny petitioners' title is unworthy of our country." Expressing clear thought in characteristically blunt terms, Douglas went on to delineate what he viewed as the unmistakable intent in the Constitution and key precedents such as Marshall's decision. They protected the civil rights of Americans, and provided safeguards regarding Indian treaty rights.[15]

Douglas was a prolific writer and world traveler, who maintained close personal ties to lifelong Yakima Valley friends during frequent visits to wild Northwest landscapes. His 36-year Supreme Court tenure (1939–75), the longest in American history, yielded over 1,200 written opinions. Several of the thirty-two books he authored offer insights into the profound influences that shaped his thinking. Born in 1896, Douglas lost his Presbyterian missionary father at a young age, and grew up in difficult circumstances in the Yakima Valley where his devoted mother nurtured her son's intellectual prowess. Douglas sought to compensate for the effects of infantile paralysis by hiking along the Ahtanum and in the rugged Cascades. He also forged close friendships with Chief Alec Shawaway, his son Alba Shawaway Kooatyahhen, and other Yakamas, who acquainted him with their culture and their regard for the natural world. Alec Shawaway was the son of the prominent *Washani* leader Kooatyahhen (Kotaiaquan)—grandson of legendary Weowicht, who had resided near present-day Parker.

In a chapter titled "Indian Philosopher" from his best-selling 1950 memoir, *Of Men and Mountains*, Douglas recalled his familiarity with Kamiakin's story, and retold several area Indian myths, including the legend of the Painted Rocks pictographs. Douglas's growing appreciation of tribal history coincided with the court's gradual shift regarding Indian rights. By the late 1950s, Douglas was contributing to majority opinions that began reversing termination policies, in spite of the court's previous tendency against intervention in such cases. In January 1959, the Supreme Court's landmark unanimous ruling in *Williams v. Lee* decided in favor of a Navaho appellant. It overturned Arizona's previous decision to affirm state court jurisdiction over the tribal system. This case—confirming tribal court sovereignty over state courts in civil matters—established the "infringement doctrine" as the basis for determining when any state law might be excluded from enforcement on reservations.[16]

Douglas became the bench's leading authority on Indian treaty rights and penned 14 opinions in Indian cases decided by the justices during his court tenure. He authored two key majority opinions on Northwest fishing rights, in which the court finally clarified the 1850s treaties language regarding traditional off-reservation fishing sites, to be held "in common with the citizens of the Territory." Douglas used the opportunity to affirm his vital interest in conserving wild fish runs consistent with his controversial "Wilderness Bill of Rights," and in restoring recognition of treaty rights contrary to erroneous Washington Supreme Court interpretations.[17]

In one of Douglas's last decisions from the bench, he contributed a concurring opinion in *Antoine v. Washington*, a case involving a Colville Indian hunting off the reservation. It ruled that the treaty right to hunt "in common" with others was unambiguous in its intent. Indians could hunt on non-reservation lands without state hunting licenses, barring situations where there was a need for conservation.

Throughout this often stormy era, Douglas routinely returned to the Northwest when the court was in summer recess, to again dwell in the places of his youth and further explore the region's wilderness areas. Douglas also frequently visited his Walla Walla alma mater, Whitman College, where a prominent stone marker on campus commemorated the site of the 1855 Treaty Council. This was the place where Kamiakin had confounded Stevens at the end of the deliberations by observing: "The forest…knows my heart." What had seemed incomprehensible to some government officials at that distant time now was being perceived by others a century later. Douglas wrote of visits among the "pine and fir that greeted the Fathers of the Ahtanum Mission." In time of need, "these trees were friends—silent, dignified, and beneficent friends" that promised "help and solace."[18]

Orphaned Elder

In June 1956, Frank George, Cleveland Kamiakin, Peter Dan Moses, and other reservation representatives participated in a site dedication ceremony for the only Columbia River dam that would be named for a Native American leader, the Chief Joseph Dam, located 40 miles downstream from Grand Coulee. Celebratory remarks were made by Governor Arthur Langlie, Army Corps of Engineers officials, and Lt. C.E.S.

Wood's son, Erskine Wood, who had lived with Joseph for a time at Nespelem when a 14-year-old boy. Cleveland and Frank George offered more sobering words.

Frank George told listeners that recent shifts in federal Indian policy were threatening the very security and treaty rights negotiated by Plateau Indian leaders decades before. The irony of George's remarks was not lost on anyone in the crowd familiar with Joseph's story—at this time when a hydroelectric project was being named in his honor.

Later, when some government officials proposed the idea of removing Joseph's remains from Nespelem and entombing them inside the massive concrete structure, tribal officials were incredulous. The outlandish proposal never came to fruition. The broad dam would span perspectives that could still be worlds apart. Also, the much heralded salmon fishery planned for the facility would never replenish the runs, which continued a serious decline in spite of the corps' expensive mitigation efforts in the Columbia watershed.

In early October 1956, an Ephrata historian and Bonneville Power Administration attorney, Nat Washington, arranged a tour of the Moses Lake area with Cleveland Kamiakin and Moses band elder Billy Curlew, documenting Indian names for geographic features and traditional campsites. In public, Cleveland typically appeared with a wide-brimmed circular felt hat wound with a scarlet or dark green silk handkerchief, with a matching bandana around his neck. He favored dark flannel shirts and sometimes wore pants festooned with a colorfully embroidered inseam.

Colville Agency interpreter Harry Nanamkin, great-grandson of Chief Owhi, translated for Nat Washington, who tape-recorded the talks with the two elders. The voice of 86-year-old Cleveland, speaking in Sahaptin, emerged strong and deep, as he patiently responded in measured tones to inquiries about camp life, tribal myths, and his relatives (he distinctly pronounced the family name as "K'amáyakun"). He and Billy Curlew expressed delight at the opportunity to visit the Rocky Ford camp northwest of Moses Lake and reminisce about past times when their ancestors traded roots and salmon for buffalo hides with tribes from the mountains.

The two men's words reflected a profound sense of loss, but also marveled at Coyote's creations across the landscape. As Cleveland walked among the ancient lodge rings at *Indupasnuwit*, he grew wistful. "*Íchna áw míimi pawyáninxana....* I am not strong like I used to be," he told Wash-

ington. "I am an orphan from everywhere. I am separated from all my homelands.... This is how it once was. Spílya made everything. Whatever he said, he did it just like that. We came to know such things through stories. He was very smart and brave. He went around, he made this [rock] sweathouse.... He was skillful and gifted. He had power and was cunning. He was someone to be reckoned with! It was awesome, and he finished it wonderfully.... My friend was skillful, intelligent, and masterful, and whatever he said, he made it. That is how it was, how Spílya was."[19]

In April 1957, a retired Elmer City sheep rancher and Kamiakin family friend, Cull White, interviewed Cleveland Kamiakin at his home in Nespelem. Cleveland related details then about his father's last years at Rock Lake. He also spoke poignantly of the family's relocation to area reservations seven decades earlier. White concluded his notes, observing that Cleveland's "dearest wish" still remained "a grant of his old home in the Palouse."[20]

The Kennedy Years

Members of the Association on American Indian Affairs joined in the NCAI's campaign against termination. An advocacy group of mostly White membership, headed by anthropologist Oliver LaFarge, the AAIA sought to protect the special status Native Americans had negotiated in the previous century. In 1958, Oliver LaFarge described the stakes in unmistakable terms: "Our federal policy does not actually aim to destroy the bodies of living Indians—although, as recent U.S. Public Health Service reports show, that is one of its byproducts—but to disintegrate their communities, their hopes, their very souls,...and hence will be from the point of view of the Bureau of Indian Affairs, as good as dead."[21]

Such candid rhetoric in a time of Cold War rivalries infuriated some political conservatives, who branded AAIA activists as Communist sympathizers, and attempts for reform as "socialist experiments." Some government officials expressed suspicion about Nez Perce leader Archie Phinney's motivation because of his anthropological studies in Soviet Russia during the 1930s. Phinney, who died in 1949, was a linguist and BIA administrator. He had studied at the Soviet Academy of Sciences in Leningrad on the advice of his mentor at Columbia University, the noted anthropologist Franz Boas.[22]

Prominent spokesmen for Native American rights, such as Phinney, LaFarge, George, and D'Arcy McNickle, had formulated a sophisticated strategy for political change in an age of American decolonialism. They invoked historic themes of

Frank George (right) with President and Mrs. John F. Kennedy and Archibald Cox, c. 1962.
WSU Libraries (Cull White Collection)

Indian patriotism, strikingly evident in recent Native American wartime enlistments. They also affirmed sovereignty rights and tribal identity ties to ancestral lands.

In the 1960 presidential campaign, NCAI representatives reached out to leaders in both major parties. Frank George met with John Kennedy, lawyer Archibald Cox (a civil rights advocate), and other Democratic strategists at Hyannis Port. George helped draft the party's platform on Indian affairs, and was named chair of the Democratic National Committee's Indian Section of the Nationalities Division.[23]

During this time, a Washington, D.C., attorney and House subcommittee staffer, Albert Grorud, was doggedly lobbying in Congress for the termination of Indian reservations. He also established a series of pro-termination "Indian Associations" in targeted localities across the country, including the Pacific Northwest. Grorud's "Associations" were an anathema to the NCAI and ATNI, who charged them with using heavy-handed methods and outside funding to advance the agendas of non-Indian special interests. Through the combined efforts of groups such the NCAI, ATNI, and AAIA, the national trend toward termination eventually was halted. By then, however, the Klamath, Menominee, and dozens of other tribal governments had been devastated by the policy, and 1.3 million acres of Indian lands were taken.[24]

In 1961, President Kennedy restated the Native American resolve in opposing termination as a principal policy goal of the "New Frontier." On March 5, 1963, he welcomed NCAI representatives to a White House reception along with Idaho Senator Frank Church, Washington Senator Henry Jackson, and other dignitaries. Beneath sunny skies in the Rose Gar-

den, the president reaffirmed a pledge that the nation's "first citizens" be able to "develop their lives in the way that best suits their customs and traditions and interest." With Frank George standing at the president's side, Kennedy emphasized improved elementary and secondary Indian education as a priority, and pledged to address the problem of unemployment on reservations.

Later recalling two figures prominent in Pacific Northwest history, Chief Joseph and Sacajawea, Kennedy noted the broader national need to address Indian education: "Our treatment of Indians…still affects the national conscience. We have been hampered by the history of our relationship…in our efforts to develop a fair national policy governing present and future treatment of Indians under their special relationship with the Federal government. Before we can set out on the road to success, we have to know where we have been in the past. It seems a basic requirement to study the history of our Indian people. Only through this study can we as a nation do what must be done if our treatment of the American Indian is not to be marked down for all time as a national disgrace."

But Kennedy's encouraging rhetoric did not readily translate into federal action. An Indian policy task force did little more than explore the promotion of Indian reservation tourism, popular in the Southwest, as a marketing strategy to strengthen reservation economies across the country.[25] Although Kennedy's Interior secretary, Stuart Udall of Arizona, also publicly opposed termination, divisions within the Democratic Party and the administration's preoccupation with other domestic issues and the Cold War forestalled a lasting resolution to the challenges of termination and economic development.

Still, in November 1963, many Indian leaders deeply mourned the tragic loss of Kennedy, whose interest in the lives of their people seemed genuine. His passing jeopardized hopes for the anticipated delivery of the administration's good intentions. During a visit to the nation's capital soon after the assassination, Joseph Garry laid a wreath at the grave of the slain president, with military escort and cannon salute, on behalf of Northwest tribes and the NCAI. To this day, Kennedy's portrait is often seen mounted on walls of homes in Nespelem, Toppenish, Lapwai, and throughout Indian country.

I Love My Country

Termination advocates had found an unlikely ally in U.S. Senator Henry M. Jackson from Washington, a Democrat. Known for his hawkish views in foreign affairs, Jackson nevertheless held liberal stands on most domestic issues. Regarding termination policy and Indian matters in general, however, Jackson took a hard line and supported measures toward Indian assimilation, which in his view was best for society as a whole.

In 1963, Jackson became chair of the Senate Interior Committee, which set the agenda for the Indian Affairs Subcommittee. In the Northwest, hope was reborn for termination advocates, who calculated that every full-blooded Colville member would receive $56,000 if all rights to federal recognition were abrogated. On the other side, "Petitioner Party" opponents, such as the Kamiakin-Williams, Paween, and Moses families, pointed out that federal officials had not considered compensation for hunting, fishing, and mineral rights, and the incalculable value of the Colvilles' "close spiritual attachment for the land." Government spokesmen appeared unwilling to do so, citing, among other factors, that the Colville Reservation was established by presidential executive order rather than through direct treaty negotiation.

The opponents of termination, with little support from agency officials or local commercial interests, had to take matters into their own hands. They were confronting what many felt was yet another "land grab" by powerful politicos. Representation of their views was desperately needed in hearings before the Indian Affairs committees; however, the most influential traditional Indian leaders were too elderly for transcontinental travel to Washington, D.C.[26]

On a spring day in the mid 1960s, George Friedlander and his sisters, Lucy Covington and Emily Peone, joined other relatives for an annual horse round-up on the family ranch near Nespelem, established nearly a century earlier by their father, Louie Friedlander. Even in their older years, the Friedlander siblings were excellent riders, and met annually to brand and inspect one of the most valued herds in the locality. Their appaloosas, paints, and bays carried bloodlines extending back to stallions brought to the reservation by the Kamiakins and Moses, and possibly even a storied ancestral mare owned by Chief Khalotash.

The family gathered near the weather-beaten remnant of their childhood home, where Mary Owhi Moses had regaled them with stories about Kamiakin and Owhi, Qualchan and Moses. Amidst the warped boards and broken panes, the Friedlanders considered the struggles of their forebears and contemplated the Colville people's current plight, lacking resources to effectively continue the battle. Determining to help affirm the tribe's hard-won treaty rights, the family decided to liquidate a substantial portion of their most treasured asset and a living symbol of their freedom and homeland—the family livestock herd.

George and Lucy immediately set about organizing the sale of cattle and horses. The proceeds enabled Lucy Covington, Frank George, and other petitioners to present their case before federal officials in Washington, D.C., and to lobby Senator Jackson, U.S. Representative Thomas Foley, and other members of Congress. In 1965, this proved to be an important factor in the BIA and the House Interior and Insular Committee decision to hold hearings in Washington, D.C., and also at Nespelem, where tribal members of all ages, bands, and affiliation could more directly participate.[27]

At Nespelem in November 1965, public hearings were chaired by Representative Foley and others. Here, George Pierre poignantly noted that a phrase heard in Congress about terminating federal trust responsibility "'as soon as possible' sounded…like doom." The widows of recently deceased traditional chiefs—Annie Paween Cleveland, Hattie Red Star Andrews, and Annie Owhi—presented their views through interpreters Frank George and Lucy Covington before a hushed audience. On November 19, when introducing these honored elders, George related that "none of the blood that courses through their veins comes from alien soil, that their forebears have always been inhabitants of the North American Continent and they feel a very deep reverence for the retention of Indian status as it now exists."

In her testimony, Cleveland Kamiakin's wife, Annie, served notice to the visiting congressional delegation that the vast majority of full-blooded Indians on the reservation expected the federal government to live up to its established responsibilities. She reminded listeners that her father-in-law, Chief Kamiakin, had "signed the treaty of 1855 on behalf of the Yakima Nation," and that her husband had "always opposed any movement to end the federal trusteeship." She further argued that "the indiscriminate relinquishment of Federal responsibilities for the protection of Indian property rights is not justifiable and would be dangerous for the tribal members…. Liquidation is merely a scheme to have Indian owned lands pass into the hands of the non-Indians."[28]

Charley Williams, son of T'siyiyak Kamiakin, pointed out that those who first came to the reservation maintained "a deep reverence for the property of the Indians," and vowed to "never dispose of it or barter it away in any manner." Williams also mentioned the loss of his son in World War II, "when the Nation was called upon to defend this country." The committee noted this remark with special significance. Other tribal members followed, expressing similar views against termination in words expressing values beyond monetary considerations. "I love my country out in the hills," elderly and infirm Madeline Moses told the lawyers and politicians. To Margaret Piatote, their home was "a beautiful reservation…worth more than any money."[29] The elders' testimony, dress, and mannerism prompted a reporter to comment on the ancient and modern worlds intersecting that day in the Nespelem school gymnasium.

The forest knows my heart, Chief Kamiakin had said. Now tribal members faced a fateful decision and spent weeks throughout the winter in conversations among family and friends considering matters of forests, hills, and hearts. Kamiakin-Moses descendant Lucy Covington spoke on many occasions, often reminding listeners, "termination is like giving away your eagle feather." When final votes were tallied, a majority of tribal members among the Colvilles opposed the termination measure. In the 1968 tribal council balloting, after a campaign that included visits by Elnathan Davis of the Klamath tribe, Assiniboine-Sioux Hank Adams, who had grown up on the Quinault Reservation, and Sioux activist-scholar Vine Deloria Jr., Colville anti-termination candidates were overwhelmingly elected.

Although termination advocates introduced bills in Congress each year until 1970, when the Nixon administration formally repudiated HCR 108, the proposals never again emerged from committee. Congress substantially laid the termination issue to rest in 1975, when an ATNI initiative helped lead to passage of Public Law 93-638, the Indian Self-Determination and Education Act.[30] The measure was heralded as the most important landmark Indian legislation since the New Deal policies of Commissioner John Collier. During the previous decade Northwest tribal leaders had contributed greatly to a change of heart by the bill's principal sponsor— Senator Henry Jackson.

Annie Cleveland (George), c. 1940.
WSU Libraries (Cull White Collection)

Palouse, Moses-Columbia, and Nez Perce Claims Cases

The Indian Claims Commission Act enacted by Congress in 1946, in response to initiatives from the National Congress of American Indians and other supporters, authorized tribes to file claims against the United States for fair compensation denied them for century-old cessions. Newly established Indian Claims Commission courts were authorized to decide the validity of the claims. Most groups in the Inland Pacific Northwest filed such cases, including the tribes on the Colville and Yakama reservations that had been party to the 1855 Stevens treaties.

Under the terms of the Yakima Treaty, the various tribes and bands had ceded to the government 8,176,000 acres for a paltry consideration of $593,000—a little over seven cents per acre. The tribes also argued that they had held lands outside of those delineated in the Yakima Treaty, and that this acreage should be compensated for as well. Constituent bands of the Yakama Nation also sought other redress through the ICC. On July 20, 1948, the Yakama Tribe had hired a Washington, D.C., attorney, Paul M. Niebell, to represent their claims against the government on behalf of the Palouse Indians. The Palouses on the Yakama Reservation claimed that 10,828,000 acres had been illegally expropriated by the United States. Sixteen months later, the Colville Confederated Tribes hired the legal firm of I.S. Weissbrodt, James E. Curry, and Lyle Keith to press their case on behalf of the Palouse and Moses-Columbia bands. I.S. Weissbrodt's brother, Abe Weissbrodt, a prosecutor of German war criminals at the Nuremberg Tribunals, played a leading role in researching and presenting the case.

To simplify the trial process, the Indian Claims Commission eventually consolidated the Yakama and Colville claims for Palouse descendants residing on both reservations. After an exhaustive examination of the evidence, the commission reported on July 28, 1959, that both groups "contain members or descendants comprising the Yakima Nation and are, therefore, entitled to present claims." At this point, the Colvilles filed a formal claim on behalf of their Palouse band under Docket 222 in the names of Cleveland Kamiakin and Charley Williams, and Docket 224 on behalf of George Friedlander and members of the Moses-Columbia band. Since the Palouse case involved lands already under consideration in Docket 161 of the Yakama Tribe, the commissioners combined this case with Docket 222 filed by the Colvilles.

In 1960, Chief Commissioner Arthur V. Watkins convened a hearing into the Palouse Indian claims case. Verne F. Ray, the eminent anthropologist who had spent much of his academic career studying Plateau tribes, served as the expert witness for the tribe. Ethnologist Stuart A. Chalfant testified on behalf of the government, presenting testimony that attempted to counter many of the Indian claims. The testimony and deliberations took months, as the petitioners and government representatives presented their cases, and as the commissioners examined volumes of evidence presented in the form of treaties, agency reports, and other documents, and oral histories that had been provided by such elders as Cleveland Kamiakin, Charley Williams, and Nellie Moses Friedlander.

A similar case was presented by the Colville Confederated Tribes on behalf of the resident non-treaty Nez Perces, who did not recognize the Treaty of 1863 that had so reduced the size of the reservation specified in the original 1855 agreement. Petitioners for this case also included Charley Williams, whose elderly wife, Alalumti (Susie Chief), was one of the last survivors of the 1877 Nez Perce War, as well as Joe Redthunder, and Harry Owhi who sought compensation for both the value of expropriated ancestral lands (Docket 175-A), and mining and related uses for the period 1860–67 (Docket 180-A). On December 31, 1959, the Claims Commission ruled in favor of these petitioning parties, and awarded the Confederated Colville Tribes a total of $7,297,605 for damages from grossly unfair compensation.

On July 29, 1963, William M. Holt, a founding member of the ICC, delivered the commission's initial opinion to representatives of the Colville and Yakama confederated tribes in the Palouse and Moses-Columbia cases. He maintained that both tribes had members affiliated with these bands, and that these tribes had legitimate claims. Holt added that awards would be made "to the tribal entity," and "not to individual descendants." He then ordered the case to proceed to determine "the acreage of the lands involved; the market value thereof as of March 8, 1859 [when Congress ratified the Yakima Treaty]; and the consideration paid." In 1964, the commissioners reported final judgment, stating that "the consideration totaling $593,000 paid by the defendant the United States government to the Yakama Nation for the cession of lands having a fair market value of $4,088,000 was so grossly inadequate as to make the consideration unconscionable."[31]

Tribal members assembled in general meetings on the Yakama and Colville reservations to decide whether to accept the proposed ICC settlements. On November 14, 1964, the Colville tribal council chairman, Narcisse Nicholson Jr., called some 200 members to order in a four-hour meeting held at the Nespelem School. The vast majority of members voted to accept the terms, and a subsequent meeting of the business council authorized Nicholson and Frank George to lead a delegation to Washington, D.C., to formally report the decision.

On December 3–5, 1964, a similar well-attended general council was convened on the Yakama Reservation at the Community Center in Toppenish, where tribal chairman Eagle Seelatsee moderated discussions, which also resulted in an overwhelming decision to accept the award. The Yakama Business Council then delegated Seelatsee, Watson Totus, and tribal interpreter and historian Alex Saluskin to testify before the ICC, affirming the assembly's decision.

Meanwhile, terminationist Albert Grorud persisted to the end in the name of the "Colville Indian Association" to forestall the Colville award. He voiced objections to the pending agreement at the ICC's final hearing on the matter in March 1965. The commissioners, however, found this position "without any basis for refusal…to accept and approve the stipulations of settlement." They then ordered the award of $3,446,700 to the Yakama and Colville tribes on behalf of the Palouse and Moses-Columbia bands.[32]

The matter of equitable distribution was carefully considered by both tribal councils in a series of meetings in 1966 and 1967. The Yakamas pressed for payment based on 1954 tribal enrollments, which favored their position by a membership of 4,067 to 697. The Colvilles sought an equal division of the award, since the commission had ruled for the purposes of judgment that both tribal entities were successors to the "Yakima Nation" as designated in the 1855 treaty. Frank George further noted that four of Chief Kamiakin's sons and two of his daughters had filed allotments on the Colville Reservation, as did many other Palouses, Wenatchis, and others. The Chief Kamiakin family's long association with both the Yakama and Colville reservations contributed to a final resolution of the matter, allocating similar benefits to members on both reservations.[33]

The Indian Claims Commission judgments meant the end of a long struggle by tribal leaders to obtain more reasonable compensation for the lands forfeited over a century earlier. The settlements also created a new economic foundation for building new business opportunities on the reservations. Tribal elders still mourning the loss of ancestral lands received

Cleveland Kamiakin,
c. 1950.
*Yakima Valley Museum
(C. Relander Collection)*

some consolation for their persistent efforts to gain redress.

Cleveland Kamiakin did not live to see the success of the Indian claims cases involving the Palouses and Nez Perces. On September 3, 1959, he died quietly in his sleep at Nespelem. Hundreds of Indians from across the Pacific Northwest traveled to the small reservation community to pay their final respects to Chief Kamiakin's last son. Two days later, the revered elder was buried in a cemetery overlooking Nespelem, a short distance from Chief Joseph's grave.

A decade later, on June 6, 1969, Charley (Kamiakin) Williams—the last hereditary chief of the Colville Yakama-Palouses—died and also was buried at Nespelem. With the passing of these elders, the band lost the last of their leaders born in the Palouse homeland and who had lived "in the old way."[34] Their Native lands had become a patchwork of

grain fields and rangelands, owned by the heirs of the first *Shuyapo*.

Northwest tribal leaders still found it necessary to confront some persistent deleterious attitudes to treaty rights remaining in the state legislature. "Sagebrush Democrat" legislators of the 1960s, such as Nat Washington, Mike McCormack, and Wilbur "Web" Hallauer, represented central Washington districts where many Indians lived. They had to mitigate recurrent pressures from commercial fishing and agricultural interests to reconsider provisions in century-old treaties.

Like Washington, Hallauer had a keen interest in regional history enhanced by his association with pioneer families in the Yakima and Okanogan valleys, where he established extensive tree farming and fruit drying businesses. Both men had read Splawn's account of Kamiakin's life—as well as writings by Justice Douglas—and were interested in locating historic places in the region associated with the chief's life.

Indian fishing on the Yakima River at Horn Rapids, c. 1975.
Richard D. Scheuerman

Web Hallauer's election to the senate in 1956 led to his subsequent appointments as chairman of the Legislative Interim Committee on Water Resources and as Washington's first director of the Department of Ecology. His work in these roles led to important laws and regulations affecting Columbia River drainage flow levels, the Yakima River Basin Enhancement Project, and complex negotiations between the tribes and developers over water rights.

Hallauer's view of the future of Indian and White political relationships held some ominous long-term concern: "The question of public importance has to do with what authority and what controls over the majority should be exercised by the minority, particularly when the relations are on a ninety-nine to one scale." Hallauer further reasoned: "We have changed the status of Indians so they're citizens in common with us and yet they have their sovereignty.... I think it's something that cries out for settlement so that it won't go on for a thousand or ten thousand years."

Such expressions contrasted with tribal leaders' insistence that fishing and other rights negotiated by Kamiakin and other chiefs in 1855 were to be held "in perpetuity." Furthermore, as Yakama Councilman Watson Totus enunciated in 1964, "we don't want to sell our rights, because my people are still growing as long as the sun is going."[35]

Wilson Hall

A remarkable cadre of dedicated 20th century historians and artists, such as A.J. Splawn, L.V. McWhorter, W.C. Brown, Anne Harder, and Robert Ruby, found common ground in their appreciation of regional Native American culture. They built trusting relationships with members of the Kamiakin family and others in the Indian community, and created an informal network of communication among themselves to share ideas and more fully understand the region's past.

One of the most endearing and influential members of this circle was Professor Herman J. Deutsch at Washington State College, later Washington State University, whose remarkable tenure spanned several decades of full-time duties (1926–62), followed by two more decades of significant contributions as a faculty emeritus. Just as his influence upon Worth Griffin had helped lead to the founding of the Nespelem Art Colony, Deutsch also inspired several generations of students in classes ranging from the study of medieval culture to Colonial America.

He always emphasized family and local contexts in studies of important individuals and events. Enrollments in his Northwest history courses regularly exceeded the number of chairs in the classroom, as students clamored to hear his lectures and anecdotes on topics ranging from Dorsey Baker's "Rawhide Railroad" to Governor Stevens' Indian treaty negotiations. He carried on an extensive correspondence with local experts, including Judge W.C. Brown in Okanogan, which led to Deutsch's groundbreaking reappraisals of many neglected aspects of regional history.

At an American History Association meeting at Berkeley in December 1950, Deutsch gave a presentation titled "Indian and White in the Inland Empire." Deutsch passionately argued that scholars had long "overlooked" the experiences of large numbers of post-war, non-reservation Indians. He cited comments by Yakima Agent R.H. Milroy in the 1880s, who said as many Indians subject to his jurisdiction lived off the reservation as those residing within the boundaries. Deutsch found it remarkable that the lives of such stalwart people had been so little studied, in spite of the ready availability of written records and oral sources.

At the time, however, many professional scholars and biographers viewed "local" and "oral" history with suspicion. Deutsch, nevertheless, endeavored to show that properly gathered and interpreted local reminiscences were essential to overall scholarly understanding. This need was especially relevant regarding Indian history, where the role of memory and oral accounts often represented alternate interpretations, as well as additions, to written accounts, the latter of which almost always had been kept by Whites.

As Deutsch learned from L.V. McWhorter and Judge Brown's intensive efforts in talking with elders such as Tomeo Kamiakin, often oral stories and memory were the *only* ones available, since most Native peoples did not have a written tradition. Deutsch noted the "delicate human perception" in the collaboration between Clifford "Click" Relander and Wanapum elder Puck Hyah Toot, whose partnership led to the completion of the tribal history, *Drummers and Dreamers* (1956). Isaac Stevens' son had left a substantial, noteworthy two-volume biography of his father, filled with the governor's perspectives on interactions with Kamiakin and other Plateau leaders. Deutsch, however, lamented the fact that Chief Kamiakin had lived twice as long as the governor and fathered many sons who retained valuable first-hand knowledge, yet nobody in the scholarly community had investigated these Indians' perspectives on the two great figures in mid 19th century Northwest history. Deutsch succeeded in demonstrating the value of reminiscence and oral history as highly significant to professional work in research and writing, and he led important efforts to cultivate wider approaches to historical inquiry.[36]

Deutsch's efforts bore fruit in the recruitment of a new generation of researchers and scholars drawn to his vision of "history." In 1977, the WSU departments of history and Native American studies jointly appointed Wyandot scholar Clifford E. Trafzer who, though raised on the dry desert tablelands of southern Arizona, formed a special attachment to the Inland Northwest from the moment he arrived. Trafzer—who rented a house near the corner of "Cleveland" and "Kamiaken" streets in Pullman—met Dr. Deutsch, who still kept office hours in Wilson Hall after a half-century of service at WSU.

Deutsch introduced Trafzer to the Kamiakins' story, and encouraged the young scholar to devote serious scholarly attention into the largely forgotten yet pivotal roles of the Yakama-Palouse chief and his descendants in history. Trafzer set out to assemble all known written sources related to the Yakama and Palouse Indian past. He also was determined to visit area reservations and conduct extensive oral histories with the remaining tribal elders still able to recall stories of prominent 19th century Native American leaders, such as Kamiakin, Moses, and Tilcoax.

Down the Dirt Road

In excursions to Lapwai, Nespelem, Toppenish, and other reservation communities, Trafzer forged a wide network of friendships among the Kamiakin, Jim, and Bull families, and learned about the special significance of family relationships in researching American Indian history. In the course of Trafzer's field research, he had a profoundly moving dream in which an elderly man digging roots in a black basalt canyon sang a song of thanksgiving and spoke to him about the virtues of the plants. During these same months, Trafzer recurrently was advised by tribal elders on several reservations to seek out Andrew George for answers that still eluded him about Plateau tribal customs and Chief Kamiakin.

Finding the medicine man involved a quest of many months, which Trafzer recalled in an introductory essay to the best-selling Doubleday anthology of Native American short stories, *Earth Song, Sky Spirit* (1992). "Andrew George, it seemed, was always on the move, his services much in demand. To me, he was an Indian phantom, a spirit, a stick person from the Northwest. Sometimes I wondered if he existed at all." But Trafzer's persistence eventually bore fruit.

On a trip with his wife and a friend to the Yakama Reservation in November 1980, Trafzer learned that Andrew George recently had been staying with his daughter. Finally, the long-awaited opportunity seemed at hand to speak with one of the last persons known to have been raised at *Palus*, and who had been closely acquainted with Tomeo, Kiatana, Sk'olumkee, and other members of Chief Kamiakin's immediate family.

"We followed the directions to take the country road down this way until the pavement ended, turn right at the yellow sign, and travel down the dirt road along the canal to the red pump house.... We went to the front door of a house that we thought was that of Andrew George's daughter. I knocked and waited. Two little girls opened the door, and I asked, 'Does Andrew George live here?' Neither girl answered. They both giggled and ran off down a hall to the left. The door opened wide, allowing the cold wind to swirl around the tidy living room. A few moments later an old man with long white hair emerged from the dark hallway.... Before I could say anything, he stepped through the open door, reached out his hands, and brought us inside. We entered his home in silence, and followed him to the kitchen table. Yes, I told myself, this is the old man of my dream. I recognized him and he knew me. I knew that he had called me to his place to listen and learn."[37]

Through Andrew George, pathways opened to Trafzer that would document the Kamiakins' experiences after the territorial wars, and acquaint him with the work of the Animal People in fashioning the Palouse Hills, and in bringing fish and roots to the lands of the Columbia Plateau. He came to understand that family and traditional religion are fundamental to understanding the course of events in Northwest frontier history, and the whole course of Indian-White relations on the Columbia Plateau. Trafzer learned that tracing family history was far more than genealogy.

With an essential lens from the Indian community looking into the past, this approach became the basis of new research for Trafzer's work with the state Humanities Commission and the National Library of Medicine. These efforts led to the publication of *Renegade Tribe: The Palouse Indians and the Invasion of the Inland Pacific Northwest* (1986), and *Death Stalks the Yakama* (1997), a study of Indian health based on largely unexamined medical records for 14 tribal bands covering the period 1888 to 1964. Trafzer credits the contributions by Andrew George and other Plateau Indian elders for his selection by the Smithsonian Institution to co-edit *Native Universe: Voices of Indian America*. This highly acclaimed volume was commissioned to commemorate the 2004 opening of the National Museum of the American Indian, on the National Mall in Washington, D.C.

Living Treasure

Andrew George (*Tipiyeléhne Xáyxayx*/White Eagle)—in recognition of his selfless and untiring efforts to share Native wisdom with children and educators of all backgrounds in the Pacific Northwest—was named Washington's first "Living Treasure" on Memorial Day weekend 1989, inaugurating a State Centennial Commission program that continues to recognize the distinguished contributions of such individuals. On May 26 at the Seattle Center, following presentations by Governor Booth Gardner and Secretary of State Ralph Munro, Andrew George spoke poignantly to a large gathering about his and the Kamiakin family role in preserving a threatened cultural and environmental heritage.

"The books say that these Coyote Stories were originated by people who imagined, but to me these things are true to fact. I have seen for myself where things happened in Coyote's time, the shape of rocks and rivers and lakes. All around today Coyote and his gifts from the land are unrecognized—unwanted—unappreciated—unprotected, and we must not allow God's blessings to be taken from our children."

Exquisitely clad in a beaded blue vest and shimmering dark red shirt, and surrounded by television cameras with a Hollywood celebrity standing nearby, the aged medicine man looked beyond the crowd and remembered Chief Kamiakin and his sons and their homelands: "The history of my family and people has been told by my uncles and other elders and is written in the ancient rocks. You cannot read it all in a book or understand it all; you can only see it. The drums, the seven drums beating and the words of the song, speak the same truths as are in the Bible. Listen, you can hear them. Truth is the same everywhere."

After the crowd dispersed and he slowly made his way across the Seattle Center in the shadow of the Space Needle, a well-wisher asked Andrew George to name the most memorable part of the day. Without hesitation the old man smiled, raised his cane skyward, and replied gleefully: "A bird sang from these trees a while ago."

He momentarily pondered the experience, as if it was a wonderful mystery from an ancient text he hoped others might know, and then marveled: "Never have I heard such a song."

Epilogue

Young Chinook, powerful and brave,
yelled his victory song!
The Wolf Sister heard the shout
and ran from the lodge.

She recognized his voice
and went to greet him.
Young Chinook took her as his wife
and they returned together
to his father's home.

The bone-tired elderly couple finally glimpsed windswept Rock Lake off to the east beyond a row of stony defiles. The pink light of summertime dusk danced on the worn, green-lichen-stained basalt columns scattered across the shallow coulees. Sk'olumkee finally broke the day's prolonged silence. "We will find the store tomorrow," he informed Pemalks. "Night will soon fall and I must tend to the horses."

Their loosely jointed wagon turned around a final bend leading toward the south shore of the lake. Off to the east, a slow moving dust cloud hovered over a yellow caterpillar tractor as a farmer headed home after laboring in a summer-fallow field. Exhausted by the long ride in the late June sun, the horses kept to their slackened pace in spite of the prospect of fresh water.

"We have enough for a fine dinner," Pemalks reassured her sullen husband as they both leaned sideways when Sk'olumkee diverted the horses onto a dirt trail.

The team no sooner left the road than Sk'olumkee reined them to a halt. Three strands of barbed wire strung on a long row of cedar posts blocked access to the lake. Suspended from the top line was a peeling black and white sign bearing familiar words, "No Trespassing." Sk'olumkee paused a moment, then shouted "*Hup-hey*" to command the horses backward. The forlorn creatures awkwardly retraced their steps several

feet before Sk'olumkee reined them right to continue along the road, while two marmots scurried ahead along the fence.

Sk'olumkee squinted down the gray-blue gravel ribbon, struggling to comprehend something unfamiliar—an enormous man-made rock pile now obscured the entrance to the grassy defile leading to where his family once lived. They passed by a trail to a boat launch, but continued eastward to examine the massive formation. They soon discerned railway tracks crowning a mountain of basalt detritus. In several minutes, they drove under the viaduct in a narrow concrete passageway, entering the familiar landscape of Sk'olumkee's youth.

He drove the team past the old Henderson home—after 69 years still painted white and displaying the original frontier Gothic gables and casements. They saw a man clad in overalls stepping from an adjacent machine shed toward the house. Sk'olumkee turned into the place and asked the rancher in broken English if he might walk up the draw behind the house to view his family's former campsite. The kindly stranger smiled upon recognizing the name "Kamiakin" in Sk'olumkee's words, obliged the old man's request, and looked on curiously as Sk'olumkee and Pemalks slowly stepped down from the spring-wagon and walked up a lane behind the house.

Sk'olumkee showed Pemalks the site where he lived during the summers of his youth. He also noted that the massive train trestle obscured a spectacular view of the lake. Returning to the wagon, they retraced their route for a mile to the flat at the lake's south end, where a short trail led to the boat launch and a public campground. A green pickup truck pulling a silver boat was exiting just as Sk'olumkee drove into the small fenced enclosure. He stopped the horses near a stony promontory that rose several feet above the surrounding prairie and traded stares with other fishermen preparing to leave.

Sk'olumkee stepped out onto the edge of the slight rocky formation. "I played here as a child," he said casually before wincing in pain as he leaned backward. Sk'olumkee's beaded leather vest stretched over the slight bend of his back. Pemalks turned around to fetch a bottle of liniment. "But this was a mountain then," he said with a laugh, "and I was chief of my brothers!"

Pemalks smiled—she was pleased that her husband's ancient memories seemed to dispel the gloom that periodically descended upon him. Sk'olumkee stepped around the wagon and raised his hands to help Pemalks down from the seat. "We'll camp over yonder," he said with a nod of his head toward some small hawthorn trees just twenty feet away. As Pemalks set about preparing the evening meal, Sk'olumkee unhitched the team and led them to the lake, where he also drew a sip of water.

He then hobbled the horses near the wagon and broke feed from a hay bale. "Hey, my *kwetala'ma*," he whispered as he patted their heads, "you have brought me home and I thank you." Sk'olumkee also opened a crumpled burlap gunnysack near the hay in the wagon and drew out a faded-red coffee can full of oats to pour on the animals' fodder.

"My travelers have brought me home," he repeated to Pemalks, who had begun a vegetable stew consisting of dried salmon, potatoes, carrots, and beans, kept for this special time.

"Are you expecting others?" Sk'olumkee witted when hovering over the ample portion of savory stew beginning to warm in the iron kettle.

"Maybe Atween," Pemalks suggested, and they both chuckled.

That night, the old couple feasted as Sk'olumkee told his wife about the events and adventures of his youth. She never before heard him speak so much about Kamiakin, the legendary chief who only existed in Pemalks' imagination and that of their many nieces and nephews.

Tonight's tales were not those she heard from others about Chief Kamiakin in battles with soldiers or meetings with a governor and Army commanders. Sk'olumkee's recollections were of a father teaching his son how to ride a dun mare, ways to stalk skittish mule deer with bow or rifle, and about solemn preparations for a youth's vision quest. These and the other stories Sk'olumkee recalled were life's lessons given by a beloved father. Only late that night when Pemalks worked the clear liquid into Sk'olumkee's arched spine did he close his eyes and fall silent, lost in thoughts of this hallowed place.

Early the following morning, Sk'olumkee silently awoke in the predawn darkness while Pemalks continued sleeping beside him. He quietly rose and dressed in his green shirt of red spangles with ruffled sleeves, and put on his leather vest and round felt hat. He drew back the canvas door flap and instantly recognized a pleasant breeze coming off the water, fresh but not cold. The stooped old man strode on the low rocky rise, listening to the familiar *wesla'yawau*, the cry of the wind from his youth. He watched the sky graying in the east as dawn came from behind a thin fog. Soon, pines and aspens emerged from obscurity in the distance.

Sk'olumkee returned to the wagon, reached into a storage box behind the seat where dried roots and berries were stored, and took out a small sack. He then turned to walk along the road in the direction they had come, returning to the narrow lane blocked by the fence. Sk'olumkee pushed against the top of the gate post to release it from a wire loop and stepped through. Leaving the gate down, he proceeded intently for several minutes to a place where the trail led eastward back to the water. He paused for a moment, turned to the left, and continued along a small path traveled by cattle and coyotes, and disappeared into the distance.

By the time her husband returned, Pemalks had prepared a meager breakfast of coffee and biscuits with the last of the camas root flour and dried berries. "Maybe that store will have some of your peppermints or licorice," she said as he walked up to the fire.

"Perhaps," Sk'olumkee replied, "but it will not taste as good as the *k'unch* you make. Look around here," he continued, "nobody has gathered the moss in these pines for years." They both stood in silence near the dying embers.

"Did you find him?" Pemalks finally asked softly.

"Much has changed," he said, "more fences, cattle trails, even an orchard there now. But yes, I walked next to him." Sk'olumkee sipped coffee from a chipped white enamel cup, then said, "Come, I will show you where our mothers and brothers rest."

Pemalks followed her husband's lead along the lakeshore to the east, before ascending a stony slope in the shadow of a steep brown-black basaltic bluff.

The trail led to a secluded bunchgrass-covered flat. Pemalks watched as Sk'olumkee paused with ambassadorial dignity to remove his hat. He then looked skyward and spoke in whispers she could not understand. Pemalks quietly stepped beyond her husband among the slight mounds of earth, and wandered toward a cluster of serviceberry bushes in the distance, where a nest of tiny wrens suddenly darted about.

As she looked back toward the lake, Pemalks glimpsed the swift motion of her husband's hand as if casting seeds in the wind. She was close enough to see him reach into the bag and spread the contents in a great arc glistening in the morning sunlight. A few moments later he limped back down the trail as Pemalks slowly followed.

When Pemalks came near the place where Sk'olumkee had stood, she looked down on a scattering of lustrous white shells and crimson glass beads.

Kamiakin and Affiliated Family Lineages

A. Kamiakin Family
B. Sulk-stalk-scosum (Moses) Family
C. Poyahkin (Billy) and Paween Families

The 19th century dates listed for births and deaths in the following genealogies are based on oral history transcripts, federal census reports, enrollment documents, probate proceedings, and records and sources held at the National Archives and Records Administration, Seattle, and in university archives and libraries. The Columbia Plateau was divided linguistically between the southern Sahaptin-speaking tribes including the Yakama, and Interior Salish peoples to the north, such as the Moses-Columbias. Many Indians of the region were bilingual due to intertribal family associations and seasonal gatherings, thus some individuals had names in more than one language. Names in Native American families, as in other cultures, are often hereditary with origins in the distant past.

To better distinguish between individuals sharing the same name, added Roman numerals—I, II, etc.—begin with the first person bearing that name identified in the oral or written record. These designations are enclosed in brackets, as they would not have been used by the people in question, and are added here for editorial clarity. Among Plateau peoples, an individual's name traditionally changed over time, marking growth from infancy into adolescence and adulthood. Whenever known, an individual's adult name is used in the following lineages.

Many individuals, particularly among non-reservation families, did not participate in federal censuses during the 19th century. Consequently, vital statistics are limited in some cases, particularly regarding those who never relocated to reservations where agency records were maintained. (A notable exception was the 1914 Charles Redfield census of families living along the lower Columbia and Snake rivers.) Because census and some probate documents give the "age" of an individual rather than a "year" of birth or death, dates for these people may vary in accuracy by at least a year.

The use here of birth year (*b.*), circa (*c.*), death year (*d.*), and question mark (?) varies slightly from common practice. Circa (*c.*) is used to indicate uncertainty about a date when only general information has been provided (e.g., "When he died in 1930, he was about 60"). A question mark (?) indicates that differing dates are provided by the sources. The most common contradiction occurs when oral histories state one year, but census records indicate a different year. In these instances, the year supplied in family accounts is used, but a question mark is added. Birth year (*b.*) and death year (*d.*) are used only when one or the other, but not both, is known, and a question mark might also apply in these instances.

The oral and written sources listed below were used to determine both dates and the name forms. The abbreviations for these sources are set in small caps in the lineage charts.

AA: Albert Andrews (with R. Scheuerman), Moses Lake, 2005.

AB: Agatha Bart (with M. Finley), Nespelem, 2007, OHA, Colville Confederated Tribes.

AD: Agnes Davis (with R. Scheuerman and M. Finley), Pullman, 2006.

AJ: Andrew J. Splawn, *Ka-Mi-Akin: The Last Hero of the Yakimas*, 1917.

AK: Alalumt'i Kamiakin and Annie Owhi (with V. Ray), Nespelem, 1971, Gonzaga University.

AS: Alex Saluskin (with B. Rigsby), Yakima, 1966.

AT: Arthur Tomeo (Kamiakin) (with R. Scheuerman), Nespelem, 1972, OHA, Colville Confederated Tribes.

BR: Bruce Rigsby Collection, University of Queensland, Graceville, Australia.

CK: Cleveland Kamiakin (with C. White), 1957, MASC, Washington State University.

CS: Cecelia Sam, Mollie Si-een-wat (with L.V. McWhorter), Yakima, 1922, MASC, Washington State University.

CW: Cull White Papers, MASC, Washington State University.

EB: Ernie Brooks (with M. Finley), Nespelem, 2006.

EC: Edward Curtis, *The North American Indian* (7), 1911.

EP: Emily Peone (with R. Scheuerman), Nespelem, 1981, OHA, Colville Confederated Tribes.

FA: Frank Andrews (with M. Finley and R. Scheuerman), Nespelem, 2006, OHA, Colville Confederated Tribes.

FH: Family Histories (Yakama), RG 75.291.1, National Archives, Seattle.

GC: General Correspondence (Yakama Inheritance), RG 75.107.2, National Archives, Seattle.

IA: Isabel Arcasa (with R. Scheuerman), Nespelem, 1981.

JD: James L. Davis Collection, MAC, Spokane.

JY: Josephine Yemowith (with L.V. McWhorter), Yakima, 1912, MASC, Washington State University.

LM: Lucullus V. McWhorter Collection, MASC, Washington State University.

MK: Matilda Kalyton, 1918, MASC, Washington State University.

RR: Robert Ruby Papers, MAC, Spokane.

SF: Sam Fisher (with L.V. McWhorter), Lyons Ferry, 1939, MASC, Washington State University.

SH: Sacred Heart Mission (marriage and baptismal records, 1860–1900), De Smet, Idaho.

SM: Sadie Moses (with R. Ruby), Nespelem, 1958.

SR: Sharon Redthunder (with R. Scheuerman), Nespelem, 2006.

SW: Sophie Wak-wak Williams (with C. Relander), Yakima, 1951, Yakima Valley Library.

TA: Tom Billy Andrews (with B. Rigsby), Nespelem, 1964, OHA, Colville Confederated Tribes.

TK: Tomeo Kamiakin (with W.C. Brown), Nespelem, 1928, MASC, Washington State University.

TT: Tanya Tomeo (with R. Scheuerman), Yakima, 2006.

WB: William C. Brown Collection, MASC, Washington State University.

A. Kamiakin (K'amáyaqan) Family

Chief Kamiakin (Kamiakun) 1800?–77,[1] son of T'siyiyak [I] *Palouse/Nez Perce-Spokane* and Com-mus-ni TK (Ka-e-mox-nith, daughter of Chief Weowicht, *Yakama-Wenatchi* AT)

1st wife: **Sunk-hay-ee** (daughter of Chief Teias, *Yakama*)
1. **Yam´naneek** (Catherine) 1837-1907 EP
   a. Hattie?

2nd wife: **Kem-ee-yowah** SW (To-me-ye-ou-wauk TK, daughter of Chief Tenax, *Klickitat*) *d.*1901? MK
1. **We-yet-que-wit** (Talking Hunter, "Young Kamiakin") 1840?–86 *m.* (1st) **Agatha?**[2] SH (daughter of Chief Húsis Moxmox, *Palouse*), *m.* (2nd) **Tallas** (Theresa Koltsenshin,[3] daughter of Gabriel and Theresa Koltsenshin, *Coeur d'Alene*) *d.*1905?
   a. (1st *m.*) Joseph? *b.*1869 SH
   b. (2nd *m.*) Ellen Chumayakan (Helen Kamiakin) *b.*1874 *m.* Louis Pe-ell (Pierre, *Coeur d'Alene-Colville*) *b.*1874 SH
      children: Catherine, Raymond, Teresa, Mary, Samuel
2. **Yumasepah** (Chamesupum SW, Mollie, Mary[4]) 1845–1920 *m.* **Peopeo-hy-yi-toman** (Whistling Bird, *Palouse-Nez Perce*) *d.*1898 (near Colfax, WB)
   a. Pe-nock-ton-my 1880–*c.*1908 *m.* Johnnie Pe-el *b.*1879
   b. Sophie Kamiakin (Atwice) *b.*1889 *m.* (1st) Tipyahlahnah Elassanin (Roaring Eagle, George Comedown, *Nez Perce, Joseph Band*) *b.*1882, *m.* (2nd) Isaac Wakwak (son of Sam Wakwak, *Umatilla*) *b.*1895
      children: (1st *m.*) Ned Comedown, Kes-les-tum; (2nd *m.*) Martha, Joseph, Nancy, Walter

    c. Ta-lats Ton-my (Telestonmy) *m.* Ko-san-yum (E-yu-mah-klt, Luke Wilson SR, son of Wolfhead *b.*1855, *Nez Perce*) *b.*1870?

          children: Hattie, Henry, George, Helen

3. **Tespaloos** (Tesh Palouse) 1858–1933 *m.* (1st) **Pas-as-pam** (Annie Kentuck, *Palouse*) *d.*1890, *m.* (2nd) **Me-a-tu-kin-ma** (Mary, daughter of Chief Bones, *Cayuse*) 1859–1931, *m.* (3rd) **Elizabeth (Eliza) Skumsit** *b.*1865 GC

    a. (2nd *m.* JD) Mul-mul-kin (Sam Tespaloos) *b.*1891 *m.* Annie, 1886–1966

          children: Jenny, Alexander

    b. Kay-yee-wach (Pete Bones, Hiyouwath Kamiakin) 1895?–1954 *m.* O-in-ta-tot-mi (Lucy)

4. **infant** MK

3rd wife: **Wal-luts-pum** MK (Why-lats-pam LM, daughter of Chief Tenax, *Klickitat*)

1. **T'siyiyak** [II] (Siyiyah, Williams) 1854?–1901? at Moses Lake WB *m.* **Ni-ka-not** 1859–1937 (granddaughter of Chief Slowiarchy the Younger, *Palouse*)

    a. Charley Kamiakin Williams (Te-meh-yew-te-toot) 1879–1969 *m.* Alalumti [II] (Susie Chief, daughter of Little Man Chief,[5] *Nez Perce*) 1888–1971 AA

          children: Edward, Ida (Timentwa/Grant/Desautel), Walter, Virginia (Andrews), Abel, Clayton

    b. William *b.*1881

    c. Mary (Ka-mosh-nite) *b.*1888 *m.* Smith L. George[6] (Tah-harts, Hay-hay-tah WB, Heheestah FA, *Nez Perce*) *b.*1867?

          children: Frank George (*m.* Annie Cleveland, daughter of Cleveland Kamiakin), Winnie, Delia (Covington)

    d. Gilbert (Na-ta-quen-et) *b.*1893 *m.* Sadie Paul JD

2. **Lukash** EP (Neu-Cass MK, Locos RR, Luke) 1858?–86 *m.* **Sinsinq't** [III] 1855?–88 (daughter of Chief Moses, 1829–99, *Columbia-Yakama*)

    a. (2nd *m.*) Qu-qua-la-que (male) CW

    b. Nellie Kamiakin Moses (Sinsinq't [IV]) 1883–1958 *m.* (1st) Louis Friedlander (son of J.H. Friedlander) 1879–1912, *m.* (2nd?) Antoine Francis 1888–1934

          children: (1st *m.*) Emily (Peone), George, Thomas, Lucy (Covington), Louis Jr.

3. **Sk'ees** EP (Sk'eec, Petescot?[7] MK)

4. **Sk'olumkee** ("Snake River Kamiakin") 1867–1949 *m.* **Pemalks** (Annie Skumsit, sister of Elizabeth Skumsit) 1861?–1957

4th wife: **Hos-ke-la-pum** CK (Aus-kil-ah-pum MK, daughter of Chief Tenax, *Klickitat*) *d.*1877?

1. **Kiatana** (Ka-you-to-nay SW, Lucy) 1861?–1946 *m.* (1st) *Palouse*, *m.* (2nd) **Ben Awhi** (Owhi, son of Sque-malks Owhi, *Yakama-Palouse*) 1854–1927, *m.* (3rd) **Que-em-le-ke** (John Hayes, *Nez Perce*) 1867–1941

    a. (2nd *m.*) Harry Awhi (Owhi) 1894–1955 *m.* (1st) Mary Mocton (*Nez Perce, Joseph Band*) 1896–1951, *m.* (2nd) Annie (Chuweah, daughter of Tom Paween, *Palouse*) 1893–1989

          children: (1st *m.*) McKinley; (2nd *m.*) Rosville (Roscoe), Martha (Judge), Dora (Francis), Bertha (Williams), Harry Jr.

2. **Piupiu K'ownot** (Bird of the Morning, Cleveland) 1870–1959 *m.* (1st) **Yup-cha-sin** (Annie Billy, *Palouse*) 1867–1965, *m.* (2nd) **Wah-pah-tan-mi** (*Nez Perce*) *b.*1885, *m.* (3rd) **Alalumt'i** [III] (daughter of Tom Paween, *Palouse*) 1885–1977

    a. (1st *m.*) Henry *b.*1899

    b. (2nd *m.?*) Peo-peo-la-om-neet *b.*1907

    c. (3rd *m.*) Clara *b./d.*1911

    d. Annie 1912–97 *m.* Frank George 1912–68

    e. Thomas *b.*1914

    f. Ruth *b.*1920

g. Ned 1922–83 *m.* (1st) Naomi (Circle), *m.* (2nd) Inez (Andrews, daughter of Tom Billy Andrews) *b.*1925

  children: Wesley, Donald, Pamela

h. Alfred Abraham 1928–53

5th wife: Colestah TK (Kohlstiat MK, daughter of Chief Tenax, *Klickitat*) *d.*1867? EP

 1. **Tomeo** (Ta-mull Mox-mox TT) 1862–1936[8] *m.* **Ot-wes-on-my** (sister of Tom Paween 1864–1940, *Palouse*), 1877–1957

  a. Theodore (Teddy Tomeo) 1896–1936 *m.* Mattie (Dick) *Yakama*

   children: Irene, Stanley, Hays

  b. Arthur 1906–91 *m.* Josephine (Lucei) *Yakama* TT 1916–84

  c. Mamie *b./d.*1911

  d.   Mary 1912–20 TT

  e. Cato 1916–74 *m.* (1st) Helen (Jackson), *m.* (2nd) Ruby (Miller) TT

 2. **Tomomolow** (Tomolio) 1865?–71? EP

1. Mary Kamiakin (1918) and Emily Peone (1981) provided the birth order of Kamiakin's children. The family surname, "Kamiakin," often was dropped in the grandchildren's generation; thus Tomeo Kamiakin's family perpetuates the surname "Tomeo" (e.g., Arthur Tomeo) and Cleveland Kamiakin's descendants use the surname "Cleveland" (e.g., Ned Cleveland), etc.

2. Although Mary Kamiakin only identified We-yet-que-wit's first wife as the daughter of the Palouse Chief Húsis Moxmox, Sacred Heart Mission records indicate the marriage of "Xavier and Agatha Chamayakan" on June 21, 1869. Elsewhere "Xavier" is listed as godfather to several of Chief Kamiakin's younger children as early as 1861. Of the Kamiakin sons listed in the available family accounts, only We-yet-que-wit would have been old enough to marry at this time.

3. After We-yet-que-wit's accidental death in 1886, Theresa Koltsenshin Kamiakin's second marriage in 1890 was to Andrew Saichan (Sijohn) of the Coeur d'Alene tribe. Andrew and Theresa had a son, Nicholas, who was called Chumayakan among the Coeur d'Alenes.

4. According to several accounts, Mary Kamiakin was a half-sister to Tespaloos as they had the same mother but different fathers (e.g., EP). Tespaloos (1911) stated that Phillip Andrews was "my sister's son" and that his father had been with Joseph in the 1877 war (WB). According to Tom Paween (1935), Andrews' father died in an accident near Colfax "75 or 80 years ago" (WB). The date of death would considerably precede the reference to Mary Kamiakin's Nez Perce husband, but the name and geographic details may be more than coincidental.

5. Little Man Chief (Koots-koots Tsom-ya-wet) and his wife, Iatotkikt, survived the 1877 Nez Perce War and were the parents of a son, Jessie Chief, who later married Hatats (1864–1964). Their son was Edward Chief (Chu-kumpts 1907–67), husband of Maggie Weipah (JD).

6. Smith L. George also was the father of Andrew George (1905?–89), Mabel, and Ruby (Williams) by his first wife, Julia (Redheart) Johnson (*b.*1882). Julia was the daughter of Palouse exiles in Indian Territory, Ip-na-mat-we-kin and Ah-na-ne-mart (Dick and Fannie Johnson).

7. This is the only known reference to a son of Chief Kamiakin by this name. However, Sam Fisher (1939) related similar details about the life of Kamiakin's son Sk'ees, so it may be that Petescot and Sk'ees, also mentioned by Emily Peone, are the same person.

8. Although census records indicate Tomeo's year of birth as about 1862, some family accounts give 1856.

B. Sulk-stalk-scosum (Moses) Family

Chief Sulk-stalk-scosum (Half-Sun *Columbia-Sinkiuse*) *d.*1848?

1st wife[1]: **Kanitsa** (Karneetsa, *Spokane-Columbia*)

 1. **Patsk'stiway** (female) *d.*1849?

 2. **Q'uetalican** (Chief Moses) 1829–99 *m.* (1st) **Silpe** (RR, *Flathead*), *m.* (2nd) **Quo-mo-lah** (daughter of Chief Owhi) *d.*1864? RR, *m.* (3rd) **Sanclow** (Mary, daughter of Chief Owhi, *Yakama*) 1820?–1938, *m.* (4th) ***Wanapum,*** *m.* (5th) **Peotsenmy** *Nez Perce d.*1902?

  a. (2nd *m.*) Qu-qua-la-que (male) CW

  b. Sinsinq't [III] 1855?–88 *m.* Lukash Kamiakin (son of Chief Kamiakin, *Yakama-Palouse*) 1858?–86

   children: Nellie Moses (Sinsinq't [IV]) 1883–1958 *m.* (1st) Louis Friedlander (son of J.H. Friedlander) 1855–99, *m.* (2nd) Antoine Francis 1888–1934 c-h. (3rd *m*.) 3 sons and 3 daughters died in infancy ᴇᴘ

    i.   (4th *m*.) Tom-quin-wit (Lucy Moses [I]) *b*.1863? *m*. (1st) Kol-kil-le-tsa-kas-nim (Johnson, *Nez Perce*, ʀʀ), *m*. (2nd) Tes-ka-sar-kow-kow (William Paul, *Nez Perce*) 1867–1917, *m*. (3rd) Ben Awhi (Owhi, *Yakama-Palouse*, ᴄᴡ) 1854–1927, *m*. (4th) Henry Wilson (son of Peopeo-hy-yi-toman and Mary Kamiakin, *Nez Perce*)

        children: (2nd *m*.) Sadie (Williams), Edward Moses; (4th *m*.) Thomas Moses

    j.   (5th *m*.) Quiltlay

3. **Sinsinq't** [I] *b*.1840s? ʀʀ *m*. (1st?) **Qualchan** (son of Chief Owhi, *Yakama*) *d*.1858

    a.   Chillileetsa[2] 1842–85 *m*. Ku-nullix (Nettie, daughter of John "Virginia Bill" Covington ʀʀ)

    b.   Charley Qualchan (Socula ᴄᴡ) 1845?–1916? *m*. Mary *b*.1850

        children: Sam Sokula (Sah-ku-lah) 1862–1950[3] (*m*. (1st) Chu-chu-walx (Lizzie), *m*. (2nd) Kist (daughter of Nahanoomed, *Yakama*) 1870–1954)

2nd wife: **Sipitsa** *Columbia-Sinkiuse*

1. **Quiltenenock** [I] *d*.1858 *m*. (1st) **Tisaqt** (daughter of Chief Tecolekun ʀʀ, *Wenatchi*), *m*. (2nd) ***Blackfoot***

    a.   Quanspeetsah *m*. Wee-ash-i-wit (son of Chief Tilcoax, *Palouse* sᴍ)

        children: Peter Dan Moses (Weashuit) 1861–1962, Joe Moses (Quiltenenock [II]) 1876–1935

2. **Kwayitsa** (Kwee-ja, Crasam) (male) 1839?–1913 *m*. **We-tu-we** *b*.1845?

        grandson?: George Haynes (Haines) *b*.1892 *m*. Christine

3. **Shimtil** (See-um-tat-quat) (female) *d*.1893

    a.   Sam

    b.   Yos-o-soken (Jack O'Socken) *m*. Minnie (Yellow Wolf, *Nez Perce*, ʀʀ) 1870–1955

        children: Jim Jack

3rd wife: **Nkiyapitsa** *Spokane-Columbia*

1. **Paq'uin** (Keelpucken) (male) *d*.1858 ᴡʙ

    a.   Ceepetsa[3] *m*. Chief Skolaskin *San Poil* ʀʀ

2. **Panekstitsa** (Louis) 1821–96 ᴡʙ *m*. (1st) **?**, *m*. (2nd) **Q'ue-matk**

    a.   (1st *m*.) Joe Moses 1866–1925 *m*. Mo-yet-at 1872?–1941 ᴀʙ

        children: Madeline Moses (Jim), Peter, Nancy

    b.   (2nd *m*.) Madeline (Kekimetsa) 1884–1930 *m*. Robert Covington (son of John "Virginia Bill" Covington) 1870–1961

        children: Eva, William, John, Eddie, Rose (Wakwak)

4th wife: **Pohamatku** *Columbia-Sinkiuse*

1. **T'cher-man-chute** (Shpowlak) *m*. (1st) **Nahanoomed** *Yakama, Kittitas Band*, *m*. (2nd) **Sk'nwheulks** (Elizabeth ɪᴀ) 1885–1940

    a.   Kist 1870–1954 *m*. (1st) Leo Thompson, *m*. (2nd) Sam Socula 1862–1950, *m*. (3rd) ?

        children: (1st *m*.) Harry *b*.1885, Sit-sim-te-tock *b*.1897, Willie *b*.1906, Margaret (Piatote) 1906–87; (2nd *m*.) Christine *b*.1916, Matilda (Madeline) 1917–2004 (*m*. Adam Bearcub Sr.); (3rd *m*.) Mary (*m*. Charley Skaminsky)

1. Order of marriages and children's births as given by Mary Moses (1918, ᴡʙ); Sque-malks is not listed.

2. As Qualchan had several wives, the affiliation of his son is not certain. Chillileetsa drowned while fording the Columbia River near Barry in 1885. His father-in-law, John "Virginia Bill" Covington, came west from Virginia in 1849 and settled in the Willamette Valley. He relocated five years later to the San Poil area, where he married a local woman, Smil-keen, and operated the post store at Ft. Spokane.

3. Madeline Covington (1961) stated that "Ceep-peetsa's sisters," or half-sisters, included Gin-na-mon-teesah, Yat-peetsa, and Cheepat (Sally Whistocken) (ʀʀ).

C. Poyahkin (Billy) and Paween Families

1. **Poyahkin** (Five Times TA) 1830?–94 *m. Yakama* TA
    a. Wiyukshenéet[1] (Jim Billy, *Palouse-Nez Perce*) *b.*1846? *m.* Hiyómatway[2] (Eyomotwy, Old Lady Grizzly Bear, *Nez Perce-Palouse, Alpowa Band*)
        1. Annie Billy (Yup-cha-sin) 1867–1965 *m.* (1st) Cleveland Kamiakin (son of Chief Kamiakin) 1870–1959, *m.* (2nd) Wi-yu-kea Ilpilp (Red Elk, *Nez Perce*, FA)
            children: (2nd *m.*) At-wa-la-tak-it, Matilda (Tillie Bob)
        2. Alice Billy (Alpiato, Wash-e-tone-my) *b.*1878 *m.* (1st) Charlie Wilpocken (Yat-ah-mo-set, son of Chief Showaway, *Yakama*) 1852?–1927, *m.* (2nd) Tom (Joe) Waters *Nez Perce b.*1880
            children: (1st *m.*) Art Wilpocken Circle, Iva; (2nd *m.*) Tom, Nancy (Broncheau)
        3. Tom Billy Andrews (Wiyukshenéet BR) 1887–1964 *m.* Alice (Tamaawalí, daughter of Little Wolf Moies, *Nez Perce, White Bird Band,* FA) 1891–1975
            children: Grant, Jasper, Omar, Thomas Jr., Iva (Bob/Saxa), Janice (Hernandez), Frank, Inez (Cleveland), Almeda BR
        4. Frank Andrews *b.*1897
    b. Peopeo-hy-yi-toman[1] (Whistling Bird, *Palouse-Nez Perce*, WB) *d.*1895? *m.* Yumasepah (Mary, daughter of Chief Kamiakin) 1845?–1920
        1. Sophie Kamiakin (Atwice) *b.*1889 *m.* (1st) Tipyahlahnah Elassanin (George Comedown, *Nez Perce, Joseph Band*) *b.*1882, *m.* (2nd) Isaac Wakwak *Umatilla b.*1895
            children: (1st *m.*) Ned Comedown, Kes-les-tum; (2nd *m.*) Martha, Joseph, Nancy (Goudy), Walter
        2. Ta-lats Ton-my *m.* Ko-san-yum (Luke Wilson, son of Heminish Húsis, *Nez Perce*) *b.*1855
            children: Henry, George, Helen

2. **Pe-nock-kah-low-yun** (The Player WB)[3]
    a. Chief Hahtalekin (Taktsoukt Ilpilp, Red Echo) 1843?–77
        1. Pahta Pahtahank ("Five Fogs") 1847?–77
        2. Wes-ins (Fisher) *d.*1893? *m.* Nan-ne-me-nicht *d.*1916 SF
            children: Ich-yich-whel-ek (Sam Fisherman [I]), Pah-ot-wal-ak-is-it (Bill Fisherman), Yoh-yoh Too-le-cas-sat (Jim Fisherman), Taneenmy (Sloutier), Chuck-louse (Sam Fisher [Fisherman] [II])
    b. Alalumti [I] AK 1845–1934 *m.* Tenoo Paween *Palouse d.*1880?
        1. Tom Paween (Húsis Paween [II]) 1866–1940 *m.* (1st) Skispum (daughter of Lew-los-le-wit, *Nez Perce-Umatilla*) 1860–1913, *m.* (2nd) Pe-yo-ots-on-my, *m.* (3rd) I-yu-to-tum (Minnie Yellow Wolf, *Nez Perce*) 1870–1955
        2. Ah-kis-kis *b.*1855 *m.* (1st) Hal-la-mish (Angry Woman, *Palouse*) *b.*1865, *m.* (2nd) Ana-chous *b.*1864?
        3. Ot-wes-on-my 1877–1957 *m.* Tomeo Kamiakin (son of Chief Kamiakin) 1862?–1935
        4. Metina (Milly RR) *b.*1878 *m.* Robert Johnson *Nez Perce b.*1869?
        5. We-ah-non-my *b.*1876 *m.* Hin-mot Ilpilp (Red Thunder, *Nez Perce*)
            children: Yo-huny-we-talick, Hal-ah-kala-keen, Joe Red Thunder

1. **Chief Húsis Paween**[4] **[I]** (Bald Head) *d.*1890? AK *m.* **Teek-ton-nay** *Nez Perce, Timothy-Red Wolf Band* WB

2. **Tenoo Paween**[4] 1846–80? *m.* **Alalumti [I]** (sister of Chief Hahtalekin, *Palouse*) 1845–1934
    a. Tom Paween (Húsis Paween [II]) 1866–1940 *m.* (1st) Skispum (daughter of Lew-los-le-wit, *Nez Perce-Umatilla*) 1860–1913, *m.* (2nd) Pe-yo-ots-on-my, *m.* (3rd) I-yu-to-tum (Minnie Yellow Wolf, *Nez Perce*) 1870–1955

1. 1st *m.* Youch-youch-pouch (Bertha Carter) 1881?–1918
2. Alalumt'i [III] 1885–1977 *m.* Cleveland Kamiakin (son of Chief Kamiakin) 1870–1959
1. 2nd *m.* Tu-kar-sey-i-yet (female) *d.*1924
2. Hat-a-mo-whil-i-ken (Hattie Paween) 1891–1980 *m.* Willie (Red Star) Andrews[5] (Cool-cool Smool-mool, adopted son of Chief Joseph, *Nez Perce, Joseph Band*) 1865–1948
   children: Ruth, Albert, Isaac, Agnes, Ida, Felix, Douglas, Rose Marie
3. U-pa-pi (Annie) 1893–1989 *m.* (1st) Percy Chuweah (son of Chuweah 1865?–1912, *Umatilla-Palouse*) 1892–1956, *m.* (2nd) Harry Owhi (Sr.) *Yakama-Palouse* 1894–1955
   children: (1st m) Mary, Alfred; (2nd *m.*) Rosville (Roscoe), Martha (Judge), Dora (Francis), Bertha (Williams), Harry Jr.
   b. Ah-kis-kis [II][6] *b.*1864? *m.* (1st) Hal-la-mish (Angry Woman, *Palouse*) *b.*1865, *m.* (2nd) Ana-chous *b.*1864?
   c. Ot-wes-on-my 1877–1957 *m.* Tomeo Kamiakin (son of Chief Kamiakin) 1862?–1936
   d. Metina (Milly) *b.*1878 *m.* Robert Johnson *Nez Perce b.*1869?
   e. We-ah-non-my *b.*1876 *m.* Hin-mot Ilpilp (Red Thunder, *Nez Perce*) *b.*1870
      1. Yo-huny-we-talick (female) *b.*1896
      2. Hal-ah-kala-keen (male) *b.*1902
      3. Joe Red Thunder 1907–96 *m.* Lucy Weipah 1915–85

3. **Atuskis** (Ah-kis-kis [I]) (ᴀᴋ) *b.*1849 *m.* **Mary** *b.*1854
   a. Wayayentutpik (male)

1. Wiyukshenéet (Jim Billy Andrews) and Peopeo-hy-yi-toman are listed here as sons of Poyahkin, based on interviews by Bruce Rigsby with Tom Billy Andrews (1964), and W.C. Brown with Alalumti [I] at Nespelem (1930). Alalumti further stated that she was "the daughter of Pe-nock-kah-low-yun, who was one of the brothers of Poy-ah-kin."
2. Hiyómatway's father was Pah-ka-pah-tan-muk (ɢᴄ) and her paternal grandmother, Sawíchi, lived at *Palus*. According to family tradition, she was said to have been a daughter of Sacajawea, the Shoshone woman who accompanied Lewis and Clark's party. Bruce Rigsby suggests that she may have been the daughter of a Shoshone captive.
3. Listing Hahtalekin and Alalumti [I] as the offspring of Pe-nock-kah-low-yun is derived from an interview conducted by Verne Ray with Mrs. Cleveland (Alalumt'i Paween) Kamiakin and from Mrs. Harry (Annie Paween) Owhi (1971): "Italican was a chief of one of the villages. He was a brother of my grandmother Alilintai" (ᴀᴋ).
4. Húsis Paween and Tenoo Paween are identified as brothers by Annie Paween Cleveland and Cull White. Húsis Paween's widow married Chief Wolf of the Palouse Tilcoax family (ᴄᴡ).
5. Willie Red Star Andrews was orphaned following the deaths of his father in Indian Territory and of his mother (1885) at Ft. Spokane, where the exiles waited for travel arrangements to the Colville Reservation (ᴀᴅ). Willie Red Star Andrews was then raised by Chief Joseph and eventually had four wives: (1st) Yow-wan-pum *Nez Perce*, (2nd) Annie Billy *Palouse*, (3rd) Annie (Ca-tal-pi) *Moses-Columbia*, and (4th) Hattie Paween *Palouse*.
6. Ah-kis-kis [II] being a nephew of Ah-kis-kis [I] and brother to Tom Paween (Húsis Paween) is inferred from an 1891 letter from Ah-kis-kis to Húsis Paween (ʟᴍ) and the 1910 Colville tribal census.

Chapter Notes

Abbreviations for frequently cited collections—

BMC   Benjamin Manring Papers, Whitman County Historical Society, Colfax.
BMP   Benjamin Manring Papers, Greg Partch Collection, Garfield, Washington.
BRC   Bruce Rigsby Collection, University of Queensland, Graceville, Australia.
CAA   Catholic Chancery Archdiocesan Archives, Seattle.
CIA   Commissioner of Indian Affairs, National Archives and Records Administration, Seattle.
CRC   Click Relander Collection, Yakima Valley Regional Library.
CWC   Cull White Collection, Manuscripts, Archives, and Special Collections, Washington State University, Pullman.
DRT   Documents Related to Ratified and Unratified Treaties, National Archives and Records Administration, Seattle.
ICC   Indian Claims Commission Papers, National Archives and Records Administration, Seattle.
ISC   Isaac Stevens Collection, University of Washington Library, Seattle.
LMC   Lucullus V. McWhorter Collection, Manuscripts, Archives, and Special Collections, Washington State University, Pullman.
MAC   Museum of Arts and Culture, Archives, Spokane.
OIA   Oregon Superintendency of Indian Affairs, National Archives and Records Administration, Seattle.
OPA   Oregon Province Archives, Foley Library, Gonzaga University, Spokane.
PWC   W. Parkhurst Winans Collection, Manuscripts, Archives, and Special Collections, Washington State University, Pullman.
RCA   Records of the Commands of the United States Army, National Archives and Records Administration, Seattle.
RRC   Robert Ruby Collection, Museum of Arts and Culture, Archives, Spokane.
SED   Senate Executive Document.
SI   Secretary of Interior, National Archives and Records Administration, Seattle.
SW   Secretary of War, National Archives and Records Administration, Seattle.
VRC   Verne Ray Collection, Foley Library, Gonzaga University, Spokane.
WBC   W.C. Brown Collection, Manuscripts, Archives, and Special Collections, Washington State University, Pullman.
WHC   Walt Horan Collection, Manuscripts, Archives, and Special Collections, Washington State University, Pullman.
WIA   Washington Superintendency of Indian Affairs, National Archives and Records Administration, Seattle.

Prologue

1. Local newspaper coverage described Sk'olumkee and Pemalks' visit to Rock Lake in June 1941. Sk'olumkee (1867–1949) was a son of Chief Kamiakin and Klicktitat wife Wal-luts-pum.

Chapter 1: Rocks that Glisten

1. G. Moulton [5], 1988:[October 16–18, 1805]. For a discussion of the terms "Yakama" and "Yakima," see B. Rigsby, 2008.
2. T. Kamiakin, oral history, n.d., LMC; A. Splawn, 1917:1–6.
3. W. Brown, 1961:67–74; G. Fisher, oral history, 2006; A. Splawn, 1917:12.
4. T. Kamiakin, oral history, 1928, WBC; E. Peone, oral history, 1981.
5. L. McWhorter to H. Taylor, January 13, 1919, LMC; E. Peone, oral history, 1981. In another version of the story both women returned and gave birth to sons; L. Mann to L. McWhorter, January 24, 1918, LMC.
6. A. Splawn, 1917:16.
7. H. Schuster, 1998:330–34; M. Hannigan to K. Simmons, August 9, 1949, Yakama Nation Library, Yakama Cultural Heritage Center, Toppenish; A. Saluskin 1955:57–58.

8. M. Jim, oral history, 1979; E. Hunn, 1990:330–31.
9. G. Fisher, oral history, 2006. The Sahaptin word *máamin* may be related to *maron*, a French Canadian term for "mustang." For additional information on the breed, see F. Roe, 1968, and F. Haines, 1955 and 1963.
10. M. Moses, oral history, 1918, WBC.
11. T. Stern, 1993:184.
12. C. Wilson [1860], in G. Stanley, 1970:113–14; M. Jim, oral history, 1979; E. Hunn, 1990:148–54.
13. A. George, oral history, 1980.
14. E. Peone, oral history, 1981; C. Wilson [1860], in G. Stanley, 1970:107; T. Kamiakin, oral history, 1928, WBC.
15. A. George, oral history, 1980; G. Lucas, oral history, 1930, Melville Jacobs Collection, University of Washington.
16. E. Peone, oral history, 1981.
17. S. Fisher [1936], in E. Clark, 1960:117–18; G. Fisher, oral history, 2006.
18. W. Lewis, 1922:108; C. Kamiakin [1957], 2003.
19. H. Stevens, 1915:402–33.
20. E. Peone, oral history, 1981; B. Rigsby, 2007.
21. A. Ross, 1849:150.
22. A. Ross, [1855] 1956:22–31.

23. A. McDonald, 1917:228–29; A. Splawn, 1917:16.
24. T. Kamiakin, oral history, 1928, WBC; S. Kamiakin, oral history, 1951, CWC; L. McWhorter, "Yakima Tahmahnawis Power; Kamiaken's Son," LMC.
25. A. Splawn, 1917:16; S. Kamiakin-Williams, oral history, 1951, CRC.
26. A. Saluskin, 1967; H. White, oral history, 2006.
27. C. Wilkes [IV], 1845:453–56.
28. W. Lewis, 1922:107–17; F. Chenowith, *Oregonian*, July 12 and 15, 1851; T. Winthrop [1863], 1913:178.
29. A. Splawn, 1917:15–16; W. Brown, 1961:76–77; A. Waller letter, April 15, 1845, quoted in R. Boyd, 1996:151.
30. T. Kamiakin, in L. McWhorter, 1940:52–53.
31. A. Saluskin, 1967.
32. A. McDonald, 1917:228–29.
33. C. Kamiakin, oral history, 1957, CWC; J. Gibson, 1985:52.
34. A. Blanchet to E. Chirouse, July 16, 1848, CAA.
35. E. Kowrach, 1992:7–10, 52–55.
36. C. Pandosy to P. Ricard [1852], in E. Kowrach, 1992:60–61.
37. G. Gibbs [1854], 1972:28; C. Pandosy to P. Ricard [1852], L. D'Herbomez to P. Ricard, September 7, 1852, in E. Kowrach, 1992:58–61,134.
38. G. Haller, n.d.; K. Richards, 1979:194; C. Pandosy to T. Mesplié, April 1853, RCA.

Chapter 2: A Highly Desirable Field

1. *Annual Report*, 1854, CIA; G. McClellan to I. Stevens, August 22, 1853, RCA.
2. *Annual Report*, 1854, CIA.
3. L. D'Herbomez to T. Mesplié, August 25, 1853, CAA.
4. I. Stevens, 1860:179.
5. Ibid., 179–80.
6. Ibid., 253–55.
7. *Annual Report*, 1854, CIA; C. Pandosy to Bishop de Mazenod, June 5, 1854, CAA; Splawn, 1917:21; C. Pandosy, in Kowrach, 1992:78.
8. C. Wilson [1860], in G. Stanley, 1970:110, 135; W. Lewis, 1922:107–17.
9. T. Kamiakin, oral history, n.d., LMC; A. Kamiakin, oral history, 1972. S. Neils, 1985:9, suggests without attribution that Kamiakin and Piupiu Maksmaks were related through their marriages to daughters of Klickitat Chief Tenax.
10. A. Splawn, 1917:21–22; C. Trafzer and R. Scheuerman, 1986:39–41.
11. C. Pandosy to T. Mesplié, April 1853, CAA.
12. W. Lyman, 1919:233–34; A. Splawn, 1917:22–24.
13. P. Durieu to P. Ricard, April 12, 1855, in W. Bischoff, 1950:162–69, 330–31; Splawn 1917:22.

Chapter 3: Peace and Friendship

1. J. Doty [1855], MAC; C. Trafzer and R. Scheuerman, 1986:43.
2. Ibid., 43–44.
3. P. Durieu to P. Ricard, March 28, 1855, in E. Kowrach, 1992:81–82; J. Doty [1855], MAC; C. Trafzer and R. Scheuerman, 1986:44.
4. J. Doty [1855], MAC; C. Trafzer and R. Scheuerman, 1986:44–45.
5. *Annual Report*, 1854, CIA; E. Kowrach, 1992:80–84; C. Trafzer and R. Scheuerman, 1986:46–59.
6. Council Proceedings, 1855, DRT; H. Stevens [II], 1901:34–65.
7. L. Kip [1855], 1897:15; H. Stevens [II], 1901:38; J. Doty [1855], MAC.

8. Luqaíôt (Lokout), in E. Curtis [VII], 1911:18–19.
9. G. Meninock, in F. Garrecht, 1928:167–78; L. Kip [1855], 1897:18; K. Richards, 1979:215–26.
10. E. Peone, oral history, 1979.
11. Council Proceedings, 1855, DRT; Kip [1855], 1897:20–21.
12. A. Splawn, 1917:32–33; Luqaíôt, in E. Curtis [VII], 1911:19.
13. Council Proceedings, 1855, DRT; J. Doty [1855], MAC; H. Stevens [II], 1901:58; Pambrun [c. 1893], 1978:95.
14. "Treaty with the Yakima, 1855," in C. Kappler, 1904 [I]:699. The "Treaty between the United States and the Yakama Nation of Indians" was ratified by the Senate on March 8, 1859, and proclaimed by President James Buchanan on April 18, 1859. The 21,000 acre Mt. Adams tract excluded from the reservation in 19th century surveys was restored in 1972.
15. J. Palmer to G. Manypenny, October 9, 1855, WIA; G. Gibbs [1857], Oregon Historical Society, Portland.
16. Council Proceedings, 1855, DRT; J. Doty [1855], MAC.

Chapter 4: Common Cause

1. *Pioneer and Democrat*, June 29, 1855; *Puget Sound Courier*, July 12, 1855.
2. W. Lyman, 1919:238; W. Trimble, 1914:18–21; H. Thoreau [1852], in B. Torrey and F. Allen, 1906:162, and H. Thoreau [1849], in B. Torrey and F. Allen, 1906:223.
3. A. Splawn, 1917:38–39.
4. V. Ray, 1973, VRC; E. Curtis [VII], 1911:39.
5. A Splawn, 1917:39; J. Doty [1855], MAC.
6. A. Splawn, 1917:41; *Weekly Oregonian*, September 1, 1855.
7. L. McWhorter, 1937:12-14; Luqaíôt, in E. Curtis [VII], 1911:23; A. Saluskin, 1967.
8. J. Palmer to Commissioner, October 9, 1855, OIA.
9. *Pioneer and Democrat*, October 12, 1855.
10. Ibid.; S. Waters, oral history, n.d., LMC.
11. A. Splawn, 1917:46–49; E. Curtis [VII], 1911:39; A. Saluskin, 1967.
12. Schna-tups Ka-lula, oral history, n.d., LMC; C. Trafzer and R. Scheuerman, 1986:63–64.
13. *Oregonian*, October 20, 1855; R. Ballou, 1938:330.
14. A. Splawn, 1917:49.
15. Luqaíôt, in E. Curtis [VII], 1911:22; Lesh-hi-hite, oral history, 1912, LMC.
16. N. Olney to J. Curry, October 12, 1855, OIA.
17. S. Waters, in C. Miles and O. Sperlin, 1940.
18. Kamiakin and C. Pandosy, "Les Yakamas aux Soldats" [1855], translated by E. Kowrach, CAA; Kowrach 1992:95–97; for another translated version, see Clifford E. Trafzer, ed., *Indian War in the Pacific Northwest: The Journal of Lieutenant Lawrence Kip* (Lincoln: University of Nebraska Press, 1999), 149–52.
19. C. Pandosy, in E. Kowrach, 1992:103.
20. P. Sheridan, 1888:62–63; *Pioneer and Democrat*, December 7, 1855; G. Haller, n.d.; J. Nesmith to G. Curry, November 19, 1855, in R. Burns, 1966:130. Lt. Sheridan, Capt. Rains, and a number of other Army officers who participated in Plateau military campaigns later became high ranking commanders during the Civil War.
21. G. Rains to Kam-i-ah-kin, November 13, 1855, in G. Fuller, 1928; W. Brown, 1961:144–45; C. Trafzer and R. Scheuerman, 1986:64–66.
22. P. Kelly [1855], in W. Bischoff, 1976; E. Chirouse letter, November 18, 1855, in *Pioneer and Democrat*, January 4, 1856.
23. F. Wolff [1908], 1915:163–65; *Pioneer and Democrat*, February 15, 1856; W. Brown, 1961:148–49.

24. P. Kelly, [1855] in W. Bischoff, 1976; A. Underwood, 1910; C. Trafzer and R. Scheuerman, 1986:67–69.
25. E. Chirouse to T. Mesplié, January 15, 1856, WIA; I. Stevens to J. Wool, December 28, 1955, and J. Wool to I. Stevens, February 12, 1856, RCA.
26. *Puget Sound Courier*, October 19, 1855; *Pioneer and Democrat*, October 26, 1855.
27. H. Stevens [II], 1901:133–40.
28. J. Doty [1856], MAC; H. Stevens [II], 1901:139–40; A. Ravalli to I. Stevens, August 2, 1856, ISC.
29. I. Stevens to J. Davis, July 7, 1856, *Annual Report*, 1856–57, SW; J. Doty [1855], MAC.
30. *Pioneer and Democrat*, January 22, 1856.
31. T. Cornelius, February 6 and March 6, 1856, Thomas Cornelius Collection, Huntington Library, Huntington, California; E. Chirouse [1856], CAA.
32. B. Shaw to I. Stevens, February 11, 1856, WIA; *Pioneer and Democrat*, February 17, 1856.

Chapter 5: Forests Must Fall

1. T. Smartlowit, oral history, n.d., LMC.
2. E. Keyes, 1884:250–54; L. Spencer and L. Pollard, 1937:297–98.
3. H. Stevens [II], 1901:205.
4. *Pioneer and Democrat*, February 8 and 29, 1856.
5. A. Ankeny to G. Curry, April 10, 1856, OIA.
6. G. Wright to W. Mackall, July 27, 1856, RCA; S. Jones, in N. Ankeny, n.d.
7. *Oregonian*, May 29 and April 14, 1856; P. Sheridan, 1888:73-82.
8. *Pioneer and Democrat*, March 4, 1856.
9. Ibid., March 28, 1856.
10. G. Wright to D. Jones, May 6 and 8, 1856, RCA; W. Bischoff, 1949:163–208.
11. G. Wright to D. Jones, May 11, 1856, RCA; Luqaíôt, in E. Curtis [VII], 1911:28–30.
12. G. Wright to D. Jones, May 18, 1856, RCA.
13. Ibid., May 30, June 8 and 11, and July 7, 1856, and G. Wright to I. Stevens, June 20, 1856, RCA.
14. W. Craig to I. Stevens, May 27, 1856, WIA; H. Stevens [II], 1901:198–99.
15. K. Cronin, 1960:41–42.
16. G. Wright to D. Jones, July 1 and 7, 1856, RCA.
17. I. Stevens to J. Davis, November 21, 1856, in V. Field, 1961.
18. W. Mackall to G. Wright, August 2, 1856, RCA; S. Plucker, 2006.
19. *Oregon Times*, August 2, 1856; B. Shaw to J. Tilton, July 24, 1856, and G. Wright to W. Mackall, October 31, 1856, RCA.
20. *Pioneer and Democrat*, October 24 and November 7, 1856.
21. "W.H.P. to Editor, August 17, 1856," in *Oregon Times*, August 23, 1856.
22. J. Doty [1856], MAC; W. Craig to I. Stevens, May 27, 1856, ISC.
23. W. Bischoff, 1950:162–69, 330–31.
24. J. Anderson, August 6, 1856, in *Pioneer and Democrat*, October 10, 1856.
25. *Pioneer and Democrat*, October 10, 1856.
26. *Oregon Times*, August 23, 1856; H. Stevens [II], 1901:209; A. Splawn, 1917:79–80.
27. *Pioneer and Democrat*, October 10, 1856.
28. H. Stevens [II], 1901:215–16; I. Stevens to J. Davis, October 22, 1856, and E. Steptoe to G. Wright, September 20, 1856, RCA.
29. A. Splawn, 1917:80–81.

30. A. Pambrun [c. 1893] 1978:104–5.
31. A. Splawn, 1917:80, 125.
32. *Pioneer and Democrat*, October 10, 1856.
33. E. Steptoe Report, June 3, 1857, RCA.
34. S. Plucker, 2006.
35. *Pioneer and Democrat*, October 3, 1856.
36. W. Craig to I. Stevens, December 5, 1856, WIA.
37. G. Kuykendall, 1911.
38. W. Brown, 1961:155; J. Owen [1857], in S. Dunbar, 1927:158.
39. H. Covington, oral history, February 5, 1958, RRC.
40. J. Archer to sister, January 5, 1856, Maryland Historical Society, Baltimore; *Pioneer and Democrat*, August 8, 1856.
41. CIA, *Annual Report*, 1859; A. Robie to I. Stevens, March 23, 1857, WIA.
42. W. Brown, 1961:183.
43. Ibid., 181–83.
44. A. McDonald, 1917:228–29; *Pioneer and Democrat*, July 25 and August 1, 1856. Olney earlier had directed Chief Factor James Sinclair at the HBC's Ft. Walla Walla to dump 1,500 pounds of ball and powder into the Columbia River in order to avoid its capture by Indians.
45. N. Congiato to N. Clarke, August 3, 1856, Early Wars Branch, National Archives and Records Administration, Seattle; J. Joset/P. DeSmet, in H. Chittenden and A. Richardson [II], 1905:748.
46. W. Bischoff, 1950:162–69, 330–31.

Chapter 6: Lake of Fire

1. J. Owen, March 25, 1857, in S. Dunbar, 1927:158.
2. J. Campbell, 1916:198–99. Campbell had come west from Manitoba with the James Sinclair party in 1854.
3. *New York Tribune*, January 5, 1857; *Pioneer and Democrat*, February 4 and 27, 1857; K. Richards, 1979:307.
4. G. Gibbs, Journal, November 29, 1857, Oregon Historical Society, Portland; R. Kirkham, in N. Clarke to Headquarters, January 1, 1858, R. Garnett, January 30, 1858, and N. Grier to Asst. Adj. Gen., May 16, 1858, RCA.
5. *Pioneer and Democrat*, March 6, 1857.
6. *Pioneer and Democrat*, February 6 and March 13, 1857; J. Archer to A. Archer, April 2, 1857, CRC.
7. *Pioneer and Democrat*, August 7, 1857.
8. Ibid., March 6 and June 19, 1857.
9. J.R. Browne to G. Denver, December 4, 1857, CIA.
10. Ibid.
11. I. Stevens, *Report*, 1858, SED 40, 35 Cong. 2 sess.
12. *Pioneer and Democrat*, November 27, 1857.
13. *Weekly Oregonian*, December 29, 1856; *Pioneer and Democrat*, May 21, 1858.
14. R. Burns, 1966:205–6. While Father Burns' account focuses on the role of Jesuits such as Joseph Joset in the events of 1858, his version of the Steptoe and Wright campaigns is among the most thorough of any published accounts.
15. E. Steptoe to W. Mackall, April 17, 1858, *Report*, SED 1, 35 Cong. 2 sess.; J. Joset, 1874, OPA.
16. *Weekly Oregonian*, June 12, 1858.
17. P. DeSmet, in H. Chittenden and A. Richardson [II], 1905, 750–51; N. Ankeny, n.d.
18. P. DeSmet, in H. Chittenden and A. Richardson [II], 1905, 750–51; E. Curtis [VII], 1911:59; A. Seltice, in E. Kowrach and T. Connolly, 1990:88–89.
19. E. Steptoe to W. Grier, May 15, 1858, RCA; J. Joset, 1874, OPA.

20. G. Palmer, et al., 1987.
21. M. Kriebel to R. Scheuerman, February 29, 2008; C. Sijohn, oral history, 2008.
22. E. Steptoe to W. Mackall, May 23, 1858, in Report, SED 1, 35 Cong. 2 sess.; N. Ankeny, n.d.; P. DeSmet, in H. Chittenden and A. Richardson [II], 1905:751–52; J. Joset, 1874, OPA; D. Gregg letter, in *Weekly Oregonian*, May 29, 1858. In 1928, Tomeo Kamiakin told Judge W.C. Brown that his father was not present at the Steptoe Battle; see W. Brown, 1961:416.
23. D. Gregg to B. Manring, February 22, 1910, BMC.
24. J. Randolf to W. Steptoe, April 8, 1861, and N. Steptoe Eldridge to B. Manring, 1908, BMP. Regarding Steptoe's medical condition, Dr. John Randolf, physician at Ft. Walla Walla and veteran of the expedition, also added, "in the fall of '58 he became…prostrated from dyspepsia, nervous debility and I believe mental trouble to a certain extent."
25. A. Seltice, in E. Kowrach and T. Connolly, 1990:101–2; M. Manring to W. LaFollette, March 30, 1916, BMC.
26. J. Joset, 1874, OPA; Ft. Walla Walla Post Return, May 1856, SW; C. Sijohn, oral history, 2008.
27. D. Gregg letter, *Weekly Oregonian*, May 29, 1858; E. Steptoe to W. Mackall, May 23, 1858, in *Report*, SED 1, 35 Cong. 2 sess.; J. Seltice, in E. Kowrach and T. Connolly, 1990:119.
28. P. DeSmet, in H. Chittenden and A. Richardson [II], 1905:755–56; N. Clarke to J. Joset, June 27, 1858, OPA; J. Seltice, in E. Kowrach and T. Connolly, 1990:112.
29. C. Frush, 1896:337–42.
30. *Harper's New Monthly Magazine*, June-November, 1858; K. Richards, 1979:310–12.
31. J. Joset, 1874, OPA; P. DeSmet, in H. Chittenden and A. Richardson [II], 1905:753–54; *Weekly Oregonian*, May 29, 1858.
32. A. Seltice, in E. Kowrach and T. Connolly, 1990:118–19.
33. Ibid., 117–18.
34. R. Garnett to N. Clarke, June 9, 1857, RCA; A. Splawn, 1917:83–84.
35. N. Clarke, June 10, 1858, in Burns, 1966:237; N. Clarke to J. Joset, June 27, 1858, OPA; E. Peone, oral history, 1981.
36. D. Emmons, 1965:389–90.
37. N. Congiato to N. Clarke, August 3, 1858, SED 1, 35 Cong. 2nd sess.; E. Peone, oral history, 1982.
38. J. Nesmith to I. Stevens, August 20, 1858, ISC; H. Guie, 1977:115, 118.
39. J. Yemowit, oral history, 1912, LMC; *Puget Sound Herald*, July 16, 1858; M. Moses, oral history, 1918, WBC.
40. L. Kip, 1859:39–40.
41. G. Wright, 1858:344–45; S. Plucker, 2006.
42. J. Smith, 1916:267–77.
43. G. Wright, 1858:386–90; L. Kip, 1859:59.
44. G. Wright, 1858:391–92; N. Ankeny, n.d.; L. Kipp, 1859:58–59.
45. G. Wright, 1858:392–93.
46. D. Jim, oral history, n.d., LMC; L. Kip, 1859:63–66.
47. Ibid., 64; G. Sohon, "Battle on the Spokan Plain—Col. G. Wright in Command and Against Combined Forces of the Indians, 1858" [drawing], Smithsonian Institution; P. McDermott and R. Grim, 2002:16–22.
48. R. Burns, 1966:294–97; E. Peone, oral history, 1982; G. Dandy, in G. Hunt, n.d.
49. L. Kip, 1859:91–92; C. Trafzer and R. Scheuerman, 1986:85–88; E. Keyes, 1884.
50. J. Yemowit, oral history, 1912, LMC.
51. T. Beall to L. McWhorter, January 6, 1917, LMC; G. Wright, 1858:400; L. Kip, 1859:102–5.
52. W. Brown, 1961:294–99; T. Beall to L. McWhorter, December 13,

1916, LMC; *Annual Report*, 1858–1859, SW.
53. *Message from the President of the United States*, 1858; J. Joset, in H. Chittenden and A. Richardson, 1905 [II]:759–60.
54. W. Brown, 1961:297.
55. M. Moses, oral history, 1918, WBC; L. Mann to L. McWhorter, July 13, 1916, LMC; J. Yemowit, oral history, 1912, LMC; W. Harney to N. Clarke, November 4, 1858, RCA; A. Saluskin, in C. Relander, 1956.
56. D. Gregg to B. Manring, October 1, 1908, BMC.

Chapter 7: Home in the Hills

1. A. Splawn, 1917:120–21; E. Peone, oral history, 1982.
2. P. DeSmet, in H. Chittenden and A. Richardson [III], 1905:968; M. Kalyton, oral history, 1948, WBC.
3. G. Fisher, oral history, 2006; C. Wilkes [IV], 1845:286. About 1800, Mt. St. Helens erupted, sending a volcanic plume northeast across the wintry landscape of the Columbia Plateau.
4. E. Peone, oral history, 1982; G. Fisher, oral history, 2006. The Ram's Horn Medicine Tree stood along a highway near Darby until 2001 when, at an estimated age of 300 years, it broke near the base in a violent windstorm. The tree was entirely removed several years later following the designation of another medicine tree in the vicinity.
5. R. Carriker, 1995:157–58; P. DeSmet, 1859, quoted in S. Thompson, 2008.
6. P. DeSmet to A. Pleasanton, May 25, 1859, RCA.
7. Ibid.
8. *Dalles Journal*, March 28, 1859; J. Owen to E. Geary, May 31, 1859, WIA; N. Clarke, *Report*, 1860, House Executive Document 65, 36 Cong. 1 sess.
9. C. Wilson [1860], in G. Stanley, 1970:96; P. Lugenbeel to J. Mullan, July 13, 1859, W. Harney to W. Scott, June 1, 1859, and J. Owen to A. Pleasanton, May 28, 1859, RCA.
10. R. Lansdale to E. Geary, June 30 and July 1, 1859, WIA.
11. T. Kamiakin, 1928, CWC.
12. C. Wilson [1860], in G. Stanley, 1970:112–13.
13. S. Waters, oral history, n.d., LMC; R. Lansdale to E. Geary, April 27 and July 9, 1860, WIA.
14. W. Gosnell to E. Geary, February 12, 1861, and W. Kapus to E. Geary, March 21, 1861, WIA.
15. A. Splawn, 1917:120.
16. A. Kamiakin, oral history, 1972; E. Peone, oral history, 1982.
17. G. Palmer, et al., 1987:94.
18. J. Mullan, 1863:104–5.
19. A Kamiakin, oral history, 1971, VRC. Impassable Spokane Falls prevented salmon from migrating farther upstream.
20. T. Kamiakin, oral history, 1928, WBC; S. Kamiakin-Williams, oral history, 1949, CRC.
21. E. Peone, oral history, 1982; G. Fisher, oral history, 2006; E. Pierre, 1938, 157.
22. T. Kamiakin, oral history, 1928, WBC; E. Peone, oral history, 1981.
23. Sacred Heart Mission Baptismal Records, DeSmet, Idaho; J. Joset, 1874, OPA.
24. A. Bancroft to C. Hale, May 15, 1864, and A. Bancroft to T. McKenny, May 28, 1864, WIA; *Dalles Mountaineer*, May 19, 1864.
25. T. Beall, 1917:83–90.
26. T. Kamiakin, oral history, 1928, WBC; E. Peone, oral history, 1982. Some modern maps identify Kamiacan Creek as "Kamiache Creek." W. Milnor Roberts in the company of pioneer developer Philip Ritz stayed at the Kentuck Trail crossing of the Palouse River on July 24–25, 1869. Roberts noted Indians in the vicinity, and the camp of "Ka-mi-a-kan, a

famous Indian Chief" six miles downstream, which indicates the family continued to reside periodically on the Palouse River even after relocating their main camp to Rock Lake. W. Milnor Roberts Papers, Montana State University, Bozeman.

27. L. Kip, 1859:128.
28. W. Winans to T. McKenny, September 1, 1871, WIA; G. Fisher, oral history, 2006; E. Peone, oral history, 1982.
29. E. Pierre, 1938; E. Peone, oral history, 1982.
30. A. Splawn, 1917:120–21; *Walla Walla Union*, August 16, 1873.
31. T. Kamiakin, in L. McWhorter, 1940:52–53.
32. S. Ross, in *Annual Report*, 1870, CIA; W. Winans to T. McKenny, February 5, 1871, WIA.
33. G. Harvey to S. Ross, May 26, 1870, and P. Winans to R. Partee, November 18, 1870, WBC.
34. E. Peone, oral history, 1982.
35. P. Winans to T. McKenny, February 5 and 24, 1871, PWC.
36. P. Winans to T. McKenny, April 13, 1871, PWC; P. Winans, n.d., W. Parkhurst Winans Papers, Eastern Washington University, Cheney.
37. T. McKenny to P. Winans, March 20, 1871, WIA; October 1, 1872, PWC.
38. A. Tomeo, oral history, 1972; E. Pierre, 1938:157.
39. Fr. J. Caruana to Fr. P. DeSmet, April 14, 1873, CAA.

Chapter 8: Deceived and Deserted

1. R. Scheuerman, 1994:55; T. Kamiakin, oral history, 1928, WBC.
2. E. Wright, 1895; E. Baughman, in *An Illustrated History of North Idaho*, 1903:20–21.
3. G. Sohon and P. Engle, in J. Mullan, 1863:95.
4. J. Mullan, 1863:14–15.
5. R. Scheuerman, 1994:55–56.
6. Hay-hay-tay [Smith L. George], oral history, 1931, WBC; M. Jim, oral history, 1979.
7. A. Cain to E. Ferry, July 26, 1878, WIA; W. Lever, 1901:360; F. Bailey, oral history, 2006; "Yakima Family History," Book 3, n.d., Yakima Agency Records, RG 75.291, National Archives and Records Administration, Seattle; W. Lever, 1901:360; F. Bailey, oral history, 2006.
8. R. Scheuerman, 1994:67–68.
9. Ibid., 68.
10. P. Winans to R. Milroy, August 31, 1872, WIA; *Annual Report*, 1872:343, CIA, quoting R. Milroy to F. Walker, October 1, 1872.
11. WPA, H. Thorp-Hattin, 1938.
12. Mrs. R. Rees to L. McWhorter, n.d., and Harry Owhi to L. McWhorter, January 9, 1916, LMC.
13. R. Ruby and J. Brown, 1965:227; S. Ross, in *Annual Report*, 1870, CIA; E. Peone, oral history, 1982.
14. E. Peone, oral history, 1982; A. Kamiakin, oral history, 1971.
15. N. Bailey, oral history, 2006; B. McRae, 1940.
16. G. Palmer, et al., 1987:27–28; J. Seltice, in E. Kowrach and T. Connolly 1990:230–31.
17. T. Kamiakin, oral history, 1928, WBC; S. Kamiakin-Williams, oral history, 1951, CRC.
18. Ibid.
19. When Ft. Colville closed in 1871, Angus McDonald moved to Montana, where he died in 1889. Pandosy died in February 1891 at the Mission of the Immaculate Conception near present-day Kelowna, British Columbia, where he had faithfully served.
20. C. Kamiakin, oral history, 1957, CWC; J. Lynch to J. Splawn, October 17, 1907, WBC.

21. E. Peone, oral history, 1982; A. Saluskin, 1967; Kiatana Kamiakin, oral history, n.d., WBC.
22. A. Splawn, 1917:121.
23. H. Painter to L. McWhorter, 1928, LMC.
24. Ka-ya-ta-ni Kamiakin, oral history, n.d., and C. Henderson, oral history, 1942, LMC; W. Brown, 1961:399–403.
25. C. Sternberg, 1909.
26. L. McWhorter to W. Holmes, December 19, 1927, and G. Callender to L. McWhorter, February 23, 1928, LMC.
27. E. Sorenson to R. Scheuerman, December 30, 1996.
28. G. Hunt, n.d.

Chapter 9: Salmon Out of Water

1. B. Owhi, oral history, 1915, LMC.
2. L. McWhorter, 1952:171–72.
3. *Annual Report*, 1877, SI.
4. Ibid.; O. Howard, 1907:255.
5. L. McWhorter, 1952:188–99; A. Josephy, 1965:512–16.
6. B. Owhi, oral history, 1919, LMC.
7. A. Josephy, 1965:565–71.
8. L. McWhorter, 1940:288–89, and 1952:525–30; J.D. Pearson, 2004, unpublished manuscript; B. Owhi, oral history, 1919, LMC.
9. L. McWhorter, 1952:539–42; J.D. Pearson, 2004, unpublished manuscript.
10. *Spokesman-Review*, May 25, 1885; S. Waters to R. Miller, May 23, 1885, WIA.
11. A. Andrews, oral history, 1961, RRC; *Annual Report*, 1886, CIA.
12. H. Covington, oral history, n.d., WBC.
13. G. Kuykendall, "Historical Essays II," n.d.
14. E. Peone, oral history, 1981; E. Burbank, 1899:181–83.
15. *Palouse Gazette*, March 21, 1879; M. Jim, oral history, 1979.
16. R. Ruby and J. Brown, 1965:86–97; E. Peone, oral history, 1981.
17. *Omaha Weekly Herald*, March 29, 1878.
18. *Walla Walla Statesman*, June 28, 1879; G. Friedlander, oral history, 1961, RRC; R. Ruby and J. Brown, 1965:185–86; J. Davis, Journal, n.d., MAC.
19. Seattle *Daily Intelligencer*, May 20, 1879.
20. E. Ferry to C. Schurz, May 16, 1879, CIA; *Annual Report* [II], 1879:155, SW.
21. *Spokan Times*, June 19, 1879.
22. *Annual Report* [II], 1879:151–54, SW.
23. R. Ruby and J. Brown, 1965:214–18; J. Davis to R. Ruby, February 12, 1962, RRC.

Chapter 10: Travois on the Trail

1. L. West, 1927:47–48.
2. A. Kamiakin, oral history, 1971; C. Kamiakin, oral history, 1956, RRC.
3. C. Kamiakin, oral history, 1956, RRC; A. George, oral history, 1980.
4. C. Relander, 1956:117–18; T. Connolly to R. Scheuerman, 1987.
5. G. Hunter, 1887:364–65.
6. C. Trafzer and R. Scheuerman, 1986:129–33. Pete Bones was identified as the son of Tespaloos, in C. Kamiakin, Harry Owhi, and Hattie Andrews, Probate Testimony of Peter Bones (Peter Gibson) Estate, September 1954, General Correspondence (Colville Inheritance), RG 75, National Archives, Seattle.
7. E. Peone, oral history, 1981; J. Grant, oral history, 2007.
8. *Annual Report*, 1884, 1885, CIA.

9. L. Covington, oral history, 1961, RRC; R. Ruby and J. Brown, 1965:215–16.
10. A. Kamiakin, oral history, 1972; E. Peone, oral history, 1981.
11. T. Kamiakin, oral history, 1928, WBC; *Annual Report*, 1886, SI; J. Davis, Journal, n.d., MAC.
12. F. Andrews, oral history, 2007; E. Latham to H. Cole, March 14, 1891, WIA; J. Davis, Journal, n.d., MAC.
13. R. Ruby and J. Brown, 1965:233; J. Casey, oral history, 1961, RRC.
14. *Dalles Times-Miner*, January 15, 1887; E. Peone, oral history, 1981.
15. T. Connolly to R. Scheuerman, 1987; A. Andrews, oral history, 2005.
16. J. Hermilt and L. Judge; 1925:20–28; J. Atkins, oral history, 1981.
17. E. Williams, oral history, 1981; N. Friedlander, oral history, 1956, VRC.
18. S. Kamiakin-Williams, oral history, 1961, RRC; B. Owhi, oral history, 1919, LMC.
19. T. Tomeo, oral history, 2006; Council Proceedings, Nespelem, Washington, June 20, 1907, VRC; E. Peone, oral history, 1981.
20. E. Peone, oral history, 1981; J. Casey, oral history, 1961, RRC.
21. N. Friedlander, oral history, 1956, VRC; *Spokane Chronicle*, July 7, 1928, and July 9, 1931; *Wilbur Register*, July 11, 1929; *Grand Coulee News*, July 6, 1936.
22. *Wilbur Register*, September 5, 1890; *Spokane Falls Review*, April 9, 1891.
23. R. Ruby and J. Brown, 1965:286–88.
24. T. Andrews, oral history, 1964, BRC; *Wilbur Register*, June 30, 1893.
25. P.D. Moses, in Council Minutes, 1911, Office of History and Archaeology, Colville Confederated Tribes; J. Mires to H. Cole, WIA.
26. A.P. Kamiakin and A. Owhi, oral history, 1971, VRC.
27. *Annual Report* 1897, CIA.
28. A. George, oral history, 1981.
29. S. Kamiakin-Williams, oral history, 1961, RRC.
30. F. Honn and R. Honn, oral history, 2006; G. Fisher, oral history, 2006.
31. E. Peone, oral history, 1982; J. Davis, Journal, n.d., RRC.
32. T. Andrews, oral history, 1964, BRC.
33. F. LeBret, 1997, MAC; *Spokane Chronicle*, October 3, 1901.
34. E. Peone, oral history, 1982. The agency day school in Nespelem consolidated with the local public school in 1935.
35. A. Tomeo, oral history, 1972; *Omak Chronicle*, May 12, 1916.

Chapter 11: Artists and Authors

1. C. Tomeo, oral history, 1963, RRC.
2. For additional characterizations of Kamiakin and other leading figures of the war period see H. Bancroft, 1890; C. Snowden, 1911; and G. Fuller, 1938.
3. *St. John Journal*, June 20, 1941; *Colfax Gazette-Commoner*, June 27, 1941; W. Lyman [I], 1919:238.
4. C. Wood, 1893:436–39.
5. J. Wehn to L. McWhorter, n.d., LMC.
6. *Yakama Republic*, October 16, 1907; J. Miles to R. Scheuerman, March 18, 2008.
7. *Spokesman-Review*, July 29, 1938; J. Creighton, 2000.
8. A. Harder, oral history, 1978.
9. J. Creighton, 2000:36–40. WSC's annual summertime Nespelem Art Colony was cancelled in 1942, after the outbreak of World War II.
10. E. Williams, oral history, 1981.
11. *Wenatchee Daily World*, July 8, 1948, and July 10, 1956.
12. A. Tomeo, oral history, 1971; E. Peone, oral history, 1982.
13. T. Kamiakin, oral history, 1928, WBC; E. Peone, oral history, 1982.
14. See E. Meany, 1918:240.

15. L. McWhorter to W. Brown, September 27, 1930, to C. Ivy, January 21, 1931, and to C. Deitz, March 27, 1936, LMC.
16. A. Kamiakin, oral history, 1972; S. Kamiakin-Williams, CRC.
17. R. Ruby to R. Scheuerman, December 7, 1981.
18. W. Henry, 1953; R. Gale, 1984:29–31; *New York Times*, October 13, 1956. Allen's Nez Perce historical-romance novels include *From Where the Sun Now Stands* (1959) and *The Bear Paw Horses* (1973).

Chapter 12: Rivers Rise

1. C. Burke, 1921.
2. Chief Sluskin, oral history, 1915, LMC.
3. Chiefs of the Colville and Okanogan Tribes, "To the President of the United States" [1925], in O. and M. Raufer, 1966:428–36.
4. P. Pitzer, 1994:227.
5. A. Netboy, 1980:72–84. On the elimination of native Columbia River salmon, see Harden, 1996. For a thorough discussion of hydroelectric dam construction impacts on Snake River salmon runs, see Petersen, 1995.
6. V. Ray, 1977; *Yakima Herald*, March 5, 1932.
7. J. DeSautel and L. Covington, in R. Young and R. Pace, 1977.
8. *Spokesman-Review*, July 6, 1941; *Confederated Tribes of the Colville Reservation Grand Coulee Settlement Act*, H.R. 4757 [1994].
9. C. Kamiakin, W. Andrews, et al., to J. Collier, April 5, 1935, and J. Collier to C. Kamiakin, et al., April 30, 1935, WIA; *Spokesman-Review*, May 5, 1934.
10. *Spokesman-Review*, February 22, 1938.
11. Chief Kamiakin to W. Horan, n.d., and W. Horan to Chief Kamiakin, December 15, 1943, WHC; Colville Agency Meeting Minutes, January 10, 1944, CWC.
12. A. Tomeo, oral history, 1972; F. Gross to G. Thomas, June 15, 1944, WIA.
13. F. Andrews, oral history, 2006; J. Grant, oral history, 2007.
14. S. Ambrose, 2001; E. McClung, oral history, 2006.
15. D. Burgett, 2006; P. Godeau, 2008.

Chapter 13: The Essence of Life

1. H. Owhi to P. Sherman, December 12, 1943, and W. Horan to L. Keith, July 19, 1947, WHC.
2. *Wenatchee Daily World*, November 21, 1947, and July 12, 1948.
3. "Meeting of the Affiliated Tribes Convened at the Colville Indian Agency," 1947, WHC.
4. *Wenatchee Daily World*, November 21, 1947.
5. A. Saluskin and W. Totus, in Portland District Corps of Engineers, "The Dalles Dam Indian Fishery: Minutes of Meeting with Yakima Negotiating Committee," April 22, 1954, Yakama Nation Library, Yakama Cultural Heritage Center, Toppenish.
6. A. George, oral history, 1981.
7. Chief Kamiakin, et al., to W. Horan, October 18, 1948, WHC; *Wenatchee Daily World*, April 1, 1948.
8. Colville Business Council, et al., "To the President of the United States," [1950]; W. Horan to C.L. Graves, May 29, 1950, WHC.
9. A. Fisher, 1999:2–17.
10. E. Peone, oral history, 1982; F. George, 1952.
11. P. Rosier, 2006; R. Ruby and J. Brown, 1970:289–92.
12. *Yakima Herald-Republic*, December 1, 1955, and May 8, 2006.
13. T. Yallup, in *Yakima Republic*, June 10, 1955; *Seattle Post-Intelligencer*, June 11, 1955.

14. *Spokane Chronicle*, August 30, 1955; J. Garry, NCAI 1955 Convention Minutes, MAC.
15. T. Hulst, 2006:256.
16. W. Douglas, 1950:133–39; C. Wilkinson, 2005:252.
17. These rulings significantly contributed to subsequent decisions in federal district court defining "fair share" and "in common" as one-half of annual harvestable salmon and steelhead. See *Sohappy v. Smith* (Belloni, 1969) and *U.S. v. Washington* (Boldt, 1974).
18. R. Johnson, in S. Wasby, 1990:200–1; W. Douglas, 1950:56–57.
19. C. Kamiakin, oral history, 1956, Office of History and Archaeology, Colville Confederated Tribes.
20. C. Kamiakin, oral history, 1957, CWC.
21. *Christian Century*, September 21, 1958.
22. W. Willard, 2004:3–4; D. Mallickan, oral history, 2005.
23. S. Simpson, 2005.
24. K. Philip, 1982; D. Fixico, 1992. See R. Scofield, 1977, for a sympathetic portrayal of termination advocates.
25. J. Kennedy, 1963 [The American Presidency Project]; J. Kennedy, in W. Brandon, 1964; M. James, 1990.
26. C. Wilkinson, 2005:178–80; C. Williams to G. McGovern, May 29, 1967, ICC.
27. E. Williams, oral history, 1981; E. Peone, oral history, 1982.
28. *Colville Termination Hearing Proceedings*, H.R. 5925 and S. 1413, Serial No. 89-23 [1965].
29. Ibid.
30. *Wenatchee Daily World*, November 7, 1965; C. Wilkinson, 2005:180–82; *Five Tribes Journal*, March-April 1975.
31. *Interlocutory Orders, Dockets 175,180, 222, The Confederated Colville Tribes and Dockets 161 and 224, The Yakima Nation*, et al., Plantiffs v. *USA*, July 29, 1963, ICC.
32. *Finding of Fact in Docket Nos. 161, 222, and 224*, April 5, 1965, ICC.
33. F. George, 1966; C. Schuster, oral history, 2005.
34. *Wenatchee Daily World*, September 4, 1959; *Yakima Herald-Republic*, June 12, 1969.
35. T. Kerr, 2001:156; W. Totus, in Committee on Interior and Insular Affairs, 1964:75.
36. H. Deutsch, 1956:44–51; H. Deutsch to R. Scheuerman, May 7, 1977.
37. C. Trafzer, 1993:1–4.

Bibliography

Books, Manuscripts, Articles, and Reports

Ambrose, Stephen E. *Band of Brothers....* New York: Simon and Schuster, 2001.

Ankeny, Nesmith. "The Cascade Battle as Told by Sam B. Jones." Unpublished manuscript, n.d. Washington State Historical Society Research Center, Tacoma.

_____. "The Story of the Steptoe Battle as Told by Lewis McMorris, Michael Kenney, Thos. Beall, and John McBean." Unpublished manuscript, n.d. Washington State Historical Society Research Center, Tacoma.

Bagley, Clarence B., ed. "Journal of Occurrences at Nisqually House." *Washington Historical Quarterly* 7 (1915):59–75, 144–67.

Ballou, Robert. *Early Klickitat Valley Days.* Goldendale, Washington: Goldendale Sentinel, c. 1938.

Bancroft, H.H. *History of Washington, Idaho, and Montana, 1845–1889.* Vol. 31. San Francisco, 1890.

Beall, Thomas B. "Pioneer Reminiscences." *Washington Historical Quarterly* 8 (1917):83–90.

Bigler, David L. *Fort Limhi: The Mormon Adventure in Oregon Territory, 1855–1858.* Logan: Utah State University Press, 2004.

Bischoff, William N. *The Jesuits in Old Oregon.* Caldwell, Idaho: Caxton, 1945.

_____. *We Were Not Summer Soldiers: The Indian War Diary of Plympton J. Kelly, 1855–1856.* Tacoma: Washington State Historical Society, 1976.

_____. "The Yakima Campaign of 1856." *Mid-America* 31 (1949):163–208.

_____. "The Yakima Indian War, 1855–56, a Problem in Research." *Pacific Northwest Quarterly* 41 (1950):162–69, 300–31.

Boyd, Robert T. *People of The Dalles: The Indians of the Wascopam Mission.* Lincoln: University of Nebraska Press, 1996

Brandon, William. *The American Heritage Book of Indians.* New York: Dell, 1964.

Brown, William Compton. *The Indian Side of the Story....* Spokane: C.W. Hill, 1961.

_____, "Life of Owhi Is Epic." *Wenatchee Daily World*, February 21, 1928.

Burbank, E.A. *The American Indian: A Collection of Portraits of Noted Chiefs.* Chicago: Thurber Art Galleries, 1899.

_____, and Ernest Royce. *Burbank among the Indians.* Caldwell, Idaho: Caxton, 1944.

Burke, Charles H. *Report of the Commissioner of Indian Affairs.* Washington, D.C.: U.S. Government Printing Office, 1921.

Burns, Robert Ignatius. *The Jesuits and the Indian Wars of the Northwest.* New Haven, Connecticut: Yale University Press, 1966.

_____. "Pere Joset's Account of the Indian War of 1858." *Pacific Northwest Quarterly* 38 (1947):285–314.

Campbell, John V. "The Sinclair Party—An Emigration Overland along the Old Hudson's Bay Company Route from Manitoba to the Spokane Country in 1854." *Washington Historical Quarterly* 7 (1916):187–201.

Carriker, Robert C. *Father Peter John de Smet: Jesuit in the West.* Norman: University of Oklahoma Press, 1995.

Chadwick, S.J. "Colonel Steptoe's Battle." *Washington Historical Quarterly* 2 (1907–8):333–43.

Chalfant, Stuart A. *Interior Salish and Eastern Washington Indians.* 4 vols. New York: Garland, 1974.

Chief Joseph. *Chief Joseph's Own Story.* Fairfield, Washington: Ye Galleon Press, [1925] 1999.

Chittenden, H.M., and A.T. Richardson, eds. *Life, Letters and Travels of Father Pierre Jean DeSmet, S.J., 1811–1873...* 4 vols. New York: Francis P. Harper, 1905.

Clark, Ella E. *Indian Legends of the Pacific Northwest.* Berkeley: University of California Press, [1953] 1960.

Clark, Stanley J. "The Nez Perces in Exile." *Oregon Historical Quarterly* 36 (1935):14–59.

Clarkin, Thomas. *Federal Indian Policy in the Kennedy and Johnson Administrations, 1961–1969.* Albuquerque: University of New Mexico Press, 2001.

Colville Confederated Tribes. *The Year of the Coyote: Centennial Celebration, July 2, 1972.* Nespelem, Washington, 1972.

Colville Termination Hearing Proceedings, House Subcommittee on Indian Affairs, H.R. 5925 and S. 1413, Serial No. 89-23 (1965).

Committee on Interior and Insular Affairs. *Indian Fishing Rights: Hearings before the Subcommittee on Indian Affairs of the Committee on Interior and Insular Affairs.* Washington, D.C.: Government Printing Office, 1964.

Confederated Tribes of the Colville Reservation Grand Coulee Settlement Act, House of Representatives, H.R. 4757 (1994).

Coonc, Elizabeth Ann. "Reminiscences of a Pioneer Woman." *Washington Historical Quarterly* 8 (1917):14–21.

Creighton, J.J. *Indian Summers: Washington State College and the Nespelem Art Colony, 1937–1941.* Pullman: Washington State University Press, 2000.

Cronin, Kay. *Cross in the Wilderness.* Vancouver, British Columbia: Mitchell Press. 1960.

Curtis, Edward S. *The North American Indian....* 20 vols. Cambridge, Massachusetts: University Press, [1911].

Deloria, Vine, Jr., ed. *American Indian Policy in the Twentieth Century.* Norman: University of Oklahoma Press, 1985.

_____, and Clifford M. Lytle. *American Indians, American Justice.* Austin: University of Texas Press, 1983.

Deutsch, Herman J. "Indian and White in the Inland Empire: The Contest for the Land, 1880–1912." *Pacific Northwest Quarterly* 47 (1956):44–51.

Dippie, Brian W. *The Vanishing American: White Attitudes and U.S. Indian Policy.* Middletown, Connecticut: Wesleyan University Press, 1982.

Doty, James. "Journal of Operations of Governor Isaac Ingalls Stevens, Superintendent of Indian Affairs and Commissioner, Treating with the Indian Tribes East of the Cascade Mountains, in Washington Territory, and the Blackfeet and Neighboring Tribes, Near Great Falls of the Missourie, in the Year 1855; Including Therein Details of the Celebrated Indian Council at Walla Walla, and of the Blackfoot Council at Fort Benton, and the Commencement of the Indian Wars 1855–8." Typescript copy, n.d. Museum of Arts and Culture, Spokane.

_____. "A True Copy of the Record of the Official Proceedings at the Council in Walla Walla Valley, Held Jointly by Isaac I. Stevens and Joel Palmer on the Part of the U. States with the Tribes of Indians Named in the Treaties Made at That Council, June 9 and 11, 1855." Unpublished manuscript, n.d. Oregon Historical Society, Portland.

Douglas, William O. *Of Men and Mountains*. New York: Harper and Brothers, 1950.

Dunbar, Seymour. *The Journals and Letters of Major John Owen, 1850–1871….* New York: Edward Eberstadt, 1927.

Elliot, T.C. "Steptoe Butte and Steptoe Battle-field." *Washington Historical Quarterly* 18 (1927):243–53.

Emmons, Della Gould. *Leschi of the Nisquallies*. Minneapolis: T.S. Denison, 1965.

Fahey, John. *The Inland Empire: Unfolding Years, 1879–1929*. Seattle: University of Washington Press, 1986.

————. *The Kalispel Indians*. Norman: University of Oklahoma Press, 1986.

Field, Virgil F. *The Official History of the Washington National Guard*. 4 vols. Camp Murray, Tacoma, 1961.

Fisher, Andrew H. "'This I Know from the Old People': Yakama Indian Treaty Rights as Oral Tradition." *Montana Magazine* 49 (Spring 1999):2–17.

Fixico, Donald L. *Termination and Relocation: Federal Indian Policy, 1945–1960*. Albuquerque: University of Mexico Press, 1992.

Franco, Jere Bishop. *Crossing the Pond: The Native American Effort in World War II*. Denton: University of Northern Texas Press, 1999.

Frush, Charles W. "A Trip from The Dalles of the Columbia, Oregon, to Fort Owen, Bitter Root Valley, Montana, in the Spring of 1858." *Contributions to the Historical Society of Montana* 2 (1896):337–42.

Fuller, George W. *The Inland Empire of the Pacific Northwest: A History*. 4 vols. Spokane: H.G. Linderman, 1928.

Gale, Robert L. *Will Henry/Clay Fisher (Henry W. Allen)*. Boston: Twayne, 1984.

Garrecht, Francis A. "An Indian Chief." *Washington Historical Quarterly* 19 (1928):167–78.

George, Frank. "Address to the Affiliated Tribes of Northwest Indians, Spokane, Washington, August 21, 1952." Unpublished manuscript. Office of History and Archaeology, Colville Confederated Tribes, Nespelem, Washington.

————. "Statement in the Matter of Disposition of Judgment Funds Realized from Awards Made by the Indian Claims Commission in Docket Nos. 161, 222, and 224, November 21, 1966." Unpublished manuscript. Office of History and Archaeology, Colville Confederated Tribes, Nespelem, Washington.

Gibbs, George. *Indian Tribes of Washington Territory*. Fairfield, Washington: Ye Galleon Press, 1972.

————, et al. "Reports on the Indian Tribes of the Territory of Washington." *Secretary of War Reports of Explorations* 1 (1854):400–49.

Gibson, James. *Farming the Frontier: The Agricultural Opening of the Oregon Country, 1786–1846*. Seattle: University of Washington Press, 1985.

Gidley, M. *With One Sky above Us: Life on an Indian Reservation at the Turn of the Century*. New York: G.P. Putnam's Sons, 1979.

Guie, H. Dean. *Bugles in the Valley: Garnett's Fort Simcoe*. Portland: Oregon Historical Society, 1977.

Haase, Larry. "Termination and Assimilation: Federal Indian Policy, 1943–61." Ph.D. dissertation. Washington State University, 1974.

Haines, Francis. *Appaloosa: The Spotted Horse in Art and History*. Austin: University of Texas Press, 1963.

————. *The Nez Percés: Tribesmen of the Columbia Plateau*. Norman: University of Oklahoma Press, 1955.

Haller, Granville O. "Kamiarkin—In History: Memoir of the War, in the Yakima Valley, 1855–1856." Manuscript A128, Bancroft Library, University of California, Berkeley.

Harden, Blaine. *A River Lost: The Life and Death of the Columbia*. New York: W.W. Norton, 1996.

Harder, Annine. *Opportunities of the Golden West*. Spokane: Ross, 1978.

Hembree, Wyman C. "Yakima Indian War Diary." *Washington Historical Quarterly* 15 (1925):273–83.

Henry, Will (Henry W. Allen). *To Follow the Flag*. New York: Random House, 1953.

Hermilt, John, and Louie Judge. "The Wenatchee Indians Ask Justice." *Washington Historical Quarterly* 16 (1925):20–28.

Howard, O.O. *My Life and Experiences among Our Hostile Indians….* A.D. Worthington, 1907.

Hulst, Tom R. *The Footpaths of Justice William O. Douglas: A Legacy of Place*. New York: iUniverse, 2006.

Hunn, Eugene, with James Selam and Family. *Nch'i-Wana: The Big River, Mid-Columbia Indians and Their Land*. Seattle: University of Washington Press, 1990.

Hunt, Garrett B. *Indian Wars of the Inland Empire*. Spokane: Spokane Community College, n.d.

————. "Report of Committee on Fixing Sites and Scenes Relative to the Battle of the Four Lakes and Subsequent March, August 31-September 6, 1858." Spokane Public Library, 1916.

Hunter, George. *Reminiscences of an Old Timer*. San Francisco: H.S. Crocker, 1887.

(An) Illustrated History of North Idaho Embracing Nez Perce, Latah, Kootenai, and Shoshone Counties. Western Historical, 1903.

Jackson, Helen Hunt. *A Century of Dishonor: A Sketch of the United States Government's Dealing with Some of the Indian Tribes*. New York: Harper and Brothers, 1881.

Jackson, John C. *A Little War of Destiny: The First Regiment of Oregon Mounted Volunteers and the Yakima Indian War of 1855–56*. Fairfield, Washington: Ye Galleon Press, 1996.

Jacobs, Melville. "Palus Dialect (N. Sahaptin)." Unpublished manuscript. Melville Jacobs Collection, University of Washington, 1930.

————. "A Sketch of Northern Sahaptin Grammar." *University of Washington Publications in Anthropology* 4 (1931):83–292.

James, M. Annette. "The Hollow Icon: An American Indian Analysis of the Kennedy Myth and Federal Indian Policy." *Wicazo Sa Review* 6 (1990):34–44.

Jessett, Thomas E. *Chief Spokan Garry, 1811–1892….* Minneapolis: T.S. Dennison, 1960.

Johannsen, Dorothy O., and Charles M. Gates, *Empire of the Columbia: A History of the Pacific Northwest*. New York: Harper and Row, 1967.

Josephy, Alvin M., Jr. *The Nez Perce Indians and the Opening of the Northwest*. New Haven: Yale University Press, 1965.

Joset, Joseph. "Account of the Indian War of 1858." Unpublished manuscript, 1873. Oregon Province Archives, Gonzaga University, Spokane.

————. "*Utrum Expediat movere missionem SS. Cordis ad Nilgwalko,*" June 1874. Oregon Province Archives, Gonzaga University, Spokane.

Kamiakin, Cleveland. "The Vision Quest." *Tác Titóoquan News* (March 2003):5.

Kamiakin, Tomio. "Chief Kamiakin." Unpublished typescript, n.d. L.V. McWhorter Collection, Manuscripts, Archives, and Special Collections, Washington State University, Pullman.

Kappler, Charles J. *Indian Affairs, Laws, and Treaties*. 2 vols. Washington, D.C.: Government Printing Office, 1904.

Keller, Robert H., Jr. "William O. Douglas, the Supreme Court, and the American Indians." *American Indian Law Review* 3 (1975):333–60.

Kennedy, John F., "Remarks to Representatives of the National Congress of American Indians, March 5, 1963," in *The American Presidency Project*, John Wooley and Gerhard Peters, eds. Santa Barbara: University of California, 2006.

Kerr, Thomas J. *Wilbur G. Hallauer: An Oral History*. Olympia: Washington State Oral History Program, 2001.

Keyes, Erasmus D. *Fifty Years' Observation of Men and Events: Civil and*

Military. New York: Charles Scribners' Sons, 1884.

Keyser, James D. *Indian Rock Art of the Columbia Plateau.* Seattle: University of Washington Press, 1992.

Kip, Lawrence. *Army Life on the Pacific: A Journal of the Expedition against the Northern Indians, the Tribes of Coeur d'Alenes, Spokans, Pelouzes, in the Summer of 1858.* New York: Redfield, 1859.

————. *[Journal] Indian Council at Walla Walla.* [1855] 1897.

Kowrach, Edward J. *Mie. Charles Pandosy, O.M.I., a Missionary of the Northwest: Missionary to the Yakima Indians in the 1850's.* Fairfield, Washington: Ye Galleon Press, 1992.

————, and Thomas E. Connolly, eds. *Saga of the Coeur d'Alene Indians: An Account of Chief Joseph Seltice.* Fairfield, Washington: Ye Galleon Press, 1990.

Kuykendall, E.V. *Historic Glimpses of Asotin County.* Clarkston, Washington: Clarkston Herald, 1954.

Kuykendall, George. "Historical Essays II." Unpublished typescript, n.d. Manuscripts, Archives, and Special Collections, Washington State University.

————. "Reminiscences and Early History of Garfield County." Unpublished typescript, 1911. Manuscripts, Archives, and Special Collections, Washington State University.

Kvasnicka, Robert M., and Herman J. Viola, eds. *The Commissioners of Indian Affairs, 1824–1977.* Lincoln: University of Nebraska Press, 1979.

LeBret, Frances. "The Ft. Spokane Indian Boarding School." *They Sacrificed for Our Survival.* Educational Exhibit. Spokane: Museum of Arts and Culture, 1997.

Lever, W.H. *An Illustrated History of Whitman County, State of Washington.* n.p., 1901.

Lewis, William S., ed. "The Daughter of Angus MacDonald [Christina McDonald McKenzie Williams]." *Washington Historical Quarterly* 13 (1922):107–17.

Lyman, William D. *History of the Yakima Valley, Washington.* 2 vols. Spokane: S.J. Clarke, 1919.

MacMurray, J.W. "The Dreamers of the Columbia River Valley in Washington Territory." *Transactions of the Albany Institute* 11 (1887):241–48.

Manring, B.F. *Conquest of the Coeur d'Alenes, Spokanes, and Palouses.* Spokane: Inland Printing, 1912.

McDermott, Paul D., and Ronald E. Grim. "The Artistic Views of Gustavus Sohon." *Columbia* (Summer 2002):16–22.

McDonald, Angus. "A Few Items of the West." *Washington Historical Quarterly* 8 (1917).

McMaster, Gerald, and Clifford E. Trafzer. *Native Universe: Voices of Indian America.* Washington, D.C.: National Museum of the American Indian, Smithsonian Institution, 2004.

McRae, Barbara Jane Matlock, "Crossing the Plains from Missouri to Washington Territory, 1874–1875." Unpublished manuscript, c. 1940.

McWhorter, L.V. *Hear Me, My Chiefs! Nez Perce History and Legend.* Caldwell, Idaho: Caxton, 1952.

————. *Tragedy of the Wahk-Shum: Prelude to the Yakima War, 1855–56.* Yakima: privately printed, 1937.

————. *Yellow Wolf: His Own Story.* Caldwell, Idaho: Caxton, 1940.

Meany, Edmond S. "Historic Gardens of Chief Kamiakin." *Washington Historical Quarterly* 9 (1918):240.

Meinig, Donald W. *The Great Columbia Plain: A Historical Geography, 1805–1910.* Seattle: University of Washington Press, 1968.

Miles, Charles, and O.B. Sperlin, eds. *Building a State: Washington, 1889–1939.* 3 vols. Tacoma: Washington State Historical Society, 1940.

Miller, Christopher L. *Prophetic Worlds: Indians and Whites on the Columbia Plateau.* New Brunswick, New Jersey: Rutgers University Press, 1985.

Moulton, Gary E., ed. *The Journals of the Lewis and Clark Expedition.* 13 vols. Lincoln: University of Nebraska Press, 1981–1988.

Mullan, John. *Report on the Construction of a Military Road from Fort Walla-Walla to Fort Benton.* Washington, D.C.: Government Printing Office, 1863.

Neils, Selma. *The Klickitat Indians.* Portland: Binford and Mort, 1985.

Netboy, Anthony. *The Columbia River Salmon and Steelhead Trout: Their Fight for Survival.* Seattle: University of Washington Press, 1980.

O'Donnell, Terrence. *An Arrow in the Earth: General Joel Palmer and the Indians of Oregon.* Portland: Oregon Historical Society Press, 1991.

Painter, Harry. "New Light on Chief Kamiakin." *Walla Walla Union Bulletin,* March 18, 1945.

Painter, Robert M., and William C. Painter. "Journals of the Indian War of 1855–1856." *Washington Historical Quarterly* 15 (1924):11–31.

Palmer, Gary B. "Indian Pioneers: The Settlement of *Ni'lukhwalqw* (Hangman Creek, Idaho) by the *Schitsu'umsh* (Coeur d'Alene Indians)." *Oregon Historical Quarterly* 102 (2001):22–47.

————, Lawrence Nicodemus, and Lavinia Felsman. *Khwi' Khwe Hntmikhw'lumkhw: This is My Land.* Plummer, Idaho: Coeur d'Alene Tribe, 1987.

Pambrun, Andrew D. *Sixty Years on the Frontier in the Pacific Northwest.* Fairfield, Washington: Ye Galleon Press, [c. 1893] 1978.

Pearson, J. Diane. "Numipu Narratives: The Essence of Survival in the Indian Territory." *Journal of Northwest Anthropology* 38:1 (2004).

Petersen, Keith. *River of Life, Channel of Death: Fish and Dams on the Lower Snake.* Lewiston, Idaho: Confluence Press, 1995.

Philip, Kenneth R. "Dillon S. Meyer and the Advent of Termination." *Western Historical Quarterly* 19 (1988):37–59.

Pierre, Ellen. "Tribal Treasures." *Coeur d'Alene Teepee* (June 1938).

Pitzer, Paul C. *Grand Coulee: Harnessing a Dream.* Pullman: Washington State University Press, 1994.

Plucker, Steven. "Troops at Ft. Simcoe, 1856–1859." Ft. Simcoe State Park Interpretive Center, White Swan, Washington, n.d.

————. "The U.S. Army's Fort Walla Walla, Its Development and Early History." Unpublished manuscript, 2006.

Prosch, Thomas W. "The Indian War in Washington Territory." *Oregon Historical Quarterly* 16 (1915):1–23.

————. "The Indian War of 1858." *Washington Historical Quarterly* 2 (1908):237–40.

Purdin, Walter. "Ka-Mi-Akin, the Great Chief." Unpublished manuscript, n.d. Yakima Valley Museum, Yakima.

Raufer, O.P., and Maria Ilma. *Black Robes and Indians of the Last Frontier: A Story of Heroism.* Milwaukee: Bruce, 1966.

Ray, Verne. "Ethnic Impacts on the Events Incident to the Federal Power Development on the Colville and Spokane Indian Reservations." Port Townsend, Washington: Prepared for the Confederated Tribes of the Colville Indian Reservation and the Spokane Tribe of Indians, Verne Ray Collection, Foley Library, Gonzaga University, Spokane, 1977.

————. "Native Villages and Groupings of the Columbia Basin." *Pacific Northwest Quarterly* 27 (1936):99–152.

————. "Tribes of the Columbia Confederacy, and the Palus." Plantiff's Exhibit No. 112, U.S. Court of Claims, Docket 261–70 (1973).

Relander, Click. *Drummers and Dreamers….* Caldwell, Idaho: Caxton, 1956.

————. *Strangers on the Land: A Historiette of the Long Struggle of the Yakima Nation's Efforts to Survive against Great Odds.* Yakima: Franklin Press, 1962.

Richards, Kent D. *Isaac I. Stevens: Young Man in a Hurry.* Pullman: Washington State University Press, [1979] 1993.

————. "Isaac Stevens and Federal Military Power in Washington Territory." *Pacific Northwest Quarterly* 63 (1972):81–86.

Rigsby, Bruce. "Changing Property Relations in Land and Resources in the Southern Plateau." Unpublished typescript, 2006. Bruce Rigsby Collection, University of Queensland, Graceville, Australia.

_____. "Comments on the Chiefly Name 'Kamiakin.'" Unpublished typescript, 2007. Bruce Rigsby Collection, University of Queensland, Graceville, Australia.

_____. "The Oral History Narratives of Thomas Billy Andrews." Unpublished typescript, 2007. Bruce Rigsby Collection, University of Queensland, Graceville, Australia.

_____. "The Origin and History of the Name 'Yakima'/'Yakama.'" Unpublished typescript, 2008. Bruce Rigsby Collection, University of Queensland, Graceville, Australia.

_____. "Some Aspects of Plateau Linguistic Prehistory: Sahaptian/Interior Salishan Relations." *University of Oregon Anthropological Papers*. No. 52 (1996).

_____, and Noel Rude. "Sketch of Sahaptin, a Sahaptian Language." *Handbook of North American Indians*. Vol. 17. Washington, D.C.: Smithsonian Institution, 1996.

Roe, Frank G. *The Indian and the Horse*. Norman: University of Oklahoma Press, [1955] 1968.

Rosier, Paul. C. "'They Are Ancestral Homelands': Race, Place, and Politics in Cold War America, 1945–61." *Journal of American History* 92 (2006):1300–26.

Ross, Alexander. *Adventures of the First Settlers on the Oregon or Columbia River*. London, 1849.

_____. *The Fur Hunters of the Far West*. Kenneth A. Spaulding, ed. Norman: University of Oklahoma Press, [1855] 1956.

Ruby, Robert H. "Return of the Nez Perce." *Idaho Yesterdays* 12 (Spring 1968):12–15.

_____, and John A. Brown. *The Cayuse Indians: Imperial Tribesmen of Old Oregon*. Norman: University of Oklahoma Press, 1972.

_____, and John A. Brown. *Half-Sun on the Columbia: A Biography of Chief Moses*. Norman: University of Oklahoma Press, 1965.

_____, and John A. Brown. *The Spokane Indians: Children of the Sun*. Norman: University of Oklahoma Press, 1970.

Saluskin, Alex. "Early Yakama History." Unpublished manuscript, 1967. Bruce Rigsby Collection, University of Queensland, Graceville, Australia.

_____. "Old Days and the Present," in *Treaty Centennial, 1855–1955. The Yakimas*. Yakima: Republic Press, 1955.

_____. "Testimony of the Yakima Negotiating Committee, July 22, 1954." in *The Dalles Dam Indian Fishery Report*, Portland District Army Corps of Engineers. Toppenish, Washington: Yakama Indian Nation Library.

_____. "The Yakima War." Unpublished manuscript, 1967. Bruce Rigsby trans. Bruce Rigsby Collection, University of Queensland, Graceville, Australia.

Santee, J.R. "Pio-Pio-Mox-Mox." *Washington Historical Quarterly* 25 (1934):128–32.

Scheuerman, Richard D. *Palouse Country: A Land and Its People*. Walla Walla: Color Press, 1994.

_____. *The Wenatchee Valley and Its First Peoples: Thrilling Grandeur, Unfulfilled Promise*. Walla Walla: Color Press, 2005.

_____, and Michael O. Finley. "Columbia Plateau Chieftain Clan Lineages." Unpublished typescript, 2008. In possession of the authors.

Schlicke, Carl P. *General George Wright: Guardian of the Pacific Coast*. Norman: University of Oklahoma Press, 1988.

Schuster, Helen H. "Yakima and Neighboring Groups." *Handbook of North American Indians*. Vol. 12. Washington, D.C.: Smithsonian Institution, 1998.

Scofield, Ruth. *Behind the Buckskin Curtain*. Seattle Pacific College, 1977.

Sebring, F.M. "Indian Raid on the Cascades in March, 1856." *Washington Historical Quarterly* 19 (1928):99–107.

Sheller, Roscoe. *The Name was Olney*. Yakima: Franklin Press, 1965.

Sheridan, Philip H. *Personal Memoirs of Philip H. Sheridan, General, United States Army*. New York: C.L. Webster, 1888.

Simpson, Sam. "John F. Kennedy's Promise to Help American Indians." *Tribal Tribune* 31 (2005).

Smith, John E. "A Pioneer of the Spokane Country." *Washington Historical Quarterly* 7 (1916):267–77.

Snowden, Clinton A. *History of Washington: The Rise and Progress of an American State*. 4 vols. New York: Century, 1909–11.

Sohon, Gustavus. "Records of the Walla Walla Council, 30th May 1855, Translated in the Language of the Spokan Indians." Manuscript 4306-c, National Anthropological Archives, Washington, D.C., n.d.

Spencer, Lloyd, and Lancaster Pollard. *A History of the State of Washington*. 4 vols. New York: American Historical Society, 1937.

Splawn, A.J. *Ka-Mi-Akin: The Last Hero of the Yakimas*. Portland: Kilham, 1917.

Splawn, Margaret. "Kamiakin's Gardens." Unpublished typescript. Yakima Valley Museum, Yakima, WA, 1918.

Sprague, Roderick. "The Meaning of 'Palouse.'" *Idaho Yesterdays* 12 (1968):22–27.

_____. "Palouse," in *Handbook of North American Indians*, Deward E. Walker Jr., ed. Washington, D.C.: Smithsonian Institution, 1998.

Stanley, George F.G., ed. *Mapping the Frontier: Charles Wilson's Diary of the Survey of the 49th Parallel, 1858–1862*. Seattle: University of Washington Press, 1970.

Stern, Theodore. *Chiefs and Change in the Oregon Country: Indian Relations at Fort Nez Percés, 1818–1855*. Corvallis: Oregon State University Press, 1996.

_____. *Chiefs and Chief Traders: Indian Relations at Fort Nez Percés, 1818–1855*. Corvallis: Oregon State University Press, 1993.

Sternberg, Charles H. *The Life of a Fossil Hunter*. New York: Henry Holt, 1909.

Stevens, Hazard. "The Ascent of Takhoma." *Washington State Historical Society Publications*. 2 (1915):402–33.

_____. *The Life of Isaac Ingalls Stevens*. 2 vols. Boston: Houghton, Mifflin, 1901.

Stevens, Isaac I. *Narrative and Final Report of Explorations for a Route for a Pacific Railroad, Near the Forty-Seventh and Forty-Ninth Parallels of North Latitude from St. Paul to Puget Sound*. Washington, D.C.: Government Printing Office, 1855, 1860.

_____. *Washington and Oregon War Claims*. Washington, D.C., 1858.

Tannatt, E.F., ed. *Indian Battles of the Inland Empire in 1858*. Spokane: Shaw and Borden, 1914.

Taylor, Graham D. *The New Deal and American Indian Tribalism: The Administration of the Indian Reorganization Act, 1935–45*. Lincoln: University of Nebraska Press, 1980.

Thompson, Albert. "The Early History of the Palouse River and Its Names." *Pacific Northwest Quarterly* 62 (1971):69–71.

Thompson, Erwin N. "Men and Events on the Lower Snake River." *Idaho Yesterdays* 5 (1961):10–15.

Thompson, Sally. "Winter on the Clark Fork, 1859." Unpublished manuscript, 2008.

Torrey, Bradford, and Francis H. Allen, eds. *The Writings of Henry David Thoreau*. Multi-vols. Boston: Houghton, Mifflin, 1906.

Totus, Watson. "Presentation on Behalf of the Yakima Tribe, May 12, 1952." *Hearings of the U.S. Sub-Committee on Civil Functions of the Army*. Yakama Nation Library, Yakama Museum and Cultural Heritage Center, Toppenish, Washington.

Trafzer, Clifford E. *Earth Song, Sky Spirit: Short Stories of the Contemporary Native American Experience*. New York: Doubleday, 1993.

_____, ed. *Indians, Superintendents, and Councils: Northwestern Indian Policy, 1850–1855*. Lanham, Maryland: University Press of America, 1986.

_____, and Richard D. Scheuerman. "The First Peoples of the Palouse Country." *Bunchgrass Historian* 8 (1980):3–18.

_____, and Richard D. Scheuerman. *Renegade Tribe: The Palouse Indians and the Invasion of the Inland Pacific Northwest.* Pullman: Washington State University Press, 1986.

Trimble, William. *The Mining Advance into the Inland Empire.* Bulletin 638. Madison: University of Wisconsin, 1914.

Underwood, Amos. "Indian Fighters of Early Days in the Pacific Northwest." *Weekly Oregonian,* July 10, 1910.

Victor, Frances V. *The Early Indian Wars of Oregon.* Salem, Oregon: Grant C. Baker, 1894.

Villard, Henry. *The Early History of Transportation in Oregon.* Eugene: University of Oregon Press, 1944.

Walker, Deward E., Jr., ed. *Handbook of North American Indians.* Vol. 12 (Plateau). Washington, D.C.: Smithsonian Institution, 1998.

Wasby, Stephen L. *"He Shall Not Pass This Way Again": The Legacy of Justice William O. Douglas.* Pittsburg: University of Pittsburg Press, 1990.

West, Leoti L., *The Wide Northwest: Historic Narrative of America's Wonder Land.* Spokane: Shaw and Borden, 1927.

Wilkes, Charles. *Narrative of the United States Exploring Expedition During the Years 1838, 1839, 1840, 1841, and 1842.* 5 vols. Philadelphia: Lea and Blanchard, 1845.

Wilkinson, Charles. *Blood Struggle: The Rise of Modern Indian Nations.* New York: W.W. Norton, 2005.

Willard, William. "The Nez Perce Anthropologist." *Journal of Northwest Anthropology* 38 (2004):3–4.

Winans, W. Parkhurst. "Stevens County, Washington, Its Creation, Addition, Subtraction, and Division." Typescript copy, n.d. Manuscripts, Archives, and Special Collections, Washington State University.

Winthrop, Theodore. *The Canoe and the Saddle: or, Klalam and Klickitat.* Tacoma: John H. Williams, [1863] 1913.

Wolff, Francis J.D. "Reminiscences of a Pioneer in the Early 50's." *Washington State Historical Society Publications* 2 (1915):163–65.

Wood, C.E.S. "Famous Indians: Portraits of Some Indian Chiefs." *Century Magazine* 24 (1893):436–39.

Wood, Erskine. *Days with Chief Joseph.* Portland: Binfords and Mort, 1920.

Works Progress Administration. *Told by The Pioneers* ("H. Thorp-Hattin Interview"). Olympia, 1938.

Wright, E.W. *Lewis and Dryden's Marine History of the Pacific Northwest.* Portland: Lewis and Dryden, 1895.

Wright, George. "Report of the Indian War of 1858." *Message from the President of the United States.* 2. 35th Cong., 2d sess. House Ex. Doc. 2, 1858.

Young, Ray, and Robert E. Pace, *The Price We Paid.* Media Services, Yakama Indian Nation for the Confederated Colville Tribes Business Council, 1977.

Manuscript Collections

Catholic Chancery Archdiocesan Archives, Seattle—Delannoy Papers.

Colville Indian Reservation, Nespelem—Colville Tribal Probate Records.

Eastern Washington University, Archives and Special Collections, Cheney—Winans and Kingston Collections.

Federal Records Center, Seattle—Colville Agency Records; Simms Letters; Yakima Agency Records.

Fort Simcoe State Park, White Swan—Plucker Papers.

Gonzaga University, Foley Library, Spokane—Ray Collection.

Huntington Library, San Marino, California—Cornelius Collection; Fort Dalles and Fort Simcoe Letterbooks.

Library of Congress, Washington, D.C.—McClellan Collection.

Maryland Historical Society, Baltimore—Archer Collection.

Montana State University, Bozeman—W. Roberts Collection.

Museum of Arts and Culture, Spokane—Davis, Doty, Ruby, and Harder Collections.

National Anthropological Museum, Washington, D.C.—Sohon and National Congress of American Indian Collections.

National Archives, Washington, D.C.—Indian Claims Commission Dockets 161, 222, 224; Records of the Bureau of Indian Affairs; Records Related to Negotiations of Ratified and Unratified Treaties; Microcopy of Records of the Washington Superintendency of Indian Affairs, 1853–74.

Nez Perce National Historical Park, Spalding Center Museum, Spalding, Idaho—Spalding-Allen Collection.

Oregon Historical Society, Portland—Geary, Gibbs, and Nesmith Collections; Oregon and Washington Territorial Volunteer Soldiers' Papers.

Oregon Province Archives of the Society of Jesus, Crosby Library, Gonzaga University—Cataldo, DeSmet, Joset, and Kowrach Collections.

Sacred Heart Mission, De Smet, Idaho—Baptismal Registers.

Spokane Public Library, Spokane—DeSmet, Monteith, and Stevens Collections; Oregon and Washington Territorial Volunteer Soldiers' Papers.

Tamástslikt Cultural Institute, Umatilla Indian Reservation, Pendleton, Oregon—Treaty of 1855 Exhibit.

University of California, Berkeley, Bancroft Library—Elmendorf and Haller Collections.

University of Oregon, Special Collections, Eugene—Palmer Collection; Nez Perce Agency Letterbook; Cayuse and Yakima War Papers.

University of Puget Sound, Collins Memorial Library Archives, Tacoma—Canse and Oregon Methodist Missions Collections.

University of Queensland, Department of Anthropology, Graceville, Australia—Rigsby Papers.

University of Washington Library, Special Collections, Seattle—Haller, Jacobs, Stevens, and Swan Collections.

Washington State Historical Society Research Center, Tacoma—Ankeny, Canse, and Milroy Collections.

Washington State University, Manuscripts, Archives, and Special Collections, Pullman—Brown, DeSmet, Deutsch, Horan, Kuykendall, McGregor, McWhorter, Oliphant, Simms, Sutherland, White, and Winans Collections.

Wenatchee Valley Museum Archives, Wenatchee—J. Brown Collection.

Yakama Nation Heritage Cultural Center, Yakama Indian Reservation, Toppenish—Oral History Collection.

Yakima Valley Regional Library, Yakima—Relander Collection.

Oral Sources

Glen Adams. Fairfield, May 19, 1982.

Albert Redstar Andrews (Redstar-Kamiakin Family). Nespelem, December 10, 2005, and June 26, July 19, 2007.

Frank Andrews Sr. (Wiyukshenét-Hiyúmpiskis Family). Nespelem, March 17 and September 6, 2006, and February 24, 2007.

Isabel Arcasa (Friedlander-Shilkohsaskt Family). Nespelem, October 17 and 31, 1981, and April 30, 1982.

Barbara Aripa (Moses-Kamiakin Family). Nespelem, August 14 and September 6, 2006.

Joe Atkins (Tye-ah-kin-Yaksum Family). Nespelem, March 13, 1981.

Horace and Andrea Axtell (Timpoosnim-Lookingglass Family). Lewiston, Idaho, May 17, 2003.

Daryll and Dorothy Bahr. Wilbur, June 27, 2007.

Floyd and Barbara Bailey. Rock Lake, February 11, 2006.

Norm and Arlene Bailey. Rock Lake, June 16, 2006.

Agatha Bart (Jim-Moses Family). Nespelem, November 18 and 23, 2005.

Fr. Thomas Connolly S.J. De Smet, Idaho. July 19 and 20, 2007.

Agnes Davis. Nespelem, September 1, 2006.

Ida Desautel (Kamiakin-Little Man Chief Family). Nespelem, October 20, 1981.

Robert Eddy. Cashmere, March 5 and December 16, 2006.

Gordon Fisher (Hahtalekin-Paul Family). Lapwai, Idaho, June 19, 2006, and July 24, 2008.

Ronald "Duckie" Friedlander (Friedlander-Moses Family). Omak, January 16, 2006.

Andrew George (George-Kamiakin Family). Toppenish, November 15, 1980, and May 5, 1981.

John Grant (Grant-Kamiakin Family). Nespelem, November 10 and 20, 2007.

Herman Harder and Henry Harder. Aspen Creek Ranch (Ritzville), May 3, 2003.

Floyd Honn. Benge, March 22, 2006.

Ray Honn. Ewan, February 2, 2006.

Rose Jack (Telekish-Jim Family). Mission, Oregon, July 20, 1984.

Charles Jenkins. St. John, June 12, 1970.

Mary Jim (Fishook Jim Family). Parker, April 2 and November 10 and 11, 1979.

Randy Lewis. Seattle, September 25, 2006.

Diane Mallickan. Lapwai, Idaho, July 15, 2005.

Earl McClung. Inchelium, August 23, 2006.

Paul D. McDermott. Gaithersburg, Maryland, February 5, 2008.

Isaac Patrick (Tilcoax-Kalyton Family). Mission, Oregon, May 8, 1981.

Emily Peone (Friedlander-Moses-Kamiakin Family). Nespelem, October 31, 1981, and April 30, 1982.

Sharon Redthunder (Comedown-Kamiakin Family). Nespelem, August 14, 2006.

Carrie Jim Schuster (Fishhook Jim-Tilcoax Family). Moses Lake, December 10, 2005.

Matilda George Sharloo (George-Shallo Family). Toppenish, July 25, 2007.

Cliff Sijohn. Plummer, Idaho, May 16, 2008.

Frank Sijohn. Plummer, Idaho, May 16, 2008.

Arthur Tomeo (Kamiakin-Paween Family). Nespelem, June 16, 1972.

Tanya Tomeo (Kamiakin-Paween Family). Toppenish, October 18, 2006, and July 25, 2007.

Joe Thompson (Ustimatee-Tamalchuh Family). Mission, Oregon, May 9, 1981.

Helen Tyler. Tampico, August 15, 2006.

Flora Wasis (Nye-White Swan Family). Mission, Oregon, July 20, 1984.

Wilson Wewah Jr. (Tilcoax-Kalyton Family). Lyons Ferry, June 16, 2006.

Hiram and Sharon White. Tampico, August 15, 2006.

Elijah (Charlie) Williams (David Williams Family). Nespelem, June 15, 1981.

Correspondence

Donald Burgett. Howell, Michigan, 2006.
Thomas Connolly. De Smet, Idaho, 1987.
Andrew George. Wapato, 1981.
Pierre Godeau. Vaux-sur-Sure, Belgium, 2008.
Mahlon Kriebel. Garfield, 2008.
Jo Miles. Yakima, 2008.
Steven Plucker. Touchet, 1985.
Bruce Rigsby. Brisbane, Queensland, Australia, 2007.
Robert Ruby. Moses Lake, 2006.
Eric Sorenson. Pullman, 1996.

Newspapers and Magazines

Alta California
Cheney Sentinel
Christian Century
Coeur d'Alene Teepee
Dalles Journal
Dalles Mountaineer
Five Tribes Journal
Grand Coulee News
Harper's New Monthly Magazine
Omak Chronicle
Oregonian
Palouse Gazette
Pioneer and Democrat
Puget Sound Courier
Puget Sound Herald
Seattle Daily Intelligencer
Spokan Times
Spokane Falls Review
Spokesman-Review
St. John Journal
Tribal Tribune
Walla Walla Statesman
Walla Walla Union
Weekly Oregonian
Wenatchee World
Wilbur Register
Yakima Herald-Republic

Index

A

Adams, George (Skokomish), 155–56
Adams, Hank, 166
Affiliated Tribes of Northwest Indians (ATNI), 154–57, 158, 159, 164
Ah-kis-kis (Palouse), 131
Ahtanum Mission
    see St. Joseph's Mission
Alamōtín (village), 68, 97, 104, 131, 151
    see also Almota (Creek)
Alexander, Chief (Kalispel), 91, 93
Allen, Henry W., 144
Almota (Creek), 106, 116
American Fur Company, 15
Anderson, Albert, 134
Anderson, J.P., 63
Andrews family, 130–31, 133, 135, 152, 165
Andrews, Willie Red Star (Nez Perce), 130, 136, 140–41, 149–51, 153–56, 165
Ankeny, Capt. Alexander, 58
Apash Wyakaikt
    see Looking Glass, Chief
Archer, Capt. James, 89
Askolumkee, 3, 18, 99, 119, 174
Asotin, Washington, 7, 32
    see also *Hasúutin* (village)
Association on American Indian Affairs (AAIA), 154, 163–64
Astor, John Jacob (Astorians), 15–16, 49
Atween
    see Askolumkee
Augur, Lt. Christopher, 89

B

Bagley, C.B., 139
Baker, Dorsey, 121
Bancroft, Ashley, 94–95, 97
Bannock-Paiute War, 122, 126, 127
Barry, Washington, 130
Battle of the Bears Paw Mountains, 118, 119–20
Battle of the Big Hole, 118, 119, 132
Battle of the Cascades, 56, 58–59, 70, 82
Battle of the Clearwater, 118
Battle of Connell's Prairie, 56
Battle of Four Lakes, 75, 83–84, 88, 98, 142
Battle of the Grande Ronde, 62
Battle of Satus Creek, 57–58
Battle of Seattle, 55–56
Battle of Spokane Plains, 75, 84–86, 89, 98, 142
Battle, Stevens (1856), 65
Battle of Tohotonimme ("Steptoe Disaster,") 75, 78–80, 87, 89, 108, 116
    see also Steptoe, Col. Edward J.
Battle of Toppenish Creek, 47, 48, 50
    see also Haller, Major Granville O.
Battle of Two Buttes (Union Gap), 49, 50
    see also Rains, Major Gabriel
Battle of White Bird Canyon, 118
Beach, L.P., 105

Beall, Tom, 80, 87, 97
Benge, Washington, 104
Bernard, James (Colville), 146
Big Thunder, Chief (Palouse), 126, 131
Billy, Annie
    see Kis-am-x'ay
Blanchet, A.M.A., 20
Blenkinsop, George, 73
Bolon, Andrew Jackson, 35–36, 45, 48, 50, 64, 71, 73, 88, 94
Bumford, George, 50, 73
Bones, Chief
    see Waughaskie
Bones, Pete
    see Kamiakin, Kah-yee-wach
Bonneville Dam, 147
Boyd, Chief Sam (Spokane), 158
Broncheau, Phillip, 152
Brooke, Lloyd, 50, 73
Brouillet, J.B.A., 45, 81
Brown, John A., 143–44
Brown, William Compton, 67, 88, 111–12, 142, 169
Browne, J. Ross, 72
Bryan, Enoch O., 139
Buchanan, Pres. James, 41, 70
Buck, Frank (Wanapum), 160
Buck, Johnny (Wanapum), 159–60
Buck, Rex (Wanapum), 160
Burbank, E.A., 120
Burke Act (1906), 146
Burke, Charles, 145
Burris, C.A., 155
Butler, Major John, 147

C

Cain, U.S. Sen. Harry, 157
Camas Lake, 18
Camaspelo (Cayuse), 66
Camp Chelan, 133
Campbell, John, 69
Caruana, Joseph, 97, 101, 109, 110
Cascades City, 19, 56, 58–59
    see also Battle of the Cascades
Casey, Lt. Col Silas, 56
Cataldo Mission
    see Coeur d'Alene Mission
Celilo Falls, 4, 19, 103, 147, 156
Chalfant, Stuart A., 167
Charlo, Chief Paul (Flathead), 158
Chase, Henry, 66
Chief, Edward, 152
Chenowith, Francis, 18, 19, 20
Chief Joseph Dam, 162–63
Chief Mountain
    see Cowiche (Mountain)
Chirouse, Eugene Casimir, 20, 37, 41, 45, 51, 53
Chumayakan, Helen, 129, 158

Church, Sen. Frank, 164
Chuweah (Umatilla), 122, 127
Civilian Conservation Corps, 149
Clarke, Gen. Newman S., 70, 72, 76, 80, 81, 82, 87
Clarke, John, 16, 49
Cleveland, John B., 155
Coeur d'Alene council (1858), 75, 86
Coeur d'Alene Mission (Cataldo, Idaho), 22, 28, 52, 63, 76, 80, 81, 86, 88, 92, 96, 101, 104
Coeur d'Alene Mission (De Smet, Idaho), 109, 110
Colfax, Washington, 106, 121, 126, 130, 151
Collier, John, 150, 166
Colonel Wright (steamboat), 103–4
Com-mus-ni (Kamiakin's mother), 7, 10
Conboy Lake
    see Camas Lake
Congiato, Nicholas, 68, 80, 81
Coolidge, Pres. Calvin, 146–47, 158
Cooper, James, 25, 27
Cornelius, Col. Thomas, 50, 53, 57–58
Corps of Discovery, 14, 39, 117
Coulee City, Washington, 130, 140
Covington, Alex, 144
Covington, Henry, 120
Covington, Lucy (Friedlander), 133, 143, 149, 154, 158, 165–66
Covington, Virgina Bill, 120
Cowiche (Mountain), 8, 9
Cowley, Henry, 124
Cox, Archibald, 164
Craig, William, 37, 52, 61, 63, 67
Crawford, John, 138
Creighton, J.J., 140
Curlew, Billy (Columbia), 157, 163
Curry, Gov. George, 47, 50, 51, 58
Cutmouth John (Cayuse), 46, 50

D
Dalles Dam, 156
Dandy, Lt. George, 86
Dart, Anson, 19
Davenport, Joseph W., 106
Davis, Elnathan (Klamath), 166
Davis, James, 133
Davis, Sec. of War Jefferson, 61
Dawes Act (1887), 145, 146, 149
Day, Lt. Edward, 47
Dayton, Washington, 66, 131, 160
DeLong, Joseph, 96, 103
DeLoria, Vine, Jr., 166
de Mazenod, Bishop, 49
DeMoy, Victor, 79
Dent, Capt. Frederick, 62, 89
Denver, James, 72
de Rougé, Etienne, 134–35
DeSmet, Pierre J., 74, 78, 79, 80, 91, 92–93, 95, 101, 110
De Smet, Idaho, 13, 109, 110
Deutsch, Herman J., 139, 169–70
D'Herbomez, Louis, 25, 26, 45
Dill, Clarence, 149
Dixons Pond, 12
Donati's Comet, 84

Doty, James, 35–37, 40–42
Douglas, Justice William O., 162, 168
Dunn, John, 64, 65
Durieu, Paul, 33, 36

E
Eagle of the Dawn (Nez Perce), 14, 32
Easton, Washington, 12
Eaton, John, 105, 110
Eaton, O.M., 45, 88
Eisenhower, Pres. Dwight, 159
Ellensburg, Washington, 16, 18
Emery, Bob, 97
Endicott, Washington, 13, 67, 104
Engle, P.M., 104
Ephrata, Washington, 125, 131
Erwin, Lewis T., 129
Ewan, Washington, 2

F
Federal Power Act (1933), 148, 149
Ferry, Gov. Elisha, 123–24
Fisher, Gordon, 160
Fisher, Sam and Helen (Palouse), 127–28, 133, 160
Five Crows, Chief (Pahka Qohqoh), 14, 64
Fletcher, Lt. Col. J.S., 120
Floyd, Sec. of War John, 87–88
Foley, U.S. Rep. Thomas, 165
Friedlander family, 133–35, 143
Friedlander, George, 133, 143–44, 157, 165, 166
Friedlander, J. Herman, 133
Friedlander, Louis, 133, 143, 165
Friedlander, Nellie, 127, 129, 133, 143–44, 167
Frush, Charles, 80
Ft. Astoria, 16
Ft. Benton, 28, 73, 103
Ft. Colvile (HBC), 17, 19, 27–28, 32, 67, 69, 71, 73, 80, 82–83, 94, 100, 149
Ft. Colville/Harney Depot (U.S. Army), 89, 93, 103
Ft. Dalles/Camp Drum, 19, 21–22, 45–47, 56–58, 61–62, 65, 71, 80, 82
Ft. George Wright, 86, 133
Ft. Lapwai, 89, 117–18
Ft. Leavenworth, 119–20
Ft. Limhi (Lemhi), 70
Ft. Na-chess, 57, 59
Ft. Nez Perces/Walla Walla (HBC), 19, 27–28, 40, 50–51, 64
Ft. Nisqually, 17, 18, 55
Ft. Okanogan, 16, 83
Ft. Sherman, 123
Ft. Simcoe, 57, 61–62, 66, 69–71, 77, 81–82, 88–90, 93, 95, 120, 127
Ft. Spokane, 120, 133
Ft. Steilacoom, 42, 45–46, 82
Ft. Taylor, 75, 83, 104
Ft. Vancouver (HBC), 19
Ft. Vancouver (U.S. Army), 19, 25, 41, 45–47, 51, 56, 58, 73, 80–81, 83, 93
Ft. Walla Walla (U.S. Army), 57, 63, 65–66, 69–70, 73–76, 79–80, 82–83, 87, 93, 97, 103–4, 112

G
Gardner, Gov. Booth, 171
Garfield, Washington, 137

Garnett, Major Robert, 56, 70, 71, 81, 82, 88, 90
Garry, Chief Spokan, 28, 32–33, 42, 52, 67, 77, 80–81, 84, 86, 93–95, 100–1, 123–24, 158
Garry, Joseph, 158, 161, 164
Gaston, Lt. William, 75, 79, 84, 89
Geary, Edward, 93
General Allotment Act
    see Dawes Act
George, Andrew, 132, 156, 170–71
George, Frank, 141, 154–56, 158–59, 160–61, 162–63, 164–65, 167
George, Smith L.
    see Hay-hay-tah
Gibbs, George, 25, 26, 42, 70
Gosnell, W.B., 94–95
Governors' Interstate Indian Council (GIIC), 154
Grand Coulee Dam, 147–49, 150, 154, 157, 160
Grange City, Washington, 126
Gray, William, 20, 92
Gregg, Lt. David, 78, 79, 89
Grier, Major William, 74, 76, 85
Griffin, Worth, 139–40, 169
Grivna, Edward, 135
Grorud, Albert, 164, 167
Gross, F.A., 151

H
Hahsilatah (Nez Perce), 118–19
Hahtalekin, Chief (Red Echo, Palouse), 41, 68, 109, 116–19, 131
Hallauer, Wilbur "Web," 168–69
Haller, Major Granville O., 46–48, 50, 58, 59, 64, 83
Hana-yah-kla-ka (Yakama), 83
Hanford project, 160
Harder, Anne Maybelle, 136, 139–40, 169
Harlish Washomake, Chief (Wolf Necklace, Palouse), 91, 104, 131
Harney, Gen. William S., 92–93
Harrison, U.S. Rep. William, 159
Harvey, George, 99–100
Hasúutin (village), 7, 32, 89
Hayes, Lt. Gilmore, 56
Hayes, Pres. Rutherford, 122–23
Hay-hay-tah (Smith L. George), 126, 141
Hayt, E.A., 123
Head, Wade, 154–55
Hembree, Absalom, 57–58
Henderson, William, 109
Henry, Will, 144
Hiachenie, Chief (Cayuse), 122
Hill, U.S. Sen. Samuel, 147
Hoecken, Adrian, 91
Holland, E.O., 139
Holt, William M., 167
Homestead Act/claims, 105, 109, 121
    see also Indian Homestead Act
Homily, Chief (Walla Walla), 122
Horan, U.S. Rep. Walt, 151, 153, 157
Horn Rapids, 6, 168
Horse Slaughter Camp, 75, 86
Howard, Gen. O.O., 117–18, 121–24, 126, 138
Huff, Roland, 111–12

Hunter, George, 126–27, 128
Húsis Kute, Chief (Palouse), 68, 78, 116–17, 119–20
Húsis Moxmox (Palouse), 107, 126, 127, 131

I
Iatot-kikt, 129
Inchelium, Washington, 148, 152
Indian Citizenship Act
    see Snyder Act
(U.S.) Indian Claims Commission (ICC), 147, 154, 159, 166–67
Indian Homestead Act/claims, 107, 109, 123–24, 126–27, 151
    see also Homestead Act
Indian New Deal, 149, 159, 160, 166
Indian Reorganization Act
    see Wheeler-Howard Act
Indian Self-Determination and Education Act (1975), 166
Irwin, Lewis, 131–32
Itseyiyi Shamkin (Nez Perce), 118

J
Jackson, U.S. Sen. Henry, 159, 164–65, 166
James, Chief Jim (San Poil), 146, 156–58
Johnson, Lt. Robert E., 17, 21
Johnson, Pres. Andrew, 109
Johnson, Robert, 140
Jones, U.S. Sen. Wesley, 147
Jordan, Lt. Thomas, 81
Joseph, Chief (Hin-mah-too Yah-let-kekt, Nez Perce), 14, 108, 115, 117–20, 128–29, 132, 134, 138
Joseph, Old (Tuekekas, Nez Perce), 32, 51, 66, 113, 115
Joseph, Pierre, 151
Joset, Joseph, 52, 68, 74, 76–81, 88, 93, 96, 109

K
Kamiacan Creek, 98, 112
Kamiak Butte, 13
Kamiakin, Alalumt'i, 160
Kamiakin, Chief—
    Weowicht (Wiyáwiikt) origins, 7–10
    family rivalries, 18, 26, 47, 49, 60
    "Kamiakin's Ditch," 19
    Kamiakin's gardens, 19, 20, 25, 142
    Indian alliances, 32–33, 49, 56, 57, 63–64, 66–69, 72, 74, 81, 83, 86–87
    meets Doty, 35–36
    Walla Walla Council (1855), 37–42, 64, 65, 73, 76, 160, 161
    Bolon's death, 45–46, 48, 64, 71, 73, 88
    war in Yakama country, 46–51, 57–58
    epistle, 48–49, 50, 64
    "Kamiakin's War," 51
    "Kamiakin's Outbreak," 60, 64
    Walla Walla Council (1856), 62–65
    Kamiak's Crossing, 13, 67, 95–96, 103
    accused in Steptoe affair, 80, 137–38
    Battle of Spokane Plains, 86, 98
    mountain exile, 91–94
    returns to Palouse, 95–97
    settles at Rock Lake, 97–101, 103
    refuses Harvey's petition, 100
    death of Tomomolow, 100
    dispute over Rock Lake camp, 106–7

death and burial, 110–13, 121, 125, 138
monument proposal, 142
Kamiakin, Cleveland (Piupiu K'ownot)—
early life, 100, 108, 125, 131
move to reservation, 128–30, 163
pow-wows and rodeos, 130, 140–41
enrollment and probate testimony, 143, 151
Indian Reorganization Act, 150
Game Code controversy, 150–51, 153
opposition to termination, 154, 157–58
founding of ATNI, 154–56
"Truman Scroll" presentation, 157–58
Spokane NCAI convention, 161
Chief Joseph Dam dedication, 162–63
as ICC petitioner, 166–67
last years, 159–61, 163, 168
Kamiakin, Colestah, 17, 82, 86, 96–98, 100, 108–10
Kamiakin, Hos-ke-la-pum, 17, 100, 108
Kamiakin, Kah-yee-wach (Pete Bones), 126–28, 132, 160
Kamiakin, Kem-ee-yowah, 17, 56, 67
Kamiakin, Kiatana, 97, 107–8, 110, 115, 129, 131, 140, 143
Kamiakin, Lukash, 120, 127–29, 133, 143
Kamiakin, Me-a-tu-kin-ma, 126, 128
Kamiakin, Ot-wes-on-my, 108, 131
Kamiakin, Pemalks, 1–3, 127, 130, 140, 173–75
Kamiakin, Piupiu K'ownot
see Kamiakin, Cleveland
Kamiakin, Skees, 110
Kamiakin, Sk'olumkee, 1–3, 97, 125, 127–30, 138, 140, 143, 173–75
Kamiakin, Sophie, 129, 133–34
Kamiakin, Sunk-hay-ee, 7, 17, 20, 95, 108
Kamiakin, Ta-lats Ton-my, 119, 133–34
Kamiakin, Tespaloos, 93, 126, 128–30, 143
Kamiakin, Tomeo, 96, 108, 128–31, 139–43, 152
Kamiakin, Tomomolow, 97–98, 100, 110
Kamiakin, T'siyiyak, 32, 108, 125, 127, 129
Kamiakin, Wal-luts-pum, 17, 32, 97, 108
Kamiakin, We-yet-que-wit ("Young Kamiakin"), 17, 67, 97, 99, 107–8, 123–24, 126–27, 129, 158
Kamiakin, Yam'naneek (Catherine), 20, 108
Kamiakin, Yumasepah, 67, 98–99, 108, 115, 119, 129
Kamiak's Crossing, 13, 67, 95–96
Kamiak's Flat, 12, 98
Kanasket (Yakama-Klickitat), 45, 56
Kash Kash, Chief (Cayuse), 138
Keller, Washington, 148
Kelly, Col. James, 50, 51, 53, 77
Kennedy, Pres. John, 164
Kenny, Sgt. Michael, 77, 78
Kettle Falls, 12, 17, 19, 49, 61, 108, 129, 147–49
Keyes, Capt. Erasmus, 56, 87
Khalotash, Chief (Kalatúsh, Palouse), 10–11, 37, 41, 165
Kip, Lt. Lawrence, 84, 86–87, 98
Kirkham, Capt. Ralph, 70
Kis-am-x'ay (Annie Billy), 160–61
Kohlhauff, Sgt. William, 61
Kolecki, Theodore, 85, 95–96
Koltenschin, Theresa, 129
Kooatyahhen, Alba Shawaway, 162
Kuykendall, George, 120

L
LaFarge, Oliver, 163
Lahoomt, Chief (Wenatchi), 39
Langlie, Gov. Arthur, 162
Lansdale, Richard, 35, 57, 93–94
Latham, Edward, 128, 132
Latter Day Saints
see Mormons
Lawyer, Chief (Nez Perce), 33, 38–39, 41, 60, 66, 72
LeBret, Frances, 133
Lee, Jason, 18, 32
Leschi, Chief (Nisqually), 26, 29, 44, 55–56, 60, 63, 82, 105
Leschi, Jennie, 105
Lesh-hi-hite (Yakama), 7, 83, 87
Levi (Nez Perce), 78
Lewis and Clark Expedition, 5, 28, 48, 51, 66, 98
Lewiston, Idaho, 89, 103, 130
Lincoln, Pres. Abraham, 89, 103
Lokout (Yakama), 7, 38, 40, 45, 47, 59–60, 65, 83, 87, 91
Looking Glass, Chief (Nez Perce), 32, 39, 40, 42, 44, 51, 52, 66–67, 72
Looking Glass, Chief (The Younger), 117–19
Lot, Chief (Spokane), 123–24, 138
Lower Monumental Dam, 160
Lugenbeel, Major Pinkney, 89, 93
Lyman, William, 138
Lynch, Jay, 142
Lyons, Dan, 126–27
Lyons Ferry, 104, 142

M
Mackall, Major W.W., 61
MacMurray, Major J.W., 128
Magnuson, U.S. Sen. Warren, 157
Mámunashat (Charley Nason), 45
Manring, Benjamin, 89, 137–38
Maranguoin (Marengo), Louis, 66
Mary (steamboat), 58, 70
Mason, Charles, 45, 46, 47
Matisse, Henry, 45, 88
Matlock Bridge, 142
Matlock, John, 96
Matlock, Preston, 96
May, Thomas, 110
McBean, John, 122, 123
McCafferty, Green, 51
McClellan, Capt. George, 25–26, 27, 28, 89
McClung, Earl, 152
McDonald, Angus, 17, 19, 32, 41, 52, 66–68, 73, 83, 94, 100, 110, 119, 147
McDonald, Catherine, 119
McDonald, Duncan, 119, 147
McDougall, Duncan, 16
McElroy, Jack, 110, 111
McKay, Thomas, 16
McKay, William, 19, 45
McKenny, Gen. T.J., 100–1
McKenzie, Donald, 19
McLoughlin, John, 19
McNickle, D'Arcy, 154, 163
McWhorter, L.V., 112, 142–43, 169
Meany, Edmond, 139, 142

Medicine Creek Treaty, 29
Meek, Joe, 48, 58
Meninick, George, 149
Meninock, Chief (*Mináynak*, Yakama), 39
Mesplié, Toussaint, 22, 33, 72
Meyer, Dillon S., 159
Milroy, Robert H., 107, 127, 169
Minote (Yakama), 97
Mires, John, 131
Mission of the Immaculate Conception (Kittitas Valley), 51
Mitchell Act (1938), 148
Miyáwax (village)
    see Cowiche (Mountain); Rimrock, Washington
Monteith, John B., 117
Montour, George, 52, 63, 65, 80
Moore, Benjamin, 128–29
Morgan, Lt. Michael, 87
Mormons, 11, 62, 70, 72, 82
Moscow, Idaho, 74, 104, 109
    see also Paradise Valley
Moses, Chief (Columbia), 21, 25, 88, 113, 125, 130–32, 138
    war in Yakima Valley, 44, 46, 82
      negotiates for Moses-Columbia Reservation, 101, 121, 122–23, 157
      relocates to Colville Reservation, 124, 127
Moses, Chief John (Nez Perce), 155
Moses, Joe, 141
Moses, Mary Owhi (Sanclow), 7, 25, 82, 88, 121, 127, 133, 142–43, 165
Moses, Peter Dan, 127, 141, 144, 150–51, 153–55, 157, 162
Mullan, Lt. John, 72–73, 84, 85, 95, 98, 103–5
Mullan Road, 72–73, 95, 96, 97, 103–5, 109, 142
Munro, Ralph, 171
Mushíil (Yakama), 45, 71, 88, 94

N
NAGPRA, 113
Nanamkin, Chief David (Yakama-Entiat), 127
Nanamkin, Harry, 163
National Congress of American Indians (NCAI), 154, 159, 160, 161, 163–64
Nesmith, Col. James, 48, 49–51, 82
Nespelem Art Colony, 136, 139–40, 169
Nez Perce War, 99, 117–20, 121, 124, 126, 138, 152, 167
Nicholas, Chief Victor (Colville), 154, 157
Nicholson, Narcisse, Jr., 167
Niebell, Paul M., 166
Ni'lukhwaqw (campsite), 13, 96–97, 109
    see also De Smet, Idaho
Nixon, Pres. Richard, 166
No Shirt, Chief (Umatilla), 138
Noble, John, 50, 73
North West Company (Nor'Westers), 15–16, 17, 19
Northern Pacific Railroad, 105–6, 121
Northern Pacific Railroad Survey, 23–26, 27, 29, 69, 73

O
Oakesdale, Washington, 74, 109
Olney, Nathan, 19, 28, 45, 47, 51, 90
Ord, Capt. E.O.C., 84, 89
Oregon Donation Land Act, 21
Oregon Improvement Company, 105
Oregon Steam Navigation Company, 104, 106

Oregon Trail, 19, 21, 27, 28, 32, 48
Oregon Volunteers, 15, 47–48, 49–51, 53, 57–58, 66, 70
Owen, John, 69, 70, 73, 80, 93
Owhi, Ben (Awhi) (Yakama-Palouse), 108, 115–16, 118–20, 129–31, 152, 165
Owhi, Chief (Yakama), 7, 20, 39, 55, 63, 72, 108, 121, 122, 127, 133, 143
    camp in Kittitas Valley, 7, 25, 26
    discord with Kamiakin, 18, 26, 47, 59–60
    Walla Walla Council (1855), 38–40, 42
    war in Yakima Valley, 44–47
    Wright campaign (1856), 59–61, 72
    Walla Walla Council (1856), 65
    miners, 81
    capture and death, 87, 92, 93, 115
Owhi, Harry, 131, 151, 155, 157, 167
Owhi, Roscoe, 151
Owhi, U-pa-pi, 131

P
Pacific Fur Company, 16
Pahka Lawash-hachit (Palouse), 115, 120
Pahka Pahtahank (Five Fogs, Palouse), 119
Pahka Qohqoh
    see Five Crows, Chief
Painter, Harry, 111
Painter, William C., 49
Palmer, Joel, 28, 37–38, 42, 45
Palouse City, Washington, 76
Palouse council (1858), 75, 87
Palouse Falls, 14, 127
Palus (village), 13–14, 16, 49, 68, 83, 87, 95, 103–4, 107–8, 115, 117, 124–33, 151, 160
Pambrun, Andrew, 37, 40, 59, 63, 65
Pambrun, Pierre, 19, 40
Pandosy, Charles Marie—
    St. Joseph's (Ahtanum) Mission, 18, 20–21, 22, 25
    Pandosy's forewarning, 29, 32, 33, 37, 66, 72, 82, 92
    Kamiakin's epistle, 43, 48–49, 50
    exile to St. Paul's Mission, 49, 61
    return to Wright's council, 61
    King George's Country, 110
Pangburn, George, 103, 104
Paradise Valley, 74, 109
Parker, Samuel, 92
Paween, Alalumt'i (Alilintai), 131, 142
Paween, Chief Húsis (Palouse), 37, 68, 108, 116, 130–31
Paween, Chief Tom (Palouse), 130
Paween family, 83, 104, 117, 130–31, 142, 151, 165
Pearson, W.H., 74
Penawawa (Creek)
    see Pinawáwih (village)
Peone, Emily (Friedlander), 133, 135, 143–44, 165
Peotsenmy, 127
Peterson, Helen, 161
Pettyjohn, John, 126–27
Phinney, Archie, 154, 163
Pierce, Pres. Franklin, 62
Pierre, George, 165
Pierre, Ray, 158
Pinawáwih (village), 13, 68, 104, 106, 116, 128, 130–31, 151
Pine Creek, 75–79, 112

Piupiu Maksmaks, Chief (Walla Walla), 20, 28
    gathers with tribal leaders, 32, 33
    Walla Walla Council (1855), 35, 37–42
    murder, 51, 53, 59, 62, 68, 93
Piupiu Maksmaks (The Younger), 57, 59–60, 62, 65–66
Plante, Antoine, 28, 52, 63, 104
Plymouth, Washington, 160
Point Elliott Treaty, 29
Point No Point Treaty, 29
Polatkin, Chief (Spokane), 63, 77, 83
Poyahkin, Chief (Palouse), 83, 116
Poyahkin family, 104, 117, 130–31
Priest Rapids Dam, 159–60
Prosser, Washington, 17
Puck Hyah Toot, 169
Puckmiakin, 129

Q
Q'omolah (Quo-mo-lah, Yakama), 7, 25, 127
Qualchan (Yakama)—
    pre-war, 7, 25
    hostilities (1855/1856), 44–47, 56, 71, 80
    Wright campaign (1856), 60
    Stevens encounter (1856), 65
    hostilities (1858), 77–78, 81–84
    execution/burial, 87, 97, 110, 130, 142
    descendants, 127
    assessment, 92, 138
Quanspeetsah, 127
Quetalican
    see Moses, Chief
Quiemuth, Chief (Nisqually), 29, 70
Quiltenenock, Chief (Columbia), 25, 44, 46, 59–60, 63–65, 66, 81, 83,
    108, 110

R
Rains, Major Gabriel, 28, 45, 46, 47, 49–51, 59, 61, 89
Ravais, Antoine, 48
Ravalli, Anthony, 28, 52, 63, 64, 68
Ray, Verne F., 167
Red Feather, Chief (Flathead), 93
Red Wolf, Chief (Nez Perce), 43, 51, 66
Red Wolf (Spokane), 44
Red Wolf's Crossing (Alpowa Creek), 69, 74, 79
Redthunder, Joe, 130, 151, 167
Reid, Thomas, 161
Relander, Clifford "Click," 169
Ricard, Pascal, 20, 32, 44
Rimrock, Washington, 8
Ritzville, Washington, 139
Robertson, Mortimer, 81
Robie, A.H., 67
Rock Creek, 95, 96, 112, 133
Rock Lake, 1, 3, 12, 14, 28, 67, 97–101, 103, 106–10, 130, 138, 142, 151,
    160, 163, 173
Rocky Ford Creek, 125, 163
Roosevelt, Pres. Franklin, 147
    see also Indian New Deal
Rosalia, Washington, 75, 77, 79, 112
Ross, Alexander, 16–17

Ross, Samuel, 100
Ruby, Robert H., 143–44, 169

S
Sacred Heart Mission
    see Coeur d'Alene Mission
Saluskin, Alex (Yakama), 6, 156, 160, 161, 167
Samuya (village), 7
Sanclow
    see Moses, Mary Owhi
Saxton, Lt. Rufus, 27–28, 67
Scholl, Louis, 61
Seelatsee, Eagle, 167
Seltice, Chief Andrew (Coeur d'Alene), 74–75, 78, 100–1, 109
Sgalgalt, Chief (Spokane), 52, 63, 77, 84
Shaw, Lt. Col. Benjamin F., 61–65, 77
Shawaway, Alec (Yakama), 143, 162
Sheridan, Lt. Philip H., 49–50, 58
Sherman, Paschal, 151, 161
Sherwood, S.F., 106, 108, 109, 138
Showaway, Abraham, 156
Showaway, Chief (Cayuse), 156
Showaway, Chief (Kamiakin's brother), 7, 36, 45, 51, 60, 67, 71, 94, 143
Showaway, Chief (Kamiakin's uncle), 7, 17, 18
Simms, John A., 106–8, 123
Simpson, Charlie (Wata-stoma-kolick), 123
Simpson, Sir George, 19
Sinclair, James, 58
Sitting Bull (Sioux), 119
Skloom, Chief (Kamiakin's brother)—
    early life, 7, 18, 20
    Kamiakin relationship, 26, 92
    meets Doty, 35–36
    Sohon portrait (1855), 40
    Plateau hostilities, 44, 46, 51, 70, 72
    Wright campaign (1856), 59–60
    Kamiak's Crossing, 67, 71
    mountain exile, 88, 91–93
    Yakima Valley, 94, 95
    descendants, 143, 156
Slaughter, Lt. W.A., 46–47
Slouthier, Carter, 133, 160
Slowiarchy, Chief (Palouse), 68, 95, 104, 108, 115
Sluskin, Chief (Yakama), 7
Sluskin (Taidnapam-Yakama), 15
Smohalla (Wanapum), 159
"Snake River Kamiakin"
    see Kamiakin, Sk'olumkee
Snyder Act (1924), 145–46
Soap Lake, Washington, 130
Sohappy, Louis, 143
Sohon, Gustavus, 42, 44, 85, 86, 104, 107, 139, 161
Sopa, Chief (Wenatchi), 16, 17
Spalding, Henry H., 21, 59, 66, 106, 117
Spencer, Chief (Klickitat), 58, 94
Splawn, Andrew J., 7, 33, 40, 95, 99, 107, 111, 139, 142, 168, 169
Spokan Garry
    see Garry, Chief Spokan
Spokane council (1858), 75
Spokane House, 19
Sprague Lake, 1, 12, 13, 32, 67, 104, 139

Sprague, Washington, 1, 99, 130
St. Ignatius Mission, 91
St. John, Washington, 13, 130
St. Joseph's Mission, 20–21, 22, 26, 33, 35, 44, 45, 48
    plundered, 49–50, 59, 61, 63
St. Paul's Mission, 49, 61, 80
Stáquthly, Chief (Stockwhitely, Tenino), 33, 42, 51, 62, 97, 156
Starbuck, Washington, 87
Steele, Henry, 128
Stellam, Chief (Coeur d'Alene), 63, 78–79, 84
Steptoe Butte, 2, 13, 75, 79, 96, 144
Steptoe, Col. Edward J., 56, 62, 63–66, 70, 74–81, 89
Sternberg, Charles, 111–12
Stevens, Isaac I., 15, 23–25, 29, 33, 105, 110
    governor, 23, 28
    travels with survey party, 27, 28, 73
    Indian councils (1855), 28–29, 35–43, 45, 52–53, 55, 73, 95
    returns to Olympia (1855), 52–53
    dispute with Army, 51–52, 53, 56–57, 61, 62, 64, 66, 72
    Indian councils (1856), 62–65
    congressional delegate, 69–70, 72, 80
    Civil War, 89
Stevens, Hazard, 15, 63, 89, 137, 142, 169
Stickus, Chief (Cayuse), 33, 52
Stuart, David, 16
Stuart, Robert, 16
Stwire, Joe
    see White Swan, Chief
Suckley, George, 27
Suxaapí (Wanapum), 44
Swaptsa (Wanapum), 7

T
Tahwat-tus-son (Cayuse), 40
Tampico, Washington, 17, 142
Táthinma (campsite), 74
    see also Moscow, Idaho
Tatshama (Umatilla), 122–23, 127
Taylor, Capt. O.H.P., 75, 79, 83, 84, 89
Tecolekun, Chief (Wenatchi-Entiat), 39, 61, 81, 83, 129
Teias, Chief (Yakama)—
    Kamiakin's father-in-law/uncle, 7, 17, 18, 95
    Kamiakin relationship strained, 18, 26, 36, 40, 60
    meets Doty, 35–36
    Walla Walla Council (1855), 38, 40, 42
    war in Yakama country, 44–45, 72
    Wright campaign (1856), 60, 61, 63
    Garnett campaign (1858), 82–83, 89
    reservation, 95
Tekoa, Washington, 109
Tenax, Chief (Klickitat), 17, 56, 58
Tensed, Idaho, 97
Thompson, Chief Tommy, 156
Thorp, Bayless, 107
Thorp, Willis, 99, 107
Three Feathers, Chief (Nez Perce), 67
Tilcoax, Chief (Palouse), 37, 41, 44, 51, 57, 65, 68, 73–83, 86, 88, 91–92, 104, 108, 130–31, 138
Time-i-tas, Chief (Klickitat), 46
Timothy, Chief (Nez Perce), 60, 74, 76, 78, 93
Tomanawash, Robert (Wanapum), 160

Tomeo, Arthur, 134, 141
Tomeo, Cato, 152
Tomeo family, 134
Tomeo, Stanley, 152
Tom-teah-kuin (Yakama), 7, 83
Toohoolhoolzote (Nez Perce), 117
Totus, Watson (Yakama), 156, 160, 167, 169
Trafzer, Clifford E., 170
Trevit, Victor, 46, 66, 71, 72, 77
Truman, Pres. Harry, 157
Truman Scroll, 157–58
T'siyiyak (Kamiakin's father), 7, 11, 12–13, 32, 67, 68, 89, 91, 111, 115, 125, 128
T'siyiyak's Place, 12, 67, 96
Tuekekas, Chief (Nez Perce)
    see Joseph, Old
Tuichalt (Yakama), 97
Two Moons (Nez Perce), 128

U
Udall, Stuart, 164
Umtuch, Chief (Taitnapam), 47
Union Flat Creek, 95, 103–4
Union Gap, 6, 49
Union Pacific Railroad, 131
U.S.-Canadian Boundary Survey, 89, 94
U.S. Exploring Expedition, 17
Utsinmalikin, Chief (Nez Perce), 37

V
Van Trump, P.B., 15, 89
Victor, Chief (Coeur d'Alene), 79
Victor, Chief (Flathead), 91, 158
Victor, Chief (Kalispel), 93
Villard, Henry, 105
Vincent, Chief (Coeur d'Alene), 63, 74–81, 109
Volunteers
    see Oregon Volunteers; Washington Volunteers

W
Wáashat/Washani religion, 32, 68, 116, 117, 128, 130, 141, 159, 162
Waiilatpu (Whitman Mission), 20, 73
Walla Walla Council/Stevens treaties (1855), 37–42, 64, 67, 70, 73, 76, 89, 95, 105, 116, 146, 161, 162
Walla Walla Council (1856), 62–65, 81
Waller, Alvan, 18
Wallula, Washington, 103, 115, 120–21, 122, 123
Wanapum Dam, 160
Warner, Olin L., 138
Wasco (steamboat), 58, 70
Wascopam Mission, 18
Washington, Nat, 163, 168
Washington Territorial Legislature, 20, 23, 45, 46, 64, 71
Washington Volunteers, 15, 45, 47–48, 49, 56, 57, 61, 62, 64, 66, 70
Waters, Stwire
    see White Swan, Chief
Waughaskie (Cayuse), 126, 128
Wawáwih (village), 41, 68, 104, 106, 115, 116, 128, 130
Wayayentutpik, 130
Webster, John, 133
Wehn, James A., 138–39

Wenatchi/Wenatshapam Fishery, 12, 25, 39, 41, 61, 129
Weowicht, Chief (Wiyáwiikt, Yakama), 7, 8–10, 15, 16, 17, 94, 162
Weowicht (Wiyáwiikt) clan, 7, 8, 10, 11, 15, 17, 18, 26, 47, 55, 88, 115, 122, 156
West, Glenn, 139
Wheeler-Howard Act (1934), 149–50, 154, 159
White Bird, Chief (Nez Perce), 117–18
White Bluffs, 71, 80, 104, 160
White, Cull, 163
White, Frederick, 71, 72
White, Lt. James, 84, 86
White Swan, Chief (Joe Stwire, Klickitat), 94, 97
Whitford, John, 37
Whitman (Marcus and Narcissa), 20, 45, 48, 59, 66, 81, 105
Wilbur, James, 95, 97, 101, 127
Wilbur, Washington, 130, 140–41
Wiley, J.W., 46, 52, 57, 58–59, 65, 71, 72
Wilkes, Lt. Charles, 17
Williams, Abel J., 151–52
Williams, Alalumti (Palouse-Nez Perce), 129, 151
Williams, Chief Charley (Palouse)—
    relocation to reservation, 129, 151
    opposition to termination, 158, 165
    as ICC petitioner, 166–67
    last years, 159, 168
Williams, Elijah, 129, 130
Wilson, Charles, 93, 94, 95

Wilson, Luke (Ko-san-yum), 119
Winans, W.P., 99–101, 106–8
Wind, Henry, 104
Winder, Capt. Charles, 77, 84, 89
Winthrop, Theodore, 18, 21, 55
Wolf Brothers, 2, 8, 14, 32, 96, 128
Wolf Necklace ("Tilcoax the Younger")
    see Harlish Washomake, Chief
Wood, Erskine, 163
Wood, Lt. C.E.S., 138, 162–63
Woodruff, Capt. Dickinson, 71
Woods, Rufus, 155
Wool, Gen. John E., 51, 56–57, 58, 59, 61, 63, 64, 66, 69–70, 72, 80
Wright, Col. George, 56, 57–66, 70, 72–73, 75, 81–89, 97–99, 110, 133
Wynecoop, Clair (Spokane), 156

XYZ
Yáamuštas (Elk's Abode)
    see Steptoe Butte
Yallup, Thomas (Yakama), 160–61
Yellow Wolf (Nez Perce), 119, 128, 129
Yemowit family, 87, 95
Yeracostchin, Eddie (Nespelem), 157
Youmas, Andrew, 109
Young, Brigham, 62, 70
Young Chief (Taitau, Cayuse), 37
Zachary (Coeur d'Alene), 79

The Authors and Photographer

Richard D. Scheuerman currently teaches and writes at Seattle Pacific University's Graduate School of Education. He holds degrees in history, Russian, and education, and has written several books and articles on regional themes, including *Palouse Country: A Land and Its People* and *The Wenatchee Valley and Its First Peoples: Thrilling Grandeur, Unfulfilled Promise*. He is a recipient of the Governor's Award for Excellence in Education, and the Robert Gray Medal for contributions to historical scholarship.

Michael O. Finley is a member of the Colville Confederated Tribes and a graduate of Eastern Washington University in history and American Indian studies. He has served as an archaeological technician and traditional cultural property coordinator for the agency's Office of History and Archaeology in Nespelem. Finley currently is a Vice Chairman of the Colville Business Council. He is a descendant of Jaco Finlay, explorer David Thompson's French-Indian guide who established Spokane House in 1810.

John Clement is a landscape photographer residing in Kennewick, Washington, and a graduate of Central Washington University, Ellensburg, where he studied cultural geography and geology. He has received over fifty national, regional, and international photography awards, including induction of his work into the National Photographers Hall of Fame. Included among his audiovisual productions is the critically acclaimed program *Four Seasons of the Drylands*.